Chasing An Illusive Dream

To
Vernal &
Veloria,

love you,

Jackie
Valero

Chasing An Illusive Dream

Autobiography by

Frankie Valens

authorHOUSE®

AuthorHouse™
1663 Liberty Drive
Bloomington, IN 47403
www.authorhouse.com
Phone: 1-800-839-8640

First published by AuthorHouse   10/27/2011

ISBN: 978-1-4670-3637-5 (sc)
ISBN: 978-1-4670-3636-8 (hc)
ISBN: 978-1-4670-3635-1 (ebk)

Library of Congress Control Number: 2011919435

Printed in the United States of America

CONTENTS

CHASING AN ILLUSIVE DREAM

An autobiography by

Frankie Valens

Introduction

I decided to call my autobiography "Chasing An Illusive Dream," and you will understand why when you read it. Some of my experiences are taken from a vague remembrance of a situation or an ordeal. Sometimes I chose to leave out certain experiences because they were not pertinent enough, or a highlight of my life. If I didn't mention an experience that you know about, maybe I purposely left it out because it could cast a negative spotlight on the people I deeply care for, or simply because I did not know about it. I want this book to make a positive statement, but also stating the facts as best as I could as they happened. Also I wanted to record events that took place in my family that either happened or could have just been tales that has been passed down from one generation to another. Some of the information I've written about are rumors and tales I had heard, and may not have even happened. I have no way of proving the stories because most of those family members have passed away, and thus I will say that it was a rumor or a tale. Sometimes my imagination went dancing!

My greatest dream before I die is to know that I made a difference, and I want to be confident in the knowledge that I had become good at something. I had no formal training in music but yet I have spent most of my life pursuing it. I took one vocal lesson from the same vocal instructor that also instructed Michael Jackson in California. When I finished my lesson the instructor simply told me that he felt I was already a professional and there was nothing more he felt he could teach me. I went out into my car and wept like a baby because I realized that my talent was God-given.

This book is a collection of notes that I've written over the span of a few years, and my attempt to help family, friends, and others to have a better understanding of my life and my family's life from the beginning. I pray that I will have the ability to express in intimate detail, the memories of both happy and painful situations and how they affected me. I am also hoping that the knowledge I gained through life's experiences over the years can help others in some profound way with my faith, and sometimes my lack of it.

The idea to write my life story came to me over ten years ago when my wife Phyllis and I were on a concert tour. We had pulled to a stop on the side of the highway in our borrowed motorhome in the mountains of Colorado and we were standing just outside the RV enjoying the beautiful scenery when I felt the Lord touching my heart, telling me to write a book about my life's experiences. I didn't take actions on those thoughts until many years later, and many experiences later.

I am hoping that this compilation of notes and pictures in this book will help capture each moment as it happened in my life or in my family's life. Sometimes I felt like I was weaving a dream of wishes and wants that was never meant to be.

A lot of research has gone into this book to help achieve my purpose, and that main purpose is to record my life so that my children and grandchildren will have a record of who they knew sometimes as Frank Piper, Frankie Valens, dad, uncle Frankie, great uncle Frankie, grandpa, and why I chose to make the decisions that were life-changing for me, including the mistakes I made that created regrets. Sometimes those decisions I made literally changed the course and direction of my life drastically. I am praying that my family takes an interest in this book!

My autobiography will help give you the background and history of the accomplishments and mistakes I made, and the incredible journey I took living life to the fullest. My feeling of rejection and the insecurities that was always present at every turn, the hurt feelings I tried to hide, and the constant fear of never being accepted or good enough to someday make a difference, is all recorded in this book. I never wanted to ever purposely cause any hurt or harm to anyone, but ended up hurting those whom I love dearly. I ask for your forgiveness. Do I have regrets, yes! The only time I had much parental influence on my children was when they were quite young when I showered them with love and attention. I ask for your forgiveness for not being there most of the time. I guess I never really grew up enough to know what parenting was all about.

Even though I became a Christian in my teens I don't feel a lot of my actions were covered under grace. Living under grace does not give us carte blanc to do whatever we please. I have learned to never compare myself and my life to others, because I have no idea what their journey is, but I do know mine. My background and circumstances may have influenced who I am, but I am responsible for who I became.

In this book you will find a record of my family history. I've traced the Piper family heritage back several generations to a town in Germany, which is now Kalisz, Poland, and another branch from Holland. The rumors of why some Pipers (or Piepers) came to America, and are we related to the famous William T. Piper, the founder of the Piper Cub airplane? Am I part Indian? All I know for certain is that I am Scott, Irish, Dutch, German, and English. Am I a relative of Wild Bill Hickok and Daniel Boone? Do I share a grandmother with Lucille Ball? In my research I found where my great-great grandpa Julius's old stone foundation was in Chase County, Kansas, along with his older brother Herman's old stone foundation and Herman's son William. Milton and Milton's wife Glenda, Alice Miller, Melvin Koegeboehn and I visited the site to take pictures.

I have also traced my dad's mother, Goldie Ellen (Mallory) Piper's roots, as well as tracing her mother, Rosa's roots. My mother, Pauline Evelyn (Day) Piper's side of the family has been more difficult to trace, but this book will include many names, and sometimes faces, of my mother's family tree as well.

It has taken me years to accomplish writing this book from months of research and the notes I had accumulated. Just a few months ago I lost most all of my manuscripts after a computer glitch wiped out all my new additions and notes I'd added since March, 2010. I was so hurt and at a loss as to what I should do, and my discouragement was at an all-time low, but I have since purchased a better program for my computer that will help me accomplish writing the rest of my story.

During the last few months of writing this book we were being sued by a family member for thousands of dollars, who singlehandedly placed a permanent split in the family by taking us to court. It's like a dark cloud that's been hanging over our heads because we do not know how the judge is going to decide over this family squabble. We also made a major move that entailed our having to scale down and move to a smaller home, and I landed in the hospital for two days after a fainting spell, discovering that I had had a heart-attack earlier on in life! What a wake-up call! My creative juices just seemed to freeze over and helped to slow my progress down in writing this book. We both have gone through cancer scares and operations.

In this book you will learn that as a child I was such a small, skinny, bashful and shy boy, and was often bullied by the other boys. I was so skinny you could count my ribs! I was too little to compete in sports and was often called names I'd rather not remember, but I've learned that sometimes being different isn't all that bad and can sometimes be a blessing. I think one of the things I was searching for most of my life was a demonstrative love from my dad that showed that he loved me, or even to let me know verbally that he was proud of me. Even up to the time of his death I felt cheated that he never told me he loved me. While I was sitting there at my dad's funeral service just before his casket was taken away for burial, I wanted to sob hysterically for the loss I felt and of the unresolved feelings I had stored up and never got resolved with him.

I also have wondered whether I was the only one in this world that felt that I was destined to do great things and accomplish many of my dreams throughout my lifetime. Every time I turned around I was always trying to achieve much more than my knowledge would take me to. I never wanted to ever underestimate what I thought I could accomplish or achieve in life. I was an inventor of sorts, but only in my mind.

Sometimes when I was just a young boy I would hear the statement that I was just too pretty to be a boy. Maybe it's because I was a late bloomer and I didn't even have to shave until I was in college.

My love of music surfaced at a very young age, but my parents either did not recognize it, find it important enough, or simply could not afford to pay for any lessons I might need to take to accomplish the goal of the musical appreciation that was festering in my thoughts and actions. My parents were too busy just surviving life with all the struggles that marriage and kids threw at them. In my lifetime I did briefly take accordion lessons, drum lessons, recorder lessons and piano lessons, but the best instrument I chose to use for the rest of my life was my vocal cords.

My early life was not always dedicated to the glory of the Lord. In truth, I spent many years in abject defiance and rebellion. Even when my father became a pastor of a church, at about the time when I was in my tenth grade in high school, I rebelled. I've succumbed to almost every deception that the enemy could throw at me. But God can use it all to His glory. It is part of my story and also a part of His story. The ultimate record of redemption and reconciliation in the knowledge that "all things work together for good to them that love God, to them who are the called according to His purpose." Romans 8:28 KJV

"The Lord is my strength and song, and is become my salvation." Psalm 118:14 KJV

Even though I have appeared in concert with many famous notables over the years, I cannot say that I actually met all of them. I was an independent, struggling artist who was a nobody in the late 60s. The singers and groups I often appeared with never emerged from their cocoons (dressing rooms) until show-time, and then quickly disappeared after their performances. It was all part of the persona. When I became well-known as an independent artist, I too learned about the importance of the persona image with body guards, girls chasing me, and riding around in limos. Because I was never a major recording artist it took years of hard work and dedication to try and make my name a household name, even though I often was mistaken for Richie Valens and sometimes Frankie Valli. Before each concert I still have to explain to people who I'm before I told them who I am. Part of my testimony is that I do not receive any royalties for any recordings I ever made. Later in life I did appear in concert with "The Byrds," "the Platters," "Crystal Gayle," and "The Boxtops," some of whom I did meet.

I learned early on that I had to be more than just a singer and performer. I learned how to emotionally connect with my audiences and entertain them, dressing like I deserved to be up there as a star, otherwise they could very well have stayed home and just listened to my music. I carried this knowledge and experiences into our ministry to bring variety and interest in our ministry concerts, but always placing the Lord first.

One of my biggest fears in life is that my own children will not come to the personal knowledge of who their Savior is and will continue leading ungodly lives. Let me share with you that our body was made from dust and to dust it will return, but our spirit lives on and it is up to us to make a decision as to where we want to spend eternity. I want to spend eternity with my family!

I've learned that peace is seeing a sunset and knowing Who to thank! I've also learned that the happiest people don't necessarily have the best of everything. They just make the best of everything that comes their way. I've learned that surviving and living life successfully requires courage. The goals and dreams I was seeking required a lot of courage and risk-taking. I learned from the turtle—it makes progress only when it sticks its neck out! I've also learned to not live in the past and not to try and dream of the future, but concentrate more on the present.

When my dad died I was struck with the pain of learning that sometimes there just isn't any more and he's not returning. Time will heal the wounds in my heart, but it won't erase the scars. So, while we have our parents, and while we still have our relatives and dearest friends, its best that we love and care for them. If something is broken, fix it. Cherish what you have while you still have it, like our aging parents, grandparents, and our friends and relatives, because they are worth it. Some friendships are worth keeping, like a best friend that moved away, or a classmate we grew up with, so I want to keep my closest friends and family close to my heart, mind, and spirit by first giving a thank you to those who helped with my being able to write this book.

I've learned that talent is God-given, be humble. Fame is man-given, be thankful. Conceit is self-given, be careful. Conceit and success are not compatible! There is no shame in taking pride for achievements and positions, but nobody gets to the top alone. It's only the lonely that are at the top who forgot to thank all the people who helped him succeed, and the ones who he met along the way that he failed to acknowledge for his success. Ego trips have dangerous destinations! Be careful!

I want to thank all my family and friends who helped to contribute pictures, articles, rumors, tales, or verbally acknowledged specific events that happened in the family that I am able to share with you now. My mother Pauline, age 89, helped fill in the blanks from before my birth to my early childhood days. She was there when I needed her as a child and she's been there for me as I write this book. Thanks, mom.

I want to thank Kimberly and Rex Butter for providing me with pictures and information from yet another branch of my family tree. I also want to thank Carla Gallmeister from the Chase County Historical Society for providing me with copies of articles that helped me piece together the historical impact my family made in Chase County.

I want to thank my second cousin, Betty Criss, my great uncle Fred Piper's daughter, who provided me with some of the Piper family history, along with copies of family photos. A thank-you to my cousin Lorena Linder in California, niece of Betty Criss, who provided me with more of the puzzle pieces of her family, including Rena's father, Marion Lawrence Piper. It is my understanding through another family member that I may have ruffled some feathers in my family tree because of stories and rumors I have heard and read about that I included in this book. I reiterate that some information was just rumors and I could not prove them right. Everything I have written is to the best of my knowledge and understanding at the time of my writing this book.

A big thank you to my second cousin Milton, my great-uncle Charles Piper's son, who so graciously provided me with some of the stories and tales that had been passed down through the family. He had copies of census records that clearly showed my great-great grandfather Julius's name. My great-great grandmother did not appear in the 1920 census because she had died in 1907. My great-great grandfather's name always appeared as "Julius Piper," and I have felt that he simply didn't want to be called August. Maybe his parents nicknamed him Julius? Even though at birth I was legally Bernard Franklin Piper, I was nicknamed Frankie, or Frank.

I want to thank my wife Phyllis for not only proof-reading my work, but also for encouraging me to pursue writing my book even after my computer crashed and I lost most of the original manuscript. We both just wanted to sit down and cry. She knows how much time and effort I had already put into writing this book, just to lose most of it because of a computer glitch.

I also want to thank my cousin Harold Van Buren for his wonderful childhood memories he shared with us about his life in Florence, Kansas.

He also shared with us a record of his family tree. A big thank you to Alice Miller, a distant cousin for her hard work.

Quoting from "The Illusive Dream" in Omnia Paratus on December 14, 2006:

"Where might you be going this fine day, my friend?
Off along an aimless road that soon must end?
Chasing an illusive dream that shines so fair,
But when found, isn't there?

I can understand your weary sigh, my friend,
There but for the grace of God go I, my friend.
Come and let Him lead you to your journey's end.
Oh, come along and walk with Him.

If without the grace of God your life should end,
And before the face of God you'd stand, my friend,
What would your illusive dream avail you then?
So, come along and walk with Him."

A special thank you to a dear friend of ours who provided the funding to get this project started. We're very grateful to you for not only your friendship and love, but also for your generosity.

Thank you to Mark Johnson for creating a wonderful book for me from my notes and pictures. Thank you for the art work and adding pictures to my book that helped to complete this book. You are not only a friend, but my brother in the Lord as well, and you know that Phyllis and I love you and Connie dearly. I say to you, "A friend is someone who knows the song in your heart and can sing it back to you when you have forgotten the words." Anonymous

All the information included in this book is accurate to the best of my knowledge at the time of my writing. My story is very unapologetic and real, and in some chapters the 'real' could very well jump out from the pages and grab your heartstrings and rip them to shreds! It is my life story with areas of family history. Can I prove that everything happened? No! I have to rely on family stories and tales that have been passed down from one generation to another. What happened to me was real and true and told in the best possible way I could, but as for family history, I'll leave that up to you to decide.

In writing my autobiography and the research it took to achieve my goal helped bring together things I had heard about when I was growing up that didn't mean anything to me then, but now as a mature man I have a greater understanding of those rumors. Some proved to be false rumors, but some turned out to be the truth, but I had to be the one to find out for myself. In writing my book there was an emotional healing that happened to me when I chose to expose myself quite openly on every page.

Reading this book is your allowing me to wander into your time and space for just a few fleeting moments. Thank you! And now my story begins.

ONE

A MATCH MADE IN HEAVEN

My mother, Pauline Evelyn (Day) Piper, was born on November 29, 1921 in Junction City, Kansas and was raised there. She attended the same Washington Grade School I attended when my family lived there and I had gone to first grade. She is now 89 years old and lives with my brother Doug in Wellston, Oklahoma. My dad, Bernard (Bernie) Hobert Piper, was born on March 19, 1920 in Florence, Kansas. He lived in Florence most of his life except from about 1923 to 1930 when he and his family lived near Trenton, Nebraska. According to rumors in my family my dad was named after a horse that his mother saw while she was standing at her kitchen window in Florence, Kansas. His sister, Joan, only remembers them owning a donkey! Dad had been nicknamed Bernie. My dad, a retired pastor, died in his sleep at age 82. To think that I could have been nicknamed "Bernie!" I had enough trouble in school with kids calling me the Pied Piper or reciting Peter Piper picked a peck of pickled peppers, etc . . .

Junction City and Florence, Kansas are about 59 miles apart and connected by highway 77. A town called Herington lies between these two towns, or 29 miles south of Junction City and 30 miles north of Florence. Herington is actually where my story begins.

My mother told me that she used to volunteer to do sewing for the NYA (National Youth Association) in Herington while she was in high

1

school. Her mother and dad would drive her to Herington from Junction City and she would spend time sewing blankets and quilts for needy people and for the servicemen. Mom met a young lady there who was also a volunteer that lived in

The original skating rink building in Herington, KS where my parents met.

Florence. Her name was Bernadine Piper, and mom and Bernadine became the best of friends.

On many occasions when the two had free time after sewing most of the day, they would walk over to the local skating rink, snap on roller skates and have fun skating. I found out that this skating rink building had quite a history behind it. According to The Advertiser newspaper, in the Thursday, June 19, 1958 edition, there was an article about Arthur C. Kelch, the man who was responsible for the skating rink died of a heart ailment. According to this article Arthur and an Ernie Johnson started the J and K Grocery Store which was housed in the Wilson Building at the corner of Broadway and Day Streets in the 1930's. During 1946 he started a building program on South Fifth Street which housed his grocery store and skating rink where he ended up adding two more buildings as well. These were completed in 1947 when he opened Kelch's Drive-In Market. Arthur was born on September 19, 1890 at Erie, Kansas and came to Herington with his parents in 1906.

Arthur C. Kelch, age 67 and owner of Kelch's Drive-In Market, died Tuesday of a heart ailment at the Herington hospital where he had been a patient since May 30, 1958.

My dad, Bernard (Bernie), came to pick his sister Bernadine up at this skating rink to take her back home to Florence when Bernadine introduced my mother to her brother Bernard, or Bernie as most people called him.

An early picture of my dad, Bernie Piper

Mom was taken by dad's appearance with his jeans and white shirt, but was turned off because he had been drinking and was tipsy. Dad loved his beer. Many years later after dad died mom told us that dad had always had a drinking problem and at one time it almost cost him his life, and it was at that time that dad decided to turn his life over to the Lord. In May of 2011 I was told that the old skating rink building that had become a bar had burned to the ground! This is the very building that my mom and dad met in over 70 years ago.

Mom and dad dated long distance for about two years. When they decided to get married on January 3, 1942 mom met dad at his parents' home in Florence and the two of them left for Burns, a small town about eleven miles south of Florence. Dad's sister Bernadine and a friend Asa

Parsonage in Burns, KS where my parents were married on Jan 3, 1942

Yarhams followed behind to be mom and dad's witnesses for the wedding, and they met at the Methodist church parsonage in Burns to get married. This parsonage had been built in 1920, and is still there today. Bernadine and Asa drove back to Florence while mom and dad drove on down to El Dorado to spend their wedding night in a boarding house, which was about a 20 mile drive from Burns. Mom told me that the boarding house was rather dumpy looking.

After the wedding night the two of them drove back north to Florence to live with dad's parents. Mom told me that this home was in downtown Florence and had no electricity or running water, no inside restrooms, just an outdoor toilet. My second cousin Betty Criss, who now lives in El Dorado, Kansas, remembers visiting that home in downtown Florence when she was just a little girl. Her father, Fred Edward Piper, was my grandpa Will's brother.

My dad's parents, Will and Goldie Piper's old stone foundation in Florence, KS

The two of them lived with dad's parents for about three months when dad received a notice that he was being drafted into the army. Remember the Pearl Harbor attack? Some quick decisions had to be made because the army wanted dad to go into training at Camp Berkley in Abilene, Texas. World War II had broken out and many young men were being drafted.

My grandma Goldie with her son, and my dad, Bernie

Mom decided to move back to her parents' home in Junction City and dad was sent to Abilene, Texas for training. Mom was

4

now pregnant with me at the time dad had to leave for Texas, and mom wanted to join dad in Abilene before he was shipped out. She told me she went to see him by bus before I was born and then one last time on a train after I was born. Dad was then shipped overseas to France. In France dad befriended an orphan girl and he tried to adopt her, but because of the war and the red tape involved, the adoption did not take place.

My mother was pregnant with me. This is my parents back in 1942.

Mom was very reluctant about staying with her in-laws because she had already

My dad holding me when I was a baby, in Abilene, TX about 1943

had firsthand experience with dad's sisters and brothers and how they would not accept her into their family easily. The only brother of dad that actually accepted mom as one of the Pipers was dad's brother Bobby, and of course Bernadine, mom's best friend. Bernadine had already married George Thomson and was not living at home, but Bobby still lived at home.

During the time my mom and dad were together in Abilene, Texas, it was later in 1942 when grandpa Will and grandma Goldie moved their family from Florence to a farm near Olathe for a short time and then to an upstairs apartment in Rosedale, Kansas, a suburb of Kansas City, Kansas. I believe my grandparents wanted to move from Florence because in September 1941 water swept into Florence as the Cottonwood River went on a rampage, the worst in 35 years, and by October the river flooded for the third time in one year!

1951 flood in Florence, KS

There was a lot of damage that was done to basements, buildings and the streets. The businesses had water standing from two to three feet deep, and very few homes escaped this horrible flooding. During the month of November, 1941 more rain fell, about 6.48 inches, bringing the year's total to 42.21 inches of rain. My grandparent's home in Florence sat right at the end of the block on Fifth Street at the river's edge. Their home must have suffered greatly with each flooding. Back then there was a bridge that spanned the river at Fifth. Today that bridge can only be accessed through another street. The street that bordered the river in front of my grandparent's home is gone and a large dike sits where the street used to be.

Then, on December 7, 1941—PEARL HARBOR! My parents were married that following January and within a few months my dad was drafted into the Army!

I wanted to know more about the town of Florence, Kansas because my dad was born there and spent most of his growing up years there, except for a few years when his parents had lived near Trenton, Nebraska from about 1923 to 1930. The town of Florence was formed in 1870 by Governor Samuel Crawford and was recorded as being a railroad community and the first town in Marion County to have a railroad in 1871. The town was named in honor of Governor Crawford's daughter, Florence, who later became the wife of Arthur Capper, the governor of Kansas from 1915-1919, and a Kansas Senator from 1919-1949. The town began to grow rapidly with groceries under tents, shops in the open air, a bank for loans from a shed, and families living in covered wagons.

Florence suffered its serious first attack in 1874 when grasshoppers plagued the plains. The insects covered the sky and land, destroying all vegetation. Then drought followed, destroying the remaining vegetation and causing a mass exodus of people from many Kansas communities. By 1875 prosperity and success came to Florence and the population numbered about 1,000. As the railroad grew, so did Florence. By 1883 an Opera House was built and opened with a gala and colorful affair in January, 1884. A water tower was built in 1887 by C. O. Johnson, a stone contractor, and water lines were laid in Florence. A large well was dug on the east side of the Cottonwood River at the end of Seventh Street. In the 1920s oil was discovered after two oil wells were drilled and the town grew from about 1,000 people to about 3,500 almost overnight.

Grandpa Will had been working on the railroad in Florence and was offered a position at the train depot terminal in Kansas City after his daughter Bernadine talked to one of the employees of a train she had been riding about her dad Will. My own dad told mom he wanted her to live with his family, so mom took a bus from Abilene, Texas to Kansas City to stay with dad's parents who had moved there in 1942.

I was born on November 7, 1942 as Bernard (Frankie) (Frank) Franklin Piper, in Kansas City, Kansas. Shortly after my birth, mom decided to join dad again in Abilene, Texas because he hadn't been shipped out yet. I had been sick with the flu, or as some called it back then, the summer complaints, with it's complications during our stay in Abilene and almost died. But mom does not regret going to Abilene because she knew that her husband would be gone for several years fighting in the war. Mom must have been a very strong and independent woman to travel the way she did on buses and trains, and not knowing whether her husband would even return alive from the war. Mom tells me that she wished she had stayed in Junction City with her own family during dad's stint in the army because she knew her own family loved her and would have taken care of her and her new baby son.

TWO

ROSEDALE

Mom was now living with dad's parents, William (Will) Otto Julius Piper and Goldie Ellen (Mallory) Piper, in an upstairs apartment over a store-front business on the main street of Rosedale, KS. The name "Rosedale" was so named because of the hills and dales in that area that were covered with roses. Rosedale is a neighborhood in Kansas City and is located in the southeast corner of Wyandotte County and the Argentine neighborhood is to the west. Rosedale is the home of Rosedale World War 1 Memorial Arch, and the University of Kansas Medical Center, which was called the Bell Memorial Hospital when I was born there in 1942. My grandparent's apartment had a back entrance from the alley and outside wooden stairs to the second floor. Even though the apartment was located in town, grandpa was raising chickens in a fenced area in their back yard by the alley.

Frankie as a baby

I can still remember playing in their back yard when a rooster got loose from the pen and started chasing me. My dad heard my frantic cries and came running to catch the rooster. The rooster had already attacked me and had me face down on the ground, pecking at my head.

I was quite young and in diapers. Dad ended up killing that rooster and the family ate him for dinner.

There was another time at this upstairs apartment that my mom, Aunt Bernadine and Grandma Piper were in grandma's kitchen peeling potatoes. Aunt Bernadine's oldest daughter, Kathy and I were still in diapers and were playing under the kitchen table. At one point mom looked under the table to see how we were doing and mom asked grandma where Kathy and I had gotten a sweet potato to eat, and grandma told mom that she didn't have any sweet potatoes. They realized that I had found what rolled out of my diaper and was taking a bite and handing it to my cousin Kathy! Oh, the sweet innocence of babyhood.

Aunt Bernadine and Uncle George Thomson used to own a two-story house right in Rosedale. Mom stayed with them for a while and enrolled me in the Whitmore Grade School in a kindergarten class only a block away. I was only four years of age. The school wanted me to start early because my birthday would fall in November of that year and I would be five. I can still remember the lunches mom prepared for me in a paper bag for school. Aunt Bernadine would throw in a banana, which was quite a treat for me, since I don't remember my mother ever buying any bananas for us before. As a treat I do remember that we often had apples.

The living here and living there with family members of dad's must have been very hard on mom. But, almost three years later, dad came home from serving in World War II and they found an apartment to live in there in Rosedale. Dad found a job working for the Louis Shutte and Sons Lumber Company in Rosedale, and he kept that job till we moved away from the Kansas City area several years later. He had eventually become their lumber yard foreman.

Across from this lumber yard where dad worked was a row of houses. The first home as you entered onto the street from across the tracks was a two-story home owned by two women who laughed and giggled a lot, and who rented the upstairs apartment to my mom and dad. The entrance to the apartment was from the front door of the house that led into an entry way. The stairs were located to the left, against the wall, and they led straight up to a small landing and curved around to the right, and the stairs seemed to disappear into the ceiling.

It was in this upstairs apartment that I remember waking up during the night and headed towards mom and dad's bedroom where they always left their door open. As I approached the open doorway in the dark, my eyes started focusing on a bright shiny object over on the left in an open closet in their bedroom where coats and clothing usually hung. I could not take my eyes off that shiny object that had an ugly face imprinted on it that seemed to be angry looking. What gave that glow to the shiny object must have come from an open curtained window where the moon or a streetlight was shining in, but at the time the only thought I can remember was that the shiny object made me afraid and apprehensive to even take another step. I stopped dead in my tracks right there at the entry way and started to cry when mom heard me crying and came to rescue me. The shiny object was just a fancy broach attached to one of mom's coats! She was always so good about hearing me during the night if I cried out or called for her.

I can still recall playing outdoors in front of this home. There was a sidewalk in front of this row of homes but the streets were just dirt and gravel. It was a dead-end street that ended at the Turkey Creek on the south end of our street. The lumber company was situated on the east side of the street and took up most of that area. Then there was what we called the 'swinging bridge' at the end of our street that led across the creek to homes on the other side on a hill which was not visible because of the trees. I was never allowed to cross that 'swinging' bridge for fear of falling off of it into the Turkey Creek.

Many times I remember watching neighborhood girls playing jump rope in the street. Now I know that they were the Hamon girls just down the block, and they lived in the only other two story house on this block. I must have been only four or five years of age at the time when I kissed Wilma, one of those Hamon girls. Later in life I found out that she married my cousin Eddie, from my mother's side of the family.

Right next door to our house on the south side was a small house with a tall fence around the backyard with lots of trees, and there were chickens being raised in the backyard of this home. Mrs. Rice lived there with her two sons, and my mom would send me over to their home to buy eggs. I can still remember standing on their front poor knocking on the door.

Down the side street that ran alongside the railway tracks beside the home we lived in was another dead-end gravel frontage road, where a two-story home was where the "Land" kids lived, right behind the two-story home we lived in. These kids were very mean kids and we tried to stay away from them. We called them the "Land" kids because that was their last name. Across the street from their home and situated right at the tracks was a railway station. I can still remember going over to that railway station that had large glass doors. Looking right into this station I could see a large grandfather clock and I could hear it ticking away. I told myself that when I got older, I wanted to have a grandfather clock in my home. My wish did come true, but many years later.

The Land kids always seemed to create fear in everyone they came in contact with. At one time the boys conned me into coming into their home to get some candy and then they locked the doors so I couldn't get back out. As a little boy, I was afraid and cried. Their mother heard me crying and asked me what was wrong, and all I could tell her was that I wanted to go back home, so she opened the door and let me out. My mother never really understood the fact that I was afraid of that family and she would often take walks right by their home. It was during one of these walks that Mrs. Land came out to talk with mom. She was holding one of her infant sons and he had a butter knife in his hands. I was standing on the ground just below this infant and when he dropped the butter knife, it landed right near the edge of my left eye, near to my tear duct gland. The knife did not damage my vision but I always had trouble from that day on with my eyes watering and my eyes became very sensitive to air pressure and temperature changes. That problem has plagued me all my life.

One day a man leading a pony came by our house and was asking all the neighborhood kids if they wanted their picture taken sitting on the pony. Mom agreed and the man sat my brother and I on the horse and then he took a picture, but my brother Doug cried the whole time. I however enjoyed it.

A young Frankie and his brother Dougie sitting on a horse in Rosedale, KS

After we moved from the upstairs apartment, dad moved us into an apartment at the back of the garage at the lumber yard that was right across the street. Many of the childhood memories are captured from experiences I had living in the lumber yard apartment.

It was in this apartment at the back in of the garage that I remember finding what I thought was a chocolate candy bar while I was playing, and decided to sneakily indulge myself in its' tasty delights and not let my parents know what I had done. They might get mad, but I found out that it was not a chocolate candy bar at all. It turned out to be a laxative, so I ended up sitting on my little potty for several hours till the laxative worked its way through my little body. For a long time after that I would not even touch a candy bar.

One morning I woke up early while my parents slept and I started playing in the apartment and found a small keychain. I discovered that if I messed with the latch I could unsnap the chain and it would become one length and then if I snapped it together again it formed a circle. All it was was just a little boy's wonderment about the uniqueness of a little key chain. Oh the multiple uses I found for that little keychain!

Then I looked over and spotted my mom and dad still sleeping. Mom was on the outside nearest to me sleeping on her back, with her mouth wide open. I wondered to myself how far down I could dangle this little chain in mom's open mouth without it disappearing. So I walked over to the side of the bed and gingerly held the open chain over mom's mouth and slowly let it dangle there for a few moments. After a short time I lowered the chain even more into her open mouth when the inevitable happened. I lost my grip of the chain and the chain fell into her mouth. All I remember from that point on was that my mother started choking and sputtering, throwing her arms out wide. Her left arm hit dad right in his face as he slept, and soon the apartment was bustling with two very upset parents. Dad was grumbling, and mom got up and chased me around the apartment to spank my little behind. I ended up crawling under their bed, crying my eyes out and wondering what I did wrong. I had to literally take an emotional pit stop under that bed. I escaped the spanking, but only because mom couldn't reach me.

I remember another moment in time in this apartment that mom and dad were arguing profusely. It just seemed like dad was yelling at mom very loudly. My dad is over 6 foot in height, but my mother is only 5 foot 2. I was afraid for my mother and walked up and stood between the two of them and defended my mother by telling my dad not to hit her. That ended the fight and I never once saw or heard them ever fight or argue over anything ever again.

My brother Dougie was born during the time that we lived in this apartment at the back of the garage, and Dougie wasn't old enough to attend school yet but he was an active toddler. One Christmas mom and dad bought him a kiddy pedal car. It was always parked at the back of the garage but in front of our apartment. To me it looked just like a miniature grownups' car with headlights and a steering wheel. They had bought me a little red wagon, and I was thrilled with it and took it everywhere. We had a family dog Trixie who had a litter of pups and I would take these pups for a ride in my little red wagon. One little puppy fell out of my little red wagon and he died from the fall. I was totally devastated.

I would often give my brother a ride in that little red wagon, but he would never let me touch his kiddy pedal car. If I came near his pedal car, he would go running into mom and tattle on me. Mom would come out and tell me that Dougie didn't want me to ride his pedal car and to please stay away from it. Even as a little boy I couldn't understand why I wasn't even allowed to go near my brother's pedal car. It just didn't seem fair.

One afternoon my grandma and grandpa Piper came to visit us and they had their grandson Gene Haney with them. Gene and I ended up playing in the sand pile at the lumber yard. The gates to the lumber yard were always locked after closing time but since we lived in that apartment we had access to the whole yard through a side door from our apartment. The sand pile was near one of the locked gates alongside a stack of lumber that had been left out overnight, and Gene and I first played in the sand pile and then played on some of that stacked lumber. It was growing dark so we both decided to just sit on some lumber and talk. I looked up into the sky and saw the moon and stars and started singing "Over The Rainbow" in my little Vienna Boys Choir voice. Gene looked at me in amazement and told me that I really sounded good and that I ought to sing for a living when I grow up. Little did I know that I would indeed become a nationally known entertainer and singer.

I attended the Whitmore Grade School, which was only a block or so away from where we lived, but I had to cross the railroad tracks to get to the school. Because of the train depot situated right near us, all

the trains would slow down and often backed up to unload, sometimes blocking the intersection for a half an hour or more. If I could make it across the tracks I then would head on out to the main street of Rosedale, turning left to walk up the sidewalk. I passed a shoe repair shop and then on the corner just beyond his shop was a small home with a chain link fence around it where a little old lady

Whitmore Grade School in
Rosedale, KS

lived. She always had beautiful, colorful tulips and irises growing in and around her chain link fence. Those flowers grabbed my attention each time I passed her home, and to this day my favorite flower is the tulip.

The playground of Whitmore Grade School was all concrete. Even the Jungle gym made of steel piping was right on the concrete. I never wanted to climb on it for fear of falling off of it onto the concrete below, and the teeter-totter and the swings sat on concrete as well. Several years ago the Whitmore Grade School was torn down and only a playground remains. The supporting stone wall around that old playground still remains to this day.

After I crossed the side street heading to Whitmore, there was a small grocery store where I often would stop after school and buy penny candy. Across the street and catty cornered to this store, was the local Rexall drug store and malt shop. The drug store was on the same side as the school and playground. I would pass the grocery store and head to the crosswalk that would take me to the stairs that led the school children up into the playground and to the front doors of the school. There were always crossing guards there to help the children to the other side of the street. The school building is no longer there but that stone wall supporting the playground is still there.

My very first friend was Peggy who also attended Whitmore Grade School. She always wore braids in her hair, what some people called pig-tails. I later met her again when I attended the seventh grade at the Rosedale High School and she still wore those same braids in her hair. I only knew Peggy at school, and on the last day of school the principal of the school called both of us into her office and told us how proud she was of the two of us and what good students we had been for her. My first accolades.

Sometimes our teacher at this grade school would march our class down the front steps of the school playground and up the sidewalk in front of the school and across the side street to the large Methodist Church building where I remember a large sanctuary with very few lights. It was dark in various places in this large room but the platform area was lit up brightly. Sunday school teachers from the church would present a program for our class using little felt figures of Jesus and His disciples that they placed on a felt board. I was amazed at wherever she placed a felt figure, it stayed where she placed it. It was here that we were taught how to sing "Jesus Loves Me." I can still hear the little voices of all the kindergarten classmates of mine singing that wonderful song.

THREE
WASHINGTON GRADE SCHOOL

We used to travel often to Junction City from Kansas City, which was about a two hour drive and 126 miles, to visit with my mother's parents. My grandma, Ida Hazel Fern (Nickell) Day, and grandpa, Charles Franklin Day, used to live in a two-story home right on the main street of Junction City, nestled between local businesses. They had a cherry tree in their side yard that produced beautiful red cherries. The home had a wraparound front porch and back porch, with a fenced in back yard. There were two front doors into their home. The door on the left led to a staircase that led upstairs to two bedrooms. The main front door led into their living room. Grandpa Day always had a spittoon sitting on the floor near him, so he must have chewed tobacco and periodically had to spit into it?

They had a large kitchen with a large table right in the middle of the room. My cousin Eddie and his brother Jimmy lived with my grandparents most of their lives and had an upstairs bedroom. They were my mother's sister, Helen's sons. She had remarried and they didn't have room for the boys in their small home, only for their daughter Emma.

It was here at my grandparent's home that we found out that my mother's brother Vernon, who was serving in the military, had died of a brain tumor while he was overseas. They had shipped his belongings and then were shipping the body home for military burial. I can still remember seeing and touching Vernon's wallet with all its contents. Grandma ended up placing all of Vernons belongings in a chest that sat at the top of the stairs. Because of that chest sitting up there, Eddie and Jimmy didn't want to go up those stairs at night because they feared that Vernon's spirit was there with his belongings. Eddie and Jimmy, my Aunt Helen's boys who were living with my grandparents at the time, took me to the bottom of the stairs and told me that they dared me to go up those dark

My mother's brother,
Pvt. Vernon Day

stairs. I wanted to show them that I was a big boy and wanted to prove to them I could do it, plus they dared me! I wasn't afraid and went right up those stairs and passed that trunk on my way to their bedroom. From that time on, Jimmy and Eddie was afraid to go up the stairs at night. Eddie and Jimmy had created such a fear within themselves over something that really didn't matter, and even though I was so young, I had no fear of something I knew very little about.

My grandparents, Charles and Hazel Day's former home in Junction City, KS

Sometime after my kindergarten class ended while we still lived in Rosedale my parents decided to move to Junction City. Dad probably thought he could make more money there, so he quit the lumber yard. Grandma and Grandpa Day had moved from their two story home on the main street of Junction City to a home on east 10th street.

Going to my grandma Day's home on east 10th street was always fun. She and grandpa had a porch swing I loved to sit on and ride. Their front yard was above the sidewalk that ran in front of their home and a stone wall helped hold back the dirt that created their front yard. I used to love to play on this stone wall, and that wall is still there but grandma's house is gone. As a young boy that stone wall seemed to be so tall, but when I drove by there when I was much older, that wall seemed to be so short. I even knocked on the front door of that home and the new owners let me in for a few brief moments so I could relive my childhood memories. That home is no longer there.

We stayed with my grandparents until dad got a job at a gas station. Dad then found a two-story home for us to rent a few blocks away from

mom's parents and right next door to mom's sister, Helen (Day) Settgast, her husband Kip, and their daughter Emma, nicknamed Sissy. Aunt Helen and her family lived upstairs in that two-story home. Uncle Kip's sister and their family owned the house he and Aunt Helen lived in and they themselves lived on the main floor. These two homes are still there today.

My mother's sister, Helen (Day) Settgast

I started first grade at the Washington Grade School, which was about four blocks away from our home. I had to walk across Washington street of Junction City to get to the school, but again, there were always crossing guards there to help. Each day I walked to school I had to stand in line with all the other kids at the side door waiting for the doors to open. Even during the coldest of winters we always had to stand outside those doors, waiting. Even after recess when the bell would ring, we had to line up at the door waiting to be escorted into our classroom. I remember losing my little silver ring with two hearts on it on the playground of this school.

This school allowed the use of a rubber hose for discipline. I don't remember ever hearing of someone ever getting hit by it but it was always the possibility that you could be hit by it if you were out of line. The rubber hose always kept the fear factor up. My mom tells me that she also attended this same elementary school when she was growing up. What a history to tell my kids and grandkids! That school is still there today!

One time after school mom and dad took Dougie and me over to the grade school to play on their swings. Somehow I lost my grip and fell backwards out of the swing and onto the concrete below gashing the back of my head and it started bleeding. I never saw my dad so worried as when he picked me up to take me to our family doctor to get bandaged up.

There was hardly ever a time when I remember much affection shown, either between my mom and dad, or for us kids. Dad wasn't the kind of guy who could show much emotion. This much attention from dad was something I just wasn't used to, but it felt good. Even today when I see a father and son hugging, I get very emotional, because I know that I never experienced it. I always wondered how it felt to have a father's hug and approval. It just seemed like the only attention I ever got from my father was when I did something wrong, then out came his belt!

I brought a permission slip home for my mom one day asking her to sign it so I could go with my class on an outing, riding in an 18-wheeler cattle truck. The teacher wanted her kids to experience the fun of riding in the back of a truck where cattle usually ride. Mom didn't want me to go so she refused to sign the permission slip. My teacher told me that my mom was the only mother who didn't sign a permission slip, so my teacher drove out to our home asking mom if it was ok for me to go, after telling her how safe it was. Mom agreed and signed the form so I could go with my classmates. It turned out to be quite fun. All of us hung onto the open areas of the sides of the cattle truck and enjoyed the short ride.

At the south end of the Washington Street in downtown Junction City was Heritage Park, complete with a stone bubbling, colorful water fountain. Mom would often take us there so we could play in the park. I can still remember listening to the water showering above us in that concrete water fountain. As the water shot up in the air, the water would change colors. The park in Junction City is still there but the water fountain is gone.

Frankie as a baby

In the first grade I developed the whooping cough and the measles and missed a lot of school. My teacher told my parents that they felt that first grade in school was an important learning and development time for me and they wanted me to repeat first grade. It was during this time that mom and dad moved back to Rosedale and I started attending Whitmore Grade School again, repeating first grade. Dad was able to start working again for the lumber company there in Rosedale.

FOUR

BALL LANE

After I repeated my first grade at Whitmore grade school in Rosedale, Kansas, dad purchased a small mobile home for us to live in. I remember that the mobile home was often parked in Aunt Bernadine and Uncle George Thomson's driveway there in Rosedale, and later dad had the mobile home moved up to Gibbs road and 49th street. He was able to rent a temporary spot right next door to Tiny's, which was a bar/ store that was run by Tiny, a very large man. On the other side of where our mobile home was parked there was a corner gas station and an apartment building. My dad's sister, Aunt Louise, moved into the ground floor apartment right across from our mobile home so I got to see her son Gene, my cousin, and we got to play together. Gene eventually moved in with our grandma and grandpa Piper and lived with them till they both passed away.

My dad's sister Louise, dad's mother, Goldie, and my dad's sister, Bernadine

It was through this man called Tiny that dad found out about a property located on Ball Lane that was for sale. Dad became interested and decided to go ahead and purchase the land and build a home on it.

We continued to live in this small mobile home until the main part of the house was built, while dad purchased lumber and supplies from the lumber yard he worked at. I'm sure they must have given him quite a deal on lumber. I remember us driving over to this property that was covered with trees and brush. The land slanted downhill and was covered with small trees and brush. I wondered how dad could possibly build a house there.

Through the middle of the property ran a small creek and then our property continued on up a small landing and into the trees. There were lots of taller trees across the creek and on back to the end of our property which slanted uphill, and there were many trees for us boys to climb.

Before long, dad had cleared out many of the small trees and brush near the front of this property and then finished the stone foundation of our new home with the help of some of his brothers. My brother Doug and I witnessed the guys building the frame walls that stood up on end and became our four walls. The original framed home had only one bedroom and an L-shaped living room. Dad must have realized that this small framed home was not big enough for a kitchen, bathroom and a master bedroom. So before we moved into this new home that he had just built, dad added on a framed building attached to our basic home that housed a large eat-in kitchen, a master bedroom and a room for a bathroom. We then moved into our new home.

Frankie's childhood home his dad built on Ball Lane in Kansas City, KS

The school year started up again and mom enrolled me at the Noble Prentis Elemetary School on 34th street. The main part of the school was an old red brick building, but while I was attending school there they were building on a whole new classroom addition. After the new addition was added onto the school, they tore down the old red brick building and started building a newer building to replace the old one.

Noble Prentis Grade School, Kansas City, KS

I attended second grade through sixth grade at Noble Prentis elementary school, and I learned how to do cursive writing in the third grade. By fourth grade we were given tests we had to write the answers to on the blackboard. I got up and started writing my answers with my left hand, as I am left-handed. My teacher surprised me by coming over to me, slapping the back of my hand and telling me to use my right hand. I failed the blackboard test and was so hurt. I told my mother about it and she walked up the next day and barged into our classroom, confronting my teacher and told her to never slap my hand again or she would have to deal with her. She told my teacher that her Frankie was left-handed and he was going to stay that way. Incidentally, my mother is left-handed too. The teacher never tried to change what hand I used after that.

At a very young age I used to love to draw pictures of what I visually saw. By the fifth grade several of the students at Noble Prentis had finger-painted drawings that drew the attention of our art teacher. She was so impressed that she sent the best paintings of her students to the Nelson Art Gallery in Kansas City to be placed on display, and one of those finger paintings was mine. I enjoyed being able to draw so well, and so life-like, but I became discouraged when someone told me that they thought that art was for sissies. From that point on I never wanted to paint or draw again.

Our home at 2121 Ball Lane had two bedrooms, one being the master bedroom and the other a small bedroom, just off the living room, that my brother and I shared. There was a room in the new addition for a bathroom but dad wasn't in a hurry to finish the room, or just couldn't afford to. There was no city sewer and dad would have to install an underground septic tank. So, for the first few years we had to use an outside toilet across the creek in our backyard. If any of us wanted to take a bath we would have to bring in a big metal tub and sit it on the floor and fill it with warm water. I always brushed my teeth at the kitchen sink, or take a glass and stand at the back door. Mom had a wringer washing machine on our small back porch. I'm sure she had to carry hot water to fill it when she wanted to wash our clothes, and then drain the water onto the backyard!

Most of my childhood memories were created while we were living at this home at 2121 Ball Lane. This half acre of land was a haven for both my brother Dougie and myself and we so enjoyed running and playing and building tree houses and forts. Early on we had no television set but mom often listed to the radio. I still remember the programs called

My dad, Bernie with Frankie, Debi, and Dougie sitting on the ground in front of the house Bernie built on Ball Lane

"Only The Shadow Knows," and "Inner Sanctum." Another program she sometimes listened to was "Amos and Andy."

My dad was an outdoorsman. He frequently took Dougie and me on fishing trips and hunting trips. Dad owned several rifles and many fishing rods. My dad would even build his own row boats in our back yard. After he finished building one, he would strap the boat on top of one of his cars and we'd head to the Missouri River, the Kaw River as the locals called it, and he would carry that small row boat down to the river's edge. Dad, Dougie and I would board the boat and dad would row out several feet into the river to see if the boat would float. If no leaks appeared then he would take us out further, maybe to a waiting sandbar island, where he'd park the boat partway upon the sandbar, and we boys would go running barefoot on the delicious sand which cradled sand between our toes. It was fun for us youngsters.

One trip we had taken out to the Kaw River is a trip I will never forget. Dad wanted to check his trout line. Since dad was a fisherman he would often bait a trout line and leave it in shallow water and then he would come back the next day to check if he had caught any fish during the night. A trout line was a long metal chain with fish hooks attached to it every few feet.

Dad launched our small row boat out into shallow water near the shore and proceeded to reach his hand over the side of the boat to feel if the trout line had caught any fish. While dad was busy, Dougie stood up and sat on the edge of the boat. I turned my head to watch dad, and when I turned around, Dougie was nowhere to be seen. I looked over the edge of the boat and saw the top of my brother's head in about three feet of water. He was sitting on the bottom of the river, just staring straight ahead, as if he were in shock! I yelled to dad and he came rushing over to pull Dougie up out of the water. Dougie was ok except that he became so afraid of the water that he never learned how to swim and was always afraid of being near the water.

Quail season came around and dad prepared his rifles for hunting. The night before our hunting trip, dad told us boys that we needed to be up by four o'clock am and eat a hearty breakfast before we headed out. The nighttime hours seemed to go by so fast and before I knew it I heard my mother in the kitchen preparing a hearty bacon and egg breakfast. I could smell the bacon frying. Dougie and I were still sleepy and really didn't want to get up, so when mom called us to come eat breakfast, I wasn't even hungry, but we both got up and stumbled into the kitchen. I knew dad had warned us to eat, but I just couldn't eat.

While it was still dark, we three piled into the front seat of dad's car. Dad brought along our family dog, Trixie, who was a good pointer. All I wanted to do was go back to sleep. If I were in the back seat, that's exactly what I would have done. Dad knew that, so he purposely kept us boys in the front seat while he drove.

We drove for what seemed like hours to a farmhouse where dad had obtained permission for us to go hunting on their property in a forest of trees at the backend of the farm. Dad parked the car and we all got out. It was just starting to get light out and dad handed me a 410 rifle. He told me he wanted me to get used to holding and shooting one since I had never handled a rifle before. I only knew how to shoot a Daisy BB gun, but dad gave me a few pointers on 'what not to do' and then he told me to place the butt of the gun up against my left shoulder. Being left-handed, it seemed awkward for me, but I had to adapt to a right-handed world.

The gun wouldn't fit up against my shoulder, so I pushed the butt of the gun up under my left armpit. The butt was so long it stuck out the back, but it was then that I could lean my cheek into the rifle to focus on a target. Dad pointed to a small bird sitting in a nearby evergreen bush and told me to aim, and when I was ready, to pull the trigger. I saw the bird right in front of my rifle, and I pulled the trigger. The rifle kicked and I felt a sudden, sharp pain on my left cheek and jawbone. As I stood there dazed and in shock from the kick of the rifle, I could hear my dad telling me that I had shot the bird. His joy turned to surprise when he took a closer look at me. I was bleeding. The skin on my cheek had been ripped away by the jolt of the gun firing. We didn't go hunting that day. We spent most of the day at the hospital. I still have a scar just below my jaw from that ordeal.

After hunting trips we often brought home rabbits, squirrels, and ducks. Dad taught us boys how to 'clean' these dead animals for cooking. I would hold the cold dead paws of their back legs up, while dad did the dirty work. We must have eaten many rabbits and squirrels and ducks during our early childhood years. Dad even cooked frog legs for himself. When I saw those legs jumping around in the frying pan, there was no way I would even touch them. We were even served barbecued raccoon on a sandwich, unbeknownst to us boys. Had I known what it was, I probably would not have eaten it.

On one hunting trip dad came across a pawpaw tree in the woods. He told us those trees were rare and the fruit even rarer. The fruit is one of the largest edible fruits and can weigh up to 5 to 16 ounces and are 3 to 6 inches in length. Pawpaw fruit seeds look like lima beans and the fruit itself usually grows in clusters. The ripe fruit is soft and thin skinned and tastes somewhat like a pear.

When Dougie and I were still in grade school, mom started sending us to a Baptist church near the corner of Douglas and Eleventh streets which was up the street from our home on Ball Lane. It wasn't much of a walk for us and we enjoyed the Sunday school classes. Right after Sunday school we'd meet by the front door of the church and walk back home together. Our attending this Baptist church actually started because of the Baptist church's outreach program. One of their volunteers, driving one of their church buses, stopped by our home on Ball Lane and talked with mom about the church. I know they were hoping that our whole family would attend. Mom and dad didn't attend, but made sure we were there every Sunday.

One Sunday, Dougie and I got up, got dressed in our Sunday best, and walked to the Baptist Church. When we arrived at the church, it looked like the church wasn't open. There were no cars parked anywhere, and the doors were locked. We stayed for a few minutes and decided to walk back home. What we didn't realize was that we had gotten to the church an hour earlier and there was no one there yet. Mom turned us around and told us to walk right back up to the church again. Dougie and I thought we had had a free Sunday and would be able to stay home and play. Mom didn't let us get by with it.

The following Sunday morning Dougie was sick, so I walked to the Baptist church all by myself. I attended my Sunday school class as usual, but after Sunday school I followed some of the other kids into the sanctuary. Church was about to begin. I had not been to a Sunday morning worship service yet because Dougie and I had always just walked home after our classes ended.

Frankie, age six

31

Something was different this time, and I felt it in my spirit. Something was drawing me into the service.

I walked into the already crowded sanctuary and someone was playing a hymn on the piano near the front of the sanctuary. I found an open seat just off an aisle to my right and sat down at the end of the pew closest to the aisle. I had never experienced a church service before, and I was really starting to enjoy the beautiful music and the singing coming from the stage area. A group of people that were sitting in chairs behind a pulpit began to sing in unison. My little heart was pounding so fast that I thought it was going to burst right out onto my chest. The song leader had us stand, and then sit, stand and then sit. What was all this ritual about? Before I knew it I saw a few guys walking down the sides of all the pews passing a plate around. When the plate was handed to me, I realized that people had been placing dollar bills in the plate. Some were even coins. This sure looked like the same kind of ritual that my Sunday school teacher did when she handed us a small wicker basket to place our coins in for an offering during Sunday school.

When the beautiful music ended, a man stepped up to the pulpit and began to speak loudly. He told stories about the life of Jesus and that Jesus was the Son of God. He said that Jesus died on a cruel cross for us. He then said, "I would rather live my life as if there is a God, and die to find out there isn't, than live my life as if there isn't, and die to find out there is." His finger seemed to be pointing directly at me when he stretched out his arm to gesture. These were the same kind of stories I was being taught in my Sunday school class. I tried to wrap my mind around what he was saying. That preacher was talking directly to me, I just knew it. But when I looked around, I realized that he was talking to all of us.

When the preacher ended his speech, he asked us all to stand. He started asking everyone if they had given their hearts to Jesus. I told myself that it sure felt like I did when my heart was still beating so fast that I thought it would literally explode. I instinctively placed my left hand over my heart to see if my heart was coming out of my chest. No, it was still there, but beating very fast. He then asked the people to come forward if they wanted to accept Jesus into their hearts. I didn't hesitate. I burst out of the pew and started walking with a purpose, down to the front. By this time there were several men standing in front of the pulpit. One of those men bent over to greet me and asked me if I believed in Jesus Christ. I said yes. He then took ahold of my right hand and led me to a door on the left of the stage area. After entering into a small room that looked like a storage room, he bent down and told me Jesus died for me and asked me to confess that I was a sinner and to ask Jesus to forgive me. He asked me if I wanted to accept Jesus as my Lord and Savior. Afterwards he admitted to me that he felt that I was too young and not knowledgeable enough to be baptized yet. l left there very hurt and discouraged. I had an opportunity to visit this same church one week-end when I was visiting the area recently, and I told a few people there that I had attended this church when I was about 9 years of age. No one seemed impressed or showed that they even cared. I would have jumped on that knowledge and made a statement from the pulpit to acknowledge that person!

Some of my greatest experiences were when our family would drive to Zarah, Kansas to spend time with dad's parents, grandma and grandpa Piper. They had purchased an acre or two of land on the outskirts of Zarah where grandpa could enjoy planting a large garden. They had built a flat-roofed house originally, and later added on a large slanted roof that became another bedroom, the only entrance to the upstairs was by climbing up a ladder on the outside of their home. Their farm house only had an outside toilet, but did have running water for the kitchen.

When we visited one week-end, I remembered that grandpa Piper had invited the family to go out to his garden to see all his radishes, lettuce and carrots. My cousin Gene and I went back into the house when I noticed that grandma had a large pot sitting on her stove covering all four burners. I asked Gene what grandma was cooking, but he said he didn't know. He told me to grab a kitchen chair, stand on it, and see for myself. I grabbed one of grandma's kitchen chairs, pulled it over to the side of her stove, grabbing a dish towel before I stood on the chair, and proceeded to reach up and grab the lid handle to look inside. When I lifted the lid only a few inches, I saw two hairy ears and hair on the top of something. It shocked me so much that I dropped the lid and ran out of the house screaming, "Grandma is cooking a monster!" What I hadn't remembered was that earlier on when we first arrived, everyone had been talking about the slaughtered pig my grandparents had butchered. Apparently they were cooking the pig's head for head cheese?

On another visit to my grandparents there in Zarah, Kansas Grandma Piper kept telling me that she could slide her bottom teeth out. I asked her to show me. She pushed her bottom false teeth out about two or three inches, and all I could do was stand there with eyes the size of golf balls, wondering how she could do that! I tried doing it myself but my teeth wouldn't budge. I can still remember my grandma because she was the one who could slide her teeth out and she always wore an apron.

A great experience was created in July of 1956 when my parents made traveling plans with grandma and grandpa Piper for a vacation. We car-pooled with dad's parents on a trip to visit grandma's brother, my great uncle Jack Mallory. Jack and his wife Doris owned and operated

34

the famous Swanky Club located on the Boulder highway in Henderson, Nevada. The Boulder highway ran through the north side of Henderson and right to Las Vegas. The Swanky Club itself sat between Henderson and East Las Vegas on that highway. Mom bought Dougie and me two pair of jeans each and a couple of new shirts for the trip. These clothes would also be used as our new clothes for school that would start in September.

What an exciting trip! I can still remember places that we visited and motels we all stayed in along the way. We probably traveled on the famous Route 66. We stayed at a motel in Flagstaff, Arizona on our way out to Nevada. When we reached the Hoover Dam we all got out and stretched our legs, and when we did, Mom took a picture of us boys standing on the Arizona side of the dam all dressed up in our new jeans and shirts.

We drove to the famous Swanky Club and we were able to meet Jack and Doris Mallory and their family. They had a son, Richard, and a daughter Sharon, who were my second cousins. In Henderson there was a street named Mallory Street. Uncle Jack Mallory, with a previous wife, had had another son who was killed in the service, and Mallory Street in Henderson

Picture of the first Swanky Club before it burned down

was named after him. Uncle Jack had divorced Doris, but remarried her after his son died. When Jack and Doris died they were buried in Henderson.

We toured the Swanky Club and ate from their smorgasbord for which they were so famous for, and then we walked back to the Mallory's two-story home that sat well behind the Swanky Club. There I met my great-grandma, Rosa Leuna (Fleming) Mallory, who must have been in her late 80s at that time. This was my grandma Piper's mother. The impact of meeting the family really didn't register with me at the time, and

My great-grandma Rosa (Fleming) Mallory with her sons Jack and John

little did I know that this would be the last time I would ever see my great-grandma Rosa alive. We heard a few years later that the Swanky Club had burned to the ground but my Uncle Jack rebuilt it on the very same spot. Little did I know that I would be working at the new Swanky Club in 1962, six years later!

What a trip for us two boys to remember for the rest of our lives! I wanted to come back to Noble Prentis Elementary and describe our whole vacation, but the teacher never asked us students what we did over the summer months.

I do remember during the middle of the night, on many occasions, that I would wake up and call for mom. It was always so dark in our bedroom and there were no streetlights on our street to help shine any light through our window, but every time I would call mom, she would always come to my rescue. Sometimes I just needed to know that she was there. Sometimes I knew it was because of a bad dream. Was I insecure? Probably! But I also knew that I did not like not being able to see anything in the dark. Back then we had no night lights.

My mother was a good cook. My dad was a meat and potatoes kind of guy and while I was growing up, we always ate well and never went without a meal. Mom did not know how to prepare spaghetti but I do remember one time she tried fixing a meal of spaghetti and we had to pour ketchup on it. The only things I remember my dad ever cooking were frog legs and sometimes fried potatoes.

On one occasion at our home on Ball Lane, I remember waking up during the night and noticed a kid standing right next to my bed with his head leaning forward in a shy manner. I thought it was my brother Dougie, just standing there. There must have been a glow from the moon coming through our bedroom window because I don't know how else I could have seen him standing there. There were no street lights on our street. I told him to get back to bed, and I turned over and went back to sleep. Was it my brother Dougie or was it a vision?

The next morning I asked Dougie why he was standing in front of my bed in the night. He told me that he hadn't gotten up at all during the night. Then I asked myself, who was it then? Was Dougie sleep walking? To this day I still do not understand who or what I saw, but I do remember having a vivid dream that same night. My dream started with me sitting in the back seat of our family car and I looked up into the sky and saw a man, dressed in a long white robe at the top of a long flight of stairs, and he was starting to descend. Then I felt as if my heart had stopped beating and I slumped over in the back seat. I didn't stay long in that position and sat back up. In my dream I recalled that I had been told many times that no one can see God face to face and live. It is so hard for me to tell anyone about this episode without becoming emotional. Was it a dream or a vision? Was the vision of Dougie a warning?

My parents often struggled financially just to keep afloat and there were many times that one of the utilities had to be shut off for lack of payment. There were many times that I had no decent shoes to wear to school and I had to wear my mother's penny loafers. Most of the time the pants I wore were so baggy, and the crotch hung all the way down to my knees. I was often embarrassed by my appearance. (I would have fit in very well with today's styles!) During my early years when we had no inside bathroom, we didn't bathe that often so I can just imagine what I might have smelled like as well.

As I sat at my chair at school tucking the crotch of my baggy pants under me so no one would take notice, sometimes I would hear snickers from other classmates and sometimes laughter and pointing. I knew that sometimes kids can be so heartless. I just wanted to disappear into a knothole and cover the hole up over me. When I was able to deliver newspapers in our neighborhood it helped me to be able to buy clothes. Later I developed a TV Guide route that gave me enough money to buy my own lunches in the cafeteria at school, instead of always brown-bagging it.

One Christmas I received a sled as a present from my parents. I knew beforehand because Dougie and I had awakened about four o'clock in the morning Christmas day, and headed out to the living room to open our presents. We had to tiptoe past our grandma Day, mom's mother, who had come from Junction City to spend Christmas with us. She was sleeping on our living room sofa.

We got all the way to the Christmas tree by the front window where I saw a sled sitting up against the tree, just what I asked for. All of a sudden we heard grandma say, "What are you boys doing up so early? Get back to bed!" I was totally startled and let out a gasp. Grandma was angry that we had gotten up so early and awakened her. We both went back to our bedroom, but that whole ordeal with grandma ruined our Christmas excitement.

It had snowed a night or two before Christmas and the streets were still covered with snow and snow-packed tire tracks. I wanted to try the sled out right away and took it out into the street, walking up to the top of the slope just beyond the front of our home and heading down the hill on my sled. The sled didn't go very far and I was very discouraged. As I walked back up to the top of the street I looked towards the crook in the bend of the road and saw someone walking towards me with a sled under his arms. Great, I can meet another kid on our street and we can sled together. As the figure came closer I noticed it was a girl. Her name was Beverly Walters, and she lived a few houses up the street on the opposite side of the street. As we talked I told her my sled was knew and it didn't go very fast. She told me that maybe my sled would go faster if the two of us got on it. I flattened myself out on the sled and she got on top of me and we slid down the hill on my sled. Yes, we did go faster and a friendship developed. Beverly was one year older than me and attended Noble Prentis as well. Sometimes I would walk to her home up the street and together we would walk to school. I had found a new friend and spent many evenings at her home playing.

On several occasions when I visited Beverly's home, her mother would make a special candy by melting down Redhots to make a gooey soft candy that was so sweet and tasty. Several times Beverly's mother would make a banana cream pie and send it home with me for our family to enjoy. Sometimes when I went to play with Beverly, her mother would make homemade dumplings. I did not know what dumplings were so her mother gave me one to eat after she had dropped it into a pan of boiling water, or was it grease, and left it to cool for me.

All through grade school Beverly and I were the best of friends. One time when Beverly walked to my house to walk with me to school, we decided to take a shortcut through the woods. I often walked through these woods because a path had been formed by others that had also taken this shortcut.

When we got halfway through the forest we decided we were not going to go to school and spent the rest of the day playing in the woods. We were playing hooky~! We stayed in those woods until we glanced out at the streets and saw fellow classmates walking by and we knew school was over. Beverly said she could write an excuse note for herself and for me, and she did. Nothing was ever said about it and we got by with it, but the guilt floated over us both like a dark stormy cloud, and we chose to never play hooky again.

When I was still in the sixth grade at Noble Prentis, Beverly was already in seventh grade at Argentine High School, the high school in our district. We didn't see each other much after that because when I was ready for the seventh grade, I started to attend Rosedale Junior-Senior High School in a different school district, only because I gave my cousin Faye Miller's address as mine so I could ride the school bus with her. Faye was my mother's sister Marie's daughter. Her family lived on Merriam Blvd in the Rosedale school district, so I had a short walk to her family's apartment from our home on Ball Lane. Faye and I would stand out on Merriam Blvd together at the school bus stop five days a week. This worked out fine until Faye and her family moved away. When Faye moved away I had to walk all the way to Rosedale High School, which was over a mile or so from our home on Ball Lane. By 8th grade I attended Argentine High School.

The Rosedale Junior-Senior High School was dedicated on March 18, 1927 and was erected at a cost of $160,000 and was one of the finest high schools in the state of Kansas in 1927 was the first year that 7th grade pupils from Whitmore, Columbian, Maccochaque, Snow and Noble Prentis attended. There were no 'middle' schools back then. After sixth grade all of us were thrown in with the high school students immediately. This school I attended is now presently the Middle School.

The first day of school at Rosedale High was a very confusing day for me because they handed each student a small orange card with many room numbers on it, which nobody bothered to explain to me what it all meant. After the opening bell rang I took all my books and that card with me and followed a crowd of kids heading to a classroom and I went in with them. The teacher immediately started a roll call to make sure every student was there. My name was not called and by that time I was too ashamed to let the teacher know that I did not belong in that classroom and was supposed to be in a different class room. But sitting in a chair in that classroom gave me time to study that card and realize that I was supposed to attend each of those classroom numbers that were listed on that orange card. In the seventh grade I never missed a day of school, but because I had not attended that one class that I accidentally missed by going to another class, I did not receive the award for perfect attendance at the end of the school year, even though technically I was there!

In seventh grade at Rosedale Junior-Senior High School, I joined the high school Glee Club. It was perhaps the first time I could really exercise my vocals and try and get more confidence by singing with a group of other students. The music teacher tested our musical skills by playing the scales on her piano. When it was time for me to sing, she started running out of keys on her piano and wondered when the key she was playing would be too high for me to sing. She stopped and asked me if I had a break in my voice somewhere. I assured her I didn't know what she was talking about, so she proceeded to play up the scales again, asking me to project a little bit more. Still no break! During her third time and asking me to almost shout, she did find a faint break in my vocal cords that meant that I was in a falsetto voice. She told me I had a very unique voice and to use it someday to become a trained singer. Little did she know how true those words were going to become.

In one of my classes I ran into that same Peggy that I knew when we were kids in the kindergarten class at Whitmore Elementary. She was still wearing those same braids. What a shock that was!

Walking home one day after school, a guy who I saw occasionally at Rosedale High, caught up with me. We talked about many subjects, and I told him about my friend Beverly, who I grew up with. I told him that she had to attend Argentine High School and I had lost touch with her. He suggested that we both go to her house, but little did I know that he had other plans.

On the way, he suggested we take a short-cut through the forest. I loved that part of the forest and often had walked through it on my way to Noble Prentis Grade School. Beverly and I had played hooky in this same forest. There was a beaten down path right through that forest where many others had walked. We started walking off the path, just having fun walking through the trees. All of a sudden he stopped dead in his tracks. He turned around and told me to take my pants down. What? He told me that he had never seen an uncircumcised guy before. He said his friends at school had seen me in the locker room in the gym and told him about it. He said that he just wanted to see one. At birth my mother didn't have me circumcised, and I didn't have that procedure done until

I was about 24 years of age. I thought to myself that this was an awful, strange request. Reluctantly, I dropped my pants. He stood there for a few seconds, looking through a mental telescope at my exposed body.

A few blinding moments later he came over to me and pushed me to the ground, holding me down so I couldn't get up. He fumbled with his pants and dropped down on top of me, crushing me into the dirt and rocks. I had heard the word rape before, but never in my wildest dreams did I ever think that this kind of thing ever happened to boys. It took only moments and he got up and ran as fast as he could out of the forest. I just sat there hurt and crying. This was something that I didn't feel comfortable telling anyone about. When I arrived home later than usual my mother asked me if everything was ok, and all I could do was lie through my smile and tell her that yes, everything was ok. It was hard for me to even go back to school the next day. I didn't know a lot about sex in the seventh grade, and it was becoming harder for me to have close friends after that. I just didn't trust anyone. I was becoming a very angry young man. I was afraid to walk to school and back home again, always avoiding eye contact with anyone.

I was given the opportunity to join a boys marching group at Rosedale high school. We all had to wear white pants and white shirt for our debut march at the school. We practiced our intricate maneuvers weekly at the school and then gave a show in the Rosedale High School auditorium, but mom and dad didn't come to that performance, and I was so disappointed and hurt.

Then, the most shocking news came. Beverly's dad told my parents that her mother had tried to commit suicide with a rifle and was in the hospital. Dad and mom took off for the hospital to see her. Before she died she kept telling the doctors and visitors that her husband killed her.

And even with her last dying breath she still spoke of the fact that her husband shot her.

After Beverly's mother's death I was told not to go play with Beverly and to stay away from their home. Beverly's dad kept Beverly occupied by taking her to the movies and such. I did stay away out of respect.

One day while walking to the store that was at the end of Ball Lane, I had to walk right past Beverly's home. It was hard for me to pass her home and not stop in, but I walked on by. On the way back home I was walking down a slope of the road just before her home and I saw Beverly standing out in her front yard near the street, facing the street, with her head down. Apparently she had been waiting for me to come. I did not know what to do because I was told to stay away from her. We were told that Beverly's dad had been trying to keep her busy so she wouldn't remember the tragic circumstances of her mother's death, so he would send her to movies and to her older brother's home, anything to keep her mind off of what had just happened. At that very moment I was torn as to what to do, and decided to walk on by without saying a word. I have regretted that moment in time and know now that I made the wrong decision. That memory of Beverly standing there waiting for me will probably haunt me for the rest of my life. I have so wanted to meet her again to tell her how sorry I am.

By eighth grade I attended Argentine High School, which must have been two or three miles in the opposite direction from our home. There were no school buses for me to ride so I had to walk five days a week to school and back. I would always look for Beverly every time I passed her home, but by this time she and her father must have moved away. I never saw Beverly again.

While attending Argentine High I started dating Joan Wax. We met when she asked me if I would be willing to dress as a sailor and sit on the back of her father's decorated car that was entered into a parade in Argentine. Joan would be dressed as a mermaid. Of course I would, and her family provided me with a sailor suit to wear and we rode on the back of her father's convertible in this parade, waving to everyone lined up on the streets during the parade. Their car came in third as the best decorated car in the parade. I was so proud and was hoping my parents would come to the parade, but they didn't.

A Boy Scout representative visited Argentine High School and sent a note home for my parents. Dad thought it was a good idea for me to join the scouts, so I did join and learned quite a bit about scouting, earning badges and learning how to tie knots. At one of our weekly meetings they held a contest to see which one of us could figure out how to pick up a coke bottle with a paper straw. We were not allowed to tie a knot in the straw, so we had to figure out how to pick up the bottle with only that one paper straw. Standing in line waiting for my turn gave me time to figure it out. I took the paper straw and bent it in the middle in two places. I lowered the straw into the bottle and then bent the straw in those two places, which created a sturdy wide area of the straw inside the bottle that helped me to demonstrate how to pick up the bottle. All the kids were amazed that I figured that out all by myself. I won the prize.

We experienced overnight camping in tents and hiking while I was in the Boy Scouts. I can still remember all the fun I had with my troop.

Then I joined a boys club called the Grey Y. It didn't seem as organized as the Boy Scouts so I didn't stay long in this club and stopped going to their meetings. All the boys ever did was meet at a building in northwest Kansas City and play basketball till our Grey Y leader came and then a little talk and we were dismissed.

At the time that my family moved into the home at 2121 Ball Lane, there were very few houses around us. We were the only house within a block or two, except the one right across the street from us where an older couple with the last name of Pierson lived. What a sweet couple! Once in a while Mrs. Pierson would ask me to go to the store for her to pick up something and she would always pay me about twenty five cents for doing her that favor. They owned a very mean dog that they kept behind a chain-link fence in their front yard. Its bark was louder than the dog was big, but the dog always informed the couple whenever someone was approaching their house.

Within the first year we saw a family by the last name of Brown, building a house next door to us on the back end of their property on the hill. It seemed as though they built it in one day and moved in the next. It was just a small cracker box of a house, sitting on wooden blocks. We never really became friends with them because they always seemed aloof. One of their kids was a retarded young boy by the name of Jimmy, and when he got mad, Jimmy would bite his own hand, leaving teeth marks. Strange~! And if he got mad at his neighbors and friends, he would throw rocks. We learned to stay away from the whole family.

One day my brother Dougie and I saw Jimmy out playing alone near our property line, and we asked him to come over. We had been playing at the far back end of our property and their home sat right across the fence. This part of our property had many tall trees, some of which we climbed and had built tree houses or platforms to sit on. Jimmy crossed over the chicken wire fence they had built near their house that separated our property from theirs, and we asked Jimmy if he wanted to climb up to our tree house. He said he wanted to, so we placed a small ladder next to the tree for him to could climb up on. We didn't think he could handle stepping on each wooden step we had nailed to the tree that we had built to climb on to reach that platform, so Jimmy climbed up the ladder to the small wooden platform that had been built on the lower limbs of the tree, and he sat down on it. He seemed to be enjoying the fact that he was up in the tree, probably for the first time in his life he had ever been in a tree. We then took the ladder away so he couldn't get back down. Dougie and I were both just being silly.

We decided to not let Jimmy come down out of the tree unless he pulled his pants down. After a little coaching, Jimmy pulled his pants down, exposing his white underwear, and then we let him come down. After Jimmy went back home, both Dougie and I laughed our heads off. What a riot! Were we being mean? Probably, but we both enjoyed the experience tremendously.

Soon, yet another house was being built at the intersection of Ball Lane and Steele Street, near the Y in the road, just down the street from us. We never really got to know who this family was but we knew one of their sons was nicknamed Jughead, so we dubbed the family as the Jughead family. Again, not a very friendly family as rumor had it, and their three sons always seemed to be in trouble constantly.

Right next door to us to the north, a family by the name of Cobb built a house, and my mother became friends with Mrs. Cobb. Mr. Cobb drove a truck for the Pepsi Company, so we would often see a Pepsi truck parked in their driveway. The Cobb family lived in this house only a few years and then moved to Topeka, and after that, we lost track of them.

My dad's sister Joan and her husband Freddie Patch moved into the Cobb's home and became our neighbors for a while. They too didn't stay long and moved. Then another family moved in. I don't remember how many families ended up living in the old Cobb's family house before we moved ourselves.

At one point I was offered an opportunity to deliver newspapers and have my own delivery route, but to do so I would need a bicycle. Realizing my situation dad decided to buy me a bike so I could accept working for the Kansas City Journal. I know he paid about $60.00 for my bike and that was a lot of money back then, so the next hurdle was for me to learn how to ride it. To this day I can still remember how frustrating it was for me to learn how to balance on that two—wheeled contraption. In a day or so I accomplished the task of not falling off of that bike and accepted the offer from the Kansas City Journal to be a paper boy for my region. I had to deliver papers seven days a week, which eventually got old, but it was great spending money on myself and I was able to buy some decent clothes to wear to school. I started feeling better about myself.

We ended up living about seven years in this home, and towards the last few years of our residence there, dad finished the inside bathroom, complete with a shower, a stool, and a sink. He had also installed an underground septic system to handle all the waste water.

My sister, Debra Paula Diane Piper, was born while we lived on Ball Lane. Dad built a special crib for her out of wood and I can still see that homemade crib. Mom used glass bottles for Debbie's milk and one time when I was teasing Debbie in her crib, she hit me on the top of my head with her glass bottle. I was seeing stars for hours afterwards, so I learned not to tease her anymore.

Dougie and I used to love to play with a basketball in our house when it was cold outside. I remember standing in the middle of our living room and Doug was standing close to a side window in the living room. We were having fun tossing the ball back and forth, and then one time he ducked and the ball went over his head and the ball went right through that side window, breaking the glass. The French windows in our home were special windows and not that easily found. Dougie didn't get in trouble, but I received a spanking with dad's belt when he got home after work.

It just seemed that Dougie always got by with murder and could do no wrong. I didn't know it at the time but Dougie was dad's favorite. It became more and more apparent as time went on when Dougie would get new clothes and special treatment. This caused me years and years of resentment. My brother and I could hardly ever get along. The spirit in this little boy's heart of mine knew that something just wasn't right. I would constantly pick on Dougie and not include him in many play times, and he would often find times to get even with me, because he knew he could.

On one week-end my parents had gone into Rosedale to a store that sold farm equipment and tools, and they ended up bringing home a whole crate full of baby chickens. We had no place to keep them so dad built a fenced in area across the little creek in our back yard and built a sort of chicken coop to house them. The chickens grew quickly and I know that some of our fried chicken must have come from some of those chickens in our back yard.

Mom killed one of the hens for dinner one day and put the head and feet into a brown paper bag, throwing it in the trash. Dougie found it and decided to have fun with me and he came outside where I was playing and opened the paper bag for me to see what was inside. As soon as I saw that head with open eyes and feet, I yelled and ran. What did Dougie do, but run after me with that awful paper bag with the chicken parts in it. Do you think Dougie got in trouble for doing this? NO.

We did not have a TV set for many years, but ended up purchasing one after we had lived in our home on Ball Lane about six years. The only thing I can remember of the old TV shows were "I Love Lucy," and many, shoot-em up cowboy and Indian movies. Somehow I always found myself rooting for the Indians. I don't know why I was always rooting for the Indians. Little did I know that later in life my research would prove that I shared a grandmother with Lucille Ball!

We never had a home phone until we moved to Winchester, Kansas in 1961. All those years of no one being able to contact us by phone sometimes became a problem. There were times when someone in my mother's family had died and we didn't know about the funeral until someone wrote us a letter. We were always having family members showing up at our door unexpectedly because they knew they didn't have a way to notify us ahead of time. When mom's brothers died, she could never be notified and sometimes didn't know about their death until years later!

My real love of music started at this boyhood home when I would listen to the radio and sing and dance to the music. I would grab door handles and chairs and brooms to dance with. My first single 45 rpm record I bought was a song titled "The Purple People Eater." From that day on I was sold out and yearned to listen to more music. Later in life I was able to record that song.

FIVE
OUR FONTANA FARM

After my sister Debi was born, mom and dad realized that they needed a bigger home, so dad placed our home on the market and they began to search for homes to buy. On the week-ends we would often drive to homes that were not in the Kansas City area, and one drive even took us all the way into Arkansas.

Every home we looked at were homes out in the country. Dad must have longed to get back to his roots, and that was farming, because by this time my dad's friend Ed Probst, from Rosedale, who lived right next door to us and sold us eggs several years ago, wanted to move with us.

Mom and dad did find a forty acre farm near Fontana, Kansas and purchased it, and Ed Probst moved with us. Fortunately our house on Ball Lane sold quickly and we were able to move. From the sale of our home, dad purchased a tractor for Doug, chickens, and a couple of pigs we named Dot and Dotty. He also purchased a few ducks.

The town of Fontana was about 52 miles south of Kansas City and near the Missouri border. We would often buy our groceries in a little town called Beagle, which was only a few miles away. Beagle had the only store in the area and this store had a pot-belly stove that helped heat it up in the winter. Local men would come and sit around the heat of this stove and chew the fat and smoke.

One day I was standing near the front door of our farm house with only the screen door closed when a car drove by. The road running in front of our farm house was a rock road that would kick up quite a bit of dust. I saw teenage boys sitting in the car, never realizing that these two boys were some of our neighbors just about a half a mile up the road, and the boys were twins, Robert E. Lee, and Roger M. Lee, actual descendants of the famous Robert E Lee. We soon became the best of friends. Roger became like a brother to me and always invited me to join them when playing baseball, or when they took trips into La Cygne to the Saturday night Teen Town dances. I was always thrilled when they asked me to join them. This family was a very well respected family in the area and helped out and got involved in many ways in the surrounding communities.

On the first day of school my brother and I had to wait at the end of our driveway by the side of the rock road for the school bus to pick us up. Right next to us at the edge of our driveway was a beautiful purple lilac bush and we could smell the aroma of the flowers when they were in bloom. When the bus arrived to pick us up and my being new and shy, no one wanted to sit next to me on the bus, and not being a very good conversationalist made it even worse. Can you imagine riding the bus five days a week to the school and back home, and no one wanted to sit next to you?

The bus picked us up and we traveled on many back roads and to many farm houses, picking up other students, before finally arriving in downtown Fontana. The high school and grade school sat right next to each other and were connected by a paved sidewalk. The high school was an old red brick two-story building, but the elementary school building was new. Our gym was located in the elementary school and doubled as the cafeteria.

I felt so out of place right from the start at this school because I was dressed as a city boy, and all these kids were all from local farms, wearing jeans and combing their hair down in their faces. I had a high tenor voice and I walked like a dancer, and I dressed impeccably. I had remembered how badly I used to dress in Kansas City as a kid and how the kids would snicker. In high school I was able to eventually dress in nicer clothes. I was well dressed here in Fontana but still out of place because all the farm boys wore bib overalls or jeans to school. To make matters worse I was not a 'joiner' and couldn't start up conversations very easily with all these students who all knew each other. I was the outsider and a city boy. I was not good at sports, and gym was one of the requirements I needed for credits to graduate. No one wanted me on their basketball teams, baseball teams, or track teams because I simply was bad at all of them, and being left-handed I really was at a disadvantage.

I remember that in Kansas City we were never allowed to wear jeans to school, just Ivy league pants. We could not wear tennis shoes, except in the gym. The girls were never allowed to wear any kind of slacks or pants to school, only skirts and dresses. The only time we could dress in whatever we wanted to was on "Hobo Friday" when the high school allowed us to wear jeans and wild shirts if we wanted to, or dress like a hobo one Friday a month. This was a shock to me that these kids in Fontana could dress in everyday jeans and even t-shirts to school. Everyone here wore tennis shoes to school. In Kansas City the only time I was allowed to wear tennis shoes was in the gym. I was freaking out with the sudden change.

All these kids knew each other and knew each other's families. I was the new kid on the block and I dressed differently and acted differently. If it wasn't for Roger and Robert Lee, I probably would have never, ever fit in. They guided me and showed me what to expect from living in the country and being accepted as one of them at the school.

My school life totally turned around when Roger and Robert invited me to go with them to the Teen Town in La Cygne one Saturday night. La Cygne in French means "The Swan." They picked me up and the family drove on over to La Cygne and parked in front of an old downtown red brick office building that had a separate door that led upstairs to a second floor. At the upstairs entryway a guy standing at the door gave us a stamp on the back of our hands and let us all in. In front of us was a large open room that had been darkened with only wall sconces lighting up the room. Chairs were all lined up against the wall on two sides of the room, and at the far end of this large empty room was a large juke box all lit up with colorful lights. Roger and Robert's family had arrived early because they had some 45 rpm records to put in the juke box for us to dance to. They were the ones that were providing all the music for the teens for dancing.

Shortly after we arrived, more teens started arriving from not only La Cygne, but surrounding towns. Everyone was dressed like they were going to a ball. The girls had full skirts with plenty of petticoats underneath, and the guys were dressed in their best shirts and freshly ironed jeans.

Robert went over and hit a few buttons on the juke box and the music started playing. At first no one got up to dance. The girls sat on one side of the room and the guys sat on the other side. This was my first time at Teen Town so I really didn't dance at all because I was too shy to ask a girl to dance. The second time we drove back to Teen Town, I decided to show everyone that I could dance. Word spread around the school and I became an overnight celebrity. Each time the high school planned a dance party, they would ask me to run the record player and choose the songs to play. At one dance party I put on the record "Rockin Robin" and asked the head cheerleader, Martha Dickerson, to dance with me. The school had planned a dance contest that night both for a fast dance and for a slow dance and I wanted to be a part of it. Martha and I won the fast dance competition and Robert Lee and his girlfriend Monita won

Martha Dickerson and Frankie were winners of the Fontana High School dance

the slow dance competition. Martha was the head-cheerleader of our school. The student council had been taking pictures that night, and a picture of Martha and me dancing ended up in the yearbook that year. After their graduation, Robert and Monita were married, and they've been married ever since and still live in Fontana. We stay in touch through phone calls.

Shortly after we had moved to our farm Roger and Robert invited me to go on a hayride one evening with a bunch of other high school kids. Not long after sunset a tractor with a trailer with its lights on and topped with hay, pulled up in front of our farmhouse with a few kids sitting on top of the hay, and I joined them. There was a lot excitement in the air and all the students were chattering away when I hopped onto the back of that hay wagon. I remember that the moon was full and lit up the night sky. Remember now, I had been a very shy guy and I didn't know anyone yet, however Roger had asked me to bring some of my 45 rpm records for them to play at the park pavilion. To this day I do not remember where that park was that we went to. It probably was in Osawatomie, or even in Paola?

The ride was fun and it was already dark outside by the time we reached our destination. The only lights along the way were the lights on the front of the tractor and the faint glow of a full moon. Once in a while we would pass lights from a farm house off in the distance. Soon we pulled up into a park and there was a covered pavilion with stone picnic tables and benches. The lights had already been turned on for us, knowing that this hayride full of kids would be arriving soon. We all hopped off the trailer and set up a record player on one of the stone picnic tables and plugged it into a plug-in close by. They put me in charge of playing the records and I stayed right there with the record player trying to keep the music going. Before I realized it most of the students had disappeared into the thick forest that surrounded this pavilion and I couldn't see any of them, even though I could hear their voices. All these kids knew each other, probably from childhood on. I started to realize that this was no fun. I was still the outsider. For me to stand here and just play records was not what I came out here to enjoy. I thought we were all going to sit around a campfire and eat roasted marshmallows and cook hotdogs over an open fire. Food had been brought but no one was ready to eat yet. They were all enjoying a trip down to the river bank that was close by.

I decided I was going to play one more record and I too was going to take a walk in the woods. I picked up the record "Lonely Boy" by Paul Anka and headed out into the woods in the opposite directly from the distant voices of the other kids. As I walked along listening to that song, I realized for the first time how lonely I really was and how I always felt like I really did not fit in with all these other kids. I could see the glow of the moon peeking through the treetops while I walked, enough light that I could see where I was walking. I ended up at the edge of a creek or a river and stood there looking out at the surface of that water, listening to the song play which said, "I'm just a lonely boy, lonely and blue. I'm all alone, with nothing to do." It was then that I broke out into tears and just wanted to fade into the darkness of that forest and never appear again.

After what seemed like an eternity, the record I had been playing stopped and it got so silent in the forest that it almost became spooky. From the distance I could hear the kids talking and it sounded like they were heading back to the pavilion. I had to force myself to walk back to that pavilion to play more songs and join in with the others. Yes, I was a lonely boy, lonely and blue, even being surrounded by other kids my age, it didn't seem to matter. I was still not one of them. I was all alone, with nothing to do. The song read the pages of my heart from cover to cover. At least when all got together in the covered shelter we began to get serious about eating and somehow that lonely feeling started to dissipate.

My feeling of not being accepted by the other kids became a real problem for me. I tried double dating with Robert and Monita and asked Linda Whitney for a date. Linda and I had become somewhat of friends when I had asked her to dance with me at one of the high school dances. She seemed to be a very good dancer and I so enjoyed dancing with a girl that could match me, step for step.

The double date ended up being an awful awkward time for me. Linda and I were sitting in the back seat and I tried putting my arm around her shoulders. Linda was not a short girl. She was actually taller than me. My arm had to go up higher than my arm pit to fit around her neck and across her shoulders. A week or so later I asked dad if I could use the family car to pick Linda up and take her on an actual date. We went on a date and tried so hard to enjoy the date and experience each other's company. I don't remember where we drove to but on the way home I ran out of gas about 2 or 3 miles from my home. Linda and I had to walk all the rest of the way to our farmhouse, in the dark, to get help. That date ended disastrously. I chose not to date anyone from the Fontana High School ever again. I knew that Linda just wasn't my type but I wanted to give it a try. Linda was a very sweet girl and we still remained friends after that, and I found out later in life that she became a prison guard.

Our farmhouse had an electric heater in the kitchen, but it also had a large potbelly stove that we often used in the winter time to help heat up our farmhouse. There was always plenty of wood on our farm to cut up into wood chunks that would fit into the stove. We lived on 40 acres of land with lots of trees and small forests and a couple of ponds, even though one was dry.

In this farmhouse there was one bedroom downstairs that became my mom and dad's master bedroom. Debbie was quite small then and she slept in mom and dad's bedroom as well. Dougie, me and Ed Probst slept upstairs in the large, open bedroom with a ceiling that slanted towards the short walls on both sides of the room. We had two beds upstairs and an old windup Victrola record player. We had an eat-in kitchen with a potbelly wood burning stove, a formal dining room, and a living room where we had an upright piano and a TV. Still, no phone service at this home either.

This farmhouse also had no inside bathroom, only an outhouse in the back yard. If we wanted to wash up we'd have to use a bucket of water that we heated on the potbelly stove. Mom cooked on a regular kitchen stove that was fueled by propane gas.

Every day of the week we all had chores to do. Feed and water the pigs, feed the chickens and ducks, and make sure that there was plenty of wood chopped up in the winter time for the potbelly stove.

Sometimes on the week-ends dad would take the whole family into town and take us all into a beer joint so he could have his beer. In one of these beer joints they had a separate room off to the side that had a juke box and dance floor. Mom and us kids went into this room and put a few quarters into the slot and I danced with mom to the music. My mother really knew how to dance, and I learned a lot from just dancing with her.

As a kid I really didn't know that my own dad had a drinking problem. I only knew he loved to drink beer, because he often drank beer at home, but the truth never came out about dad's drinking problem until after he died. It was only then that mom felt free enough to admit our dad's problem by unraveling to us the whole sordid truth about her husband, our father.

Dad could also swear up a storm. It seemed like every other word out of his mouth was a curse word. He and Ed would sit around swearing up a storm and occasionally drinking beer as well. Dad's drinking got to become such a problem that he almost died. We didn't know about the severity of his drinking problem or about his almost dying, until after he died at age 82 and mom told us the whole story. Mom kept the knowledge of that problem away from us kids while we were growing up. All we knew was that dad wanted to sell the farm and move to Junction City. He had stopped cursing and started talking about the Lord. We all thought that he had lost it mentally. I think that he feared for his life when the drinking almost cost him it, and he decided to trust in the Lord. It wasn't long after the incident that dad sold the farm.

SIX

AN AWFUL GUT FEELING

We packed all of our belongings on the farm and my dad loaded everything he could onto a simple, open, flatbed trailer he pulled behind our car. If it couldn't fit onto this trailer, then it got left behind. Two things I know got left behind at the farmhouse were our old upright piano, and the antique windup Victrola record player.

When we arrived in Junction City we stopped off at grandma Day's house first. Grandpa Day had died when we still lived on the farm. Grandma told dad about a one bedroom mobile home located in Milford, Kansas, a few miles northwest of Junction City that was for rent. There was no room for me to live with them when they moved out there to Milford so I stayed at Grandma Day's home and enrolled at the Junction City High School. I had already started part of my 11th grade back in Fontana and was able to finish my 11th grade there at Junction City High School. I was so thrilled to be back in civilization again. I didn't realize it but Newt Gingrich attended Junction City High School in his seventh grade.

Grandma Day attended the First Christian Church in Junction City, and I often went with her. I can still remember sitting next to grandma and taking her folded bulletin to look at. The church bulletins always had a beautiful, colorful picture or painting on the front cover. While listening to the preacher, I would often open up the bulletin, which brought the front page and the blank back page together. With a pencil from the pew in front of us, I would sit and draw an exact copy of that beautiful, colorful front cover, onto the back cover, only in pencil.

I started to attend the Christian church's Sunday school classes. My cousin, Emma, Sissie, as everyone called her, also attended their Sunday school classes. The same stories of Jesus were being taught, and now I began to really know who the Lord was. My mom and dad would often accompany grandma and sit with us during the Sunday morning services.

One Sunday morning I decided I wanted to be baptized. As a young child when I attended that Baptist church near our home in Kansas City, they told me that they thought I was too young, and they felt that I didn't know enough about my reasons for getting baptized. Now I was nineteen years of age and felt I knew what I was doing. This time my mom and dad were present to witness my baptism, and what a glorious day that I will never forget.

Dad had enrolled at Manhattan Christian Bible College in Manhattan and needed to spend five days a week in Manhattan taking courses. For dad to totally stop working, mom had to take a job at a laundromat in downtown Junction City. To work there would mean that mom and dad would have to move back into Junction City, so grandma found a basement apartment for us that was situated across the street from her home. Mom and dad moved back to Junction City and moved into that basement apartment and mom took the job at the laundromat. Our family was all back together again.

At Junction City High School I learned that my aunt Helen worked in the cafeteria. It was always a wonderful feeling to walk into the lunch room and wave to her behind the counter. Her daughter, my cousin Emma also attended the high school. I didn't know it at the time but a high school student, John Kaiser actually dated Emma back in high school. John and I had never met in high school but now we're the best of friends. It's a small world, and getting smaller.

Many times I would walk to the municipal swimming pool from grandma Day's home on east 10th street, carrying my trusty towel to swim in that pool. I can still picture the many times I would get out of the shallow end of the pool after swimming, grab my towel and place it over my face. The warm air from my breath filled the towel while the rest of my body was chilled by the evaporating water on my body. The warm air around my nose and mouth felt so good. To this day when I jump out of a pool or a shower and place a towel over my face, it always takes me back to those times at the Junction City municipal pool.

The former "Plaza Truck Stop" where Frankie worked as a teenager in Junction City, KS

Shortly after moving to Junction City my grandma Day told me that her niece, Layo, was looking for someone to work the midnight shift at her Plaza Truck Stop, which was located at the Grandview Plaza at the east end of Junction City. I jumped at the chance to have a job and accepted the position.

They warned me on my first night on the job to get some sleep during the day so I could work all night. Well, I did take a little nap in the afternoon, but apparently did not get enough sleep. I had Layo's son meet me at my grandma Day's home on east tenth street and we drove on out to the Plaza Truck Stop in the Grandview Plaza.

My job was to make sure the dishes were always washed and potatoes peeled for making french-fries. If there was no rush of customers then I needed to mop the dining area and the restroom. I was not allowed to order a steak dinner, but I could order a hamburger, and I also was able to drink milkshakes and colas, all for free. This job was great for the week-ends, and the extra money helped me to buy the school clothes that I so needed.

That first all night shift was very rough on me and I became very sleepy. I ended up taking time to disappear into their rest room and lock the door and catch a short nap. After the first night I quickly learned that I needed to sleep sometime during the day so I could stay up all night.

I did such a great job at the restaurant. My great aunt saw my good work and often asked me to work more hours and sometimes double shifts on the week-end. It was during one of these off shifts during the day that I got to meet some of the waitresses that worked there. One lady and I seemed to really become close friends. I got the chance to meet her two daughters, Sheryl and Janis, when they came to pick their mother up. Sheryl had auburn hair and auburn eyes. Janis had dark brown hair and dark eyes.

Sheryl and I became friends and we began to date. She attended the middle school in Junction City. After school I would meet her at the middle school and walk her home. I was often at her home during the week after school and we'd play records and dance. Sheryl didn't know how to dance at first so I taught her. Our favorite song at the time was "Will You Still Love Me Tomorrow?" Later in life I recorded that song on one of my albums.

We dated for about 9 or 10 months and were starting to get a little serious. My parents were getting concerned that the dating would interfere with my chances of going to college, and both sets of our parents tried to help us end our relationship before it went too far. To tell you the truth, I was so afraid of Sheryl's mother from a statement she had made to me, and I knew I would never go too far with Sheryl. Her mother had told me that no guy was ever going to take advantage of her daughters or she would kill them. I took that literally as the gospel truth.

My dad was offered a position as a part-time pastor of a church in Osage City, Kansas after attending the bible college a few months. Dad took the position and we drove to Osage City every Sunday for dad to preach at that small church on Sunday mornings. Sheryl rode with us a few Sundays and decided to get baptized.

After about 10 months of dating Sheryl, we both had to call it quits. There was just too much pressure being applied from both sets of our parents. After our break-up I had such a time with that awful ache one gets when a true love ends. The hurt and the awful gut feelings nagged me for quite a few months afterward. My school grades suffered during this time and I found myself not really caring whether or not I would graduate, but I was in my senior year of high school and was ready to make plans to go to college.

SEVEN

CAP AND GOWN

I was in my senior year at Junction City High School in 1961 and would soon graduate and make plans for college. My mom helped me pick out a cap and gown for the graduation ceremonies. I felt so proud. Our senior class set a date for a rehearsal so we would all know what to do during the graduation ceremony itself. The school held the rehearsal and all went well and all the students seemed to know exactly what to expect.

Frankie's graduation picture at the Junction City High School

The day before the actual graduation ceremonies, the principal of our high school called and said he wanted to come over and talk with us. We couldn't understand why he was making a special, personal visit. Mom and dad decided to wait for the principal on our front porch.

We found out the reason why when the principal drove up and parked in the street near our front porch and walked up and sat down with us. He told us that he had come to pick up my cap and gown. I wasn't going to be able to graduate with the rest of the seniors because the English teacher, Mr. Lacy, had flunked five seniors and I was one of them. No other seniors flunked, only five from this one English teacher's class. We all thought that something was strange but didn't question the principal any further.

After the principal left, we were all in shock. I was hurt beyond what any words could possibly describe. Dad was livid. He wanted to find out the real reasons this English teacher had flunked five seniors, and dad decided he was going to look up the home address of Mr. Lacy and go speak with him.

The next day was Saturday and dad told me he wanted me to go with him to talk with Mr. Lacy at his home. Dad drove us over to an apartment complex and found Mr. Lacy's apartment number and knocked on his door. Mr. Lacy came to the door almost immediately, and dad asked Mr. Lacy why he flunked me. Mr. Lacy told dad that he had warned his class that no matter what their grades were during the school year, the final exam would determine the final passing grade. He told dad that I had not gotten a passing grade on the test and he had no other alternative but to flunk me. Dad asked him what we could do so I could graduate. Mr. Lacy said that there was simply nothing he could do or we could do except for me to repeat my senior year. He walked back into his apartment and closed the door behind him, leaving us outside with a perplexed look on our faces. We two just stood there in what seemed to be a long pregnant pause before either one of us could even pick up our feet to leave his front door.

I should have seen this coming. During my senior year I did let my grades slip because I was so distracted by my time being spent with Sheryl. There were times that I totally relied on my knowledge of knowing that even if I didn't study much, I would still get a good grade. I was so confident and I assured myself that I had nothing to worry about. So what if I get a "B." It wasn't the end of the world. Little did I know that the final exam in Mr. Lacys' class required nothing less than a "C." I received a "C minus," just enough of a grade for Mr. Lacy to flunk me. It was that awful 'minus' that hurled me over the edge of that bottomless pit of despair and discouragement. That minus would forever change my destiny and my life.

Looking back I can see now what really happened. It was when Sheryl and I split up that caused my grades to suffer the most. I didn't realize it when Sheryl and I were dating, but when we split up is when I realized what 'love' is, and now I was hurting. My heart was bleeding with the pain of not having her in my life. I had never experienced the pangs of love before. Just knowing what love for a woman can feel like made me wonder if there might be someone else out there that could eventually fill that void.

The summer months after my disappointing non graduation, and no girl in my life, seemed to go by quickly when I began to spend more time with my family and friends. It wasn't long before dad told us that he had been offered a full-time pastoring position in Winchester, Kansas, a small town just northwest of Kansas City. The church would provide a decent salary for dad and provide us with a two-story parsonage to live in. I couldn't understand how dad could take a pastoring position. He was still in his first year of Bible College. Dad however thought he was qualified and the church in Winchester was confident that dad could become their new preacher and he accepted the position.

We moved before the school year began. Yes, Winchester was a very small town but it had a grocery store and a large hospital. The parsonage was a two-story old house with many rooms, including a formal dining room. There were wooden sliding doors that separated the living room from the formal dining room and a wooden staircase by the front door that led up to four bedrooms. This parsonage was about a block away from the church that dad was pastoring and the town water tower sat in our back yard.

When the school year began mom enrolled both Dougie and Debbie in school. I was yet undecided as to what I was going to do. I had no job and no prospects. When talking with mom and dad I had asked them if maybe I could enroll at the local high school and go part-time to school to take English again and maybe a few more classes. They both thought it was a great idea.

The next day I walked up to the Winchester high school and talked with the principal about enrolling at the school, and he said it was quite alright. I chose the classes I wanted to take, including English, which I hated, and started school the very next day. I was determined to finish high school so I could go on to college.

My senior year at Winchester High went without too many problems.

The reality of it all hit me like a ton of bricks when I began to realize that here I was again living in a small town with small town people's ways that I had never really grown to understand. It was hard for me to fit in again. And to double the problems that were already staring me in the face was the fact that I was a preacher's kid now. The people expected us preacher kids to behave respectfully and be the perfect examples of what 'good' kids are. I was not that young man! I had flaws. This was my first position as a preacher's kid. How do preacher's kids act? What is expected of us?

In this small town, probably like most other towns, preachers and their families are placed on a pedestal. They are treated as special people and looked up to with great respect. I almost felt like the town's celebrity at times. People would greet me as though they had known me all their lives. Everyone knew the "Piper" family as the new pastor at the First Christian Church, and I represented my family wherever I went.

Dad became friends with other Christian church pastors and one of these pastors was Pastor Vernal Johnson in Tonganoxie, Kansas. We often would drive over to Tonganoxie to attend meetings at his church. At one of the meetings I met his daughter, Margaret, and we soon became a twosome. Before long we were going steady. Everyone thought we were a cute couple. I often asked my dad for the use of his car so I could drive over to Tonganoxie to see Margaret.

On one Sunday morning my dad asked me to sing a special song during the morning service. I looked through the church hymnal and found a song I thought I could sing and asked the church pianist if she would play it for me. I stood at the pulpit and sang two verses of the hymn, Amazing Grace from the hymnal.

As I was singing I noticed some older ladies that were sitting on the front row had tears in their eyes. I finished singing and turned around and ran into the back room. Dad came after me and asked me why I had taken off so quickly. I told him that my singing was awful. He asked me why and I told him that I had seen several ladies in the front row crying. He assured me that it wasn't because I was so bad, it was because I was that good! That helped me to have more confidence when I sang.

I had been attending classes at the high school for a few months when I met Peggy Johnson, who was the baton twirler and majorette for the high school band. We became friends almost immediately. She was also new in town. We were never boyfriend and girlfriend but we were good friends. I was still very involved with dating Margaret from Tonganoxie. Peggy often volunteered to do hospice work for the hospital and for people who were dying and left alone in their homes. She took me to a lady's home where she had volunteered to visit and spend time with the lady who was dying of cancer. We walked over to this lady's home from our parsonage and spent a few minutes there and then came on back home. Peggy told me later that the dying woman had told her that I was the best looking young man she had ever met.

I joined the Glee Club at Winchester High School. Because my voice was so high I sat in the tenor section with the men. The choir director had me stand right next to the sopranos because my voice was so high and I often sang a soprano part when they needed it. Our Glee Club was chosen to participate in the State Of Kansas competition for Glee Clubs and as one of the top competing high school choirs to perform for the state of Kansas in Kansas City. While there I ran into my cousin, Barbara Thomson, who was with her choir from Bonner Springs. All the best choirs from all over the state of Kansas were then chosen to record an album featuring a male and female opera singer. I was one of the many voices on the album. What an honor.

Before long our school sent a notice out that there was going to be a dance at the school in the gymnasium. Of course I didn't realize that 'preacher kids' do not go to dances. How was I to know? My parents had never really discussed with us kids about the new rules we kids had to follow. In fact, my parents very rarely discussed any issues with us about anything. Our teaching mostly came from their example and what we could learn on our own.

It didn't dawn on me that the consequences of attending such an event would reflect back on my dad and his church. I just knew I loved to dance and really wanted to show off. I knew I could dance and this might be my chance to really show my classmates that I have a talent. Maybe I would be more accepted? Wrong!

Peggy and I went to the dance together. Peggy had become a very popular student and very outgoing. Marching with the school band helped make her known and well accepted by all the other students, even though she was new in town. The dance music was being played on a record player that a student had donated for their use at the school dance, and during the dance contest, of course Peggy and I won. We remained friends after high school and when I started college in Norfolk, Nebraska, Peggy rode up with us to attend the college as well.

In school the next day, especially in my English class, a few comments were being bantered around that felt like an over inflated ball being tossed around at an armless convention. The minister's daughter from one of the local churches in town made the most snide remarks about my attendance at the dance. Of course she had never attended any dances at the school and rarely attended any of their basketball games or football games, but she seemed to be the loudest vocally in placing judgment on me in front of the whole class. She asked me if I had gotten in trouble with my dad, and I snidely remarked, "That's none of your business," and I told her not to look at me with that tone of voice. The other students sort of snickered at the precious moment in time when the minister's daughter from the local church had been put in her place. Reality hit me like a ton of bricks when I realized that my own dad had not yet heard about my going to that school dance.

I decided I was going to tell my dad before he could hear it from someone else, so I confronted dad and told him I wanted to have a man to man talk with him. He agreed and we sat down in the living room where I proceeded to bare my soul with the truth of attending that dance.

My dad came unglued at the hinges, which I never expected. He told me that this could cost him his position as the minister of the church. What would people think? And what were you thinking? An argument of colossal proportions ensued between father and son and I was on the losing end. My thoughts felt like I was in a finished puzzle that had missing pieces! Mom kept busy in the kitchen. She just didn't seem to be the confronter that I had become and left the argument up to us. She knew that whatever her husband decided, that was going to be the law, period. He was the total ruler in our home and my mom sort of floated within that space with very little say. Dad was the tyrant, mom was the mouse. Mom was the stay-at-home mom that never learned how to drive and depended totally on dad for everything. The only job I ever remember my mom had, other than being a housewife and mother, was when she took a job at the laundromat in Junction City to help when dad was attending Manhattan Christian College.

When our argument settled down, dad made a statement to me that I have remembered and will remember for the rest of my life. He said, "One day when you get married, you will probably want to move back home to live with us." I told him, "No, that will never happen. When I leave here I will never, ever come back to live." And, I never did. I have had to do a lot of soul searching and forgiving since those statements were made. It just seemed like my dad and I were always at odds with each other about something and it was time for me to leave the nest.

I knew I had to take time away from my home and away from my dad, at least for a while. The opportunity arose when dad drove our family to Zarah, Kansas to visit my grandma and grandpa Piper. Dad's parents had moved to a farm just at the edge of the small town of Zarah. Grandpa had a garden and he grew vegetables there. My cousin Gene Haney had moved in with them and my Aunt Bernadine and Uncle George were living right next door.

We spent a day at the farm and when my family was ready to leave I told my dad that I wanted to stay there a week. My grandparents loved the idea. I stayed a week and slept upstairs in their spare bedroom. I knew that my dad and I needed a break.

My grandparents didn't have an inside bathroom. Everyone had to go out back to an outhouse. Grandma always kept a port-a-potty under their bed so she wouldn't have to go outside during the night. I accidentally spilled it one time when playing in their bedroom, yuk!

While I was at Grandma Piper's farm I decided to use hydrogen peroxide to lighten my hair. I was told that I could apply a dose every few minutes until I got the desired blond I wanted. All day long I kept applying more doses of the peroxide. Before I knew it my hair not only lightened, it was now blonde~! Well, I sure wanted to be different, but maybe not this different! I was sure making a statement. How could I return to my high school in Winchester with blonde hair now? If there wasn't already something they could talk about, now I'm coming back to school with blonde

Frankie's senior picture taken in 1962 for the Winchester High School yearbook

hair. And to make matters worse, we were preparing to have our school pictures taken.

You guessed it. The first day back at school the same minister's daughter started in on me. This time I was able to ignore her and go on with my life. Did her comments bother me? No. I went on as if she wasn't even there and turned a deaf ear. Trying to put me down to make her look better only made her look more judgmental and not willing to accept people as they are. I only gave her fodder to chew on.

My second chance at graduating from high school was the thrill of a lifetime. Now I had my diploma from Winchester High School I and was ready to tackle the world. The trouble was that I had no immediate plans to go to any college or what I was going to do to make a living. My life was up for grabs and my direction seemed unsure, and my dad and I had just been co-existing under the same roof.

EIGHT

A SURPRISE VISIT

The very next day after my graduation, my second cousin, Tharen Piper, who had been living in Kansas City, Missouri, drove to our home in Winchester in his baby blue Thunderbird. His car alone drew much attention in the little town of Winchester. He had been visiting with my grandparents in Zarah and found out that I was graduating from high school, so he offered to take me back to my grandparent's home in Zarah and try and start my life there.

I was at my grandparent's home only a few days when grandma had a visit from her daughter, my Aunt Louise. Aunt Louise asked me if I wanted to come and stay with her and her two boys. She wanted me to sit with her boys if she had to go somewhere.

Frankie and his 2nd cousin Theron standing in front of Bernie's parsonage in Winchester, KS in 1962

She lived just off Merriam Lane in Kansas City, so I went home with Aunt Louise, a divorced mother, and moved in with them. Her oldest son was Gene Haney that was already living with our grandma Piper, but Aunt Louise's two youngest boys still lived with her.

After just a few days with Aunt Louise, I got a call from Tharen who said that he wanted me to come live with him at his flat in Kansas City, Missouri. He said he would help me find a job and I could take a bus to work. Tharen drove out from Kansas City, Missouri and picked me up at Aunt Louise's home and took me back to his flat.

Tharen had been working as a TV repairman in Kansas City and made quite a good salary. His flat had one bedroom and a Murphy bed that I slept on in the living room. Tharen was my great-uncle Charlie Piper's son and Charlie was my grandpa Piper's brother.

I had met Tharen for the first time when he was a very young child and his parents lived in Decatur, Arkansas. My dad would occasionally take us on a trip to visit with them. I remember they once lived in a two-story farm on a main highway leading south out of Decatur. Their home sat right next to the highway with electric lines running right in front of their home, but their home had no electric and no inside restroom. They even kept a black snake in their pantry to keep the mice away. But I digress . . .

At Tharens's flat I had no money and no job. Tharen bought me a newspaper so I could look at the want ads, and I found a job at a garment factory in downtown Kansas City that I could train for. I applied for the job and they hired me. A bus route ran right past the flat and I was able to catch a bus to work and back every day. Although many days I had no money for the bus, I would leave earlier to walk all the way to work. That was quite a challenge when I had to cross over many freeway interchanges to get there, dodging the traffic. After my first paycheck I was able to afford to take the bus daily. At one time my cousin Leon Bowen had gotten a job at this garment factory, and my Uncle Donny Piper, dad's youngest brother, as well. It became a family affair.

Tharen loved to cruise the streets looking for women to date. We two went on one of these cruises one evening and pulled alongside two young ladies walking down the street. They actually got into Tharen's Thunderbird and rode around with us for a while. One of the girls was a Margaret and she had lived in La Cygne, Kansas where I used to go to the Teen Town there to dance. Margaret said she had gone there many times herself. What a small world. Margaret's girlfriend was Linda. Tharen started dating Linda and Tharen wanted me to date Margaret. At first I told Tharen that I was already going steady with a Margaret in Tonganoxie and I didn't want to get involved with yet another girl, especially another "Margaret."

Every time Linda came over to our flat, Margaret would tag along. Before long we were all just enjoying being together, either at our flat or walking up our side street near our flat to the park. The four of us just enjoyed having fun together. To me this Margaret was just a friend, but the imaginary lines that I had drawn in my mind that helped keep me attached to the Margaret in Tonganoxie began to blur and become fuzzy over time.

One week-end while Linda and Margaret from the Kansas City area were spending time with Tharen and me at the flat, my parents made a surprise visit. And guess who was with them? The very girl I was going steady with, Margaret Johnson, from Tonganoxie. Needless to say, I lost both Margarets that day. The Margaret from Tonganoxie gave me my going-steady ring back, and Margaret in Kansas City didn't want anything more to do with me. My parent's surprise visit that day helped change the course of my whole life, but the plot thickens.

I was starting to enjoy working in downtown Kansas City at the garment factory, and I was learning quite a bit and being trained to move up to a better position. I had been working at this garment factory for a couple of months now. On one Friday I took the bus home as usual, but when I arrived back at the flat, Tharen told me that maybe we should go visit my parents for the week-end. I thought nothing more about it but agreed that it was about time for me to spend time with my parents.

Little did I know that Tharen and my dad had already talked on the phone and dad had asked Tharen to bring me back to Winchester so he could enroll me at the bible college in Norfolk, Nebraska. Being a preacher's son gave me an automatic scholarship to attend any bible college, tuition-free! Dad had already chosen Nebraska Christian College, in Norfolk, Nebraska. When he had spoken to Peggy Johnson about going, she wanted to attend too, and so did Tharen. That's why it didn't bother him to take me back home. All this was sprung on me behind my back. I had no choice now but to go to college in Norfolk, Nebraska. It still bothers me to this day that I could not give notice at the garment factory that I was leaving.

NINE

WHO ELSE IS LEAVING?

It was not until we headed to Norfolk, Nebraska that I started to get a little excited. Peggy Johnson was riding with us and she seemed just as excited. The drive took about five hours and we arrived in plenty of time to enroll at the college.

My class picture taken in 1962 for the Nebraska Christian College.

The Nebraska Christian College provided boys and girls dorms and both of these homes were right across the street from the college. The dorms were two large two-story older homes painted white with full walk-in attics, and a full basement. Tharen and I were able to room together in the attic of the men's dorm, and we had the whole attic to ourselves. The attic became a third story of this two—story home.

NCC also provided a wonderful breakfast in their cafeteria. To participate in a breakfast the students had to be in the cafeteria by 6am. I chose to eat and would get up early every morning so that I would at least have one good meal a day. My first class started at 7am and I was prepared, especially after eating a wonderful, full breakfast. All my other meals I had to purchase at local restaurants. My favorite restaurant just happened to be only a few blocks away, but my NCC friends told me it was the devil's den and they would not go into it. The restaurant didn't sell liquor but they did have a live band on the week-ends. So why did they call it the devils den? Was it because of the rock band?

One day I decided I was going to go into this restaurant and see for myself why they called it the devils den. I sat in a booth and ordered an open-face hot roast-beef sandwich. For a little over a dollar I was able to enjoy a good hot meal. As soon as I told some of my friends at NCC, they too started buying their lunches there and sometimes their dinners at this restaurant. The only time none of us would go there to eat was on the week-ends when the band was there and people were dancing.

NCC had a curfew and all the students had to be back at their dorms no later than 9pm seven days a week. If anyone was ever caught staying out after curfew they had to sweep and mop all the floors of the dorm. Laundry was not provided at the dorm even though there was a washer and dryer in the basement. The only ones allowed to use them were the dorm parents or with prior approval from them, anyone could pay for the use of their laundry soap.

Within the first week I was able to apply for a part-time job washing dishes at a department store lunch counter at Hesteds, on the main drag of Norfolk. I was probably not fast enough for them and they let me go within days. I then applied at Giovani's Pizzeria near the railroad tracks that crossed through town and the main drag, and the owner hired me immediately. My job was to shred the cheese for the pizza, keep the dishes and silverware washed, and sometimes wait on tables. I later learned how to cook Giovani's special pizza burgers. I could only work at Giovani's on the week-ends or whenever he needed me, and I knew I had to try and find another part-time job because there just wasn't enough income from working at Giovani's alone. A friend told me about a hotel downtown that needed a bellhop and I applied for the position and got hired. All my studying for school had to be done during the day, either between classes or right after school. I had to drop my one class that I had to take at the junior college because the time I spent walking there and back was a time when I could be studying.

I was able to work every evening after classes at either Giovani's Pizzeria, or at the hotel as a bellhop. I always walked to every job because I didn't own a car. Walking everywhere in Norfolk was never a problem until it started getting colder. I had no coat. I didn't remember to bring one from home.

It wasn't long before I met a tall girl by the name of Mary Kay Poore, who also attended NCC. Her family lived in Council Bluffs, Iowa. We started to spend time together and shared some of the same classes. We'd often walk around town together and sometimes walk to the park.

NCC announced one day that they were going to let us all out of school early the next day because there was a guest speaker appearing at a local church. This church was just down the street from NCC and NCC wanted the girls to ask the guys to accompany them to this event. I knew that I would be asked by Mary Kay.

Early the next day I was up early and I headed over to NCC to have breakfast. I had just stepped out onto the porch of the dorm when another Mary, whom I had no interest in whatsoever, ran across the street and up to the front porch of the men's dorm and caught me before I could even step one foot off the porch, asking me to accompany her to the event at the church. I felt so bad to turn her down, but I just knew that Mary Kay would be asking me sometime during the day.

I attended all my classes at the school and they let us all out early so we could attend the special event at the church that was hosting a special speaker. I made my way down to the foyer of NCC and waited a few minutes for Mary Kay. When Mary Kay arrived we stood there talking for a few minutes and she said nothing about wanting me to accompany her. I told her I would see her later and I simply walked away and returned to the men's dorm.

Within the hour Mary Kay was at the front door of the men's dorm asking for me. The guest speaker at the church was supposed to be speaking within a few minutes and she's waiting till the last minute to ask me to accompany her? I was so mad I wouldn't even come to the door. For me that was the end of our relationship. We never dated after that, and I did not attend the event.

Nebraska Christian College had a college choir, which I decided I wanted to try out for. To qualify I had to audition. The day I auditioned I can still remember the pianist played the usual musical scales starting from the low end of the keyboard, graduating higher and higher to the top end of the keyboard. When the pianist started running out of keys, he looked at me in surprise. He said "Don't you have a break somewhere?" After further singing we discovered that I did have a slight break from a regular voice to a falsetto, but it was so minute that he hadn't detected it at first. He told me I was a contra-tenor. He then showed me how to always sing in such a way as to not have that slight break affect any of my tones, and I would always be able to sing right through that break without much notice at all. He later started giving me piano lessons and I was able to practice on a piano at the college music room and sometimes in the chapel. I owe a lot to this teacher whom I never really got to know after I left college and have already forgotten his name. I had developed much more of an appreciation for singing and gospel music because of him.

Peggy Johnson was the first to leave. One day she was attending all her classes, and the next day she told us that she was quitting NCC and going back home. She had already purchased a bus ticket. I gave her a hug and saw her walk down the railroad tracks towards downtown Norfolk to catch a bus.

The news about Peggy leaving NCC was so disturbing to me, and made me feel like the earth beneath me was growing unstable and starting to crumble right under my feet. The three of us had been so excited about attending NCC when we had first driven up from Winchester. What happened? When we pressured Peggy to give us her reasons for wanting to leave, she didn't want to go into detail, she just wanted to leave. The next thing we knew, she was gone. I never saw Peggy after she left, until many years later when my dad had taken a pastorate in La Harpe, Kansas. Peggy and her husband lived in a nearby town called Gas. Mom called to tell me that she had run into Peggy, and Peggy was asking questions about me. My wife and I were able to travel out to La Harpe to meet Peggy, and it was a great reunion, but Peggy had lupus and has since passed on.

Just a few weeks later Tharen told me that he too would be leaving NCC and was going back to Kansas City to resume his career as a TV repairman. He told me that he tried many times to find a job in Norfolk, especially in the TV repair business, but none were available. He said he missed his old job in Kansas City, and Tharen had already contacted his former boss and they told him that he could come back and take his old job back.

Tharen was gone within a week. I was all by myself now and it was up to me to succeed. When Tharen left NCC, NCC decided to move me from the large attic room that Tharen and I shared, to the second floor, where I'd be rooming with another student. I was not thrilled with this new roommate. He needed so much alone time and a quiet atmosphere to study in, and I just wasn't providing that need. He was in his last year of college and this was only my first year. I would always have to leave the room so he could study. He had a large fern plant in our room that it sometimes made me feel as if I were camping out in a jungle. I kept looking under my bed for snakes and other jungle animals.

After a few weeks in my new room at the men's dorm, I decided to use the dorm house phone to call my parents in Winchester. The operator came on the line to tell me that that phone had been disconnected. What? I thought maybe I had dialed a wrong number and decided to try calling the number again. I got the same message. Now I really started to get concerned that something was wrong. I called the long-distance operator to give me the phone number of Mr. Moon there in Winchester. Mr. Moon was one of the elders of the church dad was the preacher of. Mr. Moon told me that my dad had accepted a new pastorate position in Hinton, Oklahoma and had moved the family there. Mr. Moon didn't have a phone number for dad but he told me that he would try to find it and call me back the next day.

That night I cried myself to sleep. How could my own parents move away and not even call me to tell me they were moving? I had such pains in my stomach during the night that I felt like it was on fire. Mr. Moon from Winchester called me the very next day. He had found my parent's new phone number there in Hinton, Oklahoma.

I had so many mixed feelings about calling my parents. How could I call them when I was having such a heavy feeling of abandonment. The rejection level also surpassed any and all the rejection I had ever felt from my dad over the years. I always knew in my heart that my dad always seemed to favor my brother Doug, and now all those feelings of abandonment and rejection seemed to crash down on me like a ton of bricks. I never felt that my mother favored any of us kids, but the favoritism that dad showed for my brother was always so apparent. Doug told me many years later that he knew our dad favored him.

The call to my mother was almost more than I could handle. I tried to hold back the tears but the tears started flowing anyway. Our conversation about their moving almost seemed as if it was no big deal with mom or dad that they had moved and not notified me. Mom told me that they were going to give me a call when they had gotten settled in the parsonage. I had no idea at that time but this ordeal helped me to sever my ties and apron strings to my parents. I was totally on my own now and I had to be responsible for my own support. My parents had not given me any kind of financial help for college and I knew that I would need to pay for everything if I wanted to continue attending NCC.

I knew that part or all of my tuition to attend NCC was from a scholarship fund provided by Christian colleges for people in the ministry, and their children. Nothing was ever discussed with me about the financial agreement or about any amount I might have needed to attend NCC and how much, if any, had or was needed to apply towards my tuition, either from my parents or from NCC. The president of NCC told me that there were people that had donated funds to help defray my expenses at the college.

After the discussion with the president of the college I just assumed that I would attend my classes as usual and not worry about the funding because there were many anonymous donors who had such a heart for the students. Even though I didn't know where the funding was coming from I was excited that someone out there wanted to help me. I asked mom if she and dad were the ones that the donations were coming from and she said no.

At one time some of the guys from NCC asked me if I wanted to ride with them to the local dairy queen. I readily accepted because I didn't have a car and had to walk everywhere, so I joined them and we headed towards the dairy queen. While in the car I overheard the guys talking about getting banana splits. I had never had a banana split or even heard of one so I kept my mouth shut for fear of being teased. When we pulled up to the drive-up window and ordered our banana splits I was totally surprised at what a banana split really was. I enjoyed every bite. I knew growing up I had led a very sheltered life, and now this confirmed it.

TEN

GIOVANI'S PIZZARIA

One of my favorite part-time jobs in Norfolk, Nebraska was working at Giovani's Pizzaria by the railroad tracks. It just so happened to also be a favorite hangout for most of the college kids, both from the local junior college and NCC. Giovani's Pizzaria not only served pizza, but also spaghetti and pizzaburgers. My favorite pizza was the sauerkraut pizza.

I came into work at Giovani's one evening and he had advertised an all-you-can-eat spaghetti dinner special. The dining area had several tables and just as many booths in it and it was starting to fill up fast. In one booth was a couple of college girls from the junior college and they had ordered the all-you-can-eat spaghetti meal. I delivered the plates to their booth and within a few minutes they motioned for me to bring them more spaghetti. After about a third trip to their booth I was wondering to myself if Giovani had made a big mistake by offering this special meal, and would he be losing money. I just had to leave the worrying to Giovani.

After the third trip to their booth I was starting to joke with the two girls about eating so much spaghetti and got to know them as Linda and Joyce. I found out that Joyce was attending the junior college and was from New Jersey. She was renting a room at Linda's family home.

The very next night the two girls came by Giovani's again and they decided to sit down at the counter. They didn't order the spaghetti plate, they ordered pizza burgers this time. I went ahead and decided to fry the burgers myself. When I did make the burgers I would always add more of the special seasoning powder on top of the meat when it was cooking on the grill, making it even tastier. They both loved the burgers. We struck up a conversation and within minutes I found myself asking Linda for a date. I must have looked cute in my white apron, splattered with tomato sauce and bits of cheese that I had just grated in the back room. Linda told me she would love to go on a date with me, and she asked me to come over to their home when I had an evening open and didn't have to work at one of my part-time jobs. The only night I had open that week was on Sunday evening.

A few days later Linda called me at NCC to tell me she was in the hospital with mono, the kissing disease. I immediately went to be by her side. When I arrived, Linda told me the real truth about her accepting my date proposal. She told me that she already had a boyfriend and was mad at him for giving her mono and had dated me out of spite. I just sat there next to her bed with my heart on my sleeve deciding what to do next. Then Linda told me that she thought it would be great if I would date her roommate Joyce. She said that Joyce was so far away from home and was looking for things to do in Norfolk. At first I just couldn't think about dating someone else when I had just been dumped, but after a little bit of deliberation I told her that it might be ok. Linda said she'd send Joyce over to the pizzeria that evening so we two could make plans and get acquainted.

I was working in the back room that evening shredding cheese when Joyce arrived at the pizzeria, and she sat at the end of the counter nearest to the entrance to the back room where I was working. When

I had finished grating the cheese I came out to see if I could help wait on tables, when I saw Joyce sitting there all by herself. We struck up a conversation and became almost instant friends. I found her personality bubbling and intriguing, because I always had a thing for very out-going women. My mother was just the opposite. She was always quiet and reserved.

Joyce and I spent many evenings together just walking down sidewalks and to the park. I would walk down to the home she was staying at and we'd stand on the home's wrap-around porch and talk, sometimes sharing a kiss or two. During one of my visits there she invited me in and led me to the living room where the rest of the family was already sitting.

Joyce and I sat next to each other on the sofa and I placed my left arm around her shoulders, letting my arm drape across her neck and down onto her left arm. It wasn't long before Joyce jumped up and threw me down onto the sofa and pushed me down and flat onto my back. She lifted up my shirt and started tickling my stomach. What I hadn't realized was that my arm had not draped just across her neck and down her left arm, my arm and hand had rested on her breast, and when I thought I was squeezing her elbow I was actually squeezing her breast. She had taken it long enough. The whole family was all there witnessing this whole event. I was so embarrassed I couldn't see straight.

Joyce's girlfriend's family told us about their son who was the lead-singer of a band that had just recorded a single and had a gig on Friday evening at a night spot in Norfolk. We were all invited to go with the family to help celebrate their son's debut single. When we arrived and I heard their son's singing, and his band, I so wanted to be a lead-singer of a band. My dreams did come true but not until many years later.

A few months rolled by and it started getting colder out. I had not prepared for winter and did not even have a coat. It didn't dawn on me when I came to Nebraska to bring a coat with me. Joyce and I were walking one evening in downtown Norfolk and she saw how cold I was and offered to buy me a coat. Her parents were sending her about twenty five dollars a week to live on, so she wanted to use some of those funds to help me keep warm. We found a coat with a matching hat and I was so thankful that I now had a coat to wear.

When the Christmas break came NCC told us we could either stay at the dorm or spend a week at home. I knew I could not afford to pay for a bus ticket to Hinton, Oklahoma and was prepared to stay the week at the dorm, when Joyce told me that her best girlfriend, who had been dating a black man, offered for me to stay at her mother's home in Albion, Nebraska. The bus ticket to Albion was far less expensive and I purchased a ticket and spent Christmas with Joyce's girlfriend's widowed mother. I actually did not spend any nights at the girl's mother's home. I stayed with friends of theirs, although I did spend every day at her mother's home. Her mother readily accepted me and often tried to talk to me in private about having me try and break up her own daughter and the black guy she was dating. This man had already tried out for the Harlem Globetrotters and had been accepted. All he had to do was take a physical. Her mother was a retired school teacher and she had such an issue with her daughter dating a black guy. Her mother actually locked her own daughter and me up in the master bedroom after we had simply gone in to listen to music and fell asleep on the bed. It was a while before her mother would let us out. Needless to say I couldn't wait to get away from that home and onto a bus back to Norfolk. We all later discovered that when the black guy took his physical for the Harlem Globetrotters, the doctors found out that he had leukemia.

Staying at the men's dorm at NCC was starting to wear on my senses. My roommate insisted on it being so quiet in our room all the time that he wouldn't even sit and try and get acquainted with me. I was just a distraction for him. I ended up moving from that dorm and into a private home where I only had to pay five dollars a week to stay in a family's spare bedroom. This family treated me as if I was part of their

family, sometimes inviting me to share a meal with them. After I had left college and moved from place to place, I always sent a Christmas card to this family from wherever I was living at the time. I even drove to Norfolk one time, many years later for a visit, but the woman's husband had died and she had moved in with her daughter and had developed Alzheimer's. She didn't even recognize me. My heart just felt like it had broken into millions of pieces and I knew that we could never correspond again.

Frankie with his mother Pauline, in Hinton, OK during college break.

Before I knew it Spring Break had come and we had time off again to either stay at the dorm or make other plans. I decided to take a bus to my parent's home in Hinton, Oklahoma. I spent a week there rediscovering who my parents were and toured the little town of Hinton and the Red Rock Park just south of town. Dad told me he wanted to take me to Mount Scott. He said Mount Scott is a mountain all by itself. From the top you can see the whole town of Lawton and see many miles in all directions. We stopped at the top of Mount Scott, I got out and walked over to an edge and was thrilled to witness what my dad had told me about.

Many years later and after my dad had passed away, my wife and I were asked to go with friends of ours from Duncan to the top of Mount Scott. At first I had not connected the dots, not knowing that this mountain was the same mountain my dad had taken me to when I was still in Bible College. When we arrived at the top of Mount Scott I began to gasp. This is the same exact spot my dad had driven me to over forty years before and now here I am standing in that same exact spot. My heart just seemed to shed tears on its' own accord as my spirit loomed with excitement at just the thought that I was making my own personal history here by visiting this same location. No one else could experience what I was experiencing at that very moment in time.

One day at NCC all of the students congregated in the chapel to listen to one of our classmates preach. As I sat there I asked another fellow student if we all had to preach at one time or another. He shook his head yes and told me that it was one of the requirements. I whispered back to him that I wasn't attending Bible College to be a preacher. All I wanted to do was to either go into music or into teaching. He told me that we all had to take Speech and this was one of the tests, to see if we could handle getting up in front of people. My heart just sank. I was way too shy to get up in front of people and I knew right then and there that I could not stay at NCC any longer. I had to get out.

Many years later while Phyllis and I were on a gospel concert tour, we scheduled a concert at the First Christian Church in Norfolk, Nebraska. While in Norfolk, I wanted to show Phyllis the new location of the Nebraska Christian College. We visited the new NCC building and went directly to the admissions office, where they located my original admission papers from 1962, on which I had stated that I loved to sing, but was afraid to get up in front of people! Little did I know that many years later I would be singing in front of 30,000 people and our music would be playing all around the world.

A few weeks went by at NCC and then I got the surprise of my life when I got a visit from my cousin Tharen. He had quit his job in Kansas City and was heading to Dallas to apply for special training at the Curtis Mathis Company and had driven all the way north to Norfolk. He had sold his Thunderbird and was driving a small Chevy, and had come to ask me to go with him to Dallas. I jumped at the chance and immediately quit NCC. I saw this as another opportunity for me to get some kind of special training. I met up with Joyce and told her what an opportunity I had and I would stay in touch. Tharen told me to forget her because there was more fish in the sea. I did not forget her and we did send letters back and forth after Tharen and I got settled.

ELEVEN
THE SWANKY CLUB

When Tharen and I arrived in Dallas, Tharen found the Curtis Mathis plant immediately and we drove up and parked near the front entrance. We entered the reception room of the plant and Tharen told the receptionist that he was applying for the special training that the school was offering for TV repairmen, so she handed him an application and he began to fill it out.

After Tharen filled out the application he handed the forms back to the receptionist and we waited for him to be called in. He didn't want me to immediately fill out an application, because he said he was going to check it out first. Within a few minutes Tharen was called in and he disappeared behind closed doors.

I waited in that reception room for what seemed to be like an eternity, becoming a little concerned. What I didn't know was that Tharen was going through not only a very intense interview, but had to subject himself to a lie-detector screening. I knew very little about my cousin Tharen but what I knew about him already was enough to fill two books full of regrets.

After about two hours Tharen appeared from behind the closed doors and told me that he decided he didn't want to go through the training and we needed to go. We did leave the Curtis Mathis building but we sat in the parking lot for a while, and he told me that he had had to take a lie-detector test. He also told me that he had lied all the way through the test but he passed it anyway. It didn't dawn on me till weeks later what really may have happened. He probably had flunked the lie-detector test but just didn't want to admit it.

As we sat there in the car Tharen asked me if I had any ideas on what we should do next, asking me if we had relatives we could go to that might help us get a job and get settled somewhere. I remembered that I had a great uncle, Jack Mallory, who owned the Swanky Club near Las Vegas. He was my Grandma Goldie (Mallory) Piper's only living brother, and maybe we could get a job working there. Tharen thought it was an excellent idea, so we immediately headed for Nevada.

I had received a letter in 2005 from a Greg Jones who is a relative of mine but I don't know how. All I know is that my great uncle Jack Mallory is his grandpa. The letter he sent to me read, "My grandparents came to Las Vegas back in the 1940s and were famous for serving the first buffet. Yes, we can make that claim! The place was called the Swanky Club in Henderson. The year was 1948 and the club belonged to Jack and Doris Mallory. There wasn't even a chicken purveyor in town back then, so grandpa Jack had to fly to Kingman, Arizona to bring back chickens. The Mallorys had also built and owned Sunrise Cedars, and Mallory's on the corner of Owens Avenue and Nellis Boulevard. Mallory's was originally called Bob and Pearl's Supper Club. My mother attended the original Basic High School when Henderson was called Basic. I (Greg Jones) was born at the Sunrise Hospital when it was a two-story building. My sister was born at the Women's Hospital, which is no longer there. My father, Bill Jones, worked at Bill Laden Lincoln Mercury and Walt Epreck Dodge as a car salesman and was in television commercials. On the week-ends he would take us to the barbershop on Charleston Boulevard and then we would buy our meat at the Panorama Market next door. We lived in Bonanza Village, which was an upscale neighborhood back then. There used to be nothing between Henderson and the Showboat Hotel and it took about a half an hour to get to Henderson. Sunset Road was really hilly, and my dad would go real fast over those hilly roads and make our stomachs drop while we squealed with delight. My first job was as a busboy in the coffee shop at the original MGM Grand hotel right before it burned down. When Elvis appeared at the International Hotel (now called the Las Vegas Hilton) the city went crazy. I've been a chef in town almost all my life. I have six children: Keyshie, Kenyon, LaRecee, LaQueshia, Anthony and NaAsia. Now my granddaughter, Saipress, is expecting her first son and my second grandchild." Signed, Greg Jones.

I am hoping to reconnect with Greg Jones and try to find out how he is the grandson of my great-uncle Jack Mallory.

It took Tharen and me several days of driving to get to Nevada and to Las Vegas. We drove day and night to get there with each of us sharing the driving, and while one slept, the other would drive. Tharen even picked up a hitch-hiker who helped us drive to Albuquerque, New Mexico, where he wanted to be dropped off at.

We drove over Hoover Dam and through the town of Boulder City on our way to Las Vegas. When we crossed over a hill that leads to the valley where Las Vegas sits, we were both so amazed and excited when we caught our first glimpse of Las Vegas and the whole valley the city sat in. On the north side of the city was Sunrise Mountain, and to the south was Mount Charleston. What a sight to behold! "There's sin city," Tharen exclaimed as we approached.

When we passed the main road leading into Henderson, which was on the left, Tharen spotted a large sign on the right side of the highway, perched on the roof of a building that simply read, "Smorgasbord." When we got a little closer we noticed that there was a larger sign in front of the building that simply said "Swanky Club." The Swanky Club was located at 920 N. Boulder Highway in Pittman, which is now a part of Henderson. I later found out that they were in business from 1947 to 1984.

We had arrived in the early afternoon when business at the Swanky Club was slow, so we parked, and entered in by the back door, which led directly into the kitchen. This building was a different building than what I had remembered when I was there with my family back in 1956. My Uncle Jack had added on a motel right across the parking lot, and a mobile home parking area just behind the Swanky Club. Their two-story family home still sat at the very back end of

My grandma Goldie Piper's brother Jack, and his wife Doris's Swanky Club in Henderson, NV

the property, as I remembered it, and to the left of their large home sat a small cottage with a chain-link fence around it.

As Tharen and I walked through the Swanky Club kitchen, heading for their main dining area, my Uncle Jack spotted us and greeted us. I reiterated to him who I was and that I was his sister, Goldie's, grandson. We three sat down at one of the dining tables and got caught up on family news. Tharen then asked him if there might be some job he could do at the Swanky Club. My uncle Jack said, yes, and he hired him right on the spot. Uncle Jack told Tharen that he would pay him a dollar an hour and he could eat a meal from the smorgasbord. He provided us rooming by allowing us both to stay in that small cottage building that sat on the left side of his own home.

Tharen started working every day for my Uncle Jack, and I sat in the little cottage every day wondering what I was going to do. I would often just walk out into the countryside enjoying the balmy weather. My uncle hadn't offered me a job, so Tharen told me that maybe I should go up to the club and ask Uncle Jack for a job.

It was only a few days later when Tharen got a call from his family in Arkansas telling him that his dad, Charlie Piper, one of my Grandpa Piper's brothers, was dying. Tharen discussed the problem with my uncle Jack of his needing to leave right away and asked him if I could have the job instead of him. Uncle Jack first did not want to agree with me staying behind, his feeling that he would need to be responsible for me, because I was only twenty years of age. I asked Uncle Jack if I could do the same job that Tharen had been doing, and finally, Uncle Jack offered me Tharen's old job. Tharen then drove back home to Arkansas, but his dad had died before he could get back there.

I loved living in the dry climate, and I loved living on my own and working at the Swanky Club. I loved that little cottage that was just perfect for me to live in. I was simply in seventh heaven. I could even walk to work.

My job description at the Swanky Club required me to be at work at 6:30am. Much of that time was spent sweeping and mopping all the floors and cleaning the restrooms. After all these chores were finished, I was through for the day until evening when I had to come back to bus the tables and wash all the dishes during their busy time.

I was paid a dollar an hour and received ten percent of all the tips the waitresses took in. I also got all the free food I wanted to eat from the buffet bar, and my housing. What more could a guy want?

Every day after I finished working at the club I was so thrilled to retire back to my little cottage behind the Swanky Club. I only had a small window swamp cooler that was located at the back of my little home to help the cottage cool. There was a small kitchen and a very small bathroom with a shower. I had a large picture window in the living room that had no curtains on it, and my uncle had provided a sleeper sofa for me and a small kitchen table. The rest would be up to me. I later bought curtains for the picture-window and a small orange colored chair to sit on.

One afternoon after finishing my morning chores at the club, I decided to take a walk into Henderson and see what I could find there to help furnish my little cottage. I found a store that had a wonderful orange colored saucer-shaped chair and found floor length plastic drapes with orange in them to compliment my chair. In yet another store I found a TV that I wanted to purchase. It looked awfully heavy but the store had free delivery. The TV cost $100.00 and I didn't have that much money on me at the time, but when I told the store who my uncle was they approved a loan for me through a local bank and I could pay twenty dollars a week until it was paid off. When I walked into the bank to make my last twenty dollar payment, the bank clerk told me that my credit with their bank would probably be the best credit rating I would ever have in my entire life. I was never late with my payment, and I always walked into Henderson to the bank weekly to make my payment in person.

One early morning when I was sleeping on my sleeper sofa I heard a rumbling sound and couldn't figure out what the noise was. I got up off the sofa and opened my front drapes, looking towards the Swanky Club, and I felt a sudden jolt hit under my feet. It was a rolling earthquake! It startled me because I had never experienced an actual earthquake before. The quake itself didn't last long, however, and I was able to go back to sleep.

The next morning while I was working at the club, I asked my Uncle Jack about the earthquake. He told me that the weight of the city of Las Vegas and the weight of the man-made lake, Lake Meade, was causing the ground to sink about an inch or so a year, thus causing earthquakes.

Every morning when I would go into work at the Swanky Club, I'd meet up with my Uncle Jack. Almost every morning we would both eat cereal with Elberta peaches on them. I had never had canned fruit before, and especially Elberta Peaches. They are the best. Thank you, Uncle Jack.

The Swanky Club float at the beginning of the Henderson, NV parade

Discussion at the club started focusing on a yearly parade held in Henderson. Uncle Jack always entered either a float or a decorated car for the parades and now he wanted to build a float for the Swanky Club and asked me if I would drive the float in the parade. What fun! I not only helped him build the float, I drove it from the Swanky Club into Henderson for the parade. Miss Henderson adorned the float in her bathing suit, and the Swanky Club's pianist/organist played music on the float.

During the parade I sat in a special hidden seat for the driver, and I could barely see over the decorations. I experienced the most extreme heat anyone could stand because all the heat from the motor came right up through the one area I was sitting in and almost roasted me. My sneakers were so hot you could almost fry an egg on them.

TWELVE

THE MALLORY LEGACY

Francis (Frank) Marion Mallory, my great-great grandfather on my grandma, Goldie Ellen (Mallory) Piper's side of the family was born on December 9, 1849 in Rock Run Township, Stephenson County, Illinois. His parents were my great-great-great grandparents DeWitt Clinton Mallory, who was born on January 20, 1807 and died on November 4, 1827 in Ohio, and his wife Elleanor (Brown) Mallory, who was born on August 9, 1807 and died on May 5, 1870 in Illinois. My great-great-great grandpa DeWitt's parents were my great-great-great-great grandparents Jasper and Harriet (Newton) Mallory). Jasper was born on May 1, 1784 in the USA, and died in 1808 in Connecticut. Harriet (Newton) Mallory was born on July 7, 1791 and died in 1868 in Monroe, Ohio. Jasper's parents were Joseph & Susanna (Pond) Mallory, my great-great-great-great-great grandparents. Joseph was born in 1750 in the USA and died in 1784 in Connecticut. Susanna was born in 1755 in Connecticut and died on February 17, 1812.

Following Susanna (Pond) Mallory's family line takes us to her parents, Peter and Mary (Hubbard) Pond, my great-great-great-great-great-great grandparents. (I can trace Mary Hubbard's family tree all the way to England and Ireland in 1592 and 1596.) Peter was born on January 22, 1718 in Bradford, Connecticut and died in 1765 in Detroit, Michigan, while Mary was born on January 18, 1725 in Boston, Massachusetts and died on June 16, 1761 in Milford, New Haven, Connecticut. Peter's parents were Samuel and Abigail (Goodrich) Pond. Samuel was born on July 1, 1679 in Connecticut and died in December, 1726 in Connecticut. Abigail was born on November 13, 1685 in Connecticut and died in 1721 in Bradford, Connecticut. They were my great-great-great-great-great-great-great grandparents. The great's get so full that I prefer not to refer to any of the rest of the family as greats.

Samuel Pond's parents were Samuel Sr. and Miriam (Blatchley) Pond. Samuel Sr. was born on March 4, 1648 in the USA and died on January 30, 1718 in the USA. Miriam was born on May 1, 1653 in Connecticut and died in 1694 in Massachusetts. Miriam's parents were Thomas and Susanna (Ball) Blatchley. Thomas was born in 1615 in England and died in December 1674 in the USA. Susanna was born in 1624 in Connecticut and died on December 16, 1677 in the USA. Susanna (Ball) Blatchley's parents were William and Mary (Harris) Ball. William was born about 1573 in England and died in April, 1648 in the USA.

Another Samuel Pond, the senior of the two Samuel Ponds was born in 1617 in Groton, England and married Sarah (Ware) Pond. This Samuel died on March 14, 1654 in the USA, and Sarah was born in January of 1617 in the USA and died on July 6, 1665 in the USA. Last were Samuel Pond Senior Sr.'s parents which were Robert and Mary (Ball) Pond. Robert was born in 1587 in England and died on December 20, 1637 in the USA. Mary was born in 1585 in England and died in 1637 in Massachusetts. We actually share a grandmother with Lucille Ball, the actress and comedian.

Lucille was born Lucille Desiree Ball in Jamestown, New York on August 6, 1911. Her father Henry, an electrician, died when she was four years of age, and her mother Desiree, worked several jobs while Lucille and her younger brother Fred were raised by their grandparents. Desiree then married Ed and became Lucille's step-dad. Lucille entered in a dramatic school in New York, but her classmate Bette Davis received all the raves and Lucille was sent home because she was too shy. She will be best remembered as the "I Love Lucy" character, which became the most popular and universally beloved sitcom of all time.

My great-great grandfather Francis (Frank) Marion Mallory married my great-great grandmother, Mathilda Ellen Grimsley. She was born on December 12, 1854 in Montevallo, Vernon County, Missouri. Mathilda's parents were my great-great-great grandparents, John Brumet Grimsley, born on July 2, 1827 in Illinois, and died on September 22, 1899 in Missouri. Nancy Ellen (Taylor) Grimsley, who was born in 1830 in Kentucky and died in 1868 in Vernon, Missouri. Francis Marion Mallory was a farmer, although he had enlisted as a musician on August 17, 1861 in CO G, 36th infantry Reg IL., and discharged September 22, 1864. He died December 12, 1928.

My great-great-great grandpa John Brumet Grimsley's parents were Fielding and Susan (Brumet) Grimsley. Fielding was born in 1804 in Illinois and died on September 25, 1847. Susan was born in 1804 in Virginia and died on March 22, 1873. Fielding Grimsley's parents were William and Anna Margaretha (Strickler) Grimsley. William was born in 1768 in Virginia and died in September, 1831 in Illinois. Anna was born on December 20, 1776 in the USA and died in 1831 in Illinois. Anna Margaretha (Strickler) Grimsley's parents were John and Magdalena Buckner (Kauffman) Strickler. John was born in 1733 in Chester, Pennsylvania and died in 1801 in Massanutten, Virginia. Magdalena was born in 1744 in Lancester, Pennsylvania and died in 1805 in Rockingham, Virginia. Magdalena Buckner (Kauffman) Strickler's parents were Martin and Barbara (Stover) Kauffman. Martin was born on January 1, 1708 in the USA and died on May 17, 1749 in Virginia. Barbara was born in 1714 in Pennsylvania and died on May 17, 1749 in Colorado. Barbara (Stover) Kauffman's parents were Jacob and Sarah (Boone) Stover. Jacob was born in 1688 in Pennsylvania and died in 1741 in Virginia. Sarah was born on February 29, 1692 in England and died on November 20, 1743 in the USA. Sarah was Daniel Boone's aunt, and Daniel Boone's father was Squire Boone, Sarah's brother. Their grandparents were George and Mary Milton (Maugridge) Boone. George was born on March 19, 1666 in Maine and died on July 27, 1744. Mary was born on December 23, 1669 in England and died on February 2, 1740 in the USA. DANIEL BOONE WAS MY COUSIN.

Daniel Boone was born on November 2, 1734 near Reading, Pennsylvania to a family of Quakers and never learned to read or write. Daniel's grandfather had come to America from England in 1717. Daniel's father was a weaver and a blacksmith. When Daniel was twelve his father gave him a rifle, and his career as a huntsman began. By age fifteen his family moved from Pennsylvania to the Yadkin Valley in North Carolina that took over a year to travel to. At age twenty he left his family with a military expedition in the French and Indian War. At age 23 he got married and eventually had ten children.

In 1769, when Daniel was 35, he traveled into Kentucky exploring as he went. Kentucky wasn't even a state yet. He is responsible for the exploration and settlement of Kentucky. In fact, it was seven years before the United States even became a country! In 1788 he moved into what is now West Virginia. While Daniel was in West Virginia he tried to persuade other families to go west with him into Kentucky. One of those families was the Criss family, my second cousin Betty's husband Ramon Criss's family. Ten years later Daniel traveled into the Missouri region. He lived in Missouri for the rest of his life and died of natural causes at his son Nathan's home on Femme Osage Creek on September 26, 1820 at age 85, a few weeks shy of his 86th birthday and was buried beside his wife Rebecca.

When Daniel and Rebecca were out walking she told Daniel that when she dies she wanted to be buried there, only a few miles from their home, on the bank of a small stream called Teuque Creek. A quarter of a century later they were brought back to rest at the Frankfort cemetery, or were they? The actual graves were unmarked until the mid-1830s. Were the wrong remains mistakenly taken?

I have met a direct descendant of Daniel Boone in Wichita, and his name is Daniel Boone! He and his family attend the Central Christian Church. Daniel and his son, Nate, sing in a quartet together. Nate is not only a singer but a songwriter and composer. He wrote a song and arranged a composition for the church orchestra for their upcoming Fourth of July celebration in 2011.

One of my great-great grandparents Frank and Matilda Mallory's sons was my great grandfather, John Francis Mallory, who was born on August 8, 1876 in Freeport, Illinois. I do know that John had at least one older brother, Dewitt Clinton Mallory, who was born on June 29, 1874 in Missouri and died in January of 1965 in Chicago and was a long time railroad worker.

John Francis Mallory married Rosa Leuna Fleming in Virgil City, Missouri on February 21, 1897. In September 1897 she and her husband traveled by covered wagon to Trenton, Nebraska and lived on a farm southeast of Trenton, and almost a day's drive into Trenton by covered wagon, or about 17 miles. My great-grandpa John would take his daughter Goldie, his oldest daughter and (my grandma), into town about every three weeks to buy supplies such as flour and sugar, and the rest of his kids were upset because none of them got to go into town. Grandma Goldie was born on November 7, 1899 in or near Culbertson, Nebraska.

My great-grandparents John and Rosa owned over 150 horses, some of them being wild horses, but some were draft horses and valuable. Most of the land they lived on was mainly pasture. The barns on my great-grandparents home were so large that they made the house look like a small doll house. They kept an eight foot king snake in one of the barns where they kept their grain to keep the rats, mice and rabbits away.

One day while their son Elsie (my great-uncle Jack) was out disking in the field, he left the horses standing in the heat in the middle of the field while he went swimming in the creek. His dad caught him and beat Elsie so bad that he couldn't get out of bed for about three days. My grandma said her brother decided to never do that again.

My grandma Goldie said that her dad had at one time hired a man during harvest time to work for them but he left them for a couple of years then came back to work again, and they decided to have him live in the main house, while the other 20 to 30 men slept in the bunk house. After harvest the hired hand that stayed in the main house slipped away during the night, leaving behind bloody clothes hidden behind his bed. After receiving a newspaper a few weeks later there was a story of a man that tried to rob a bank in a neighboring town. He had gotten shot and had gotten away. My grandma thinks it was probably the hired hand living in their home!

On February 21, 1947 John and Rosa celebrated their golden wedding anniversary. I met my great-grandma Rosa in 1956 when my family took a vacation to Henderson, Nevada and to her son, Jack Mallory's restaurant, the Swanky Club. Rosa had been living with her daughter, Bertha for about eight and one half years in Henderson, Nevada. Rosa was born September 30, 1876 in Matoon, Coles County, Illinois. Her parents were David and Rebecca Ellen (Davis) Fleming. Rebecca's parents were George Wiley Davis and Arminda (Maloney) Davis. John Francis Mallory died at age 70 on July 30, 1947 in Trenton, Hitchcock County, Nebraska following a lingering illness. When my great-grandfather John passed away they found $40,000 in his suit jacket! Great-grandpa John had told his daughter Goldie, (my grandma) in front of all his other children that he would make sure that Goldie would be taken care of when he died. My grandma Goldie never saw a penny, and great-grandpa's will was never found, if he even had one. My great-grandma Rosa died on December 21, 1960 at the home of her daughter Bertha, in Henderson, Clark County, Nevada at age 84. Both she and John are buried in the Trenton cemetery, Trenton, Nebraska.

Their nine children were, John (Brad) Francis Mallory, Jr., who was born on November 29, 1916 at their farm in Trenton, and died on December 29, 1929 at the age of 13 following an operation for appendicitis, and is buried at the Trenton cemetery, Trenton, Nebraska. Grandma Goldie said that when her brother got sick her dad sent one of the hired men into town to get the doctor. The doctor came out to their farm in his car and stayed overnight. The next day when the doctor drove back into town he took my grandma Goldie to school in his car. No one in the area had ever seen a car up until then and her classmates came out of the school to see the car. Grandma told us that it was like riding on a cloud.

Another son was Elsie (Jack) Ellsworth Mallory, I knew him only as my great-uncle Jack. He and his wife Doris L. Mallory, owned and operated the Swanky Club in Henderson, Nevada. Jack was born on May 7, 1904 in Trenton, Nebraska and died on October 26, 1990 in the Nathan Adelson Hospice in Henderson, Nevada at the age of 86 with alzheimers. He and Doris had moved to Las Vegas in 1946. Doris L. Mallory was born on July 6, 1911 and died on January 11, 1997. Both are buried at the Palm Memorial Cemetery in the Suncrest section in Henderson, Nevada. I want to thank Gerry Perry, who is the Nevada Tombstone Project manager, for providing these pictures.

Tombstone of my great uncle
Jack and aunt Doris Mallory

Two of Jack's sisters lived on Mallory Street in Henderson. Mallory Street had been named after one of my great uncle Jack's sons who died while serving his country. One of Jack's sisters who lived at 20 Mallory Street was my great-aunt Bertha Maybelle (Mallory) Connelly, who was born on March 10, 1902 in Trenton, Nebraska. Another sister was my great-aunt Pearl (Mallory) Pfluger who also lived on Mallory Street. I never got to know my great-aunt Pearl while living in Henderson, although I had met her on a couple of occasions. My great-aunt Pearl owned the Bob And Pearl's Supper Club on Nellis Boulevard in Las Vegas. In contrast, my great-aunt Bertha often invited me over to their home in Henderson to either spend time with them or to have dinner. They often went to a spirit-filled church on Sundays and invited me to go along with them.

My great-uncle Jack Mallory's sisters were, Bertha Maybelle (Mallory) Connelly, born on March 10, 1902 in Trenton, Hitchcock County, Nebraska, and married Rev. Charles William Connelly, who was born on October 16, 1897 in Litchfield, Nebraska. Bertha lived the last 15 years of her life with her daughter Rosemary (Connelly) Spencer in Vacaville, California and died on February 20, 1982. Pearl (Mallory) Pfluger married Robert (Bob) Pfluger. Sylvia Leota (Mallory) Walker was born on November 15, 1899 in Sedalia, Pettis County, Missouri and married Raymond Walker. Cleo Josephine (Mallory) Morris was born on May 17, 1910 in Trenton, Hitchcock County, Nebraska, and married Theron Adams Morris. Jack's only brother John died at age 13 of appendicitis.

My grandma Goldie Ellen (Mallory) Piper was born on November 7, 1899 in or near Culbertson, Nebraska. While the war was going on, the newspapers were encouraging people to write to the boys overseas, and Goldie, being a teenager, decided to write to William (Will) Otto Julius Piper. They wrote back and forth for over a year, and decided to get married after he got out of the army. Somehow he made it to Trenton, Nebraska after the war ended, either by train or horse, or maybe his father's covered wagon, we don't know for sure. At first Will was not welcome at Goldie's family farm near Trenton. Her father kept chasing him away. When my grandma Goldie married Will Piper her father ended up giving them a good team of draft horses because Will's side of the family had nothing. It took Will and Goldie about 14 days to get to Kansas to stay with Will's family until they could get a place of their own. Grandma Goldie died on June 19, 1966 a few days after she and grandpa Will were involved in a car accident. Her funeral was held on June 23, 1966 at the Amos Family Chapel located at 10901 Johnson Drive in Shawnee, Kansas and she was buried at the old Monticello Cemetery in Johnson City where Grandpa Will is buried. Grandpa died on July 7, 1974 after suffering a stroke and had been placed in a nursing home in Desoto, Kansas until his death.

My great-aunt Bertha, who lived in Henderson, Nevada, showed me a Mallory small parts catalog that was continuously being sent to her every month from the Mallory Factory in Detroit, Michigan. Her uncle, Phillip Rogers Mallory, better known as Marion Mallory, had invented the famous Mallory Coil that created the way for airplanes to fly, and he invented the Mallory Battery, which later became Duracell batteries. Phillip R. Mallory died in 1975 at the age of 90. Three years later, the Mallory Battery Company and the Duracell name were acquired by Dart Industries. It has been purchased by an assortment of corporations since 1996 but Proctor & Gamble owns the brand name, as of this writing.

The story about the Mallory family had its roots starting back in the 1920s when my great-great uncle, Phillip (Marion) Rogers Mallory, a businessman, had teamed up with scientist, Samuel Ruben, to create innovative battery products. Marion Sr. was born on April 4, 1893 in Nevada, Missouri and died on December 26, 1963. He had only a fourth grade education.

Phillip R. Mallory was a manufacturer of tungsten filament wire. In 1964 the Mallory Battery Company, as it came to be known during WWII, introduced the Duracell brand —the first highly successful alkaline battery. The company continued to produce standard batteries under the Mallory label for some time while also selling the more expensive, but longer lasting Duracell alkaline type. Phillip had married his secretary Louise and she died in 1988. They had two children, Marion "Boots" and Jean Louise.

In 1980, five years after Phillip (Boots) Mallory, Jr.'s death in a car accident, the company changed its name to Duracell International and Boot's sister Jean Louis Mallory inherited all of the Mallory fortune. In a newspaper article dated May 16, 1989 Jean Louise Mallory had donated $1,500,000 for a new wing for the Carson/Lake Tahoe hospital. She had also donated $250,000 each to the American Heart Association, the American Cancer Society, and the University of Nevada/Reno. The company continued to improve its product line by incorporating features like the "Power Check" element, which gave the user an idea of how much power was left in the cell, and showed expiration dates. In 1996, Duracell merged with Gillette. Today, Duracell is the second largest battery company in the world.

Phillip Rogers Mallory's parents were Henry R. Mallory and Cora (Pynchon) Mallory. Henry R. Mallory's father was Charles Henry Mallory who was the first president of the Mystic River National Bank in 1851 in Mystic, Connecticut. In 1864 he founded the First National Bank of Mystic Ridge and purchased its entire stock of $100,000 and became president of the bank. Four of his sons served as directors from 1870 to 1893, the one son being Henry Rogers Mallory, my great-great uncle. Henry became associated with his father in the shipping and commission house of Charles H. Mallory and Company, and served as a junior partner in the firm. He became their president in 1890 when his dad died, and he continued as their president until 1906 when the Mallory family sold their steamship interests to Charles W. Morse who merged the Mallory Line with several other lines.

The ship "Henry R. Mallory" was built in 1916 and was one of the newest and largest American steamships, until it was converted into a transport vessel. It was a cargo ship of 6,422 gross tons. It was the first American ship to transport American troops and supplies to France, and was used during WW1 and WWII. It was sunk in WWII after being hit by a torpedo. His ship was the first to sail from the United States to India, China, and Australia. His father, Charles Henry Mallory, helped build thirty gunboats for President Lincoln during the civil war.

Henry Rogers Mallory died at Winter Park, Florida on March 4, 1919 at age 74, and is buried at Greenwich, Connecticut in the Putnam Cemetery. There you will find a very impressive marble memorial honoring Henry Rogers Mallory.

Most of the Mallory collection was donated to the University of Nevada located in Reno by Jean Louise Mallory in 1994.

My grandma, Goldie Ellen (Mallory) Piper, had come from a family steeped with history and money but she chose to marry a poor dirt farmer, my grandpa, William (Will) Otto Julius Piper whom she met while writing to him while he served in WW 1. Grandma Goldie's brother, my great uncle, Elsie (Jack) Ellsworth Mallory, had borrowed a million dollars from his uncle, Philip Rogers Mallory, so he could start his own business in Las Vegas, the Swanky Club. Another sister of grandma's, Pearl (Mallory) Flueger, also borrowed money so she could start the Bob And Pearl's Supper Club on Nellis Boulevard in Las Vegas. When my great-grandma, Rosa Leuna (Fleming) Mallory died, her estate was to be divided amongst all her siblings, which included my grandma, Goldie Piper. My grandma never received any inheritance.

THIRTEEN

DODGING A BULLET

I had been working at the Swanky Club for a few months and decided to walk into Henderson one afternoon after my morning chores so I could spend time with my great-aunt Bertha and great-uncle Charles. Finding Mallory Street was so easy for me back in 1964. Now, when we recently visited the area, I could hardly find Mallory Street.

Frankie standing beside his great-aunt Bertha Connelly's home on Mallory Street in Henderson, NV

When I got to my great-aunt Bertha's home she told me that she had heard that the army was starting to draft young men who were not married, and my dad had always warned me about enlisting. He had suffered being shot in WWII and he didn't want his boys to witness what he had witnessed and he tried to always discourage us from joining the military. He had a Purple Heart to prove it. Knowing I had been in constant contact with Joyce Biondo, the girl I left behind in Norfolk, Nebraska, I told my great-aunt Bertha that I should try and get married right away.

Joyce had already finished her year at the junior college in Norfolk and had flown back home to New Jersey, but we had been writing letters back and forth, staying in touch. In one of my letters I asked her if she would marry me. I told her that we could meet in Oklahoma if her parents could bring her out, and I could take a bus to Oklahoma from Las Vegas. My dad was a pastor of a church in Hinton, Oklahoma and he had already agreed to marry us, so Joyce wrote back and said yes, she would marry me.

We set the date of July fifth to get married and that started everything into motion. Joyce's dad said that that was a perfect time for them to drive out to Hinton, Oklahoma especially during the Fourth of July holiday. I purchased a bus ticket to Weatherford, Oklahoma from Henderson, Nevada and my dad said that he would come and pick me up when the bus arrived.

When I told my great-uncle Jack and my great-aunt Doris about my plans to get married, they were both excited. Aunt Doris asked me if I was planning on coming back and I assured her that I was because I wanted to resume my job at the Swanky Club. Since I didn't own a car I really didn't know how my new wife and I would be able to come back, except by bus, but we'd work it out.

I arrived in Weatherford by bus a few days early and was able to spend time with my parents at their parsonage in Hinton. Joyce's dad called my parents to tell them that they were just a few days out and would be there a day or so before our wedding date. He made plans ahead of time and had reserved rooms at the Tradewinds motel in Weatherford for their family, and even paid for our wedding night in the wedding suite for the night of July fifth, as a wedding gift to us.

Joyce and her family arrived at my parent's parsonage a couple of days before the wedding. When I saw Joyce, I realized right then and there that I really did not want to get married. I knew I had made a big mistake. I just wanted to disappear into thin air and not have to worry about the awful situations I had created. How does one get out of a situation that you and both of your families have spent months preparing for? Joyce's family had driven all the way out from New Jersey, and I had traveled all the way from Nevada just to be here and get married. Do I dare just tell Joyce and her family that I had changed my mind and didn't want to get married? Then, the thought of being drafted hit me like a ton of bricks. I told myself that I just couldn't back out. Somehow it would work out, or at least I had convinced myself it would.

The realization that I was going to actually get married started to jar my senses. I didn't know how to treat a woman. What was expected of me? All I could think of was that we were going to be living together as husband and wife and we would be traveling together out to Nevada to live. I knew also that my wages at the Swanky Club were just not enough money for the two of us to live on. Then I pictured the two of us living in that small cottage behind the Swanky Club, and that's when the starkness of coming to terms with my own reasoning hit bottom. I knew I couldn't back out of this marriage and I had to somehow find another job.

My dad told us that we had to have blood tests and would need to drive into Anadarko. He loaned me his car so Joyce and I could drive there. Since I was only 20 years of age, I had to have special approval from my parents to marry. I would not be 21 till November 7th.

While waiting at the clinic in Anadarko for our blood tests results, we had discussed the delicate subject of her needing something to keep clean after our wedding night. I knew very little about feminine hygiene but I remembered seeing, in my mother's possessions, a douce bag. Was that what all women used? Somehow in the vacancies of my memory banks about such matters, I knew that we just had to purchase one. Our driving from one drug store to another in Anadarko, asking if they had this item, kept me red-faced and perplexed. I just wanted the experience to end. After finding one we sort of laughed about it all. We did have some good times together.

Over the years I do not ever remember much about my parents ever discussing or teaching us kids about finances, our need for education, or our career goals. Not much was ever discussed about sex, let alone, relationships. Now I wish that they had sat us down and talked frankly to us about all these issues. My idea of marriage was that the woman stayed home and cooked and cleaned for the man, and did all the laundry, just like my mother. I always thought that the man worked and provided housing, did all the outside chores, and if he wanted to have sex with his wife she gave in to him willingly.

There was very little kissing or hugging between my mom and dad that I can ever remember. Was kissing and hugging a taboo? Were all those things only done in the dark and hidden behind closed doors? I always witnessed our friends and relatives kissing and hugging. Why wasn't more of that practiced in our own family!

At the last minute my dad informed us that he didn't want to unite us in marriage until Joyce was baptized. What? Why was this sprung on us at the last minute? When I told Joyce, she reluctantly said she would, but I knew she was frustrated, as I was, that this was just one more thing we had to do before we could marry. She was Catholic as were her parents. They believed that children get sprinkled as a baby, but my dad insisted that Joyce get baptized by immersion. I later discovered that the Catholic Church did not recognize our marriage because we were not married in the Catholic Church.

We all headed on over to the church, which was right next door to their parsonage, and dad led us up to the platform where the pulpit sat. None of us could see a place to baptize anyone, but dad lifted up a trap door under where the pulpit sat and beneath it was the baptismal, a sunken large metal tub, of sorts, that was filled with water. Dad asked Joyce to head to a back room to change into white garments she could be baptized in, then he disappeared behind another side door to change into clothes he could baptize her.

After dad reappeared, he was wearing hip boots, and Joyce appeared in a white soft frock. Dad stepped down into the sunken large tub and asked Joyce to join him. I noticed, as all of us were as we were standing around the sunken metal tub area watching the baptism that Joyce was crying. I didn't know why until after our marriage that Joyce just did not want to get baptized, and especially in an awful, sunken metal tub under the floor.

The wedding went without a hitch. The church people had decorated the basement for our wedding reception and had prepared a wedding cake for us. My parents congratulated us and Joyce's dad came over and handed us a check for $500 that his mother in Masbeth, New York had given to him to give to us as a wedding present, along with two tickets to the New York State's World's Fair. We thought that maybe Joyce's grandmother Biondo was hoping that someday Joyce and I would come back to the east coast and use the tickets.

We decided to try and find a used car and use the funds that Joyce's grandmother had given to us so we could drive back to Las Vegas. We shopped around at several used car lots in Oklahoma City and found a two-door Studebaker sedan for $200.00. It was one of the few cars on the lot that we could afford. This Studebaker had a special metal awning over the windshield that made it look unique. We didn't realize it at the time that the brake lights did not work.

Joyce and I decided to drive on over to Weatherford to check into the Tradewinds motel. We said goodbye to my parents and my brother Doug and got into our used car that had temporary paper plates on it. When we arrived at the Tradewinds I was prepared to pay for a motel room but the clerk told me that my father-n-law had already paid for our room. The clerk couldn't give us the wedding suite we were supposed to be in because the motel had doubled booked, and because of the mix up the motel wanted to give us the larger honeymoon suite on a different floor, as a bonus.

Unbeknownst to us, Joyce's brothers had planned all evening long to heckle us by knocking on our honeymoon suite door and running away. What they didn't know was that the manager had moved us to another room on a different floor. The door they were knocking on was another young couple's honeymoon suite! We enjoyed a peaceful night's sleep, undisturbed.

The next day we said goodbye to Joyce's family and started our drive out to Henderson, Nevada. I was afraid that the car wouldn't make it that far, but the car surprised us and actually got us to Henderson.

When we arrived in Henderson I was afraid that my great-uncle Jack Mallory would not take me back and I was very apprehensive about driving over to the Swanky Club. Before I had left the Swanky Club for Oklahoma to get married, I had made friends with a family who lived in Henderson, so I drove directly over to their home and we two spent the night on their sleeper sofa. They told me that I should go and ask my uncle for my job back. I took their advice and we drove over to the Swanky Club and Uncle Jack did give me my old job back. Joyce and I moved into that little cottage where I had lived behind the Swanky Club and I started work the next day.

We had to sleep on a sleeper sofa in that little cottage because that's all we had. The first meal Joyce prepared for us she got all excited about because this was the first home cooked meal she had prepared. Every day I would walk up to the back entrance to the club, work for a few hours, then come back to the cottage and we'd drive into Henderson to shop or go to a matinee movie. I didn't have to be back to work until evening. We had no utility payments at the cottage and no upkeep whatsoever, and our yard was a desert.

When I came into work one morning my great-uncle Jack told me he had heard on TV that they were drafting not only single guys, but married guys with no children. It just seemed I was constantly dodging a bullet not to get drafted, but I was ok because Joyce told me she was pregnant. I took her to our family doctor and he confirmed it. However, Joyce was so upset when she found out she was pregnant that she got back into the car and lit up a cigarette. I was so mad at her for smoking that I threw my arm out over her stomach in a fit of anger. Joyce knew I didn't approve of smoking and she told me she had quit, but what I didn't know was that she had smoked all the way up to our wedding day.

On the week-ends at the Swanky Club they had an entertainer by the name of Phyllis Dilly, who played both a piano and an organ at the same time. Joyce and I got to know Phyllis and her husband because they lived in a mobile home almost right in front of our cottage behind the Swanky Club.

Phyllis Dilly and her husband came over to our cottage one evening and told us that they were moving from the mobile home into an apartment in Las Vegas and wondered if Joyce and I would like to rent the mobile home. We jumped at the chance and we moved in almost immediately. We were so thankful to have an actual bed to sleep in now. It was a cute little home with a shower, a stove with an oven, and a wonderful kitchen area complete with a kitchen table. We could now buy our own groceries and not have to depend on our one free meal at the club every day.

Our 'honeymoon bliss' first home behind my great-uncle Jacks' Swanky Club in Henderson, NV

One afternoon when I had finished working at the Swanky Club, I went back into our little bedroom to relax. I stretched out on the bed on my back with my arms under my head. Joyce walked in and jumped on the bed, and the bed frame broke immediately. When I told my Uncle Jack about the mishap, he never stopped teasing us about what he thought actually happened on that bed!

When our anniversary came around I wanted to treat Joyce to a wonderful meal, I decided to take her to my great Aunt Pearl's "Bob And Pearl's Supper Club." I thought it would be a great evening with wonderful food, and we could see my aunt Pearl again. Aunt Pearl knew that I had been working at her brother's Swanky Club. I had met my aunt Pearl on many occasions, but seldom by myself, only during family functions, so I called her Supper Club and made our reservations.

Bob and Pearl's Supper Club was located on Nellis Boulevard, just west of the Swanky Club and north of East Las Vegas. Joyce and I both got dressed up for our dinner date and headed on over to the Supper Club. I was so excited with the anticipation of meeting my great—aunt Pearl again and eating at her Supper Club, because I had never been there before. This would be a great opportunity for my great-aunt Pearl to meet my wife.

When we arrived at the Supper Club I parked our car and we walked up to the entrance of the club and gave our names at the door. Yes, we had reservations, and the hostess seated us. I could see my great-aunt Pearl as busy as a rabbit dodging bullets, trying to wait on people, making sure her customers were happy, and also making sure that her waitresses were doing their jobs. Bob and Pearl's Supper Club, with its Smorgasbord, reminded me so much of the Swanky Club, very similar in nature, and with the same type of menu and salad selections on the buffet.

Joyce and I had a wonderful Smorgasbord meal, but what I had been hoping for was that my aunt Pearl would comp. our meals. When Joyce and I were first seated at our table I had told our waitress to tell my great-aunt Pearl that Joyce and I were celebrating our anniversary. I was family, and I hoped family members would get special treatment, but aunt Pearl came over to our table once and congratulated us, made a little small talk and then flitted off to resume her mad house dashes.

We finished our meal and we were handed our check, I left a nice tip, and we headed to the cashier to see what arrangements may have been made. There were no special arrangements made for us and my aunt did not even say goodbye to us. Needless to say, we never went back.

Joyce and I had not been living behind the Swanky Club for very long when I decided I wanted to take her on a guided tour inside Hoover Dam, so I chose a day during the week when there was a slow time at the Swanky Club and we took off for the Dam.

On the way to Hoover Dam we both noticed a sign on the side of the road that said 'Helicopter Rides, Five Dollars." I told Joyce that I had never been on an airplane, let alone a helicopter, but I wanted to try it. She was not interested at all in a helicopter ride but she saw souvenir shops, so I had her attention. We stopped and walked through many of the shops, ending up at the ticket booth for the helicopter rides. I purchased a ticket and waited for my turn at boarding, but the helicopter wasn't on the landing pad. The copter must have been in the air somewhere over Lake Meade giving someone else a ride. However, soon we heard a whirling sound and we spotted the helicopter flying over a small rock hill, and we watched it as it made a landing onto the concrete strip, the rotating blades coming to a complete stop.

Within minutes I boarded the helicopter and got strapped in, while Joyce waited on a nearby bench for my return. Inside the cabin of this helicopter all I could see was nothing but windows, all the way to the floor of the helicopter. My feet were almost touching the glass, and I became a little bit nervous because I was the only passenger. The pilot started the engines and I could hear the blades above us start their circling cycle, and within minutes the helicopter rose straight up in the air and took off so quickly that I felt like I had left my heart back at the launching pad. My mind was in total shock as I tried so hard to grasp the reality and the excitement of it all. Was this actually happening? What was I thinking?

In seconds we were flying over jagged rock formations and rolling hills, as the pilot guided this over-sized dragonfly to places that only birds should be allowed to fly. Lake Meade was looming up before us and I thought for sure we were going to crash land somewhere out in the middle of the lake, but no, we flew over it and headed towards Hoover Dam. What a sight for sore eyes! There was nothing below us now but water. We approached Hoover Dam and the pilot took a sharp right and we headed just above the jagged rocks and flew above the highway leading us west and back to the launching pad. The pilot landed the craft and I got out, bent down and kissed terra firma.

I met up with Joyce and we decided to drive on over to Hoover Dam and take a guided tour. It was such a beautiful drive, especially when we started to descend down the hill to where the Colorado River flowed. The big massive concrete wall ahead of us was the famous Hoover Dam. What a sight! There were many parking spaces, both on the Nevada side and on the Arizona side. We parked on the Nevada side and took a wonderful tour through the dam. We were shown, amongst so many interesting areas of the dam, large turbines that help generate electricity that create the power to light up all the surrounding towns and the city of Las Vegas.

When we started heading back to Las Vegas we took a side trip and drove on down to Lake Meade to take a quick dip in the water. We had already planned on taking a dip if we had the time. We parked our car, went and changed into our swim wear and headed on down to the water's edge. The coolness of the water felt so good, especially since it had been so hot out. We splashed around in the water for a while and decided it was getting late when the sun started going down over the hills. When Joyce stepped out of the water, she noticed that she had lost her wedding band somewhere out there in the lake. I stepped back into the water where she had been swimming, trying to feel anything that felt like a ring in all that sand and mud, but we never found it. We ended up having to buy another gold wedding band for her.

FOURTEEN
DISHARMONY

My forty dollars a week salary and the tips I made didn't seem to stretch as much now since I had a wife. I received free meals at the Swanky Club but Joyce couldn't eat there unless we paid for her meal. She was pregnant and I began to realize that we were going to need more income and a larger place to live. The strain on our marriage was starting to show now. It just seemed like we were always at odds with each other and constantly bickering over something.

I started driving into Las Vegas every afternoon in search of another job, and a gas station offered me a job working only part time pumping gas every afternoon. I not only was working at the Swanky Club every morning and every evening, I was now working in the afternoon as a gas station attendant. The long hours started getting to me after only a couple of weeks. I gave my Uncle Jack notice that I had found another job and we moved into Las Vegas to a one bedroom apartment. The only furniture we had was what I had bought when I had lived in that little cottage before Joyce arrived.

When I read that the Seven Eleven stores were taking applications for management trainees, I jumped at the chance. I took the exam and passed with flying colors and started working at one of their stores on west Sahara Boulevard. The Seven Eleven manager wanted Joyce and me to move closer to the store, so I found an apartment almost within walking distance of the store and we moved to an upstairs two-bedroom apartment.

I loved working at the Seven Eleven store, feeling confident that I would someday become a manager of one of their stores. Except, one evening at about eleven pm when I had gotten off work, I heard that our store had been robbed about eleven thirty pm. I went in the next day and quit. That could have been me being held up at gunpoint.

I needed a job badly and just happened to walk into a Shop-n-Go convenience store a few blocks from our apartment and asked the store manager if there was an opening. I told him about my experience working as a manager trainee for the 7-Eleven stores and why I quit. He told me he did have an opening and I could start the next evening. I was thrilled to have a job and came in early to get the layout of the store and to get specific instructions on their store policies. It was the Christmas season and he needed an extra person to man the store if he needed to take off for any reasons. I remember I worked through Christmas eve and New Year's eve while he took off. The day after New Year's he came up to me and told me that he had to let me go, because a married friend of his who had several children needed an immediate job. He made the statement to me that he knew I'd understand. No, I didn't understand, after all, I only had a pregnant wife at home.

After quitting the Shop n Go store I started working full-time at a super market just off the Las Vegas strip. I worked mainly in the liquor department but helped out bagging groceries occasionally. One day I noticed on their bulletin board that the bakery department was looking for help. I told Joyce about it and she immediately got hired in their bakery department. We were able to ride into work together daily.

It wasn't long before Joyce started working that she began spotting in her clothes. The job required her to lift heavy donut trays. She immediately had to quit her job or lose our baby, so our family doctor told her to stay in bed for a few months, except to go to the restroom. Joyce did stay in bed for a few months, until the doctor said she could get up and around. When she got the approval to be active, I'd come home after work and she would be gone. Not even a note! I often was frantic as to where she was and what she was doing. I would take off in our car searching for her and never would find her, but she would eventually come home late at night, not telling me where she had been or what she had been doing.

Her taking off again and again started to wear on me. One evening when I came home and she was gone again, I drove over to her best girlfriend's home asking if Joyce was there but her girlfriend told me she wasn't there when in reality she was. Joyce was eight months pregnant and was walking all over the neighborhood late at night.

Our disagreements developed into disharmony and started to mount higher and higher. I realized that the friction between us was like sandpaper, and we both had made a big mistake by getting married. I know Joyce missed her family and often would just sit and cry over what I thought was nothing. I really wanted out, but now she was pregnant, with my child.

While I was working in the liquor department at the super market on the Strip, I left to go into the grocery story area to help bag groceries when I noticed that many of the cashiers were crying. I asked what was wrong and they told me that President Kennedy had been shot. What a shock! Some news reports said that they thought he was still alive and other reports said that he had died. We just all stood there in silence and disbelief at the news.

Working at the super market was so much fun and I enjoyed stocking the liquor bottles on the shelves and in their walk-in refrigerators. When I wasn't busy I would go into the grocery area and help bag groceries. The tips were wonderful and an added bonus.

I had to quit my job at the super market when the manager realized that I was only twenty years old. I was not even allowed to work with liquor. I immediately got another job working at the Review Journal newspaper, located on Main Street in North Las Vegas. I was much closer to our flat, and on some days I could even walk into work, weather permitting.

We finally were able to move from that depressing apartment and into a beautiful flat in North Las Vegas. This apartment was all furnished. The landlord even asked us if we wanted to be in charge of receiving everyone's rent every month, and he would give us a discount on our rent. Joyce did not want the position because she said she didn't want people constantly coming and going out of our apartment after our baby was born.

I read in the newspaper that a Las Vegas company was auditioning singers for a commercial so I decided to go and audition. When I arrived each person was taken into a room and questioned first and then we were asked to sing "Black Bird" a cappella. They told me I did a great job, but there was one more tenor they needed to listen to. At the end of our session they had chosen the other tenor, and after the meeting when I started to drive home and feeling a little disappointed, the other tenor asked me if I would give him a lift home. I not only was rejected, but now I had to take the guy home that was chosen over me! Talk about a feeling of humility! The winners were going to have an all-expense paid trip to Hollywood to record the commercial, where many doors could open for possible future commercials and movies! I was 'this' close to becoming famous but again, was I chasing an illusive dream?

We were just getting ready for bed one evening when Joyce felt a sudden pain. It startled her at first but we both realized that she was having the beginnings of labor. I drove her to the hospital but the hospital said it was false labor pains and sent us back home. Within a few hours the labor pains came back again and we took off for the hospital again.

Our daughter, Jennifer Sue Piper, was born on July 1st, 1964. We took our new daughter home and within a day received a visit from my mom and dad, who had driven to Las Vegas from Hinton, Oklahoma to see their first grandchild. We had a great reunion.

After Jennifer was born we wanted to move to another apartment that was even closer to my job at the Review Journal. We found a one-bedroom flat fully furnished and affordable, and Jennifer spent her first Christmas and her first birthday at this flat. We placed Jennifer's crib in our bedroom, and each time she would turn over or make a sound, we were both awake.

Our relationship after Jennifer was born had not changed much and we were still at each other's throats. During one of our verbal fights, I accidentally hit Joyce's TV tray and knocked it into the Christmas tree and knocked the tree over. We had quite a mess on our hands to clean up, and I felt so bad and wondered how far these fights were going to go.

I worked at the Review Journal for a year and earned a one-week vacation, so I immediately wanted to make plans to take Joyce and our daughter Jennifer to Disneyland in Anaheim, California. Joyce apposed the whole idea and fought me tooth and nail, but with much coaching I finally convinced her that it was ok for us to go. Not having any extra funds to travel anywhere, I would have to dip into that week's wages to afford our trip.

The whole vacation trip turned out to be a trip from hell. Joyce made the whole traveling experience a disastrous event, always complaining about whether it was warm enough in the car, or it was too cold. I was either going too fast, or not fast enough. I knew we couldn't afford to spend the night at a motel in Anaheim so we spent several hours at Disneyland and had to drive back to Las Vegas that same day.

The only remembrance I have of our visit to Disneyland was when we had walked up to a vendor who had a monkey that was trained to take food out of someone's hands. A crowd had gathered and we thought it would be fun to feed the monkey, so Jennifer fed the monkey and then Joyce wanted to. Joyce held out her hand to feed the monkey, and as she did she bent down a little to be a little more on the same level as the monkey. The monkey came over to Joyce and looked at her with an inquisitive look, jumped towards her and pushed her backwards, and Joyce fell onto her backside, laughing. I told myself that there is justice in this world.

We walked around Disneyland until the sun started going down when we decided we needed to leave so we could drive all the way back to Las Vegas.

At our flat in North Las Vegas we got to know some of our neighbors. One of those neighbors was Rick Sparks and his wife Shelly, who kept offering us to move into their spare bedroom. Rick wanted me to go with him to Los Angeles to apply for a job there because he knew I wasn't thrilled with the job I had at the Review Journal. He had a sister who lived in Hollywood and was married to a funeral director, and he knew we could stay with his sister while we scouted around the L.A. area for jobs. Joyce could stay with Shelly at the flat in North Las Vegas while Rick and I traveled to Los Angeles.

Joyce and I decided to give up our flat and we moved in with Rick and Shelly. All we had to do was share the grocery expense and a percentage of their utility bills. We had no other expenses now and we could save money. Joyce was pregnant and was not enjoying the thought of her being pregnant again, which was just more fodder for us to argue and fight about.

FIFTEEN

HOLLYWOOD

Rick and I chose a week-end to drive on out to Las Angeles. Why we decided that I would use my old car to drive there I cannot remember. I was still driving the old Studebaker two-door sedan and I didn't think my car would make it that far.

The drive from North Las Vegas to Hollywood, California had been about a four hour drive. Rick had his sister's address and knew just where to turn off of Santa Monica Boulevard to drive straight to their home. He asked me if I had ever been to the ocean before and I assured him I hadn't, so he took over the driving and we headed down Sunset Boulevard going west. I remember the beautiful palm trees, all the well-manicured lawns, beautiful homes along the way and the beauty of Sunset Boulevard. Rick told me that we were only within a mile or so of the ocean and then he said, "There it is." From a distance all I could see was a bluish, grey backdrop just beyond the trees and the homes that were just ahead of us. Rick told me that that was indeed the ocean, and I just sat there in the car staring in amazement, like a child with a new colorful toy. I was twenty one years old and I was seeing the ocean for the first time.

Rick drove us all the way to the end of Sunset Boulevard where we could actually be at sea level and at the water's edge. My spirit just loomed inside of me as I marveled over and over again how awesome God is. We spent a few minutes there at the stop sign where we would have to turn either right or left, but I just didn't want this experience to end. However, we did have a goal in mind and that was to visit with Rick's sister and her husband to get help in knowing who to contact in the Los Angeles area for a job, so we had to turn around and find the turnoff that would lead us to Rick's sister's home.

Meeting Rick's sister and her husband was such a treat. They had a beautiful home in the hills of Hollywood overlooking the Santa Monica freeway. From their front picture windows we could see the lights of Los Angeles. I was kind of hesitant about shaking the hand of a Funeral Director, but realized that his hands are always sanitized. They were both very friendly and made us both feel right at home. Rick's sister had friends who worked at a large Presbyterian Hospital in Los Angeles and made arrangements for Rick and me to go and fill out applications.

I found a parking lot about three blocks away from the hospital and parked my car. Rick and I walked up to the employment office of the hospital and filled out our applications. Soon after we handed in our finished applications we were both called in for an interview, and the supervisor hired us right on the spot as Inhalation Therapists trainees. We were both thrilled to have a job.

As we left the building, we both had forgotten where I parked my car. This hospital took up the whole entire city block and we had forgotten at which entrance we had come into the building. The whole city looked the same from all sides of the hospital, so we decided to circle the hospital one block at a time in all directions and then spread out and include walking two blocks away in all directions. When we finally got to a three block radius walking in a circle around the hospital, I spotted my blue Studebaker sitting in a car lot. I almost wanted to cry. It was at that point that we both decided we had just enough time to drive back to Las Vegas and spend some time with our wives before starting our new jobs.

By the time we had driven back home to our flat, spent a few hours with our wives, and started our drive back to Los Angeles, we were both so sleepy and tired. He would drive and then I would drive, but each time either of us got behind the wheel, we found ourselves wanting to fall sleep.

It was in the early, early morning about four am when we both knew we just couldn't drive another mile without falling asleep at the wheel. I was sleeping in the back seat when Rick decided to pull over and park on the side of an all-night gas station where he could curl up on the front seat and sleep. He thought that maybe after we both had slept for an hour or two we could get up and head on into Las Angeles to start our new jobs. We overslept and got into Las Angeles mid-morning, way

My dad's sister Joan with her husband Fred

after the time we were supposed to start our new jobs, and the supervisor told us we were both fired before we even started. I told Rick then that maybe we could go visit my Aunt Joan, one of my dad's sisters, and her family up in Northridge, California, and maybe they could help us get a job.

We left downtown Los Angeles and headed on up to Northridge. We found my Aunt Joan Patch's home and we stopped by to visit with them for a while, and she told us we could spend the night at their home. We then decided to try driving around the area to see if we could fill out applications for jobs. We lost track of the time and by the time we got back to my Aunt Joan's home, they had gone to bed, so Rick decided maybe we could drive around in the area and just sleep in my car. He found a small forest and pulled my car up under some of the trees where we slept until morning.

I remember waking up in the back seat and looking out my car window and seeing oranges growing on a tree. When I looked out the opposite window I saw grapefruit growing on those trees. When Rick realized I was awake, he got up and stared in disbelief that in the dark of night we had pulled into an orchard. We jumped out and picked some of the fruit and then we knew we had to head back to Las Vegas and not worry about going back to my Aunt Joan's home.

We returned home defeated and beaten down. Neither one of us felt that we had accomplished much and we both had lost a job of a lifetime because we had made bad decisions. Joyce had wanted us to move back to New Jersey, anyway, and her parents were willing to help us get started there. Now might be a good time to finally make that big move.

We returned home and I told Joyce that we needed to do something quick because I was not happy with my job at the Review Journal. It was like pulling teeth to get a raise and I just grew tired of my position there in the printing department.

My old Studebaker started giving me problems, so I went to a local used car dealer and traded my old Studebaker for a Nash Rambler station wagon. It didn't take us long to pay off the balance on the loan of the Nash Rambler, and when I paid the last payment on the Nash I decided to call it quits at the Review Journal. I knew I couldn't give them a notice or they might let me go that same day, because I needed my last paycheck to help pay our traveling expenses to New Jersey.

We had no home and we were living in the spare bedroom of our friend's apartment. I didn't care about my job and we both decided we had had enough and wanted to move. Joyce contacted her parents and they told us to come on out, so I worked all week at the Review Journal, picked up my check on Friday after work, cashed my check, and we made our plans to leave on Saturday for New Jersey.

SIXTEEN

THE HORRIFIC JOURNEY

Joyce and I packed what little we had left into our Nash Rambler station wagon, leaving the back of the station wagon cleared for our daughter, Jennifer. If she became sleepy, we simply laid her in the back, where we had placed blankets and pillows, knowing that she would sleep peacefully. Everything else we had owned in North Las Vegas we gave away. All we took with us were our clothes.

We left Las Vegas and headed east to Kingman, Arizona. There I turned onto highway 40 that would take us all the way eastward through Arizona. When we reached Flagstaff, the weather turned ugly, with the temperature dropping and heavy north winds. It was then that I realized that the cold wind was coming right through my driver's side of the car, seeping through the ill fitted door frame and dousing me with chills. It was getting harder and harder for me to drive when my hands were so cold. Although the heater in the car seemed to work fine the cold air engulfing me kept fighting the warmth, and the cold air kept winning, but this made me even more determined to keep going to keep my family safe.

When it started getting dark I decided to keep on driving and try and get as far as I could, but then I realized we needed to find an affordable motel before I got so tired that I wouldn't be able to stay awake. Sometimes on this highway 40 the towns were very few and far between and I didn't know if I would find a motel when I really needed to. I drove until about eleven pm and knew then that I had to rest and try and gather my strength for the long haul that was still staring me in the face.

The next day we headed through New Mexico and into Oklahoma where I had made plans for us to stop and visit my parents. My dad had been offered the pastorate of the Wellston Christian Church in Wellston, Oklahoma. I knew that we would change highways in Oklahoma City and would be heading to highway 44 and eventually onto highway 70. Highway 44 would take us to the Wellston exit, and that exit was about twenty four miles northeast of Oklahoma City. We could probably make a brief stop and spend an hour or so with my parents, this being the second time they could see their first granddaughter. Jennifer was about a year old now and was walking. She had beautiful blonde hair and was showing signs of being left-handed, just like her dad.

My parents were so thrilled that we had stopped. Mom wanted to serve us dinner and made her famous white milk gravy to put over potatoes. I remember growing up with this same kind of gravy recipe, but Joyce gagged when she tried eating it. She just was not used to that kind of home cooking. Needless to say, Joyce didn't eat much.

Our visit with my parents there in Wellston was much too brief. I could tell that Joyce was feeling more and more uncomfortable and wanted to leave, so we ended up staying only a couple of hours and headed on up to Joplin, Missouri where I tried to find another affordable motel so we could spend the night. To do so I had to turn off of highway 44 onto a side road that led into Joplin.

As I drove along heading towards Joplin, I spotted what looked like a very affordable motel, but when I pulled into the office area to pay for the room, Joyce came unglued. She had noticed that the parking lot itself was paved with some kind of, what looked like, roofing shingles, and she argued with me about staying overnight, wanting me to get a refund. I thought the motel itself looked clean and new and there was nothing wrong with our staying overnight, and since it was already after dark, I didn't really feel like driving further on into Joplin to try and find yet another motel. She finally gave in, but not until her attitude helped steal every precious moment of my excitement away from me for the entire night.

It just seemed to be getting harder and harder for us to ever agree on anything. My jaded thoughts kept hitting me over the head like a sledgehammer, telling me to take her to her parent's home and leave her there. Another part of me said, hey, Joyce is ok just the way she is. I am ok just the way I am. We just do not belong together. Whatever it took however, I was willing to try and work things out.

After a very sleepless night for me that included much worry and built up stress, we headed for Saint Louis early the next day. I was becoming more excited the further east we traveled. I had never, in my entire life, ever traveled east of the Mississippi river, so this would be a first for me.

We traveled all the next day, crossing the Mississippi, and through a blur of states that were just stepping stones to where I wanted to be in a day or so. In Harrisburg, Pennsylvania I should have stopped and called Joyce's parents for specific directions from that point on but I thought we had to go through Philadelphia first.

I drove us towards Philadelphia and found a very quaint motel on the north side of the city. We called Joyce's dad from there and he told us that we should have taken highway 78 that ran northeast out of Harrisburg. It would have cut off many more miles that we now would have to travel.

SEVENTEEN
MT. FREEDOM

After spending the night north of Philadelphia we headed on east and crossed the Delaware River that led us into New Jersey. We had no other choice now but to take the Jersey turnpike north. I have always had a very bad sense of direction and can get lost at the drop of a hat but somehow, with the directions we had written down that Joyce's dad gave us, I found their home on the outskirts of Rockaway, New Jersey.

Joyce's parents were renting a farm house that sat on several acres of land on the north side of Rockaway. A creek ran right through the property and they had a couple of horses roaming around in fenced areas behind their home. It

The old Biondo home in Rockaway, NJ

was so picturesque. I had a dream about horses and riding in a boat up a small river before we even thought about moving out east. That dream would come true at this very farm!

I found it was very interesting meeting Joyce's family, or shall I say "the clan." Joyce was the oldest of five siblings. All her brothers, Bob, Richard and Donny were all still living at home, and she had one younger sister, Janet. Her parents told us we could move into their master bedroom upstairs until we could make other plans. I'm sure that the sleeping arrangements for all had to be adjusted while we were there.

Joyce's mother was an excellent cook and the meals she served everyone were always so tasty and memorable, especially since she served Italian dishes and sometimes German Potato Salad. She worked outside the home at a Sears catalog store and dressed to the nines. Joyce's dad was CEO quality with an education to match, but didn't hold down any kind of a job the whole time I knew them. He seemed the supreme head of the household and father and had become a chain-smoker. Everyone in that household had great respect for their father but I'm guessing that they also feared him. I don't know how we survived living a month or so in that house where her dad kept filling the house with smoke. Maybe that's why I was always sick or had a stuffed-up nose.

There were times when Joyce's mother had spent hours preparing meals for all of us, just to have her own husband tell her that he didn't like the food she had prepared. She would never say a word but go right back into the kitchen and prepare a whole different meal just for him. I couldn't understand someone who could treat a spouse like that, but realized that there had to be a whole lot of love floating around in that dense cigarette smoke he constantly surrounded himself with, for a wife to succumb to the pressures he often threw at her.

Most of Joyce's family seemed to accept me. The one exception was Joyce's brother Bob. Bob had shown me nothing but aloofness and distain from the beginning. It was as though he was trying to discredit me for anything he could possibly grasp ahold of, to show the family that his sister should not have married me. Those uneasy feelings were always present with me when Bob was around, and my feelings would later prove to me that I was right. I had, and have always had, an uncanny sense about people when I first meet them, and can sense what their personalities are like and what they're capable of doing, right from the start.

We had only been at Joyce's parent's home about three days when someone handed me the want ads from their local paper. When searching through the want ads I found an ad asking for someone to do printing and mailing for a company located in Whippany. They were replacing someone who was retiring, so I called them and made an appointment the next day for an interview. It would be nice if I could gain employment, especially now with Joyce getting further along in her pregnancy. I got directions from Joyce's dad and headed to Whippany.

My interview went really well and they hired me right on the spot. The company was the Suburban Propane Company, the largest independent propane gas company in the world. The company wanted me to start out in the printing and mailing department and then move on up to accounting. Little did I know that I would be spending the next eight years working at that company, never achieving a higher position than what I started out as.

One day we received a call from Joyce's grandma Biondo from Masbeth, New York asking us if we had a chance to use the two tickets to the New York World's Fair, reminding us that she had given us those tickets as part of our wedding gift. The World's Fair was only open for a few more days, so we decided to use the tickets. We drove into New York City and attended the fair on the very last day it was open. It was an experience I will never forget, especially waiting in line at the Catholic Pavilion to get in, when I became impatient and a guy behind me told me "Patience Is Virtue." No one could get into the pavilion until a famous cardinal arrived first. After waiting about a half an hour, a large stretch limo pulled up and the cardinal got out, dressed in all his regal attire. It seemed like everyone there wanted to kiss his ring. I was not impressed.

Meeting Joyce's grandma Biondo was a highlight of my life. She was such a gracious, caring and loving person and I knew right away that I was going to love her, but Joyce and her whole family were constantly making fun of their grandmother because of her intricacies. Maybe she loved her family too much? Every time Joyce's grandparents came out to New Jersey for a visit her grandmother would bring a gift for everyone, including every animal. Joyce and I took a trip into Masbeth, in downtown New York City when her grandmother invited us in for a seven course meal and spend time with them.

The story goes that her grandparents used to own the apartment building they presently lived in but lost it during the depression and were now renting the upstairs apartment. Joyce's grandparents were cousins that married. Her grandmother said she didn't want to change her last name, so she married a Biondo and never had to change her last name. At the seven course meal I became dizzy and had to lie down. They proceeded to tell me that on a bad smog day in downtown New York it was like smoking a pack of cigarettes to a non-smoker. As I was lying on the sofa recuperating I noticed a beautiful artificial fireplace with a large beautiful ornate gold colored mirror hanging over it. Her grandmother came over to me and told both Joyce and I that when they die they wanted us to have that fireplace and mirror. I was so glad to find out that even after my divorce from Joyce that our oldest daughter

Jennifer did inherit the mirror and has it hanging in her bedroom. Don't know what happened to the fireplace though.

After working for Suburban Propane for a month Joyce and I wanted to find our own place to live. We found an ad for a home in Mount Freedom and decided we'd like to look into it. Upon further inspection we found this home was actually divided into three separate homes, or apartments. One apartment was at the front of the house, one was just behind the front apartment, and the third apartment was in the basement that could only be reached by walking around to the back of the house. The apartment in this home that was for rent was the apartment just behind the front apartment on the main level, with a side entrance.

My first wife and my first home in Mt. Freedom, NJ

We gave them a deposit and our first month's rent and moved right away to Mount Freedom. Joyce was pretty far along in her pregnancy, and I was content in knowing that the health insurance I had at Suburban Propane would handle the cost of a pregnancy.

Our one claim to fame by living on this particular street in Mount Freedom was that we had heard that Marlo Thomas's hairdresser's mother, lived only two doors down from us. Mount Freedom was mainly inhabited by wealthy Jewish people who often migrated each summer to Mount Freedom to spend time in their summer homes and cottages.

Joyce started to have labor pains and I drove her to the Morristown hospital, but the doctors would not let me into the delivery room or even to see her, until after our son was born. Brian was born on April 29th, 1966. I walked into Joyce's hospital room to see how she was doing and she was not very responsive and I became very concerned. The doctor told me that he feared that Joyce was suffering from postpartum depression that some mothers develop shortly after giving birth. He said it shouldn't last long but if it does I was to let him know.

All Joyce could muster up to tell me was that we had a son. We didn't have a name for him yet but a visiting nurse handed me a baby book of boy's names and asked me to thumb through it. At first I thought it was so very impersonal to choose a name from a baby book, but as I sat there thumbing through the book I decided to start at the beginning and see if there would be a name that would stand out. I got to the name Brian and told Joyce that I would like to call our son Brian, giving him my middle name as well. Our son became Brian Franklin Piper. I have since given that precious little baby book of names to Brian, who now has a family of his own.

After bringing Brian home from the hospital I had to be both mother and father to him for the first couple of weeks of his life. The postpartum depression finally cleared and we started to become a family again.

My mother called me one evening, something she rarely did when I was married to Joyce, to

"Frankie, with is children, Jennifer and Brian at their home in Mt. Freedom, NJ"

tell me that my grandpa and grandma Piper had been in a car accident and grandma was in the hospital. Mom told me that grandma had been thrown from the car.

When mom gave me the phone number of the hospital, I called right away. My Aunt Bernadine answered the phone in grandma's hospital room and told me what had happened. She told me that a gravel truck had been coming down a hill and didn't see the stop sign, driving straight through it, broadsiding my grandparents car straight on. I asked Bernadine if I could speak with grandma, and that was the last time I ever heard grandma's voice. She died that night. I hung up the phone and cried like a baby. I knew I could not afford to fly out to the funeral and I would never see her again. Grandma Piper was special to me and I loved her so much. We shared something in common because I was born on her birthday, November 7th.

EIGHTEEN

ROCKAWAY SALES

After a training period at Suburban Propane, the older man, Al, that I was replacing, retired. I remembered that he had shared with me many times the fact that he had been working part-time in the jewelry department at Rockaway Sales, so he suggested I try and apply for a part-time job there as well. I took his advice and stopped by Rockaway Sales on my way home from work one day. I got hired right on the spot to work in their Sporting Goods department.

The Rockaway Sales Department Store became my part-time job. They hired me to work in their sporting goods department as a floor salesman. I could choose what nights I wanted to work, except during the holiday season when the store expected me to work more hours. I loved my job there, partly because I was always meeting new people, and partly because I was learning more about sporting goods than I had ever learned in my life-time.

When the Christmas season neared, my sporting goods manager, Jack Weinstein, hired a couple more guys to help out. I was able to help train the new floor salesmen on where everything was located, on what aisle and what shelf. I had learned how to sell bowling balls and shotgun ammunition. I knew the differences in the sleeping bags and their fabric.

150

If I could have made this my full-time job I would have, except the pay was always just minimum wage.

One of the new floor salesmen Jack Weinstein hired was an older man, Mr. Barone. Mr. Barone learned quickly everything I taught him about the department. One evening when there was a lull in customers, I was standing in the back storage room behind the counter, singing to the piped-in music being played over the store's speakers, when Mr. Barone overheard me singing and commented that he thought I had a good voice. He went on to tell me that he was the manager of his son's band and they were looking for a lead-singer. Immediately my ears perked up and I wanted to know more about the band.

Mr. Barone asked me if I would be interested in auditioning for the band. At first I thought to myself that I really didn't have the time to be auditioning for a band, and I didn't think I was even qualified. I had just checked into continuing my college courses with Pace University and wondered whether I could possibly take time away from the evenings and afternoons I could be studying.

I decided to go and meet Mr. Barone's band. It was Saturday and I had most of the day free. I met Mr. Barone in the parking lot of Rockaway Sales and followed him to 18 Stephen Place right there in Rockaway. As we neared the home I could hear a band rehearsing. The whole block must have heard this band rehearsing. We both parked out front and I followed Mr. Barone to the back of the home and up a few stairs to their back door.

Mr. Barone knocked on the back door and an older lady answered the door inviting us both in. By this time the band must have been between songs and I couldn't hear any band music. We were standing in the kitchen of this home. I found out later that this home was the lead-guitarist, John Bowden and his parent's home. To the left was a doorway that led to some old wooden steps to the basement, and Mr. Barone told me to follow him down the staircase. As we neared the bottom of the stairs I noticed straight ahead of me a set of drums with a kinky haired guy sitting behind them. I later found out that this was Mr. Barone's son, Bob Barone. Mr. Barone proceeded to introduce me to not only his son sitting behind the drums, but also to Tom Slack on the bass guitar, and John Bowden on lead-guitar. No one could have been more nervous than me at that very moment.

John, on the lead-guitar, asked me if I had done any singing before and I told him first that I had loved music since I was too young to even walk yet. I mentioned the fact that I'd sung in choirs and had sung solos, and I told John that I wanted to hear the band play. John told Bob about a song he had in mind and I sat down on a folding chair to listen. The only lyrics I remember coming from this group of guys were "Hey, hey, you, you, get off of my cloud." I had remembered it was a song recorded by the Rolling Stones. These three guys sounded really good and I was really impressed. I wanted to embellish every last note.

After the guys played a song for me, Mr. Barone came over and asked me what I thought. What could I say? The band was fantastic! Bob then stepped out from behind his drums and walked over and grabbed a 45 RPM record and handed it to me. I looked at the title of the song about the same time that Bob asked me if I thought I could sing it. I told him that I thought I could if I had time to practice it, so Bob told me to take the record home and come back the following Saturday and sing the song for the band during their rehearsal. The song was "Unchained Melody" by the Righteous Brothers. John stepped in and told me that they had some gigs coming up in a couple of weeks and they needed a front lead-singer.

I took that record home and sang with it every chance I got. I'm sure my wife and kids were getting pretty tired of listening to it and to me singing it. On my way home from work one evening I began to break out in song while driving, hoping I could remember all the words, when all of a sudden, hearing my own voice, I realized for the first time that I had a vibrato. Immediately I broke out in tears. Maybe there was hope for me, and I began to realize for the first time that I had a shot at becoming this band's lead-singer. I knew I had rhythm because I spent most of my life dancing, but now I just might become the lead-singer of a band?

As the week came to a close I was flying high on cloud nine with the anticipation of my auditioning for this band. I so wanted to sing this song straight from my heart, letting the band know that this song had touched my heart. When Saturday rolled around I couldn't wait to drive over to John's home to audition for the band. I didn't even know what the name of the band was. I hadn't asked and no one thought to tell me.

As I drove up to John's home again, I could hear the band rehearsing already. It was then that I really started to get nervous. I parked in front of their home and walked around to the back just like I had done before and tried knocking on the door. The music was so loud I didn't think anyone would hear me, but Mr. Barone was already there and he was in the kitchen when I knocked and let me in. He looked more nervous than I felt when he took me back down those old wooden stairs again. The band was still playing a song when I came into the basement, so I grabbed a folding chair and sat down. The guys let me know they knew I was there by a simple nod of their heads and a smile.

The guys finished playing and John asked me to step up to a microphone that was already in a mike stand they had placed in front of the drums. John asked me if I thought I was ready and I told him that I was as ready as I would ever be. What I hadn't noticed yet was that they had invited a young gal to play on a keyboard, just for this audition. Mr. Barone came over to me and told me that he had big plans for this band and wanted to get the band into nightclubs. He told me that he was hoping upon hoping that I could be their lead-singer.

I walked over to the microphone and the band began to play. I realized that this would be the first time I ever sang a song in front of a live band. Immediately I recognized the song the band was playing. This was "Unchained Melody." These three guys and the keyboardist all sounded so good. Could I live up to the expectations they had for me? The next thing I knew my voice began to have a mind of its own, and I just followed behind, enjoying where my vocals were taking me.

When the song ended, my emotions had been spent, and I had very little left to even comprehend what might happen next. For a few pregnant moments it just seemed like no one wanted to say anything. Everyone wanted to bathe in the accomplishments they individually felt for having done a great job. I turned around to catch a glimpse of each band member one by one, and I saw an expression of emotion in each guy that was so close to tears that if one more musical note had been played would have sent the tears flowing over the dam. Tom had damp eyes and tried to speak but the few words he tried to speak were not even comprehensible.

Mr. Barone had been pacing the concrete floor of the basement the whole time the band was performing, and didn't settle down until the very last note brought an end to the song. He stood there just staring at all of us and blurted out to the band, "We have our lead-singer. Welcome to the Eminent Domain, Frank." It dawned on me for the first time that I had not known what the name of the band was, until now. Mr. Barone gave me a list of songs that he wanted me to perform with the band in just a week. What songs I didn't have time for, the rest of the band members would need to sing. Our concert required us to perform for two hours. Would I be ready for the first show?

When I left the band and drove on home, I was so excited. I couldn't wait to tell Joyce that I had become the lead-singer of a band. I never thought I had enough vocal talent to even be considered to sing in a band, and now I was in a band. That shy little boy from Kansas City who thought he would never amount to anything would now be singing in front of many groups of people. I said to myself, "If only my high school friends could see me now."

My excitement came to a screeching halt when I arrived at home and explained to Joyce that I had auditioned to sing in a band and became their new lead-singer. The anger that I felt from her was so thick I could cut it with a knife. She did not like the idea of me traveling with a band when I already had a full-time job, a part-time job and was studying on Monday evenings for college. I would literally not be home much anymore except on Monday evenings to study. I would be able to stop by to eat dinner after my full-time job in Whippany, and then head on over to Rockaway Sales to work until ten pm. On week-ends I would be practicing with the band and performing gigs with them.

I learned about five songs to perform at our first gig. The band picked up the slack and performed the rest of the music. Since I couldn't play an instrument I found a tambourine in a local music store and learned how to use it. I had a great sense of rhythm and added quite a bit to the band's overall sound. I later taught myself how to play the bongo drums. During most of our practice times I learned to form a harmony so I could back up the other guys when they sang lead.

At one of our rehearsal times Mr. Barone made an appearance and told us that he had signed us up to perform at a Battle Of The Bands that was being held at a local high school gymnasium. He wanted us to perform only the best songs that we could muster up and told us he would prefer that our band perform last. He said that people have a tendency to remember what they hear last.

When we started to set up at the high school to perform we noticed about four other bands were also setting up at different locations in the gym. We decided to set up under the basketball hoop where we would be dead center. No one else wanted that spot.

Bob was setting up his drums when my wife's brother, Richard, came over and wanted to help us set up. I had not realized that he attended this high school. If Richard was going to stay and listen to all the bands play, then he will certainly hear us too. No one in my family had ever heard the Eminent Domain band play. This would be a first.

Since our band would be performing last, our band members could watch and listen to all the other bands' performances. I must admit that most of the other bands had a great sound. We all thought that we probably didn't have a chance to win. I knew that there were judges but there were also cardboard ballot boxes sitting on a table with the name of the band pasted on the front of each box. Every now and then I could see a student walk up to one of the ballot boxes and place a folded piece of paper into it. After a while I lost track of the ballot boxes and wanted to focus my attention on what kind of music these bands were playing.

Frankie's first rock band "The Eminent Domain."

Now it was our turn to perform. We all took our positions and decided that all we could do was to just perform the best we knew how to do. After all, our drummer, Bob, had taught many of the other drummers how to play their drums. What a comforting thought that started to well up inside of me, and helped me to have a little bit of peace at a time when I really needed it the most.

After our performance we knew that even if we didn't win, we did our best. We were all just so excited to actually perform in front of so many people. Richard came running up to us and said, "Hey guys, look! Your ballot box is over-flowing. The Eminent Domain has won." We learned that this was just going to be one of the first of many performances that would be history making for the group.

NINETEEN
A WHITE BOMB

At Suburban Propane I had joined their company credit union and decided to have them take out a forced savings from my weekly paycheck. My funds would grow and maybe Joyce and I could buy our own home, using the savings as a down-payment. I had many ideas for these funds.

One day a brochure was handed out to the employees, and I noticed that I could purchase a car through the credit union and have the funds automatically deducted out of my paycheck. I made an appointment with the credit union and discussed the idea of my buying a car this way, and the credit union approved my loan. I had impeccable credit at that time. Since the credit union was carrying the loan, they recommended that I go to a Buick dealer that they had pre-approved and order a new Buick. Within a week I had a new all white Buick to drive. I was so proud of that Buick. Joyce and I already had a white Ford LTD that we kept for her to drive but now we had to make room in our driveway for two cars.

One week-end Joyce and I were getting ready to take a trip over to her parent's home and I had carried Brian out to our new Buick and stood him up on the front seat. I sat down next to him as we waited for Joyce and Jennifer to join us. They were taking a little bit of time so I decided to go back in to see why they hadn't come out yet. Just as I opened the side door of our apartment to go in, I heard a thud. I ran back outside and saw my new Buick up against a tree. Brian had taken the car out of gear and the car had rolled forward into a tree. I ran to the car to see if Brian was ok. Joyce and Jennifer came running to see what had caused the noise. We were all greatly relieved when we realized that Brian was not hurt and there were no dents or scratches in the fender. I knew then that I could not leave any of our kids alone in our cars ever again, and I feared for the day when Brian would actually start driving.

At Suburban Propane the company decided to hire extra help in my department, and the new man and I became friends. But there was always something in the back of my mind that kept telling me that there was something sinister about this guy. I just couldn't put my finger on it.

The new guy and I started to car pool. I had to always drive into Morris Plains to pick him up but that was no problem, since it was almost already on my route to work. One day while driving to Morris Plains to pick him up, I was getting ready to make a left-hand turn at the intersection when all of a sudden, a car from the opposite direction illegally passed on the right side of a car at the intersection and slammed into the passenger side of my new Buick. The thud was sudden and loud. The impact jarred my body and caused damage to my lower back. I was so shaken up and in shock that I cannot remember my drive on into Whippany. I knew it was too late to pick up the new guy, so I drove straight to Suburban Propane.

I was close to tears when I arrived at work. My new Buick was bashed in but drivable. I pulled into my regular parking spot and headed on into the building. Who confronted me and started yelling at me, but the new guy, asking me why I didn't come by and pick him up. He had to take a taxi to work. When I explained what had happened, he backed off and realized he had made a big mistake. A few weeks later I came into work early only to find the new guy in the restroom with a needle sticking in his arm. He was a drug addict, and the company fired him immediately. My first impressions of him and my feelings of something sinister about him were true. I later donated that Buick to Joyce when we separated. She called it the 'white bomb,' because the car gave her so much trouble.

TWENTY
FRAGILE GLASS

I knew that eventually I would have to give up my part-time job at Rockaway Sales, or give up the band. One of them would have to go. The band was starting to get busy and the strain of having to practice and perform with the band, plus my trying to work evenings in the sporting goods department was starting to take its toll on me.

The holiday season at Rockaway sales was a busy place, and my boss had to hire more floor salesmen and asked me to help train them. One short well-dressed guy always seemed to hang onto every word I said. He sometimes seemed to be a little bit too friendly towards me. Again I started to sense an uneasy feeling about him, but what was it? Little did I know at that time that Bob, Joyce's brother, was probably paying this new floor salesman a fee to see if he could entice me into some kind of a homosexual encounter. I was so naïve that I did not even see this whole scenario unfolding.

After work one evening, this short well-dressed new floor salesman asked me if I could take him home. At first I said no, but he kept telling me he had no other way home. I finally agreed, but I decided it wouldn't take me long to drop him off and then I could go on home.

On the way to his home we passed a small lake and he asked if we could pull over. It was after ten o'clock in the evening and there were very few lights on this road. As we sat there, he mentioned to me that the lake at night was beautiful with the moon casting a light across the surface of the water. We continued our idle chatting when another car pulled up beside us. I looked over and it was Bob, my brother in law. He didn't say a word but stared straight ahead. I knew then and there that Bob was trying to create some kind of a situation to discredit me and have me kicked out of the Biondo family. I was not gay and never have been, but Bob would not give up on me. I quickly started my Buick and drove away from the lake, taking the guy home. I told him I did not appreciate what he had tried to accomplish through my brother-in-law and to never ask me for a ride again. The guy never showed up for work the next evening. Did Bob send him to the sporting goods department just for this one purpose? Bob continued his escapades for years by trying to constantly create more scenarios. It was hard for me to even be around him after that.

The Eminent Domain band kept trying to improve and expand the kind of music they were playing and wanting to become a show band. At one of the battle-of-the-band performances we came in second. A band called "Canary" came in first. They were a show-band with special lighting, and the drummer would throw his sticks up in the air and catch them. We knew then and there that we had to become a show-band. We practiced for the next few weeks perfecting a new show to present. The band decided to add a female singer, one who could sing solos but also be able to harmonize with me. The band found Robin, a local Jewish woman. She didn't have much of a range but she had a good voice. We were able to share the spotlight and harmonize on several songs. One time I came into practice and Robin had practiced with the band behind my back and had learned a few new songs. Somehow I felt that

Robin planned these secret practices. I felt in my heart that she wanted to become the only lead-singer of the Eminent Domain. I didn't want to think that my band would do such a thing to me, so I eventually stopped coming to practice.

On the bulletin board of a local grocery store I saw an ad advertising a band wanting a dynamic lead-singer with a wide vocal range. I called the number and drove over to the lead-guitarist's home in Denville. The band was called "Iron Mule." The group had already been recognized because of their harmonies, their showmanship, and their writing abilities. They had just lost their lead-singer to another band and had a big show scheduled at the county fair. The group "Iron Mule" was scheduled to back up Jerry Lee Lewis in one show, and then turn around and back up the Stone Ponies. I helped make those engagements a reality. I was disappointed that the band came to a complete standstill when the county fair ended. What was I going to do now? I had to find another band that was at least active.

I auditioned for the "Fragile Glass" band. Their drummer had been trained by my former drummer from the Eminent Domain, Bob Barone. One practice with this band and I knew I was at home. The Fragile Glass band was a very popular band but unknown, who didn't have a lead-singer. All the guys in the band would take turns singing either lead or back-up, and not one voice in particular stood out. When I came into the band, the band focused on show-casing me. They had a manager that only wanted to be called Mr. Bee, although I never knew for sure what his full name was.

I quickly learned to be not only a singer, but an entertainer as well with this rock band. I dressed the part and acted like a celebrity. I developed a unique way of singing with a 'tear' in my voice that helped captivate the audience to the point that I felt I had them in the palms of my hands. There were many times I became so caught up in my own song that I would become emotional. I had to make-believe that I was sincere or the audience had enough perception to know that I was just acting, and somehow I knew that they felt my emotions through my vocal rendition of the song because of the responses I received. I just knew that I was set for stardom.

TWENTY ONE

AN ARRESTING EXPERIENCE

Our former home in Lake Hopatcong, NJ

Joyce and I had an opportunity to move to a duplex in Lake Hopatcong. It was a much newer home with two bedrooms and a full basement. We checked the home out and jumped at the opportunity to rent it. We loved this home and felt like we had made the right choice in moving there. My drive into Whippany would be a little bit of a longer commute but it didn't matter to me. Joyce enrolled Jennifer in ballet at a dance school nearby and Joyce was hoping that Jennifer would take to it. She didn't. Jennifer cried every time she had to go to practice, so we let her quit.

I found out that the Two Guys Department store was just down the highway a few miles from Rockaway Sales and had been advertising about a part-time opening in their music department. I took off from work early one afternoon and applied for the job, and they wanted me to start the following week. To start work in this music department, which they called the Records Department, was a dream come true. I would get the chance to listen to new albums and singles as they were brought in for distribution. I quit Rockaway Sales and started working at Two Guys in their Records Department. In those days we only had 33 1/3 rpm records, and 45 rpm records.

At Two Guys I made quite a few friends. Most every employee would end up at one time or another in our Records Department, shopping for music. When a new album came in recorded by the new group "Three Dog Night," we were able to open one of their albums and play it over our loud speakers in our department. They had just released a new single as well called 'One,' and we were able to be one of the first to listen to the single.

Many of my new friends at Two Guys would invite me to their parties but I would always refuse. I really didn't have the time to be out partying late at night. On a few occasions I did muster up the courage to visit a party or two, but only to make an appearance. Some of my friends started asking me when I was going to throw a party. What? How could I throw a party? Most of these friends that were asking me, were single people. I was a married man with a wife and two kids at home. Then I realized that we had that large basement downstairs. Why couldn't I decorate it and invite a few friends over!

When I shared my idea with Joyce, she emphatically was opposed to the whole plan. I kept telling her that my friends were expecting me to throw a party, and all Joyce would do was become silent and not answer. She had already made her mind up and that was that. I just wasn't going to let that deter me and I went ahead making plans for a few friends from Two Guys to come over on a Saturday night. I even invited my old band members from the Eminent Domain to come and play live music. A friend who I knew could dance became a go-go dancer that danced in a special decorated area in our basement that was specifically made for a go-go dancer. I had crepe paper hung everywhere and balloons. This was going to be a night for everyone to remember. I just had to outdo all the others when it came to partying. The only thing I stipulated was that I was not going to provide any booze. If anyone wanted to drink, they'd have to bring their own.

After I arrived home from my job at Suburban Propane, Joyce had left me a note that said she and the kids would be gone for the evening and were at her mother's. Joyce had never gotten to know any of my friends from any of my jobs. We very seldom ever invited anyone to our home. Joyce was a stay-at-home mom and I was the husband who was always gone, either working or spending time with friends I had made.

My friends starting arriving at about seven and I greeted them at my back door so they could come directly down into the basement where I already had the band playing. There were about fifteen of us having a wonderful time, some dancing and some just sitting at tables just chatting. Some had brought chips and nuts to snack on and I provided the soda pop. All of a sudden there was a hard knocking at the back door. I ran upstairs to see who was knocking so hard. It was the police. Joyce had called the police to inform them about my party. The police told all my friends to leave and they took me down to the police station for questioning.

I was fined $50.00 for allowing beer into my home when there were some present that were under twenty one, and then the police let me go. I personally did not provide any form of beer, only soda pop. When I arrived back home from the police station, I was livid. Joyce hadn't returned home so I just figured that they had spent the night at her mother's. If she had come home that same night I really don't know what I would have done. Her coming home the next day at least gave me time to cool off. This episode only tightened the tension string a little tighter in an already troubled marriage that had very little chance of surviving.

I began to spend even more time away from home. I just couldn't stand to be around Joyce. We were always at odds with each other and very seldom ever agreed on anything. I just wanted out. The only ties that kept me with her was the fact that I loved my kids so much.

One day at Suburban Propane I received a frantic call from Joyce to tell me that Brian had started a fire in the stairwell of our home leading to our basement. She had caught it in time but some of the wooden stairs were slightly charred. When our landlord heard about it he wanted us out of the house. We had to start looking for another place to live before the end of the month.

As we drove around Lake Hopatcong looking for a place to live, we saw a small light blue colored house with a cute covered front porch with a 'For Rent' sign posted in one of its front windows. At the bottom of the sign was a phone number to call. We drove over to a small grocery store nearby and called the number, and the owner said he would meet us at that little house in just ten minutes. We turned around and drove back to the cute little house and parked out front. The owner came and we toured the home and thought it was a great place to live. It had two bedrooms, an eat-in kitchen, and a fireplace in the living room. I didn't like the color of the outside of the house but I knew I could change it. We both figured out that we could place bunk beds in one of the bedrooms for our two children, and we would take the other. We moved in on the first of the following month.

What we thought was a creek running through the back yard was really a small swamp. Our home didn't have city sewer or even a septic tank. All of our waste drained directly under our cute little house in a crawl space. After we moved in, it was too late to back out. The more we complained, the more the owner ignored us. Although we couldn't smell what was being dumped into our crawl space under the house, I knew it was there and building up. It was bound to create problems down the road. If there was a city sewer system, then we had a horrible leak that the owner would not fix. We knew that we would have to make the best of what we had, until we had time to find another place to live.

On the first day of school while I was at work Joyce had walked Jennifer and Brian to the nearest school bus stop and left them there to catch the school bus. Brian got tired of waiting for the bus and simply walked back home. Joyce ended up having to drive him to school the first day. I didn't know about this incident until I came home after work, but I thought it was kind of funny.

I decided to quit working at the Two Guys Department store and I concentrated on spending most of my time singing in the Fragile Glass band, and spending time with my friends. I had to leave the raising of our kids totally on Joyce's shoulders. The band was starting to get busier and I was learning to be quite a showman for the band, and had to be gone so much of the time.

The few times I had to spend with my family were the times that I tried to help my daughter Jennifer learn her math skills. She was having a problem in almost every aspect of addition and subtraction. For the life of me I just couldn't figure how she just couldn't understand what came so easily for me. I decided I just had to try a simple procedure that I knew would work. I told her to start counting on her fingers by barely tapping her fingers on her desk top to add or subtract the numbers. This technique worked for her and she told me just recently that she still sometimes uses that same idea I had shown her when she was so young.

One evening a new movie was being shown on TV called "Born Free." Jennifer decided to sprawl out on our carpet to watch, while Brian crawled up behind my bent knees to watch the movie over my hip. If you've ever watched this movie you will know that the movie can sometimes move you to tears. Brian sat and watched the movie so intently and didn't want to miss any part of it. After the movie ended and the credits were showing, Brian was so emotional and said "Why daddy?" At first I didn't understand what he meant, but then he continued. "Why daddy, do I feel like crying?" I immediately sat up and told my son that it was ok to cry. In fact, I wanted to cry too. The family depicted in the movie had to let their pet lion go to the wilderness to learn how to live on its own. Later in the movie, the family did meet up with their pet lion again, just to discover that the lion had made it on its own, and even had a family of his own. The tears we wanted to shed were not only for the sadness of having to let your pet go, not knowing if it was dead or alive, but also were tears of joy, because now you knew that he was ok and he didn't depend on you anymore. Parents can sometimes feel the same way when they have to let their kids grow up and move away from home, not depending on your nurturing them.

It is just too bad, when I think back, that I didn't spend more time with my children. They were so precious, like sponges, grasping onto every word that was said. Our jobs, as parents, are to try and help them grow and mature into responsible adults. I myself was not even mature enough to even have kids of my own. I know I married too young and felt like I had missed out on so many things single people do that married people cannot do. When Joyce and I started drifting further away from each other, emotionally, I decided to just go ahead and live like I was single again. Not to purposely have affairs, but just to start having fun and going out with my friends. I know I had married Joyce to get out of the service. Later I found out that Joyce married me to get away from home.

During one of our heated arguments that we so often had, I blurted out to her that I wanted a divorce. It was then that the stark bold words hit both of us for the first time that the reality in those few words could become the finality of the marriage. Joyce's eyes glossed over with tears. It was one thing for me to think those kinds of thoughts, but now it was spoken. I then felt so bad that I had purposely hurt her that I just wanted to crawl in a hole and pull the hole in with me. Neither one of us took any action. I tried to forget the words I had just spoken. If I said it, then I must have been feeling it. And yes, at that very moment I didn't want to be married to her anymore.

I know that I had learned to love Joyce in spite of our differences, but the differences seemed to overshadow the shallow remnant of what could or should have been. Even though I had blurted out "divorce" in the heat of the moment I knew that I just could not go through with it. I loved my children too much. There was no way I was going to leave them.

During our first winter at this cute little house on the west side of Lake Hopatcong, I wanted to take Jennifer and Brian to the Hopatcong State Park and go sledding. It had snowed the night before and the kids had flying saucer sleds that I wanted them to use at the park. The park had a few hills alongside their parking lot that I knew Jennifer and Brian would love to slide down.

I parked my car and took the kids' flying saucer sleds out of the trunk. We walked over to the side of the parking lot and walked up the side of the snowy hill to the top where we could position the sleds. We were standing there for a moment pondering which one of the kids would go down the hill first, and Brian decided he would go first.

Brian slid down the hill and then walked back up the hill with his sled. By this time we were all standing there waiting for Jennifer to hop onto her sled to slide down the hill. She just stood there as though she couldn't decide whether to go down the hill or not, and I kept asking her to get onto her sled. A part of me thought that she might be a little intimidated by the height of the hill and wasn't sure she wanted to take the plunge.

Just about that time a couple of snowmobiles came roaring by behind us at the top of the hill. It distracted both Brian and me enough that neither one of us had noticed that Jennifer had hopped onto her sled and had gone down the hill. By the time we both looked around, I saw people running over to Jennifer and surrounding her as she lay on her flying saucer sled at the bottom of the hill. Her sled had slid onto a part of the parking lot. I didn't know what was going on. Before Brian and I could get back down to the bottom of that hill, someone had carried Jennifer over to one of the cars and placed her on the hood of it. That car was our car, the white Buick. Why would someone take my daughter and place her on the hood of my car?

When Brian and I approached our car, a crowd had gathered around the front of my car. I could barely see Jennifer lying there on her back on the hood. I heard someone say they thought the warmth from the engine would help keep her warm. I asked a lady standing nearest to Jennifer what was going on. She told me that this little girl had been run over by that pick-up truck, as she pointed to a nearby tan colored pick-up truck parked only a few feet away. My shock grew to over-whelming as I told her that that was my daughter.

I looked closely at Jennifer and it didn't seem to be anything wrong with her, as my heart had already started to skip beats from the shock of it all. An ambulance drove up and loaded Jennifer onto a stretcher, and one of the attendants asked me to follow behind the ambulance as they drove to a nearby hospital. How was I to get word to Joyce? One of the attendants took down our home phone number and he apparently called Joyce while we were in route.

Newspaper article dated 2/1/1971. Frankie's daughter Jennifer had been run over by a pick-up truck at a state park.

Following an ambulance was the last thing I thought I would be doing today. The siren's constant blare coming from that ambulance ahead of me, with its constant flashing red lights, seemed to be a constant reminder to me that my daughter was in strangers hands right now and I didn't know what damage my own daughter had received from being run over. I drove in complete shock and disbelief behind that white metal box with wheels that they called an ambulance, for what seemed like an eternity. I just wanted to hold my little girl and tell her that everything was going to be alright.

We reached the hospital and the ambulance pulled into the emergency entrance to the hospital. I parked in a nearby parking stall. Brian and I ran up to the emergency entrance just to see Jennifer being escorted quickly into awaiting interns at the door and then they disappeared behind closed doors. All Brian and I could do was to wait in the lobby for further word. My mind was racing so fast that I barely remember Brian sitting there with me.

Joyce arrived within a half an hour with tears in her eyes. All the attendant had told her was that her daughter had been run over by a pick-up truck and she had been taken to the hospital. I assured Joyce that I didn't know anything at all about Jennifer's condition. We just sat there in silence until the doctor came out to give us an update.

He told us that our daughter had been very lucky and that there was no visible trauma anywhere on her body. He said that the flying saucer shaped sled helped prevent Jennifer from being seriously injured. The way Jennifer traveled under the rear wheels of that pick-up truck protected her body when the wheels traveled over one side of the sled onto the other side, barely touching down on her little body. Apparently her head and feet were not in a direct line with the wheels, just her torso. The doctor wanted to keep Jennifer overnight for observation and would let us know the next day if she would be free to go home.

Both Joyce and I were able to take Jennifer home the next day. To this day, when I think of what could have happened, I can still get very emotional.

TWENTY TWO
CREATING AN IMAGE

My quitting my job at the Two Guys Department Store gave me much more time to study and attend my classes at Pace University. I tried very hard to get a concert date for my band at Pace, but never succeeded. I did have enough connections at the college to get our band a performance at another school, Fairleigh Dickinson University. Anytime I could secure concert dates for the band only helped Mr. Bee, making his job a little easier. He always received a fee if he booked the gig or not. I received accolades.

At the time of our gig at the University, our band did not realize that an agent from a record company had been there to hear us perform. One of the few things I remember about that gig was that I had been bitten on my behind by a female student when I had bent down to secure a few cables near the front of the stage.

Most of our music during our gig at Fairleigh Dickenson was geared around the early BeeGees and the Rolling Stones. We must have impressed the agent, because he came to another gig of ours at a local night club. Again, we didn't know he was there until a cocktail waitress informed us. She told us that an agent from Sunburst Records had been sitting at a booth the whole evening. We were hoping that he would stick around till the end of our gig so we could meet him.

At the very end of our performance the band laid down their instruments on the stage and we retired to the back room to rest and ask for drinks. Our drinks were always soda pop. A few moments later a middle-aged man appeared at our dressing room door asking us if we had a manager. We told him that our manager was Mr. Bee. At that very moment we knew that Mr. Bee was somewhere in the club, but we didn't know where. He was a guy that was always on the move and couldn't sit still. For me there was just something in my spirit about Mr. Bee that made me always have a feeling of mistrust. Was it mistrust, or was it something else? I just couldn't readily put my finger on it, but I often felt uncomfortable around him. I had always depended on my first instincts of people when it came to my knowing what kind of a person they were. I knew in my heart that I would one day find out the reason for my having those uneasy feelings.

In a few moments Mr. Bee came rushing into our dressing room to tell us that a record agent was out in the club. He stopped his speech in mid-sentence when he noticed that this agent was already in our dressing room, sitting right next to our drummer. He was chagrined. The PR executive from Sunburst Records, an independent label, spoke directly to Mr. Bee, offering the band a recording contract. He needed for us to make an appointment to come into his office for specifics. The whole band was very excited about the possibilities. After all, our lives would be changed forever.

Mr. Bee made an appointment for the band for the following Monday evening when all the band members could be there. The meeting with the record executives, at that time, seemed to me to be a blur of wistful thoughts that have since refracted from my memory banks as to what really happened during that meeting. All I could see then was a contract. What that contract said, I don't remember. All I wanted to do was to sign the contract, along with all the other band members and our manager. It seemed like we didn't care about reading all the fine print. We just wanted to get the show on the road. If Mr. Bee did read all the fine print, he never mentioned to us what all the requirements were, or what could possibly happen down the road.

After we signed the recording contract, the Sunburst PR executive started suggesting minor changes and additions in regards to our band. He wanted to change my name to a stage name, to protect the band and me from the female fans that they felt could cause problems down the road, not only for the lead-singer, but maybe for the whole band. Since I sang Richie Valens songs and had a voice like Frankie Valli, he came up with the name "Frankie Valens." We would start advertising "Frankie Valens, and The Fragile Glass Band." After the first single or two, we chose to push the "Frankie Valens" image only. He specifically told me that my stage name was only to be used in regards to our concerts and touring. I was not to be called "Frankie Valens" at home or at any job. He told me not to mention that I was married and to not even wear my wedding ring during the touring. At the time, I didn't care about demands. I just wanted to be a star. He told all of us that Sunburst Records often had recording artists that major record companies wanted and Sunburst would sell their contract to them. That was going to be a possibility sometime down the road. At that time he said that the stage name would be legal and I'd be using it all the time.

I drove home with my head in the clouds, but I didn't feel free to share all this information with my own wife. She seemed to not want to support me in any kind of a musical adventure at all. She thought this love of music I had would be a phase that I would soon get over. Joyce even came to one of our earlier concerts that was held in a school gymnasium, and she grabbed a chair so she could sit right in the middle of the dance floor all by herself. Dressed in a large floral top, she purposely wanted to draw attention to herself, but I pretended not to know who she was.

TWENTY THREE
SASKATCHEWAN

In the beginning, most of our concerts were in local night spots and bars. Sunburst wanted to expand our concert touring to other states, and possibly other countries. They booked us on an extended concert tour to Saskatchewan, Canada. The only way I knew I could go on such a venture was to ask for a week's vacation from my full-time job, or quit. For this tour Sunburst decided to add a flute player that also played the saxophone.

I didn't know how to tell my wife. What would be her response? I so often wouldn't tell Joyce anything about the band for fear that she might make an appearance or try to cause problems.

In the few weeks before the concert tour was to begin, I started to spend more time away from home and with the band, or with friends that had become our roadies. A friend of the band was Dave, who I started to spend time with. We so enjoyed playing records at his parent's home. Dave's brother had such a large collection of 45 rpm records, and kept his own top 40 listings just from playing his own music. Dave knew how to play keyboards and wanted so much to someday join our band, but he just wasn't qualified.

One Saturday Joyce sent me to the store to pick up a half gallon of milk. Before going to the store, I headed on over to Dave's house so we could listen to music. I was gone for a few hours and then stopped by to pick up the milk Joyce had asked me to get and returned home. She was very angry with me when I returned so late, and she told me she wanted me out of the house. A part of me was so relieved that a decision had been made to end this whole charade of a marriage, yet another part of me started to realize the finality of it all and what was I going to do, and where was I going to live?

I walked into our bedroom and grabbed a few of my clothes, along with my shaving gear, and threw everything in a paper bag. Joyce told me to go in and say goodbye to Jennifer and Brian, but since it was after their bed-time and they were already asleep, I worried that they might have overheard our huge fight, so I opened their bedroom door and walked over to their bunk beds. Jennifer stirred a little and I thought that maybe she had been awake to hear her parents arguing, and I had to reach up to Brian's bed and touch him to let him know I was there. Joyce stood behind me watching the whole painful scene unfold. It was so hard for me to say goodbye to my children. I loved them so much. To this day, I can still remember each heart-felt moment I shared with my two loving children on that last day I would ever live in their home.

I had nowhere to go. I had no home and no preplanned ideas of what I would be doing on my own. After this eight-year marriage I sort of wanted this to happen, but when it actually did, I just broke down and cried like a baby. Over the years there had been a bonding and a familiarity in our marriage that I had grown used to, whether it was a good experience or a bad one.

When I had time to think of all the experiences Joyce and I had had together over the eight year span of our marriage, there were many good times we shared, but there were just as many bad experiences that weighed heavily on my mind. Joyce often made fun of my feet because I have high insteps. She said my feet looked deformed. When my mother called, Joyce would make fun of her by telling the kids that their buck-toothed grandma was on the phone, anything and everything she could say that would constantly be stirring up strife and discord. She made fun of my high tenor voice, asking me if I was going to sound like that for the rest of our lives together! Those kind of degrading remarks were hard to shake off.

The first night of my homelessness I slept on a friend's pool table in their basement. The second night I slept on my old bass-guitarist's sofa. After that, everything seems to blur in my memory. I was always able to show up on time at my job in Whippany with them not even knowing I had been kicked out of my own home. I would sometimes come in early at work and shave with cold water in the company restroom. No one knew about my problem until Joyce called my work one day while I was out to lunch and left a message to have me call her. My only salvation at this point was still having a full-time job and singing in a band. Because of my band I had to quit my part-time job.

Sunburst took us into their recording studio and we recorded "This Magic Moment" as a single. They wanted a single record so we could be promoting it on our Canadian tour. Sunburst sent our single into radio stations to see if they would play their independent label, and some radio stations picked it up and started playing "This Magic Moment." One radio station invited us to their radio station for an interview. Some of the guys stayed out in the car to listen to 'live' radio on their car radios. The blonde girl who appeared in "The Summer Of 42" movie was also being interviewed. When the guys heard our song being played on their car radios, we could hear them shouting for joy with the excitement they felt at that very moment.

My one and only salvation was my band's upcoming concert tour to Canada. I took a week's vacation at Suburban Propane for this tour. Sunburst Records provided us with two vans for the tour. One van would house the band members, a body guard, and manager, while the other van carried our sound equipment. We drove day and night to arrive at Regina, Saskatchewan, Canada, for a New Year's Eve gig at the Sahara Nights Club.

We arrived in Regina on New Year's Eve day, the day of our gig, and we set up our sound equipment that afternoon. I wanted to wear new shoes for our first gig and decided to go shopping at a nearby mall, but my manager would not let me go without a body guard. I found a shiny new pair of black shoes to wear and took them back to our dressing room at the club.

Just a few minutes before eight pm, my band left our dressing room, which was by the side of the stage, and headed out to get their instruments ready for our opening number. I stayed behind, waiting for my band to introduce me. A few minutes later I heard the band playing and then I heard them introduce me. I came running out and jumped upon the stage area that was perhaps about two feet above the floor, and ran across to the center of the stage where my microphone stand was. I ran up to the microphone stand but missed it and I slipped and fell flat on my backside! At that moment in time I was in total shock and was hoping that no one noticed! I got up again and ran back to the waiting microphone stand just to fell down again, in the opposite direction! It was my new shiny, slick, new black shoes! Somehow I was able to regain my composure and finish the first set. I know my band members must have been in stitches each time I fell. I later found out that the club owner thought that they had hired a comedian!

Our whole evening really went well. People were dancing and having a good time. This was New Year's Eve and everyone wanted to celebrate the coming in of the New Year. We were playing along and not paying much attention to the time, when all of a sudden I noticed my watch showed five minutes after mid-night! Oh my goodness. I whispered to our lead-guitarist that we ought to try and do a countdown to mid-night. No one probably noticed that we were already into the New Year. We started our count down "ten, nine, eight, seven, six, five, four, three, two, one! Happy New Year," we yelled. No one ever noticed the mistake we had made.

The next day we traveled on up to Saskatoon, over one hundred miles north of Regina. We had a two-night gig at the "A Four Club." During the two nights we were in concert there, the temperature dropped so low that the radios warned people not to go out into the night air or their skin could freeze. We took that to heart and stayed in all day and all night. We still had crowds at each of our performances. The Canadians are used to the bitter cold.

We soon had to pack up our equipment and drive even further north to the town of Prince Albert. We had been told that there was a large prison there, and the club we were booked in just so happened to be called "The Pen." The stage area looked just like a Las Vegas style stage, complete with wrap-around red velvet curtains, and the area seemed to be at least ten feet above the auditorium floor.

When we arrived we set up our equipment behind the closed curtains. At eight pm we started our first song while the red velvet drapes opened to reveal our band. It was the first time we could see the audience, and it looked like the auditorium was packed. We had heard that Miss Canada was out in the audience and she wanted my autograph.

During our first set of music, we started performing "Rockin' Me Baby," by the Steve Miller Band, which was a very upbeat song. During the musical interlude I decided to jump rope with my microphone and cord. The spotlights were so bright that I just couldn't see where the end of the stage was, and I accidentally fell off the stage. The band continued to play but I could hear them asking where I was. The spotlight that had been following me, decided to follow me all the way down to the auditorium floor, where I finished singing the song. Thank God I wasn't hurt by the fall. After our performance I went out into the audience and introduced myself to Miss Canada, but for some unknown reason she didn't ask for my autograph and I didn't offer her mine.

TWENTY FOUR
SHOWCASED

The Canadian tour was so successful that Sunburst Records had already started planning a Las Vegas appearance. They had contacted the Sahara Hotel and they wanted to showcase us in concert.

When our band drove back to New Jersey from Canada, I had no place to call home. I was so tired of staying with friends, and decided I had earned enough to rent my own apartment, so I found a one bedroom apartment and moved in right away. This apartment was perfect for me and I could live alone and enjoy my career with the band. Joyce and I were separated, but neither one of us had filed for a divorce. We tried to reconcile a couple of times over the next year or so, but it just never worked out. I was missing my kids and could only see them once a week. Where was my life taking me?

Sunburst Records was now planning the Las Vegas tour. The only way they could book the two-day tour was to fly our band out. I had trouble trying to take a week off again from Suburban Propane, but when I told them all I needed was three days, they agreed. I didn't tell them why, just that I needed to take a trip.

Sunburst was thrilled about the record sales of "This Magic Moment" and wanted to follow it with yet another single of "Smoke Gets In Your

Eyes." We went back into the studio and recorded another single. We had two singles that our agent said would help cement our credibility in Las Vegas. We flew to Las Vegas and the band stayed at a motel right across the street from that super market that I had worked at when I had lived in Las Vegas years before.

The next day I knew that we were to be showcased at the famous Sahara Club, in their Lipstick Lounge. We practiced our vocals in our motel room and we hadn't left our room all day. I was getting rather hungry, when one of the guys threw a small red apple onto the bed where I was resting. I took one look at that apple and I knew I was worth much more than this. I knew that God created that apple and it was perfectly formed. That's the way He created me, perfect in every way. How could I go on taking this abuse of not taking care of myself and always wanting the attention? I was starting to enjoy the special attention of being a pop-singer in a band. Girls were screaming and wanting my autograph, and I started to develop a celebrity attitude. I didn't realize that people and positions in life can have a profound effect on the way our minds accept and grab onto the attention that is thrown at us. The record company had created a persona that I had to live up to, and it was starting to become who I was.

That night at the Sahara Hotel I felt more like a star than I'd ever felt before. Surely this had to lead to something even bigger. I asked myself, "Do you really want something bigger? Could I really handle anything more? Do I deserve to receive all this applause?" My thoughts would take me back to my childhood when I was so shy and withdrawn. I had often been picked-on by my other classmates in grade school for not having the proper clothes to wear. In high school I was able to earn money and buy my own clothes, but It was then and only then that I started to come out of my shell and was accepted by my well-to-do friends. They never learned about who I used to be and where I lived. All they knew was that I was this well-dressed guy who knew how to fit in with the in-crowd. I became a stuck-up snob in high school. I know now that all that was a big façade that I had created because of my insecurities.

We flew back to New Jersey and I had to face my hum-drum life again. It was getting harder and harder for me to resume my job at Suburban Propane, and the record company told me that eventually I would have to quit my full-time job because it would only hold me back when they booked us on extended tours. Even though I wanted to quit, I had financial security and benefits at Suburban Propane and I had been on my job for seven years. The benefits included two weeks earned vacations, an excellent health-care plan, sick days, and a good salary. All I had with Sunburst Records was a chance to sing and tour and create extra money to spend. They knew that I would not quit my full-time job unless they sold my contract to a major record label.

I had earned my degree in accounting and had been looking forward to moving up to a better position in the finance department at Suburban Propane. The only trouble was, Suburban Propane had hired a new personnel director that did not want to promote me above what my position already was, in spite of any degree. There were no openings in their accounting department, and this new director would often have me help out in the mailroom, delivering and sorting the mail. I was also told to help out in their printing department that included shipping supplies out to their various branches. Somehow I learned to love the printing department and spent most of my time there. He was trying to discourage me so I'd quit. I'd only help out in accounting if someone else was out sick or on vacation. He thought that my salary was above more than I was worth, so why he was looking for a reason to get rid of me, I could not understand.

TWENTY FIVE
IT WASN'T A DREAM!

Two singles didn't seem to be enough recordings for Sunburst and they wanted us to record yet another single, hoping that one of these singles would catch the ear of a major record producer. They had put all their faith in this one single we recorded called "She Cried."

Our record company/booking agency booked our band into a wonderful night spot in Wilkes-Barre, Pennsylvania for a two night gig. We hadn't performed much in Pennsylvania so we were all looking forward to this trip. Sunburst had made arrangements for us to perform at a large hotel lounge and the hotel provided the band with three rooms for our over-night housing. I was excited and couldn't wait for the week-end. The hotel even provided our band with a stretch limo to make a grand entrance the night of our first performance.

We used the two vans that the record company provided for us and we drove the eighty nine mile trip into Wilkes-Barre. Mr. Bee came with us and tried to divvy up the rooms so that there weren't too many guys in one room. I was surprised that he had booked the two of us into the same room all by ourselves. He had never done that before. We had always had three or four guys in one room, some sleeping on roll-a-way beds, some on the floor. The guys unloaded their overnight gear and we headed to the hotel lounge and set up our equipment for that night's performance.

Before our first night's performance we left our rooms and got into the waiting limo on the side of the hotel to make a grand entrance. What a huge success. We made our way into the hotel lounge with screaming girls all around us, and in the lounge we received much applause. People started dancing the minute we started playing, and they were having such a wonderful time listening to our renditions of popular songs. We had already recorded three singles, "This Magic Moment," "Smoke Gets In Your Eyes," and "She Cried." The one song that most people loved and wanted for me to perform over and over again was "This Magic Moment." Their second choice was "The Lion Sleeps Tonight," which I had never recorded, but was part of our show. Everyone that heard me sing "the lion song" told me that I sounded as good as or better than the original artist. Our booking agent was making long range plans for us to record that song as a single, but not until we had promoted our latest single, "She Cried."

During our second night of performing, we had a full house, and there was so much excitement in the air. All the guys in the band were performing at their best, and some of the younger girls in the audience would start screaming every time we reappeared on stage after our break.

After our successful evening of concert and music, we left by a side entrance to the waiting limo. The girls followed us, screaming all the way. Little did they know that we were just going to drive around to the other side of the hotel and retire to our rooms.

All the guys decided to come to our room first to celebrate and rejoice over what seemed like the most wonderful, fun-filled two nights that any one of us had ever had before. We partied for several hours before we all got so tired and sleepy and had to call it a night. Mr. Bee told the band that this was just the beginning. Bigger plans were already being made by Sunburst Records for us to appear on American Bandstand, as well as being an opening act for the Temptations and Victor Borge. Mr. Bee informed us for the first time that Sunburst Records had hired him on as a PR/booking agent for them. At first we were a little surprised and wondered how that would affect us, but Mr. Bee put us all at ease when he mentioned that his position with our band had not changed any and that our success could only get better.

The guys in the band left to go to their rooms for the night, and just Mr. Bee and I were left in our room. I went into the restroom to brush my teeth and put on my pajama bottoms. Mr. Bee had given me the bed while he slept on a roll-a-way bed that had been brought into our room earlier. We talked for a while and he told me some of his long-range plans for the band. He came over and sat on the edge of my bed to continue his conversation. Before he left my bed, he stood up and bent over me and took my hand to shake it, telling me that he was proud of me and that I was going to become a big star. I felt he lingered there a little too long, looking into my eyes. I was starting to get an uneasy feeling in the pit of my stomach about that whole close encounter. I just turned over and went to sleep with one eye open all night. Not really!

Sometime during the night I remember what I thought was a very exciting dream I was having, to the point of orgasm. Just at the time of my orgasm I started to wake slowly enough to be aware of my surroundings. Was I having a wet dream? No, there were fingers wrapped around my male member. Someone's hand had been masturbating me while I was sleeping. By then my eyes opened wide just to find Mr. Bee sitting on the floor next to my bed with his head and his hands under my covers. I jumped up and asked "What are you doing?"

That was the end of our friendship. I was so hurt and angry. I do not remember all I had said to him but I do know that I wanted out of that band and away from the whole music scene. I think I actually told him he was fired. I probably had no right to fire him because he was now working for Sunburst Records.

I couldn't sleep the rest of the night and sat in a chair over in the corner of our room. By morning I couldn't even look at him. I knew we all had to ride home together, but it was not going to be easy for me to have to be in his presence for the hour and a half ride back to New Jersey. I was afraid to tell the other band members for fear that maybe they would think that I had somehow instigated it. All I knew was that I had to tell somebody. I didn't want to be in the band anymore and I was sick and tired of the whole idea of being a rock star.

I was very quiet during the ride back to New Jersey. We stopped at the record company's main office building where we had parked our cars for the week-end and I jumped out first, hoping not to have to say anything to anyone about what just happened. Before I could reach my car, Mr. Bee came over to me and apologized for his actions, and pleaded with me not to leave the band, and to please not say anything about what had happened during the night. He told me that he didn't know his actions would upset me the way they did and that he would never try that stunt again. I could see he was totally repentant, but I had already made my mind up. I was going home and never coming back. He had caught me when I was sleeping and vulnerable. What I thought was a good feeling and exciting, turned out to be so wrong.

After quitting my band cold turkey, I decided I never wanted to talk about that whole experience ever again. The hurt of being betrayed weighed heavily on my shoulders and I didn't want to have to explain to anyone the reasons why I quit. The reasons were all too embarrassing.

For three weeks I cried myself to sleep, wondering what I was going to do for the rest of my life. I still had my full-time job at Suburban Propane, but it was in jeopardy with the new personnel manager they had just hired. He was always looking for a reason to let me go.

I decided to pick up the pieces and I found a singer-songwriter, who also played acoustic guitar. We joined up together and started singing in coffee houses and small bars. We were another Simon and Garfunkel. He sang lead and I formed a harmony above him. Our audiences started growing and we were often requested to perform at more places than we could possibly book. He had a full-time job and his wife didn't like the idea that her husband was out performing. She ended up talking her husband out of performing, and that ended our short-lived stardom.

TWENTY SIX
A CHANCE ENCOUNTER

I decided to hire an attorney to file for a divorce from Joyce. My attorney told me I could file using abandonment as the reason for the divorce. When Joyce had kicked me out of the house, I had nowhere to go and no place to live, and that is considered abandonment. After I filed for a divorce, my attorney told me that a divorce in New Jersey would not be finalized for a year after filing. This being New Jersey law, that would give the couple time to have a reconciliation. I was in no hurry to obtain the divorce and I was content on living by myself and working my full-time job. I had quit the band and spent most of my time hanging out with friends.

The new personnel manager further diminished my position at Suburban Propane when he hired a new woman, Ina Kay, in the finance department. I was no longer needed to help out. He made sure I spent most of my days in the mailroom or in the printing department. I had nowhere to go but down.

I was helping out in the printing office, which was in a separate building, when I saw the new woman running into the main building. The guys I was working with told me I ought to try and get to know her. They knew I had filed for a divorce and I was soon going to be a single guy again.

My opportunity to ask the new employee out on a date came when Suburban Propane planned a company party. Once a year they planned a dinner and a show for the company employees and this year the play "The Unsinkable Molly Brown" was playing at the dinner theatre. Suburban Propane made reservations for all its employees to attend. What I didn't know was that married couples could not work at Suburban Propane together, so if the two of us were to become a couple, one of us would have to leave. It was just a thought.

I took a lunch break one Friday and headed over to the company cafeteria. There right in front of me in line was this new employee buying her lunch. I came up behind her and asked her if she had plans to attend the company party. She told me that she had not made any plans to attend at all, so I asked her if we could go together. I didn't even know her name yet. When I asked her what her name was she said, Ina Kay, and I asked her for her home phone number so we could stay in touch.

The following week I had been asked to guest sing at Aunt Kate's night club during their talent night. I called Ina Kay and asked her if she would go with me. I picked her up and we headed on over to Aunt Kate's. The Pawns were the house band and they had heard that I had done some recording and wanted me to come in as a special guest star, so I sang the song "School's Out" by Alice Cooper. Ina Kay didn't seem at all impressed with the whole scenario, but this date turned out to be a good way of getting to know each other. Here I was getting involved with the very woman who was hired to work full-time in the same department that I was hoping to get into, and I was shoved out because of her. Somehow though, none of that bothered me when we started to date.

The company party was our first official date. I picked up Ina Kay at her home and we drove to the dinner theatre together, where they had a wonderful live band that played great dinner and dance music. It would be the first time that she and I danced together. It turned out to be a wonderful evening and we started seeing each other more often after that.

Ina Kay was a divorced woman with a son, Jeffrey. She had a home in Denville, near the Denville Lake. I met her son, Jeffrey, during one of my visits to her home, and I liked him instantly. He was only about five years old, but little did I know that Jeffrey had many social problems that I would later discover. It started to become a real problem during my early relationship with his mother.

One evening I drove over to spend time with Ina Kay and Jeffrey. I stayed until Jeffrey went to bed, and it was then that she proceeded to tell me the whole story about her ex-husband and the problems that were created because of him. I don't feel at liberty to write here the whole story, because I don't want to be casting a negative spotlight on the people that I deeply care for. If I were to expose the revealing truth of who Jeffrey's dad was, it might damage my relationship with Jeffrey, whom I adopted as my own son.

Just a few weeks into our relationship a new revelation came to me about why Jeffrey had acquired so many behavioral problems. I happened to meet Ina Kay's controlling sister and her controlling parents. I had an instant dislike of them, and they didn't like me either. My spirit within me was telling me that these people were not to be trusted.

My first impressions proved to be right about Ina Kay's family. Almost immediately they started creating strange and bizarre behavior patterns when they realized that I was starting to have a relationship with Jeffrey and her. They would park in front of her home and stay there in their parked car until I left. One evening I decided to stay until they left, and I ended up falling asleep on her sofa. When I awoke early the next morning, her parents had driven away sometime during the night. I just could not believe the bizarre actions her family was expressing towards me. Sometimes while parked in their car, they would even sneak up to her front door and leave a wrapped gift for Jeffrey, with a personal note, before they drove off.

I finally got to meet Ina Kay's parents when we decided to drive out to their home in Chester, New Jersey for a visit. I could sense that her parents were being very polite, but distant. Her grandmother lived there in the same household. Over the years I have met many strange people, but I just wasn't prepared for this kind of a family. Some of them would talk under their breath so not everyone could understand what they were saying, causing others to have an empty feeling of being ignored and talked about. Bizarre is the only word that comes to mind. If I was to have any kind of a relationship with Ina Kay and her son, I knew I would have to move them as far away from New Jersey as possible, before we all got swallowed up in this same kind of strange behavior.

TWENTY SEVEN
I WAS SO TORN!

The personnel manager of Suburban Propane called me into his office and had a stern talk with me about dating an employee. He told me he saw the two of us dancing and sitting together at the company party and he reiterated to me that if we were to ever get married, one of us would have to leave the company. I knew right then and there that he was trying to intimidate me even more to try and get me to quit. I wasn't going to buy into it. He had nothing to fire me over and I had no reasons to leave.

Ina Kay and I started to spend more and more time together. My divorce had become final and I was able to make future plans. At Suburban Propane I had built up a substantial savings in my credit union account and I wanted to try and use those funds for a down-payment on a house.

The three of us decided to drive around Lake Hopatcong. We headed on over across the River Stix Bridge in Lake Hopatcong on the north side of the lake to try and find homes for sale. We found a raised ranch for sale on a hill overlooking Lake Hopatcong, and we contacted the listing real estate agent. An agent came out immediately and gave us a tour of the home, and we both fell in love with it immediately. I applied for a home loan and was approved, and we signed a contract and wanted to move in right after the closing. My credit was impeccable and I had several credit cards.

I had been in touch with my parents in Colorado when I bought this home and they were so disappointed that we were not moving out there. Dad told me he had a job lined up for me working for his best friend who was an insurance agent for a multi-line insurance company, and we could stay with my parents until we found our own place. Somehow it all seemed so tempting, especially with my job at Suburban Propane being in jeopardy because their new personnel manager was trying everything he could to get rid of me.

Ina Kay had placed her home on the market and it sold almost immediately. Now we had her funds and mine for any expenses we needed. We both decided that it was a good idea for us to pack up everything we owned, rent a U-Haul truck, and move to Colorado.

I decided to go into the main office at Suburban Propane the next day and give them a two week notice in writing. The personnel manager was so excited he let me go that very same day, paying me a two week salary and severance pay. A year later I found out that the company also let him go.

I had just bought a home in Lake Hopatcong that we never had a chance to move in to, and now I've decided to place it on the market, and we were moving to Colorado to work and live, and we could buy a home there.

I knew I had to set up a meeting with Joyce, Jennifer and Brian. My emotions were running high and I knew it was not going to be easy having to say goodbye to my children. Every time I thought about moving out of state and I started to feel bad about it, Joyce's statements came back to haunt me when she said she didn't want a part-time father hanging around and she certainly didn't want an ex-husband hanging around. She admitted to me that she really never wanted a husband, but she wanted children, and in those days that is how you got children.

I called Joyce and asked her if I could come over and see the kids. I needed to tell her that I was moving, so she thought it was a good idea for me to spend time with them. I drove on over to the home where she had rented an upstairs apartment that had a back entrance, and when I arrived I knew I could not tell her I was moving out of state. When I spent time with my kids there, I knew it was going to hurt me deeply if I couldn't see them on a regular basis.

Joyce had gone in to another room and had fallen asleep. I spent quality time with the kids but it was starting to get late and I didn't know where their mother was, so I asked Jennifer if she would go and find my coat I had taken off earlier. She disappeared into one of the bedrooms and came back with my coat, looking at me very inquisitively with a puzzled look in her eyes. I asked her what was wrong and she told me that when she went to get my coat, it was under her mother's legs. When she pulled it from under her mother's legs, it partially awoke Joyce and she must have thought it was me, getting my coat, and she said, "Frank, I love you." I was so torn at that very moment, just hearing those words, and a flood of emotions started running through my mind. I knew I had to either take action and go into her, or ignore the fact that I had even heard it spoken. What was I supposed to do?

My first thoughts were that I had already become involved with someone else and was restarting my life over again. I had even purchased a home. Many times in the past I tried to talk Joyce into our buying a home together, but she didn't seem interested in wanting to. We had even looked at a couple of homes together. Then the memories of what Joyce and I had gone through over the past few years came barging into my thoughts, uninvited, choking out any remnant of my ever wanting to restart this broken and damaged marriage all over again. I knew I just didn't want to go back to where we were. I knew that we didn't like each other, and our differences were just too great of a chasm between us now.

I left without talking to Joyce, but it was so hard to leave my children behind. I hadn't even told them yet that I was moving out of state. I just sat in my parked car in front of their home, and I began crying like a baby. My spirit was broken and my feelings were in turmoil. If I had had a closer relationship with the Lord then, I would have cried out to Him in anguish.

I had drifted so far away from my beliefs when I married Joyce, who was a devout, but non-practicing, Catholic. During one brief moment of my life when I was trying so desperately to fit into the Biondo family, I even consulted with a Catholic priest. I sat down with him to discuss the possibilities of my joining the Catholic Church. When the priest came to the part where we would have to get remarried because our wedding was not recognized by the Catholic Church, I came unglued. We had been married by a pastor, my dad, in his church, and we had two children of our own. This priest was telling me that his church didn't recognize our marriage? Needless to say, that episode only added one more log onto a smoldering fire of a troubled marriage. At this Catholic Church I realized that they held musicals and I decided I'd join their volunteer choir. The coral director asked me to dress up as a sailor and sing "Mr. Lonely."

Again, I knew I had to confront the fact that Ina Kay and I were

Frankie dressed as a sailor for a musical at a benefit concert in NJ

moving out of state, and I needed to inform my children. Our moving van was already packed and we were ready to head to Colorado. When I made one last ditch effort to call Joyce, my insides became agitated and remorseful. As much as I so wanted to start my life all over again with a new job, I just didn't know how I would be able to say goodbye to my own children. Maybe I could fly them out to spend time with me later on?

I finally called Joyce to tell her that I had been offered a position with an insurance company in Denver and I had to move soon, so we made plans to meet with her and my kids at the Hopatcong State Park. I wanted Joyce and my children to meet Ina Kay and her son, Jeffrey.

At the park I played with my children. We ran and skipped together. We even walked down to the over-flow area of the dam to play on the rocks. Little did I realize that this encounter would be the last time I was ever allowed to see or talk with my children. Even after our move to Colorado I would often try and phone Joyce, wanting to talk with Jennifer and Brian, but she would always tell me that there was no one there that wanted to talk to me. Jennifer later told me she remembers her mother saying that. When Joyce told me that she didn't want a part-time father to her children hanging around, and no ex-husband hanging around, she meant it. When she told me this our kids were sitting in the back seat of the car, hearing everything that had been said.

I hugged my children and gave them a kiss on their cheeks when we said our goodbyes. Joyce took the kids and they got in the white Buick I had left them, and they drove off. We drove close behind them and followed them up the ramp that led onto highway 80 heading west. After we entered onto the highway we passed Joyce and the kids. I honked and waved to them as we sped up, and the kids saw me and waved back. It was so hard for me to hold my emotions in tack when I saw their little faces disappear from view as we got further and further away from their car. That was the last time I saw or spoke to Jennifer and Brian until they became adults.

TWENTY EIGHT
AN UNEXPECTED KNOCK

My son Brian told me years later when we were able to meet, that he remembered waving to me from their car, not realizing that he would not see me again for over 35 years!

Our trip to Colorado was uneventful except for the fact that Ina Kay had never seen oil wells before. If you travel through western Kansas, you will see oil wells all along highway 70. She wanted to stop and take pictures now and then to send back to her family in New Jersey.

Ina Kay's first taste of Denver was the suburb of Commerce City, where my dad was pastoring a Christian Church. Maybe her bubble had burst after her expectations and the anticipations of us moving to the Rocky Mountain region, and to the Denver area, was not what she was expecting at all. She must have felt pretty disappointed in this portion of Denver. The town is called Commerce City for a reason. This portion of the Denver area contained most of the factories, plants, railway interchanges, and commerce, and sometimes the air smelled like soot and smelly shoes. My parents lived in one of those suburbs in a parsonage provided for them by the church.

My parent's way of life was very simple. We stayed with them for a few nights, sleeping in two separate rooms, until we could make proper arrangements to get married. I asked my dad if he would give us the honor of marrying us, and he was delighted to.

We had a simple marriage ceremony in the sanctuary of dad's church in Commerce City with only a hand full of family there and decided we needed to find an apartment to live in until our home in New Jersey sold. I knew I also had to call the insurance company to tell them we had arrived in Denver, and that I wanted to get an interview and fill out an employment application with them, which would include a battery of tests and personal scrutiny of my life.

The next day I drove into Lakewood, a suburb of Denver, and did an interview with the insurance company that my dad had recommended, and they hired me after I was asked a battery of questions that used a microscope to examine my life and thoughts. This insurance company made one request and that was that I needed to live in Lakewood where their office was, which meant that we had to find a home in Lakewood.

Needing an immediate place to stay, we moved into an upstairs apartment in the Thornton area of Denver, but after a few months we found a four-level home, with four bedrooms and two fireplaces in Lakewood, near 6th Avenue. I could almost walk to the office.

Every week-end we would drive over to Commerce City to attend the church my dad pastored, and we soon became members there. After a few months, the church board asked me if I would direct their church choir, and lead their congregation in praise and worship. I then not only directed their choir, and led their praise and worship, I also chose all the hymns being sung, as well as printing the church bulletins and the church newsletters. I was nominated Chairman of the Board and became my father's boss!

My position with this life insurance company meant that I had to make cold calls daily. I never felt comfortable making calls to perfect strangers. Some of the information given to me to make these cold calls was referrals given to the salesmen by our managers, and new salesmen lived on a monthly draw that morphed into earned commissions. Eventually my salary would disappear, leaving me to depend on whatever commissions I had earned that month. I was always aspiring to more than I could deliver.

Daily I worried whether or not I was living up to what this company expected me to accomplish. Was I making enough cold calls? Would my commissions run out before I've earned enough in sales to live on only my commissions? Most of the clients I had to contact were pastors and their families. I was surprised at how many pastors this insurance company turned down for life insurance because of something in their past.

When I had interviewed with this company, I realized that this company's policy was that no one that ever had a drinking problem could ever purchase life insurance with this insurance company. I knew that there was no problem with me since I hardly ever had a drink in my entire life, and I didn't even like the taste of it. My problem was that this insurance company had turned down a widow's request for her husband's life insurance when he died, because apparently when she informed the company that her husband had just died, the company's spies called around to all her neighbors, family, and friends, asking if this lady's husband had ever touched a drink. One of the widow's relatives told the spy that this man had had a drink about fifteen years ago at a family reunion. That was just enough information for this life insurance company to deny her claim. I was livid. I had only been with this company less than two months, but I just couldn't stand the thought of a widow having to come up with funds to bury her own husband, especially since they had been making their monthly life insurance premiums all those years. I turned in my resignation and quit that same day.

I applied to be a salesman for the Teton Life Insurance Company, and my application went through and I had to take special training in Cheyenne, Wyoming. Why I chose to pursue another career in insurance sales, I do not know. I did not even last a month with this company.

Ina Kay and I were still living in our four-level home on Dudley in Lakewood, and we had also just purchased a repossessed double-wide mobile home in Northglenn. Our plans were to rent our own home to a deserving family, and move into the double-wide. Four guys who were skiers had answered our 'for rent' ad and we rented our home to them, packing up our furniture and moving to Northglenn.

We moved to the double-wide mobile home in Northglenn and really started to enjoy the roominess and freedom of living in a mobile home park. The mobile home had been upgraded with all new skirting around it, and it had a beautiful, large covered porch on the front that doubled as a carport.

We had an unexpected knock at our door one evening, and the guy at the door asked us when we were going to make another payment on the loan. We asked him, what loan? He told us about the loan we had taken out for the new skirting and awning that his company had installed a few months ago. We told him that we were the new owners and we didn't know anything about a loan. He told us that if we didn't make a payment within 30 days, they were going to come and repossess the awning and skirting. We were totally in shock and called the bank where we had purchased this loan. We had bought this home through a foreclosure and the bank was not aware of a pending lien against the mobile home. It was their huge mistake. They thought the best idea for them to save face, was to have us sign the mobile home back to the bank and move out. We would be free of the debt without it hurting our credit rating, so we decided to take their offer and we moved back to our four-level home on Dudley. The four guys renting our home understood our problem and moved out so we could move back in.

I applied for a job in downtown Denver at the M. L. Foss Company in accounts payable, and they hired me that same day. Now I was able to start using some of the skills for which I had been trained. I loved accounting and every aspect of it, and it was such a joy for me to go into work every day. The parking was a problem for me daily, however, and I had to pay to park five days a week, which was getting old. Almost every lunch break I started applying for work somewhere in downtown Denver. I made out an application at the AT & T Company and they called me about an opening, but the pay was much lower than what I was already earning, so I turned the job down.

Another company where I applied was an accounting firm that processed other firms accounting problems. The pay was better and they wanted me right away. I would be doing double entry bookkeeping and accounting, and I would be replacing a pregnant woman who was leaving permanently to take care of her new baby. She would train me, so I immediately gave a week's notice at M. L. Foss and started this new job. This however was the biggest mistake of my life.

The pregnant lady training me did not like the idea of a man taking her place, and she totally made my life miserable every day. I was so uptight every day that I ended up having tight muscles in my neck and could hardly move it. It just wasn't worth it for me, so after a few months of pure hell, I quit.

TWENTY NINE
A MUSICAL HERITAGE DESTROYED

We loved our home on Dudley but it was so noisy to go outside into our backyard because of the traffic noise coming from Sixth Avenue that ran right by our home. We started looking for homes further north of downtown Denver, and found a new home subdivision being built in Thornton. We applied for a loan on a new construction and got the loan, and we were able to watch our own new home being built. We sold our home in Lakewood and moved to our new home in Thornton when it was completed. Bringing sod in and building a fence around our property I felt was such an accomplishment. We planted fast growing trees, and placed an above-ground pool in our fenced-in yard.

A friend of ours told me I should apply at the Samsonite Luggage Company located in east Denver. She said that Samsonite doesn't advertise much because they can't handle the high volume of applicants on a daily basis, so I took her advice and drove over there and applied. Part of the screening for any office job was to take a typing test, and I typed 67 words per minute with three errors. Then I took a 10-key test. The lady told me to enter numbers as long as I could, or until the buzzer went off. When she came back, she saw a whole stream of 10-key paper strung out onto the floor, and asked me what had happened. She probably thought that I might be able to add up a few columns on the 10-key and not be able to have time to do more, but she didn't realize that I was fast and accurate. I made history at Samsonite for being the first male or female to ever get that high of a score, and typing on a 10-key, left-handed. I was hired immediately.

At Samsonite I was placed in the New Accounts division with a chance to move on up to accounting. All the new customers had to come directly through me. I would check their Dunn and Bradstreet Reports, along with their credit history, and after the client met all the criteria required by Samsonite, I would create an internal account for them, assigning a tracking number.

We received a phone call from my Aunt Bernadine that my grandpa William Piper had died. Aunt Bernadine asked me if I would be one of the pall-bearers. She told me that all the pall-bearers would be grandpa's grandsons. In July, 1974 we headed to Kansas City and I became one of the

Tombstone of my grandparents, Will and Goldie Piper

pall-bearers for grandpa. He was buried at the old Monticello cemetery not far from Zarah where he and grandma had lived. It was such an honor to be a pall-bearer for my grandpa.

When Ina Kay lost her full-time job in downtown Denver, I suggested she apply at Samsonite just to see if they would allow married couples to work together at the same company. Samsonite hired her and she started working in another department and in the same building I worked at, so we were able to car-pool into work together.

It was during the first few months of Ina Kay's employment at Samsonite that she had gone to our family doctor to have a checkup because she was not having her periods. It was then that the doctor told her that she was pregnant. Upon further examination of her, he informed her that the embryo had attached itself low in her abdomen, so he suggested that she quit her job and stay off her feet as much as possible if she wanted to have a safe pregnancy.

Ina Kay gave notice and quit immediately. We were both ecstatic about her pregnancy, but were worried about the unborn child. I was especially thrilled about the possibility of becoming a father again. I knew I had lost my precious son and daughter to a doomed marriage, and a mother that refused to let me communicate with them over the years. I tried and tried to understand, from her viewpoint, what her reasons were. In my mind however, I brought back to remembrance two statements Joyce had made to me after our divorce. One was the fact that she didn't want an ex-husband hanging around, and secondly, she didn't want a part-time father of her kids hanging around. She emphatically made those two statements clear to me.

Was history bound to repeat itself with a troubled pregnancy? My thoughts went back to the problems my first wife Joyce had had, when she started having problems early on in her pregnancy with our daughter Jennifer. And now, Ina Kay was having problems with our first unborn child. Each time, the embryo had attached itself low in the uterus, but she was able to stay home and have peace, knowing that she was doing all she could to protect her pregnancy.

I earned a week's vacation after my first year at Samsonite and decided I wanted to take Ina Kay and Jeff to see where I had attended Nebraska Christian College in Norfolk, Nebraska. We ended up in the

Kansas City area to not only visit my boyhood home on Ball Lane, but to meet some of my relatives. When we pulled up in front of 2121 Ball Lane, my boyhood home, a man came out to greet me who had to talk through a hole in his throat. I was so uncomfortable that I did not let my family out of the car.

We then drove through Nebraska and headed to Norfolk, Nebraska, so Ina Kay and Jeffrey could see where the college was that I had attended. When we arrived in Norfolk I drove directly to where the Nebraska Christian College was, and where the two dorms were that housed the male students and the female students. As we rounded the corner and drove up to the front of the college, I was in shock. The Nebraska Christian College I had attended was now a mortuary! Where was the college? We drove by Giovani's Pizzeria where I had worked during my college days, and the building was no longer there. I lost some of my joy and excitement about my trying to relive and remember some of my past.

My dad's sister Bernadine, and her husband George

We headed on down to Winchester, Kansas where many of my favorite memories would often come flooding back into view. I reflected upon my graduating from the Winchester High School and receiving my high school diploma. I had participated in the school's Glee Club and was a witness of their receiving accolades from the state of Kansas. My singing was birthed on the platform of that Christian Church in Winchester where my dad was the pastor.

We then drove on down to the Kansas City area to the suburb of Lenexa. I wanted Ina Kay and Jeffrey to meet my Aunt Bernadine and Uncle George. We found their home and we had a wonderful visit. When we started to leave, I began walking down the stairs towards their front door, and Ina Kay was at the top of these stairs wearing her white boots. I knew the bottoms of her boots were slick. She started to take her first step down those stairs when her foot slipped and it hit the second stair with a thud. Neither one of us gave a second thought to the incident because the slip only startled her for a moment, however, that jolt was just enough that probably had started the dislodging of the embryo in her womb. The long drive back to Denver proved to be the last driving force that cemented our baby's doom. The real severity of the problem didn't surface until we arrived back in Denver.

Before we had taken this trip we had made plans to leave our Schnauzer dog behind on chains in our unfinished basement, along with plenty of water and food that would last her for a couple of days. We had storage boxes that were nearby and I didn't think that she would even be interested in checking them out. But when we arrived back home our dog had gotten into an open box that contained my record collection and had bitten on them enough to break them, scattering them all about the room. Apparently she had been upset that we had left her behind and she tore into anything that was within the scope of the length of her chain. All my 45rpm records that I had recorded were all broken in pieces. All my autographed records that other artists had given me as a memento were all broken. There were fragments of vinyl records everywhere, and I just wanted to sit down and cry. I had no proof of my ever recording a record, and the record company was no longer in business.

While at my desk at Samsonite one day my spirit started troubling me as I was working diligently taking calls to set up numerous new accounts. The phone on my desk went silent for a while, and I was a little relieved to have some time to work on other projects that had been piling up in my inbox, but all of a sudden my focus went directly to my phone and I couldn't take my eyes off of it. It was a though I was being hypnotized by just the presence of my own black phone sitting on my desk and not ringing. I knew in my spirit that something was terribly wrong, but I didn't know what.

Suddenly my phone rang and it was Ina Kay crying hysterically and uncontrollably. She said she had had some problems with bleeding, and had decided to drive to the hospital's emergency room. When the doctor at the hospital examined her, he told her that she could have had a miscarriage, but he wasn't positive until further tests were taken. I told her not to worry and I would meet her there. I informed my boss about the emergency and left quickly so I could be there by her side.

The drive to the hospital was like having to drive all the way to the moon and back. I just wanted to get there as quickly as possible and not have to fight traffic all the way. My thoughts were going a mile a minute with the questions I had about the whole situation that was unfolding before me. My emotions broke through many times during that horrendous journey to the hospital when tears would often flood my eyes. I felt so bad for Ina Kay because I knew how badly she wanted to have more children.

I arrived at the hospital at the emergency entrance and asked the attending nurse what room my wife was in. They had taken her up to the second floor, so I walked to the elevator that took me to the second floor. I got off the elevator and headed in the direction of Ina Kay's room. As I was approaching the entrance to her room, a nurse was just leaving, holding in the palms of her hands a bloody mass, about the size of a goose egg, wrapped openly in a white cloth. I know now that I was probably not supposed to witness what the nurse had in her hands, but I did. It was our child's embryo. The nurse had not told Ina Kay that she had just lost her baby. They lied to her by telling her that her body still tested that she was still pregnant, probably knowing that she could emotionally fall apart. That was such a cruel joke to play. They were only postponing the real truth from her for the moment. I, of course, didn't have a clue as to what was really going on.

The doctor told us he wanted her to spend the night so he could keep a close watch on her. He had to have known that Ina Kay had just lost her baby. Why didn't he tell her so? Why didn't any of the hospital staff tell her? She wasn't told until the next day!

I went home and had a very restless night. Did I witness the remnants of a miscarriage, and did I actually see our baby being carried away by an attending nurse? All these questions seemed to constantly bother me as I drove to work the next day. Within an hour after arriving at work, my phone rang. Ina Kay was hysterical again and in tears. The doctor finally told her at the hospital that she had had a miscarriage. Why did they wait until the next day to tell her? Those questions will always haunt me for the rest of my life. I started to distrust doctors and hospitals.

She had trouble getting pregnant again so we both decided to have our family doctor check us both out. Ina Kay checked out fine. The doctor called me in and told me he needed to test me. I first had to give him a sperm sample. Yuck! Then he called me back in again and told me to pull down my pants and bend over because he wanted to check my prostate. I bent over as he requested me to do, but as I glanced around at the doctor, I noticed that he was putting rubber gloves on. What was he going to do? A quick jab with his middle finger into my backside answered my question. That jab was enough for me to want to jump right through the ceiling.

I found out that my prostate gland was enlarged. The doctor placed me on special medicine and told us to go home and try again within a week. After that first week, she became pregnant again. We were both excited that we were going to have another baby. Somehow we knew that this was going to be a perfect birth.

Our son, Mark Eric Piper, was born on June 24, 1975. For the first time I was able to witness the birth of one of my own children. When Mark emerged and took his first breath, the doctor had him held up enough for both of us to witness our new son. I wanted to cry with joy, but an awful thought kept creeping through my mind reminding me that I was going to eventually disappoint my son someday. Mark, those awful thoughts did come to fruition and I am so filled with regret over my past mistakes, but I ask for your forgiveness.

We were both enjoying our suburban life in our new home in Thornton. We had our son Jeffrey, whom I wanted to make plans to adopt as my own. We had Mark, and now all we needed was to have a daughter.

Ina Kay's son, Jeffrey, was not my biological son. Although I had carefully accepted him into my heart as my own son, legally he was not mine. We consulted with an attorney who had us appear in court for the adoption. The judge threw out the case because he had just received a letter from one of Ina Kay's family in New Jersey that stated they were against my adopting Jeffrey. We walked out of the courtroom in total despair and with a feeling of defeat. We both knew how controlling her parents were and how jealous Ina Kay's own sister, Peggy, was of her own sister for having a child, when she herself had had a miscarriage and had divorced her own husband. We both had a feeling that Peggy had always secretly hoped that she someday could take Jeffrey away from Ina Kay and claim him as her own son. All speculation of course.

The judge did not reveal to us the paper that showed who had signed it or submitted it, but we knew instinctively that it was Ina Kay's family. Our attorney told us to change counties and appear before a different judge, and he set a court date in a different county where we appeared and the judge granted the adoption. We decided to change his name from Jeffrey Allen, to Jeffrey Bernard, and finally my family name of Piper. Jeffrey was legally my son now. Although Ina Kay's family was only able to place a temporary road block, her family was still trying to control us from afar.

THIRTY
A SHOW BAND

I was starting to miss my love of music and singing in a band. Dare I try and pick up the broken pieces from the past and try another stab at music? I didn't want to discuss this issue with Ina Kay. I was in fear of being questioned from her about my past as a pop-singer, and the reasons why I chose to quit. I didn't want to tell anybody because those days were in the past and they needed to stay there. I had started a new life and was starting to accept the fact that I would not be singing professionally anymore as a pop singer. It was a deep dark secret that I purposely chose to hide from the possible scrutiny of prying questions that would be uncomfortable for me to answer.

While thumbing through a Denver newspaper one evening, I came across an ad for a new show band that was starting up and needed five front lead singers. I called and made an appointment. I drove over to Aurora to an apartment building and I asked myself, why would a band be starting up in an apartment complex? Would I be able to qualify enough to be accepted into this band?

I found the apartment number and rang the doorbell. I walked into a room full of potential singers from every walk of life, sitting on furniture or on the floor. One man was a school teacher in Arvada. There was about six guys at the meeting, all wanting to know if this really was something they could be a part of. The leader was Lenny Mayday from Pennsylvania. His girlfriend, Bonnie Magda, was an excellent self-taught keyboardist that could really play Boogie—woogie and pop music like it was second nature to her. Lenny was the perfect front man with a voice like Bill Medley from the Righteous Brothers.

Lenny started singing the 50s song 'Barbara Ann' a cappella, asking the guys to join in. Lenny loved the sound we all produced and proceeded to tell us about his old band in Pennsylvania, and his future plans to start a new show band in Denver. His old band was called "Tom Slick, and the Converted Thunderbolt Grease Slapper Band." The name Tom Slick came from the cartoon character whose car was called the Converted Thunderbolt Grease Slapper. Lenny was the infamous "Tom Slick." His old band out east consisted of former college students and friends of both Bonnie and him. Lenny wanted to reproduce his old show again with an all-new band with five front lead singers, and it would still be called "Tom Slick, and the Converted Thunderbolt Grease Slapper Band." All the guys that attended the first meeting became a part of the show, either as one of the five front lead singers, or as one of the band members.

When I came home from the meeting with the band I told Ina Kay about it. Somehow I knew in my heart that she thought that this would be nothing more than just a hobby for me, and probably saw it as potentially becoming extra income. Little did she realize that this new venture for me was the fulfilling of my life-long ambition to express my love of music that had been interrupted by a ghastly experience back in New Jersey. I had hopes of this band becoming my salvation from my dead-end job at Samsonite. Maybe I was just chasing an illusive dream, hoping to become a star again someday. My first love had always been music, but my second love was in the accounting field.

Lenny told me that it might take a few months before the rehearsals began for the Tom Slick show band. He had the five front lead singers, but needed a band to play the instruments. I was ready to start, but now I would have to wait, and decided to try and find a temporary band that I could be a part of.

I auditioned for a band in east Denver, called "Photon," a hard rock band, and I didn't know if I would even qualify to become their lead singer. At the first session, they had me sing a James Gang song from the late sixties, but they loved what they heard and asked me to come to rehearsals. I learned later that this band never intended to go out and play anywhere, they were content just to be practicing in the basement. The band had started creating their own songs with their musical arrangements, but lacked lyrics and a lead singer. They recorded one of their original songs onto a cassette and I took that cassette home and created lyrics for the music, and when I came back to a rehearsal session, I sang those lyrics as the band played their musical creation with me calling the song, "Time Of Confusion." They were stunned at how well my lyrics fit in with both their musical arrangement and their style, and I, along with the Photon group went into a local studio and we recorded the song onto a master tape. Somehow I ended up with that master recording to hold onto for safe keeping.

When I got word that the Tom Slick show band was ready to rehearse, I immediately quit the Photon band and started rehearsing with Tom Slick.

THIRTY ONE
A PRETZEL TREE

Ina Kay was pregnant again and we found out it was going to be a girl this time, which meant that we were both excited to be having a daughter and the excitement was for different reasons. Hers was because she so wanted a daughter. My reasons were that I already had a daughter, but knew that I may never ever be able to find her or talk with her again, and our new daughter would be replacing those empty, sad feelings that would always creep up on me when my thoughts would reflect back to my little Jennifer. My heart would tear up when I could see in my mind's eye the last time that I held her in my arms. I knew I could never replace my precious daughter, but now I had another opportunity to have another daughter to love.

I started rehearsing with the Tom Slick show band. We not only had to learn 50's hits from the past, but we were also learning intricate choreography movements. As many years as I had been involved with bands and singing, these were the most intense, grueling rehearsals I had ever had to endure. Lenny had big plans for this new show band, but if this new band was anything like his old band in Pennsylvania that he kept comparing us to, then we were going to be a hit. He kept telling everyone to develop a character and become that character on stage.

Lenny had found fantastic band members to back up the five front lead-singers, and he created nicknames for everyone. I was their first-tenor and crooner and became "Frankie Monroe," or the "Girls Dream." The name Monroe was taken from the singer Vaughn Monroe. Another front lead-singer, Gary Zugschwert became "Ziggy Swartz." Our bass singer, Richard Hansen, became "Rumblin' Rich." The baritone singer, Charles Rubel, became "Chuck U," and second tenor, Bill Durie, became "Hot Rod Bud."

Our band members were not spared from having nicknames either. Our drummer, Gary Wardell, became "Boom, Boom." Our keyboardist, Bonnie Magda, became Bee-bop Bonnie. Our lead-guitarist, Billy BB Wells, became "Baby Face." Our bass-guitarist, Phil Basile, became "The Smirk." The group later added a sax player who also played the flute, Steve Craig, who became "The Westside Story Kid."

After rehearsals one evening Lenny sat us all down and told us he had already booked us into a small bar in Thornton called "The Pretzel Tree," a new family restaurant and bar. We had been rehearsing for about three weeks and he felt we were ready to perform our first musical show. He told us that we had to dress in any kind of a 50's style outfit and grease our hair down like they did back in the 50's.

The Pretzel Tree was only a few miles from our home in Thornton. The restaurant and bar was popular for its Bavarian pretzels and the new hot, soft pretzels, and the owner, Don Ciancio, booked our band for two nights. Don advertised our appearance by stating, "While you're at the Pretzel Tree you can hear the great entertainment of "Tom Slick and the Greaseslappers" whose rollicking and sentimental renditions of the fabulous 50's music makes this group one of the most popular bands in Colorado." Don told us later that he was taking a chance on us because he simply had not heard us, or heard of us. The restaurant and bar had a dance floor but no stage area, so with no stage area, we had to set up and perform on the dance floor.

Our first night's performance didn't draw much of a crowd because no one knew about us yet. We still performed the same kind of a show as if we were singing and playing in front of thousands of people, but the second night was standing room only. Don Ciancio was thrilled and we were thrilled, and he booked us for the following week-end again. Lenny told the band that this was only the beginning.

The following week-end when we came to the Pretzel Tree to set up our equipment, Mr. Ciancio had built a stage area for us. He told us that if the crowds grew any larger, he'd have to start booking us for more nights during the week.

With five front lead-singers, there was hardly a song that we couldn't learn, and our music selections grew and grew. We created skits, geared around a specific song that would help bring a whole new meaning to the lyrics. We were 'music video' before 'music video' was ever invented! We were definitely ahead of our time. I would belt out my rendition of "Donna," and "The Lion Sleeps Tonight," and Lenny and I would harmonize famous songs by the Righteous Brothers. We always received standing ovations. Each front lead-singer not only sang solos but also harmonized. We were becoming like the 50's group "Sha Na Na."

Because Lenny was such a showman, we all began to blossom into incredible entertainers. He helped to bring out the best of each singer, and now, dancer and actor. I had been a pop-singer back in New Jersey, but this venture surpassed any performance I had ever accomplished then. If the popularity grew any more for the Tom Slick show band, I knew that we would become a top act within months.

I knew I could never mention to Lenny or any band member about my past. Lenny was the leader and he was the star of his show band. I didn't want to mention who I had been and make him feel like I could try and steal his thunder. I just wanted to be one of the guys. It troubled me on many occasions when people would request "Frankie Monroe" to sing. There were many times I just wanted to scream out that I was 'the' Frankie Valens who sang a couple of hit songs back in the late sixties.

But I had great respect for Lenny, a good singer and great performer, as well as a good businessman and organizer. He knew how to handle all the finances of the band and kept the band running smoothly.

The Pretzel Tree was always crowded during our many engagements. Don thought for sure that the fire marshal would shut him down, but because of all the local police and their families often hanging out there, he never got into trouble. The police also enjoyed our show.

During one of our performances at the Pretzel Tree, Lenny announced that it was Frankie Monroe's birthday. Some of the local police, still in uniform and carrying their pistols, came over to me while all of the front five lead-singers were singing, and lifted me up above their heads. They pulled my pants down and paraded me all over the dance floor. I had been wearing bright red underwear, and was so glad I wasn't wearing plain white boxer shorts.

As a new band, we were able to perfect our show at the Pretzel Tree. We were able to try out new musical skits, new choreography, and add new songs. Lenny created a new skit based around the musical lyrics "Tell Laura I love her." The song lyrics told the story about a guy's girlfriend that got hit by a train and died, and was sad about losing her and wanted to join her soon. Lenny had friends of the band build a special wooden box that looked somewhat like a simple wooden coffin, and lined it with red velvet cloth. He had me dress as a young woman, and I had to lie down in that box with the lid closed, while the remaining front lead-singers carried the box all the way from the band's dressing room to the stage. They placed that wooden box in front of the band and then lifted the lid, showing me lying there with my arms crossed in death. Lenny proceeded to sing his sad song, dripping his tears and sweat over me. At the end of the song, I stood up as if his singing had somehow brought me back to life. The people loved the skit. I would then run to the dressing room to change out of those clothes and resume the show.

We often changed our costumes between breaks with each set having a different theme. Sometimes we presented the 'Prom Night' when we all dressed up in light blue tuxedos. Another set was 'Glitter Grease.' We all would come back wearing a special colorful jumpsuit that I designed, with each guy wearing a different color. After I started singing "Chapel Of Love," Lenny decided he wanted me to dress in a wedding gown, so he and all the back-up singers would place a veil over their faces and dance a can-can behind me again. We were again music video before music video was invented.

The Tom Slick show band

The members of my former rock band, 'Photon' visited our show one evening at the Pretzel Tree and asked me if I wanted to come back to be their lead-singer again. They informed me that they had sent a copy of the song, "Time Of Confusion" we had recorded in the studio, to a talent scout in Hollywood. This song was the very song I had written the lyrics to, with me singing the lead, and the talent scout was interested in having the band come out to record an album, using my song as the title song of the project. As much as I so wanted to go with them, I knew I had already made my choice to sing and perform with the Tom Slick show band. The Photon band members asked me if I would give them back the master reel-to-reel recording of the song, and since I had no reason to keep it, they came back the next night and I gave them the tape. I knew that when I gave back the master, it meant that I had lost all rights to my own lyrics.

We finally outgrew the Pretzel Tree. Don Ciancio knew that we as a group had to move on and spread our wings. He knew that his business had grown and had made a lot of revenue because of us, but he couldn't hold us back. The offers kept pouring in for gigs, TV appearances, radio, and touring. Only two of us band members were married, Ziggy and myself, and we were probably holding the band back from touring full-time.

Our next gig was at a favorite night-spot in Denver called 'Saturdays.' This club had hosted many famous people and musical groups in the past. We had just finished a very successful gig at the Pretzel Tree and were ready for another venue with a new audience, so Saturday's booked us for the whole week. Monday evening we featured a limbo contest with prizes. Tuesday we had a jitterbug jamboree. Wednesday we featured a Twistomania with prizes. Thursday we had a pie eating contest and extravaganza. Friday we presented a Tom Slick tee shirt and panty parade with prizes. And Saturday, our last night we featured acrobatics and a magic show, complete with prizes, with special printing on Tom Slick tee shirts, panties, and pencils.

The billboard advertising the Tom Slick band appearing at Saturday's nightclub

Monday night at 'Saturdays,' Lenny decided he wanted us to make a lasting impression on the audience and he came out dressed as a little old lady, and he proceeded to squat on stage sideways as if going to the restroom outdoors. An announcer came over an intercom saying "Tired of the same old crap? Sit back and relax. You are now witnessing a new show and a new era in music. We at Saturdays are proud to present the incredible "Tom Slick and the Converted Thunderbolt Grease Slapper Band!" I knew Lenny had guts, but this was even too much for me, but the people loved it.

One evening at Saturdays I started to sing a Richie Valens song called "Donna." The lighting at Saturdays was mainly coming from wall sconces surrounding the ballroom, along with lit candles on each table, and I noticed at the far end of the room a couple sitting together at a table. I couldn't quite see their faces, but I could see from the wall sconce lighting, a long blonde haired woman sitting next to someone that had much shorter hair. As I sang "Donna" I decided to really get more into it, and got down on one knee and reached out my hands toward the beautiful blonde, to let her know that this song was about her. She was my long lost Donna. This was the last song of our set before we would be heading back to our dressing room for a break. At the end of my song and so close to crocodile tears, I stood up. When the house lights came back on I could see a much clearer vision of what this blonde-haired girl looked like. I stood there in shock! The beautiful blonde turned out to be a long blond-haired biker and his chick. I quickly ran off that stage and hid in the dressing room.

The very next night things went from bad to worse. We had an all new audience on Saturday night at 'Saturdays.' There were many people on the dance floor and the house was packed. We performed our first set and took a fifteen minute break. Lenny wanted us to begin our second set with me singing "Chapel Of Love," so I came out dressed in a wedding gown, and the other singers had veils over their heads and across their faces, performing a can-can dance. Towards the end of the song, an intoxicated older man walked up to the front of the stage and asked me for a dance! After that incident I told Lenny that I was just too uncomfortable dressing as a woman, but it seemed like Lenny enjoyed the attention that the skit produced. It drew a lot of laughs. He told me that if anyone could pull it off and be convincing, it would be me. He always knew that whatever song I sang, or whatever musical skit I performed, I always gave it my very best and with a whole heart, even when it was uncomfortable. The hardest performance for me was having my wife in the audience when Lenny had me dress as a woman.

THIRTY TWO
CHOOSING TO QUIT

It was growing more difficult for me to go back to work at Samsonite. Many times I had had only a few hours of sleep after performing with the Tom Slick show band, and I still had to work eight hours a day, five days a week. The mornings at work always seemed to work better for me than the afternoons. After lunch I would often become sleepy.

One of our front lead-singers, Bill Durie, or as we called him "Hot Rod Bud," wrote lyrics in the 50s style and had the band put it into music. We all loved the song that was simply called "Rock And Roll Days" and we decided to take that song into the studio and record it. The band ended up recording Bill's song on one side of the single, and recording "Blue Moon" on the flip side. With a new single and a very successful band, Lenny wanted the band to be picked up with a local booking agency that would open more doors for us, because I know Lenny wanted the band to spread its wings and fly. My friend Ziggie and I were the only two married band members. We both knew that we were very limited on any travel plans the Tom Slick band might create.

A single 45rpm record of the Tom Slick oldies band

229

Lenny met with the A & R Booking Agency in Denver to see if they would be interested in taking us on as a new client. At first they were not interested, but Lenny invited them to one of our concerts to see us perform, and when a representative was sent to witness a performance, he invited us back to the A & R Booking Agency office where Lenny signed a contract that gave the Agency permission to advertise and book us. I referred some of the Canadian nightclubs I had performed at as a pop-singer to the A & R Booking Agency, not revealing to them the fact that I had performed at these clubs as Frankie Valens.

Ina Kay was now eight months pregnant with our daughter. What would I do if this booking agency booked the band on an extended concert tour? I began to kick myself because I had referred places in Canada that I knew booked entertainment. Would this A & R booking agency actually contact those nightclubs? I was thankful that the early bookings did not reflect any Canadian tour.

A & R booked us at a pig roast in McCook, Nebraska. They turned around and booked us at the Bunny's Lounge in Denver and the Colorado School of Mines in Golden. They contacted Tulagi's in Boulder and booked us for two week-ends in a row. The University of Colorado in Boulder heard about us and booked us for a one afternoon concert for their students, one concert being at the Nu Gnu in Vail, Colorado. One of our biggest concerts was at the Turn Of The Century dinner theatre in south Denver. Little did I know that later on I would soon be working in their accounting department. The concert dates were starting to keep the band busy almost every week-end.

With Ina Kay at home now, she wanted to help out financially by doing day-care in our home. I thought it was an excellent idea. She advertised in the local Thornton paper and was able to find parents who needed someone to watch their children during the week when they had to work. We had a fenced in backyard that was perfect to let children run and play, and the extra income was proving to be very helpful.

At Samsonite I received a frantic call from Ina Kay that I at first could not understand what she was trying to say. Then I realized that she was telling me that the police had come into our home and had handcuffed her and were going to take her to the police station for questioning, and she told me they wanted to take our kids along with them as well. I told Ina Kay not to let them do anything until I got there.

I tore out of that building at Samsonite like a flash of lightning. When I pulled up in front of our home, police cars were blocking the driveway. I ran into the house just when the police had handcuffed Ina Kay and were ready to take her away in the squad car. I kept asking questions as to why, and all I could get out of anyone was that one of the children had gotten burned with hot water, and they were accusing her of child abuse and neglect. I was in shock! When the police tried to take my kids with them I told them no, because I was their father and they were going to stay with me. The police knew by my attitude that I must have meant business so they agreed to let me keep our kids at home.

The parents of this little girl ended up suing us for over one million dollars in damage. Apparently the little girl was in our main bathroom and standing on the closed lid of the toilet, reaching over to the sink to try and turn on the water to wash her hands. She had tried to turn on the faucet but couldn't, but her brother had come in turned on the hot water and not the cold, ending up scalding his sister's hands. It was a total accident and nothing that could have been prevented unless Ina Kay had been with this little girl every second of every hour she was in her care.

After that incident with this lawsuit we were sitting ducks waiting for the next shoe to fall.

I knew we had to move from that home and try to get a new start somewhere else in the city of Denver. We put our home on the market and bought a home in Aurora, Colorado, a suburb of Denver, and our home in Thornton had doubled in value when I had partly finished our basement, adding two more bedrooms, a family room, and another bath.

To my chagrin Lenny informed the band members that A & R had booked a month's concert tour to Canada, thanking me for referring the contacts to A & R. I panicked! How could I possibly take off from Samsonite for a month! I also realized that my wife was eight months pregnant and could possibly give birth before I could even finish the tour. The band needed me badly because no one in the band could sing the high notes and harmony like me, and I had solo songs that only I could sing. I was so enjoying the band, but was I still trying to create another illusive dream? Could I finally be recognized as a talented pop-singer and eventually be signed onto a major record label, if not as a solo singer, then maybe as part of a band? Should I take the chance, knowing that nothing is set in concrete or even guaranteed in the music industry? Should I just turn my back on the one element in my life that really mattered, my love of music and entertaining? All these decisions weighed heavily on my heart.

Lenny sat the band down before one of our rehearsals and informed us that this concert tour to Canada would be a sacrifice we all would be making in order for the band to grow and to mature. Then Lenny focused his attention on both Ziggie and me, telling us that we two had more of a sacrifice to make since we were the only two married men in the group. Ziggy didn't hesitate. He told Lenny that he would give a two week notice at his job to go on this Canadian tour, and I had no choice but to either give notice at Samsonite or leave the band. I had a big decision to make. Ziggy had not discussed this issue with his wife first, he just made that all important decision on his own, but I wanted to have time to go home and discuss it with Ina Kay. Lenny guaranteed me that if my wife went into labor while we were on tour, the band would fly me back home, wherever they were playing.

Ina Kay's concern was over the fact that we would not have a guaranteed weekly income and no health insurance. She also knew that the potential of a much bigger paycheck from concert dates and record sales could bypass whatever salary I was willing to accept at Samsonite. I was so afraid to give any kind of a notice at Samsonite, but all I knew was that I had to leave Samsonite without any notice and go on the tour to Canada. I couldn't look back. I finally had to make a final decision to stay or to go, and I decided to go on tour with the band.

The last day at Samsonite proved to be a very trying day for me because I knew I would not be coming back. I just couldn't bring myself to tell anyone, let alone my boss. I kept asking myself if I had made the right decision, or was I going to regret this decision for the rest of my life! The indecisions in my mind probably looked like a jigsaw puzzle with a couple of pieces missing.

THIRTY THREE
A PREMATURE BLESSING

It was really tough for me to have to say goodbye to Ina Kay, Jeffrey and Mark, knowing that I wouldn't see them for over a month. Ina Kay was in her eighth month of pregnancy. Should I torture myself with guilt for having to leave her right now? Was this some kind of a selfish ambition that threw a shadow over my reasoning? What was I thinking? I knew it was too late to turn back.

When the guys came to our home in Thornton to pick me up, I took my metal chest that contained all my clothes and personal effects, out to the waiting van. My children didn't even know I was leaving. I just couldn't tell them for fear that it would just break my heart into a thousand pieces and I would be crying up a storm. As I went back into our home to kiss my wife and hug the kids, Jeffrey must have been downstairs. At least I didn't see him. Mark was walking through the kitchen on his way to our backyard, and just seeing Mark made my heart leap with sadness. I wanted to grab him and hug him until I couldn't hug him anymore, and I told Ina Kay that it was totally impossible for me to say anything to my boys.

Our concert tour started in Rapid City, South Dakota and then on to Spearfish. The next stop was in Bismarck, North Dakota. Our tour was taking me farther and farther away from my wife and children. I missed them so much during those first few days.

We crossed over into Canada in the wee hours of the morning, taking highway 40 north, and then in Saskatchewan, it became highway 47. Over the next few weeks we traveled to Estevan, and from there we drove on up to Saskatoon for a two week gig. Our last stop in Canada was Prince Albert, near the Prince Albert National Park.

On the way during the wee hours of the morning a deer ran in front of our van. It hit with such a thud that it threw me onto the floor from the back seat where I had been sleeping. The van's radiator had been hit and radiator fluid was running all over the highway. Back then we had no cell phones to call for help. All we could do was to try and coast downhill to the nearest town to get help. We could see the lights of a town downhill from us and not that far away. The mechanic had us back on the road again and heading to Prince Albert within a couple of hours.

In Prince Albert I knew I had laundry to do so I asked one of our road crew, Bob Rasmussen, to take me to a laundromat nearby. We had some free time during the day to tour the town or to sit back and relax, and I had laundry to do.

We found a laundromat building only a few blocks away from our motel, and as I was doing my laundry I noticed a police car pull up to Bob Rasmussen's van. When Bob saw the policeman, he left me in the building to go see why the policeman was standing next to the van. Evidently the policeman had noticed an open container of beer sitting on the dash of the van, and in Canada, it is a dry state in Saskatchewan and no one is allowed to have open containers of beer or liquor. No one is allowed to drink anywhere but in a bar or a restaurant. If you purchase any kind of beer or liquor, you have to drive straight home with it. You cannot stop anywhere after you've purchased beer. Bob had to appear before the chief of police and pay a huge fine for having an open container of beer on his dashboard.

We were into our third week of this tour when I received a late night call from Ina Kay, telling me that her water had broken. We both knew that she was not due for a few more weeks, so I ran to Lenny's room to tell him I had to leave. A couple of band members immediately got into one of our vans and drove me all the way back down to Saskatoon, where I caught a red-eye flight to Calgary, British Columbia. From there I had to wait for another red-eye flight out of Calgary that would take me straight into Denver, Colorado.

My waiting for flights at the airports, and my two airline flights took all night, and I arrived in Denver early the next day. I thought for sure that Ina Kay would have given birth by the time I got there. A friend picked me up at the Denver airport and drove me straight to the hospital.

She had not even given birth yet. She was not even due for delivery for a few weeks! The doctors were afraid that she could have a dry birth. If the baby was to be born now, it would be premature.

After another day her doctor wanted to induce labor, so I dressed in a protective garment with paper shoes and joined Ina Kay in the delivery room. I wanted to be there to witness our baby's birth.

Heather Ann Piper was born on January 27, 1977. Although I don't remember much about the actual birth itself because of the tears in my eyes, I wanted to dance for joy. Out of the corner of my wet eyes I saw the doctor holding up a small baby with flailing arms and legs, crying at the top of her lungs. They quickly rushed her off to be placed in an incubator, and the next time either one of us could see Heather was in the incubator. I walked up to that incubator and saw my little bundle of joy and knew that I would love her for the rest of my life. She was such a premature blessing.

I was not able to stay long after the birth of our Heather, because I had to get back and join the band at the tail end of their concert tour. Having to leave that hospital just ripped my heart out, but I had made a commitment to do the tour with the band. I flew out of Denver to Rapid City, South Dakota and joined up with my band again.

Our daughter Heather was still in intensive care at the hospital in Denver. The first time I could visit her at the hospital was when I had finished my tour. I was in shock at several shaved parts of Heather's scalp, and the wires running here and there. As we both stood by that incubator, Heather was really starting to squirm a little. She ended up turning herself over onto her back. Our daughter was such a strong little baby and seemed so determined to get out of that incubator, and seeing her struggle only made me want to love her and protect her more than I already did.

When Heather was finally released from the hospital she still had those shaved areas of her scalp that neither one of us was pleased about, so we immediately went out and bought several bonnets for our little girl, and she became our 'bonnet baby.'

I had once read in a digest that babies actually can hear their parents and siblings voices while still in their mother's womb, and they can often react to a familiar voice. I am convinced that when Heather did not hear her father's familiar voice for a period of time, she reacted and wanted to get out of that womb and be with her dad. When I reappeared at the hospital after Ina Kay's water had broken, Heather started to hear that familiar voice again and must have relaxed in her mother's womb. At that time I felt she was content to wait until nature took its course, so it was not until a few days later that the doctor had to induce labor. By all standards, when Ina Kay's water broke, she should have given birth to Heather within a few hours, but it had been much longer than that. No one will ever convince me that this is not what happened. To this day, there has been such a special bonding between my daughter Heather and me.

THIRTY FOUR
MAYDAY! MAYDAY!

Our booking agency informed us that they had booked our band for an extended eastern tour, which would take us all the way to Pennsylvania and back. I had a feeling that Lenny probably wanted to show off his new band to his former band members. I did not want to go, because I wanted to spend more precious time with my family and our new born baby daughter. I knew that I had made a huge mistake by quitting my full-time job at Samsonite and I needed to correct the mistake by taking a firm stand. I also knew that I had to either quit the one thing that my heart so loved and to take a full-time job, or stay with the band, and possibly lose my family from having to spend so much time away on tour. My decisions were torn at the seams and becoming less than clear in my mind of what was the right thing to do.

If I were to accompany the band on the eastern tour, one of the concert dates booked was in Wilkes Barre, Pennsylvania. Wilkes Barre was not far from New Jersey where I knew my two oldest children lived with their mother, Joyce. Could I possibly inform them that I was going to be in concert just an hour away from them? I had a phone number for their mother, but I knew that if I tried to call her, she might tell me again that there was no one there that wanted to talk with me, since over the years I had tried so many times to contact my children, but I kept getting the same response.

Somehow I just couldn't make the decision to quit the band. My love of music was so strong. I knew in my spirit that if I gave up the band, I may never have such an opportunity again to fulfill my greatest ambition of becoming an international recording artist. I had already turned my back on my first opportunity of stardom when I gave up my stage name of Frankie Valens and my band in New Jersey. It was just an unfortunate incident that had occurred with my agent that helped me make the decision to quit. That choice to quit however would forever be the catalyst that was constantly trying to create war in my mind, and trying to arrest my subconscious for making wrong decisions.

The start of our eastern tour was fast approaching. I had decided to travel with Tom Slick but drive my own car and car-pool with the band's vans. Ina Kay and I discussed that possibility and we both agreed that it was a very good decision just in case I changed my mind to tour and wanted to come back home. I knew that Lenny did not like the idea that I would be separated from the rest of the band. When Lenny or any band member had an issue with another band member, or simply wanted to resolve an issue, he would call a meeting and the whole problem would be discussed with everyone involved. I had never been called onto the carpet or reprimanded before, and felt I had never given them any reason to, because I had become a model band member, although I also knew it could happen because Lenny hadn't agreed to my driving my own car on this tour.

The first concert date for our eastern tour started at the University of Colorado in Boulder. Ina Kay decided she wanted to support me by driving up to the university, and followed me as I drove our Pinto station wagon, then after the concert she would drive on home and I would join the band members and drive behind them for the rest of the tour.

During our 50's concert at the university it became apparent that Lenny had not assigned me any solos to sing. All I did was participate in the choreography and sing harmony when someone else sang a solo. He seemed very cold to me that whole evening, avoiding me like the plague.

After our performance, the band retired to the dressing room area to change clothes and, as I figured what might happen, Lenny called a meeting to order. At first I wasn't sure for whom the meeting was for, or what the meeting was about, but a little uneasy voice in the back of my head kept whispering to me, telling me that something was amiss and that this meeting was going to be about me. I had already told that little uneasy voice of mine that if this meeting started pointing a finger at me, I wanted no part of it and I would quit.

All the meetings in the past with Lenny and his band members meant that someone was going to be reprimanded, and the whole issue would be brought out in the open for the whole world to witness. The whole sordid, trumped-up charges would be dissected and looked over like a fine tooth comb and with a very powerful microscope. Whatever the charges were, this confrontation would need to be short-lived if it was about me because I knew I would walk.

The little uneasy voice in the back of my head was right. Lenny told the whole group that we all needed to discuss a few problems that had been festering with some of the guys in the group over Frankie's actions. He said the air needed to be cleared so we could continue on the concert tour. I sat there in a numb state, not being able to feel anything but shock and then remorse for what I knew my decision had to be, and I told Lenny to stop right there. There would not be any kind of a discussion about me or my actions because I quit! I grabbed the metal locker that held all my clothes and personal effects, and I walked out the back door of the university, never to sing with the Tom Slick band again. My first thought was "Mayday, Mayday, I'm in trouble here," but that was absurd! "Mayday" was Lenny's last name. How ironic.

I waited next to my Pinto station wagon for what seemed like an eternity, waiting for Ina Kay to come from the auditorium where she had been sitting watching the concert. I was antsy and wanted to get as far away from this band as fast as I could. When she saw me standing next to our car, she wanted to give me a hug and tell me goodbye, but I informed her that I had just quit the band, and she stood there in shock. At first I don't think she truly understood the finality of it all and that I had actually quit, so I told her to follow me home and we would discuss it there.

As I was driving back home I felt such anger and frustration building up over the whole situation that had just occurred, and I began to realize that the main reason for Lenny wanting to confront me was the fact that he wasn't happy with the idea that I wanted to drive myself. He was no longer in charge. I had bucked the system by attempting to establish my own identity, and in doing so, I was in charge, not Lenny. He was the driving force that made the Tom Slick group tick, and without him I'm sure the band would cease to exist. I found out later that the band fell apart on the castern tour and all the band members split.

For about three weeks after leaving the group, I cried myself to sleep every night, feeling sorry for myself. I knew I had to eventually come to grips with life and reality and try to place all the shattered puzzle pieces of my broken dreams back together again. I truly thought that I had been living in some kind of an illusive made-up fantasy world that really did not exist, except in my dreams, but I was enjoying spending more time with my children that I hadn't had time to do before.

I took a job working in downtown Denver in the accounts payable department at the M. L. Foss Company, working in the bustling heartbeat of the metropolis of Denver, exciting as it was. The thoughts I had of ever singing again were gradually being pushed back into the hidden recesses of my mind, and I decided to let life take me to wherever it would let me go.

THIRTY FIVE
ADOPTION RUMORS

We were still waiting for the next shoe to drop over the million dollar lawsuit from the family who sued us over their daughter getting hurt while in the care of Ina Kay at her Day Care Center in our home, knowing we could lose everything with one stroke of a pen. The police who had come to our home originally told us that they had been given conflicting stories from Ina Kay as to what really happened, which is why they had handcuffed her and taken her in for questioning.

The real story of what really happened came to light when Ina Kay was able to talk with our attorney. She told him that she was taking care of both this little girl and also her older brother, and when she had made lunch for the kids, the little girl had run into the main bathroom to wash her hands. To reach the sink she had to stand on top of the stool lid and lean over onto the edge of the sink, but she still couldn't turn on the water so her brother had come in and turned it on. He had accidentally turned on the hot water instead of the cold. Without him knowing or having time to understand what he had just done, his sister leaned over and placed both of her hands under that hot scalding water. Ina Kay heard the little girl scream and came running, so when she called for help, the authorities suspected child abuse and had to report it as such.

We had to get a fresh start by moving as far away from Thornton. We had read where there was a new housing development in Aurora, Colorado on the east side of the city of Denver, so we took a drive over to the real estate office in Aurora and signed a contract on a new construction, with the contingency of our home selling in Thornton.

Our home in Thornton sold quickly. The value of our home had doubled in value because I had finished the basement, and we were able to put a minimum down-payment on the home in Aurora, and still have funds to pay cash for a new Monte Carlo. On closing day we were thrilled to be living in a brand-new home and driving a brand-new car.

Our new home was a bi-level home that had a two car garage, two and a half baths, three bedrooms, and a formal dining room. The lower level had a half bath and an open family room with a fireplace, and within the first year I closed in part of the family room to make a separate bedroom for Jeffrey. I fenced in the back yard and put trees and bushes in the front yard and back yard with river rock around our sidewalk and driveway.

At M. L. Foss I was growing weary of constantly having to beg for raises. When the company hired me in their accounts payable division I was hoping to move up to full accountant. This company could only afford one accountant and he was my boss, and this was turning out to be another dead-end job. I applied for a job at the main office of AT & T in downtown Denver and was hired, but decided I couldn't take the job because it was minimum wage.

After reading the want ads in our local newspaper, I found a position for an assistant accountant needed at the Turn Of The Century dinner theatre in Denver, so I filled out an application there and was called in to do double-entry bookkeeping. Finally I was able to use some of the knowledge I had gained with my accounting degree. Looking back I can still remember when I had sung with the Tom Slick group at this very theatre, and little did I know at that time that I would be coming back and working in their accounting department. What a small world!

We started attending a local church where we both started singing in the choir, but it was hard for me to let loose and feel comfortable about singing again. I was still reeling from the bad experiences that continually kept invading my memory banks, telling me not to get too involved again or I could get hurt. My love of music was still there, just suppressed.

We both loved our home and were starting to settle into the neighborhood, but trouble started brewing when our oldest son Jeffrey would disobey us by continually inviting friends in after school when we told him not to. We both worked and couldn't be home right at 3pm every day to be there when the kids came home from school, and I was at wits end as to how to handle it. I have always believed in 'spare the rod, spoil the child,' but I did not like the idea of spanking my kids. They just knew that when I told them not to do something, they obeyed. Not Jeffrey. It just seemed like he was always trying to push all the boundaries, especially with me.

Somehow I just couldn't put my finger on why we were starting to have so much trouble with Jeff, and the troubles were starting to affect our marriage. I hated the many times I had to always be on Jeff's case about something. The truth finally came out. We found out that Ina Kay had mentioned to one of our neighbor ladies that I was not Jeff's real dad. I had adopted him. We didn't want to tell Jeff yet, because he was only 10 years old and we felt that he was too young to understand why

I wasn't his biological dad We wanted to wait to tell him until he was old enough to know and understand all the reasons why. I knew that I had to sit Jeff down someday and tell him all about the facts of life, then maybe he would fully understand why I chose him to be my son. Our father–son relationship was never the same after that.

Having trouble with Jeff seemed to always keep Ina Kay and me at odds with each other. There were times when I had wished her parents and sister had won when they had tried to stop my adopting Jeff. I knew they wanted him and would do anything to get him away from his own mother and me, and I told Ina Kay to reconsider sending Jeff out to her family, but she never would. The spikes just kept digging deeper and deeper with each new problem with him. I was at wits end. There were times when I just wanted to walk away from Ina Kay and leave her to the problems that were being created by our oldest son. How could I walk away now? We had our other children to consider.

Adopting a child is not always easy and sometimes can cause more problems in the long run. I just didn't want Jeff to be going to school using a last name that wasn't mine, which is why I adopted him by giving him a middle name that was part of my birth name so he would never forget who his father was.

THIRTY SIX

SHOWSTOPPER

At the 'Turn Of The Century' nightclub I was a salaried employee, and I loved going to work. Every day we employees were allowed to eat at the lunch buffet in the restaurant area, and on a couple of occasions I was able to meet some of the celebrity guests when they came early to have lunch or to have a drink at the bar. I met the famous group "The Lettermen" when they sat to have coffee before their show began, and when Ricky Nelson appeared, I was able to get free tickets to his performance. I took Ina Kay to see Tony Bennett perform. This seemed like the perfect job.

It wasn't until my boss started wanting me to work longer hours that I started to become concerned. Was he taking advantage of me? I noticed that he had started turning more responsibilities over to me, including interviewing and hiring new personnel and allowing only myself or him to handle all the deposits and cash. He also knew I had the bookkeeping knowledge to work out any double-entry problems that came up. He felt confident enough to go on vacation and the accounting department would run smoothly, because I was a dedicated employee, although I was being overworked. I realized that I had to get out of there.

For my next job I decided to go to a head-hunter, hoping to be hired into a wonderful company with plenty of benefits. Wrong! The first interview they sent me on was the Mid-Continent Company, located near the old airport in Denver. With a short interview they hired me to work accounts receivable in their accounting department. After I accepted this job I wondered why I took the job, because they had very few benefits and very few paid holidays.

The controller, David, was my new boss, who was in charge of the accounting department. After a few weeks he noticed how well I had handled the accounts receivable and turned over all the reconciling of the bank statements to me.

When I started reconciling bank statements I noticed that some of the physical printed checks were missing. How does one misplace a cashed check that was written by the owner of Mid-Continent, or a check that our company received? I had no choice but to list those checks as still outstanding. When I handed the bank reconciliation in to David, showing that I couldn't find some of the actual checks, his response was that he didn't seem concerned that some checks were missing. I knew enough about accounting to know that if a check is missing you ask the bank for a duplicate copy because that would show if that check actually was cashed or if it was missing. I was concerned but knew that if it didn't matter to my boss, who was a certified accountant, then I needed to leave the worrying up to him.

Somehow I found myself confiding in David that I had been a singer back in New Jersey several years ago. When I told him I was the Frankie Valens, he got excited. David had been looking for a venue to support financially, as a tax write-off, and when he heard that I had been an entertainer, he told me he wanted to offer to fund all the costs, including purchasing a complete sound system. He wanted to provide all the advertising materials and purchase a van for the band to carry the equipment in.

I just wasn't sure I wanted to try and recapture the stolen dreams I had of ever recording with a major record label and becoming a household name. I knew that if I were to pursue another musical venture, I would be exposing my past to my wife and the whole world. Was I ready for this to happen again? How would I explain the main reasons why I left the music scene and couldn't use the Frankie Valens name because it belonged to Sunburst Records? Was I able to use that stage name again? Could I legally?

Somehow I knew that David had to have been very knowledgeable about investments, and the potential of what a successful band could generate in income, and he stated to me that he wanted to eventually quit working full-time and concentrate totally on managing the band. Maybe my dream of becoming a pop star could eventually come to fruition! Was there still hope? David started unveiling to me all the possibilities that could happen if I would just take his advice and turn everything over to him for guidance, and for me, this seemed like a dream come true.

David wanted me to register with a local modeling agency and have a portfolio made. He said movie producers, booking agents and record producers go through modeling agencies to cast people for a new film or for TV advertising spots, maybe even modeling clothes.

Within a week the modeling agency called me to let me know they had cast me as an extra in an upcoming movie called "Ice Castles," starring Robby Benson. After I finished that filming, the agency called me again to tell me that they had cast me as an extra in the movie "Every Which Way But Loose," starring Clint Eastwood.

David wanted me to start advertising for band members, and the first response I received was a husband and wife team, Al and Cindy Knipe. Al played drums and had been with Reed Williams and the Fantasy Band, and his wife Cindy had sung with the O'Solo Mio singers. John Thornburg became my bass player, and Stephen Graham, who had recently moved from Chicago, became my lead-guitarist. Joe Mueller, an older man, came in as my keyboardist, and later added music to lyrics I had written that I titled "Lord Ivy." The last person to join my band was Bob Rebholz, who played a mean alto sax and flute. David wanted to pay each band member a fee for coming to the rehearsals, and whereas I had not personally ever heard of being paid to practice, but I thought it was an excellent idea. We decided the best place to practice was in our double-car garage in Aurora.

At the beginning my new band had no official name. David informed me that it was up to me what I wanted to call my band. I told him my dream was to have props that depicted an old museum, and I wanted artificial marble columns alongside the stage with ivy on them, maybe even a styrofoam statue standing in the background rounding out the theme. Even though I wanted the band to be called the "Ivy Museum," we eventually became the "Showstopper" band.

The Ivy Museum rock group

David and I flew to southern California and visited the main office of Carvin, manufacturers of sound equipment, where he purchased a complete sound system which included three stage monitors. While in southern California, we visited a company that produced mannequins, because we were looking for a statue for the band. After we had been shopping for the band we were heading to the airport to fly back home and David mentioned to me that we both needed to take a break and maybe fly to Mexico for a few day's rest. I told David that I had always wanted to go to Acapulco, so when we arrived at the Las Angeles airport, David booked us two flights to Acapulco, Mexico.

Several weeks before he and I had flown to Mexico, I had had a dream about being in Mexico. I saw myself somewhere in Mexico, below Mexico City. I could see a map of the area, as if I were looking at the terrain from somewhere in the sky. Next, I was shopping at a clothing store and found slacks hanging on a wall on display. I found a pair I wanted to buy, but when I looked at the price tag on a pair of the slacks it showed a price of $1,040. I immediately was in shock and walked away. Then I found myself walking down a huge flight of concrete stairs that was outdoors and many people were around me walking in the same direction, and ahead of me was David. He told me not to let a stranger hold my camera. Then when I came to the bottom of the stairs I found myself looking over a concrete wall, down into a narrow wet area where I saw crabs crawling, and when I immediately looked up and ahead of me someone was jumping off a cliff into deep water.

Was my dream a forewarning? Everything I had dreamt had come to fruition. We did fly to Acapulco, which is located southwest of Mexico City, and David and I did go shopping in a clothing store and I had walked up to slacks on display and yes, one pair of slacks showed a price of 1,040, but the price was in pesos, not American dollars. We took a tour of Acapulco and drove over to the famous cliff diver's tourist area and parked our rented car. A tour bus had just pulled up as we were starting to walk down a long concrete flight of stairs, and David was ahead of me as were many of the tourists who were also heading in the same direction. I stopped and looked ahead of us and I could see the cliff where the divers did their show of jumping off into the rushing water below, and I wanted to take a picture of it. My hands were so full of brochures and camera equipment that I couldn't get into my camera case to retrieve the camera to take a photo. Just about that time a local Mexican guy approached me and told me he would be happy to hold my camera so I could lay the brochures down and take a picture, but David saw the exchange going on and he came over and grabbed the camera out of the guy's hands. David warned me that this sort of exchange goes on all the time and the guys will run off with your valuables.

In my dream we proceeded walking down the concrete stairs to the bottom and right in front of us was a stone wall surrounding the concrete landing where everyone would stand and watch the cliff divers. When I looked over that wall, I saw crabs crawling in the narrow passageway and on the stone wall. Was my dream really a vision of what was about to happen, and also a warning?

While in Mexico I did purchase a carved out mask made entirely out of tree bark as a souvenir. I had no idea at the time that some items from foreign countries can often bring with them some kind of a spirit that can cause havoc in your life. I still feel to this day that that one carved mask from Mexico sent a guy to prison, caused a bankruptcy, lost a home to foreclosure, had a car repossessed, helped a couple divorce, and splintered a family that would never mend again.

After we arrived back in Denver, David admitted to me that he had become a little over-zealous with his spending with the traveling and major purchases for the band, and although he had adequate funds, most were tied up in investments. We still needed a utility van to carry the band's equipment.

Somehow David made plans, unbeknownst to me, to borrow money against my new Monte Carlo to purchase a utility van for the band. Ina and I had paid cash for the new Monte Carlo when we sold our home in Thornton, but it wasn't long before a white utility van was parked in our driveway. I did not know at the time that a loan had been placed on my new car. How he was able to accomplish such a loan I do not know to this day.

David booked the band into a couple of local nightclubs and a country club in the Denver area, and the concerts were very successful and well received. He told us that the next step would be to record an album, which would give the band credibility and possibly spawn singles. He immediately contacted his friend, Larry Prater, who owned Jetisson Records in Denver. Jetisson Records was created by Larry to help new artists record music by pre-selling their albums, which would help pay for their studio time. Larry had been the keyboardist for the famous "Cascades." "http://www.youtube.com/watch?v=bQstQST1GiM" www.youtube.com/watch?v=bQstQST1GiM who's biggest hit was "Rhythm Of The Rain."

In the recording studio at Jetisson Records, Larry Prater sat both David and me down in his office to discuss what music we wanted to include on my album. Larry told me that since I was the lead-singer and star of my own band, my voice needed to be included in every song on the album.

My first recording choice was to re-record my single "This Magic Moment." When Larry heard that I had already made it into a single in New Jersey, he told me that if we were to re-record that same song, we should reggae it up. Other songs I wanted to include were, "I've Got This Feeling," "Donna," "Cool Magic," and "Monday, Monday." My lead-guitarist had written a song called "I Just Want To Play For You" and I asked him to record and sing lead to his own song. I also asked Stephen to also record "Betty Lou," which I knew no one in the band could sing that song like he could.

Cindy talked me into recording "Smoke Gets In Your Eyes" because I had been performing this song in each of our concerts and it had become one of her favorite songs. I wasn't sure I wanted to record that song again because there was no way for me to change the style in which I had sung it on my first recording in New Jersey. I still needed to find more songs for the album.

At home I was thumbing through some of my old 78 rpm vinyl records and came across a song titled "A Cup Of Coffee, A Sandwich, And You," sung in the old megaphone style. It was a male and female duet which I knew Cindy and I could record together, so we included that old song, recorded originally in the 1920s on the album. Cindy wanted to record one of her favorite songs, "I've Got The Music In Me," and I knew she had the voice for it and the recording came out great. When I asked her to sing "Stupid Cupid," she told me she really didn't like the song but would record it for me. If you listen to the LP recording, my voice can be heard throughout the whole album, because if I wasn't singing lead, I was singing back-up vocals.

At the studio we met another group that was recording all their own original compositions. The group was the D. L. Velarde Band, a husband

and wife team recording with band members who were friends of their family. When they heard my vocals they asked me if I would sing a first tenor harmony on a couple of their songs. Their album was called "The Other Side Of Yesterday," and they included my name on their album credits as background vocalist.

After my band finished recording the album, we decided to take a break from the many hours and days we had spent in the studio. David wanted to throw an album release party that would help advertise not only the band, but give recognition to the new album as well. David had every intention for this to be the comeback album that would launch Frankie Valens back onto the scene.

David found a local restaurant that agreed to host the party and wanted to play the record for all his customers as well. Many of our friends came to the party, including some of the choir members from my church who had sung back-up vocals on my "Lord Ivy" song. Amongst the crowd was Phyllis, who knew some of the choir members. She told me later that my stage name of Frankie Valens had never been mentioned at the album release party. David had only mentioned the release of the Showstopper album. She didn't realize that I was indeed Frankie Valens.

If you listen to the "Showstopper" album, the first three songs are recorded almost to perfection, but after that, the quality of the music goes downhill quickly. It's because the owner of the record company, Larry Prator fired his recording studio engineer to give his own son a job at this record company. Larry's son did not have a good ear when it came to music and he let all the voices go off-pitch and didn't balance the vocals out properly with the music, which is why the album went nowhere. It was awful! I am proud of the first three songs, but I cringe when I hear the rest of the album. My comeback album was a flop. Because the album didn't make it, the band didn't make it. We had just hired a new booking agency and he had changed our name to "Showstopper" because we had turned into a show-band, but the album killed us.

THIRTY SEVEN
OFF TO JAIL

Larry Prator asked me if I wanted to work at Jetisson Records as one of their public relations representatives when my band wasn't performing. This was a dream come true for me!

Both David and I decided to quit our jobs at Mid-Continent to help focus our full attention on the future of the band and the record company. I gave my notice first, and then David gave his notice. With David quitting his job, this gave the owners of Mid-Continent Refrigerator time to discover there were missing documents and missing checks that had been in his possession.

I had already started working at Jetisson Records and had been on my new job only a few days when I received a disturbing phone call from the police. They were asking me questions about David, which I readily answered. Apparently the owners of Mid-Continent had been watching David for months before he quit, but they couldn't pin anything on him until they were able to go through his locked desk drawers after his departure. The company said they had proof that David had been embezzling from their company and wanted him brought in for questioning. He was arrested and placed in the county jail.

I just could not believe that David was capable of embezzling. They had to be wrong. Was this some kind of a colossal joke? When I awoke one morning to discover my Monte Carlo missing out of our driveway, I still couldn't believe it. When I started to call the police that our car had been stolen, Ina Kay informed me that the car had probably been repossessed. My Monte Carlo was missing, the white van was missing, and David was in jail. What more could happen?

David was allowed to make one phone call and he called me. He asked me if we would place a lien on our home so his bond would be paid and he could go free. I still could not believe that he was guilty so I went down and paid his bond through placing that lien on our home. When David was released from jail he came to our home and told me he had to sell the sound system to help pay his attorney fees. I knew that without the sound system, I had no band, so my band disbanded and I was again a singer with no future and no hope. I had been chasing an illusive dream again and never wanted to repeat the same mistake. I decided to start my own band.

I know my wife tolerated the times I spent with my music and the bands. I was so grateful she never said much, but there were times when she would turn off all the electricity in our home so the band would have to quit practicing and go home. I know she often would make deliberate calls to band member's families with distorted and confusing information, and I always felt that she was placing facetious ads in local papers advertising that the band was replacing some of its band members. If Ina Kay and I had a huge disagreement, she would call my parents and they would come over immediately, which made me even more upset because I didn't want my parents involved in our family dispute. If I was so unhappy with a situation and wanted to leave, she would threaten me with contacting my first wife. Why, I don't know. I do know I had learned to love Ina Kay over the years and we had become the best of friends. She was a hard worker and a wonderful mother of our three children, but I knew we were growing further and further apart. When she made the heart-wrenching statement to me that she had hoped that this music hobby of mine was over and we could get back to a normal way of life, I felt she had totally ripped out my heart and had stomped on it. How could she believe that this was nothing but a hobby for me? Her words were like a sharp jagged knife in my side that was being twisted to create more pain. Maybe I had been selfish over the years when I had such a desire to express myself musically, but this definitely was not a hobby. I just stood there in disbelief and could do nothing but turn around and walk away. I know that if she truly knew how much she had damaged our relationship with that statement, she would have not said it. I know she loved me and was trying so hard to make it all work out, but a wedge had been placed in my heart and it would take time to heal.

In our marriage it came to the point that if we had a huge disagreement, I would leave the house and not come back for hours. Soon the hours turned into overnight and then I found myself moving out of our home altogether. Was it the will of God for me to leave? No! Was I being deceived by the Devil? Yes! When I left my wife I would always feel guilty and start to realize that I did love her and I missed my children. I knew they would suffer if I wasn't around. What would my oldest son Jeffrey do? I wouldn't be there to enforce restrictions on him. I had no trouble with Mark and Heather minding us when they were told no, but would Jeffrey go off the deep end and start drinking, taking drugs and staying out late? I knew in my spirit that he was capable of doing a whole lot of mischief that I didn't want to even know about. Why couldn't Jeffrey see that I loved him as my own son? Why was he so content on being self-destructive and wanting to push all the wrong buttons with me? His rebellion was almost more than I could handle at times.

THIRTY EIGHT
A GIFTED LADY

The sorrow I felt for unwittingly creating my own solitude by leaving my family made me want to wallow in my own self-pity at times, giving me some kind of a false sense of needing reassurance that I had done the right thing. Why was I purposely trying to create drama in my life? I could very well have stayed in my marriage and pray that the Lord would give me the ability to set my musical interests aside as a non-important factor in my life, or go full throttle and throw all abandon to the wind and pursue the most Important factor in my life, music! Why couldn't I just have it all? Why was it so hard for me to find a mate that shared the same interests!

Even though I was attending a church, I felt very little spiritual guidance coming from the pulpit or from the friends I had made at church. I often witnessed how some people were treated when rumors started flying around about them. If anyone in the congregation had a personal problem, that person might be ostracized and cast out in the cold, naked and bruised. Instead of having an understanding of what that person might be going through and showing a little support, the people in the congregation seemed to want to stab them in the back. I learned early on that if I created drama or rocked the boat, I too would be the next target for their fodder. Were all churches like this, or was this church an exception?

I loved singing in the church choir and singing a solo when asked. The choir director asked me to sing in her ensemble called "Heaven Bound." We were able to guest appear in many local churches in the Aurora, Colorado area. I loved singing in her ensemble. I then started a teen ensemble and I called them The Inspirations. The choir director informed the choir during one of our choir rehearsals that she had invited a pianist, Phyllis, to play for the choir and assist her in directing the choir. We were all very apprehensive about any changes, but wanted to welcome a new chance to be a part of singing new arrangements.

Phyllis started the following Sunday and played piano for the church and for the choir. It almost seemed like it was love at first sight when I saw her for the first time. Now I realize that it only takes about a fifth of a second to fall in love, at least according to Dr. Mercola. He says that when you fall in love, 12 areas of your brain work together to release euphoria-inducing chemicals. This just could not have been love because I was already spoken for, but my thoughts just seemed to keep washing up onto her shores.

I started realizing how gifted and talented this lady was. I noticed how well she conducted herself when she played piano for the choir and when she played special piano pieces. In a couple of weeks the choir director asked me if I would sing a solo. I turned around and asked Phyllis if she would sing a duet with me. She told me that she hadn't done much singing but would gladly sing with me. I decided to sing the song "Pieces" because I had the musical tracks for it, so we rehearsed the song a couple of times, and then presented it that following Sunday. The duet we performed helped start a musical and personal friendship that would change the course and destiny of my life and our lives.

After a few weeks, our choir director was showing signs of her insecurities when she started creating rumors about Phyllis, telling some of her friends that she felt Phyllis was trying to take over the whole music department. Most of the choir sensed that our director was just feeling a little threatened by the incredible talent the new pianist had, but she followed up by not showing up at some of the choir rehearsals and Phyllis would have no alternative but to step in and help direct the choir and play the piano as well. The games had begun.

Jealousy had revealed its ugly head and the choir director eventually stepped down. Phyllis had no choice but to assume all the responsibilities of the music department. I know now that the stepping down of the choir director was just a temporary solution for what she was planning to do later. All she needed was a reason.

More rumors started surfacing after I had gone to the church to help prepare the building for Sunday morning's services, and Phyllis had come to the church about two hours later to make copies of the choir's special hymn. I was in the church office and was just about to leave, and she was somewhere in the sanctuary, I assume, at the time the church secretary dropped in to make copies of the bulletin handouts, but I left shortly after she arrived. The church secretary assumed the worst since Phyllis and I were both at the church at the same time, even though we were in totally different parts of the building. She started new fodder for the old choir director to have, and new ammunition to shoot at not only Phyllis, but now me. I had had enough of this childish, back-stabbing group who called themselves 'Christians,' and I walked away. If I had had a closer walk with the Lord at the time, I would have known to instinctively to go to Him in prayer, asking for direction. It just seemed to me at the time that the old choir director had won.

For about three or four weeks I did not know what had happened to Phyllis, whether she was still at the church or if she too had quit. I had taken a position at a concrete pumping firm in southwest Denver as assistant controller and lost touch with most of my friends. I had lost a lot of weight because I was separated from my family and missed many meals, and since I didn't know how to cook for myself, if I didn't eat out, I didn't eat at all. Was I the cause of the problems that Phyllis was now facing?

I decided to contact some mutual friends, Gil and Barbara Hutchens, who were friends of Phyllis, who also knew me. I was curious to know if Phyllis had also quit the church. Barbara was very helpful and told me that Phyllis had indeed quit the church and had been working with her Avon business out of her home, and working a temporary job in downtown Denver. I found myself wanting to contact her.

My new boss at the concrete pumping firm who was also the controller, told me about a church he and his wife were attending in Arvada, and invited me to join them for one of their Sunday morning services. I met up with them at the church that following Sunday and sat with them through the services. I could feel the spirit and the excitement that was being generated, not only from the platform, but from the congregation. The experience was sending my spirit into hyper drive. I knew something was different and I could certainly feel the spirit of the Lord there. This church was far from being dead and lifeless, it had spirit. Dare I trust myself to let go and let God? With this newfound experience I was ready to turn my life over to the Lord.

After much thought I decided that I wanted to contact Phyllis because I wanted to tell her about the church in Arvada that was full of spirit. When I reached her by phone and told her about the church, she said she'd try and come on Sunday.

All week long I felt myself becoming anxious for Sunday to roll around so I could experience that overwhelming feeling of the Lord's presence at that church. When Sunday came, I drove to the church and couldn't wait to park and enter into the sanctuary, and there were always crowds of people there all wanting to experience what I had only experienced once.

When I arrived in the sanctuary the orchestra and praise team had already started so I quickly grabbed a seat towards the back of the sanctuary. The people were standing with their hands in the air praising and worshipping. I felt a little uncomfortable because I had never held my hands in the air. During the greeting time the pastor told the people to greet one another in brotherly love, and a guy came up to me and gave me a big bear hug. And then more people came by and gave me a hug. Wow! Was this what Heaven was like?

As we all sat down and the announcements were being read, I happened to glance to my right and noticed Phyllis, sitting way over on the far side of the sanctuary. With all these people sitting all around, normally there would be no way for me to even see her, but it sure looked like a path had been made right through all those hundreds of people and hundreds of pews, for me to see Phyllis sitting there. We made contact after the services and decided to have lunch together, ending up spending the whole afternoon in Arvada at their city park. We wanted to wait around town and attend the church's evening services.

After attending the church for a while I met four guys who were attending the church's bible college and they were renting a house together there in Arvada, so I told them I was looking for a place to live and they invited me to move in with them. Driving home from church every Sunday from Arvada to Aurora was getting old, and my living in Arvada would save me from having to make that long drive to Aurora every Sunday. Phyllis and I often went to church together and I'd drive her back home to Aurora.

After two years and my divorce had finalized I continued to live with my four male friends in Arvada. I had decided to take a few college courses at the bible college where the guys were attending, and started losing interest in chasing Phyllis. I was starting to enjoy my new found freedom and wanting to get on with my life.

THIRTY NINE
A PASTOR WAS ARRESTED

I stopped calling Phyllis and decided to concentrate on spending more time with my studies and forget about all the musical interests I had had, knowing that it would be hard for me to try and recapture something that might not have happened anyway. I had just sat down at the dining room table in the house that five of us guy rented to grab a bite to eat when the phone rang. It was Phyllis. We hadn't talked for several days so I was surprised to hear from her. She first asked me if I was sitting down, and I told her no, I had had to get up to answer the phone. She told me to go sit back down. I did. The next thing I heard was Phyllis asking me to marry her. What? She told me that she felt I was starting to slip away and she was afraid I would eventually, so I quickly accepted her proposal and a few days later we set our wedding date for August 15th. How could I get married? I had just been laid off my job at the concrete pumping company.

Because we wanted to get married so soon, our own pastor of our church would not marry us unless we accepted counseling first. We both felt we had already been around a few corners and had already been there and done that, and decided to find another pastor that would marry us. A pastor of some friends of ours at a church near the old Denver airport said he would marry us, and our friends Gil and Barbara offered to stand up for us as witnesses.

When Phyllis and I met with the pastor at his church to map out our wedding plans, that awful feeling came over me that there was something about this pastor that I just couldn't put my finger on, but I knew that there was something not right about him. He led us on a tour through the church and showed us the sanctuary. But he also told us that many couples just wanted to get married on the church's well-manicured lawn

Frankie and Phyllis Valens' wedding day in August 1985 with their friends Gil and Barbara Hutchens

with the beautiful evergreens. We both agreed and made our plans to get married in that gorgeous setting. The pastor went on to tell us that since the church was so close to the airport, a plane could fly over, and if it did, he would have to wait for it to pass over before he could resume the ceremony.

On the way to the church to get married, we both forgot to bring the marriage license and we had to turn around and go back to get it. When we did arrive at the church we stood in the green grass on the front lawn of the church, along with our witnesses, Gil and Barbara, with the beautiful evergreens surrounding us, while the pastor started the wedding vows. Sure enough, a plane flew over during our short, 10-minute ceremony and the pastor had to stop the wedding vows until the plane was gone.

My intuition was right about the pastor. Less than a year later, we saw a news bulletin on TV about a pastor that had been arrested for pedophilia. That was the same pastor that had married us! The church where he was pastoring had a Christian school and a Day Care Center that apparently was too tempting for him. One day that pastor has to stand before our Almighty God and account for what he had done to innocent children. I would not want to be in his shoes.

Phyllis was renting a small home in Aurora and we decided to live there until we could find another home, hopefully nearer to our church in Arvada. Her home was a small home and in the middle of the main floor was a staircase leading down into an unfinished basement she used mainly for storage.

The first night of our marriage we had such an argument that I stormed out of the bedroom. Phyllis thought I had left the house. What she didn't know was that I simply walked downstairs to cool off, but while I was in the basement, Phyllis started playing on her piano. That piano music was so soothing I fell asleep on the basement floor. Not knowing where I was, she became frantic and had gone out looking for me, driving all over the surrounding neighborhood trying to find me. I awoke a few hours later and came back upstairs. All of a sudden I was there, standing in the living room. Phyllis turned around and saw me she, and being in total shock, asked me where I'd been. I told her I was just down in the basement sleeping. Apparently she had not seen me walk down the stairs into the basement, and although she was considerably relieved, she was somewhat angry with me for pulling that stunt!

Somehow my marriage to Phyllis was allowing me to come out of a deep sleep or a fog that I didn't know I had been living in all those years. I almost felt like an animal that had been let free out of a cage. Why did these feelings suddenly appear to me? I know I had been hiding from my fears and problems and my lack of self-worth by accepting positions I knew I was overly qualified for just because I didn't think I deserved anything better. I had hidden my desire to expound on my interest in music because those I had around me thought this love of music was a fad or a hobby and I would quickly get over it and get back to a normal life. But now somehow my spirit knew that I would be able to live a life that I had always been searching for, and to be able to live with someone who equally shared this love of music that I had suppressed for so long, but longed for. Maybe with Phyllis I could be more than I was and be what I dreamed to be. Surely I was no longer chasing an illusive dream now.

FORTY

THE TREE BARK CARVING

Our long drives on Sunday mornings from Aurora were becoming tiresome and we found ourselves wanting to live closer to the church we attended in Arvada. We did eventually find a small two-bedroom "gingerbread house" just west of the church and fell in love with it instantly. We had a fenced in back yard and an underground watering system, a fireplace in the living room and a beautiful laid-out kitchen. We lived so close to our church that we could walk to it when the weather was agreeable, and I often walked over to attend classes that their Christian college offered.

The choir directors at the church had started announcing to the choir that they needed volunteers to participate in their upcoming Christmas cantata, so to receive solo singing parts we had to audition. Phyllis and I were a part of the choir and decided we wanted to participate.

The musical director brought Phyllis in first and then it was my turn. Again, I had the same problem as I had in college when I auditioned for the college choir. When I sang the pianist was running out of piano keys on the upper keys of the piano. She asked me where my break was. She told me to sing again as she kept playing higher and higher on the piano. Again, she heard no break in my voice. She told me that I was probably a contra tenor with no break, or such a faint break that no one could

271

tell when I graduated into my falsetto voice. When she told me it was certainly a gift, I wanted to cry.

I had no full-time job but had signed up at various temporary employment agencies that I knew would keep me busy by sending me on temporary assignments, but there were many times when I didn't have assignments and I would stay at home practicing my solo parts for the pageant. It was during one of those times that a strange, unexplainable thing happened to me.

Sometime in the afternoon I had decided to lay down on our sofa and take a nap, and I fell asleep on my left side, facing the back of the sofa. I don't know how long I had been napping when all of a sudden, between my being awake and not fast asleep, I felt the presence of someone, or something in the room. I lay there motionless for what seemed like an eternity, wondering to myself if Phyllis had come home and I hadn't heard her come in, or if it was someone else that I was not aware of. Was I still asleep or was I awake? Then I felt a finger touch my right shoulder. I immediately jumped up and started looking around the room to see who had touched me. All our friends knew I was a person who startles easily and sometimes would laugh when they saw me jump.

There was no one in the room and there was no one else in our home. Did I just imagine something touching me, or was this some sort of a spirit that was in our home? I knew about evil spirits and how they can sometimes create problems, but why and how would something like that ever be in our home? We were both Christians and attended church. How did this evil being get invited in? We discussed this incident with one of the associate pastors in our church and he volunteered to come over and talk with us and offer a time of prayer with us.

The next evening the associate pastor and his wife came over to our home and sat down on our sofa. I repeated the story about the incident to him and he tried to educate us more about spirits and what we should do if anything like that ever happened again. He asked to use our restroom, which was down the hall, and when he didn't come back right away we became concerned, until we looked down the hall and saw him standing in the hallway staring at the far wall at the tree bark carving I had hung there. I had brought that tree carving of a face back with me when David and I had flown to Mexico.

We asked him what was wrong. As he stood there, he asked us where that wall hanging came from. I told him I had purchased it in Mexico. The expression on his face seemed to show a great concern for our safety. He told us to get that wooden carving out of our house immediately because he said that he felt evil spirits were attached to that carving and they were causing many problems in our lives. He prayed with us and then left.

I know Phyllis was concerned enough to want to get that carving out of our home as soon as possible, but I didn't think it would do much harm to wait until the morning, so we went to bed, but neither one of us to fall asleep. She kept telling me she felt an urgency to get that wooden carving of an evil face out of our home. It was then that we both decided it was time to take it and drive it somewhere and get rid of it. I grabbed it off the wall and we both hurriedly headed out to the garage.

As we tried to open the side door leading into the garage, the door made an awful scratching noise and frightened us. I was so frightened I almost burst into tears, but this time Phyllis had to be the strong one. We quickly got in our car and drove over to a local grocery store where I jumped out and threw that wooden carving in the dumpster. A huge amount of relief flooded over us to let us know, beyond a shadow of doubt, that we had rid ourselves of the awful evil that we had allowed into our home, and we started to enjoy more peace now, probably for the first time.

It was becoming more of a joy for us to be a part of the Christmas pageant at the church. We enjoyed every musical rehearsal, and performing not only vocally but also the drama that had been incorporated. We felt ourselves growing spiritually and becoming an integral part of the church family.

One evening when we had both gone to bed, Phyllis decided to go sit at her piano and play. She had chosen the song, "I Surrender All," which she felt most people didn't really mean that when they sang it, but that was what was in her heart now. The music so touched her own heart that she started to weep. It was then that she realized that she was playing for the Lord and she began to feel a sense of freedom to worship Him, not only in song but in the spirit. That spiritual worship time she spent with the Lord would dramatically change her life forever in how she worshipped. She had received her baptism of the Holy Spirit. I so wanted what she had.

A few weeks later I was in the kitchen and I turned on our portable cassette tape player to listen to a gospel group perform. When the song "Silent Love" started to play, the message in the song so touched my heart I began to cry, and tears began running down my cheeks. To my left, I saw a vision of a man wearing a long white garment, holding his hands out towards me and floating towards me. What I saw defied all logic and reason. It was as though there were no walls and I was peeking into the spirit world to witness such an event. Through teary eyes I kept my eyes focused on the vision of that man moving towards me, and I so wanted to welcome him with open arms and just about then, Phyllis walked into the kitchen and it disrupted what I was experiencing, and I didn't want her to see that I had tears in my eyes.

Some friends from our church in Arvada told us that their elderly mother had a home in Wheat Ridge that she wanted to rent out because she needed to move in with them since she was having trouble getting around. The rent was much less than what we were paying in Arvada so we told them we'd be happy to rent her home. We hated moving from our cute little "gingerbread home" in Arvada but wanted to help our friend's mother. We hadn't lived in her home very long, however and she decided she wanted to sell it, so we had to move out. We didn't know what to do. We were totally at a loss.

We mentioned our problem to our friends, Vince and Mary, who had been a part of the Christmas pageant, and we told them that one of Phyllis's sisters had offered to help us move out to San Diego where she and her husband lived and they would help us get started. Since we needed to move out of our home in Wheat Ridge, we were ready to go. Vince and Mary said they too wanted to get away from Denver and would share the cost of renting a U-Haul truck, so they offered to drive the truck and we followed behind in our little Volkswagon Beetle.

Vince and Mary and their teen-aged son rode in the U-Haul truck all the way to San Diego, while we were in our car. Most of our furniture and personal belongings were packed in the back of that truck, along with Vince and Mary's belongings, and our little beetle vehicle was packed all the way to the ceiling and to the back window.

We arrived safely in San Diego and drove straight to the two-bedroom apartment that Phyllis's sister had arranged for us to rent. Vince, Mary and their son had to move in with us until they could find a place to live. I don't care what you say, but having two couples living in the same apartment with two wives sharing the same kitchen can sometimes create problems, and it sometimes did, but we all survived it.

The apartment we all shared was not far from where Phyllis's sister's family lived and we sometimes walked to their townhome to practice a make-shift quartet. With Phyllis's sister singing alto, Vince singing bass, Phyllis singing soprano, and me singing tenor, we created quite an ensemble.

One evening we walked over to Phyllis's sister's townhome to practice, and then about 10pm Vince, Phyllis and I headed back to our apartment, walking along the sidewalk and enjoying the cool evening air. The streets were pretty well lit, and driveway entrances to apartment complexes and townhomes along the way were also lit up. As we three were crossing over a driveway leading into one of these apartment complexes, we noticed a big tarantula spider sitting on top of one of the short stone walls on the driveway entrance. There were special spot lights that lit up the stone walls and some of the bushes that sat in front of them, making our visibility of that spider quite clear. Vince picked up a small stick and threw it at the tarantula causing it to bound over the back of the wall, disappearing into the darkness, after which he commented that they frequently run in pairs. We three continued walking past that stone wall along the sidewalk when all of a sudden Phyllis let out a blood-curdling scream and scared me to death! She felt something brush around her leg and she figured it was the other tarantula! After recovering from the scare a black cat swiftly walked away! We all had a good laugh over it and walked on home to our apartment, still all in an uneasy state of fright.

The apartment living with another couple and their teenaged son had taken its toll on us and we decided we needed to move to another apartment, so we found an upstairs apartment across from a hospital on Zion Avenue with an outside wooden stair entrance, that was a two bedroom with two full baths. It was at this apartment that I was able to talk to my two oldest children for the first time since they were small children. Phyllis had encouraged me to contact them through Social Security, and Social Security sent my letter on to Jennifer and she responded. Through our letter writing we set aside a time one evening when the two of them could call me. When I heard their voices I wanted to sit down and cry, and that first contact in about 20 years opened up a few more doors for us to stay in touch for many, more years to come.

A temporary agency with whom I had signed with sent me to the E.F. Hutton Life Insurance Company in La Jolla, a suburb of San Diego, for special training. I loved that job and was hoping to get hired on full time, but when my boss read my resume and the education I had, they wouldn't hire me, because the only jobs they had available were data entry jobs.

My daughter Heather and I have had such a special relationship even if it was just talking on the phone long distance. I'd call her in the evening and walk out into the exposed hallway in front of our apartment and head on down to the end where the wooden stairs led to the sidewalk below. I stood at the top of those stairs talking with Heather, looking up at the moon, asking her if she could see the moon, and she told me she could. We were both looking at the moon at the same time but in totally different states, so we decided that the moon would be our connecting spirit when we missed one another. To this day, every time I see the moon, it still reminds me of when Heather and I talked on the phone. We ended up sending her an airline ticket to fly out and spend a week with us, and I took her to Disneyland. Those are memories that will always be with me.

Phyllis and I decided that the cost of living in San Diego was so high and growing more expensive by the day, that we wanted to move back to the Denver area. We started saving our money until we knew we had enough to ship all of our belongings by truck and we drove our Volkswagon Beetle back to Denver. We had to drive by night because the car had a tendency to overheat. The night we left we saw many brush fires on the hillsides and it was a feeling that we were escaping from hell.

When we arrived back in Denver our friends, Joe and Carol from the church we had been attending in Arvada, invited us to stay with them until we could find a home of our own. A couple of days later the truck arrived with all of our belongings, and we were able to store everything in their garage.

We found a two-story home on Coors Street in Arvada and were able to move from Joe and Carol's within a couple of weeks, and we resumed attending the church we had attended before. At that time we were poor as church mice. I began working through a temporary agency at minimum wage, as was Phyllis when she could get work. One of the many items we didn't have was a microwave, a luxury not provided us.

We had been at this home just a few days when we looked out our kitchen window and saw a microwave sitting out on the curb in the front of the house across the street from us. Dare we dream that it might still work? Why did that family throw it out? The microwave was a rather large one and looked heavy to carry. Being new to the neighborhood and not knowing anyone, we decided to wait until the next day, hoping it would still be there and we could get help in bringing it over to our house and see if there was any life left in it.

It snowed during the night and when I looked out our window I saw snow all over the top of that microwave. There was our 'hope' all covered with that wet stuff, probably sealing its doom. But undaunted, I decided not to wait any longer, so towards evening I went over and picked it up to bring it to our house. I carried it as far as our garage but the weight of it just became too much for me and I dropped one end of it onto the concrete floor. Our now dwindling jewel was on the concrete floor! We figured we had just sealed the fate of our dream.

However, my determination was still alive, so a bit later I braved it again and brought it into the house. We didn't know at all if it would work, so I called a handy man who we were hoping could maybe help us determine the possible useability. This friend guided us over the phone; first, plug it in; if a color came up on the readout, it might still be working; we told him what color came up on the readout, it was orange—that meant something—also meant there was power; had to set the clock before it would function at all; did that; he said to place a cup of water in it and press start. The water started boiling! We were ecstatic! God had resurrected that old discarded, snow-covered, dropped-on-the-concrete microwave for us! We told a friend our story and the next day an ad in the newspaper for that exact microwave showed the cost of our free microwave was $549.00! And we used this microwave four years!

Our church presented a huge Christmas Pageant, and we were again privileged to be a part of another wonderful presentation. A local cable TV came in and filmed the pageant so viewers throughout the Denver area could enjoy the fruits of our labor. After the last performance the music directors informed us that they were moving away, and this was a shock to everyone but we understood that they had been offered another position in another state.

When the music directors left, Phyllis applied for the music position, and although there were others that the church leadership had also been considering for the full-time, paid position, Phyllis was fully qualified. When the church leadership made their choice and made an announcement to the congregation, however, their choice was another couple. We decided at that point that it was time for us to leave and try and find another church where we could be an integral part of the music department.

One day Joe and Carol asked us to come over for dinner. They had been wonderful friends of ours but they knew we were not attending their church anymore, so after dinner we were sitting talking at their kitchen table when Joe asked us why we left. We told him that we felt the Lord had shown us that there was a spirit of control at the church and the Lord had moved us on. Joe started yelling at us, and all Carol could do was sit there in disbelief at how Joe was reacting. We were so upset by the rude and appalling manner in which we were being treated, we got up to leave, and Joe screamed at us all the way out to our car and we drove away. Within a year, Joe died of cancer at age 52. When we heard the news that Joe had died, we remembered a particular bible verse that the Lord had shown us, because the bible clearly states in Psalm 105:15 KJV "Touch not my anointed, and do my prophets no harm."

FORTY ONE

A TEMPORARY AUDITOR

One of my temporary job assignments was at a firm on the southwest side of Denver. When the temporary employment agency sent me to this firm they told me that my job would entail auditing and data entry. Little did I know that most of my duties would be mainly data entry and making hundreds of copies on a copy machine. I knew I was worth more than this and wondered why I had found myself working at minimum wage for a temporary employment agency! After all, I had extensive education in accounting and business administration! Was this some kind of punishment because of the past life I'd lived? Did I not deserve anything better? Many times I told myself that If I could only afford to leave all this accounting behind and pursue my musical career again, I would be content for the rest of my life.

The firm I worked for was in a building that was identical to a building right next door. If I wasn't paying much attention, which I often didn't, I found myself entering the wrong building and going up the wrong elevator to an identical floor but not the same office that I was working in. I've always joked with people about my not having a sense of direction.

Many of our friends kept asking me why I continued to work at minimum wage when I could have been earning a lot more as an accountant or a bookkeeper. All I could tell them was that I had applied at so many prestigious firms and corporations in the Denver and surrounding areas, but never could find employment. Phyllis and I figured that 'a' job was better than no job at all.

I answered a want ad one week-end for a precious metals brokerage firm stating that they were looking for someone with accounting skills, along with 10-key experience, to work at their office located in a bank building in Littleton. The ad went on to say that there could be a possible advancement to become an assistant to the controller, so I made an appointment and interviewed for the position. A few days later, the company called for me to come back for a second interview but this time, please bring my wife. After meeting with us I received a call telling me that the company had hired me. I realized that all my hard work and dedication, working at minimum wage and making hundreds of copies on a copy machine, paid off.

I loved going into work at the bank building every day, but for me to go to work daily, I had to drive all the way from Arvada heading east on I-70, drive through that awful Denver mousetrap (the junction of I-70 and I-25), and battle all the morning traffic south on I-25. The traffic never let up all the way into Littleton. After a few months the morning and evening commute started to get to me, which led us to look for a home closer to my work so the commute for me wouldn't be as far. We moved the following month when we found a condo located only a few miles away from Littleton Boulevard where the bank building was located.

FORTY TWO
THE ULTIMATE TESTING

Because I worked for a precious metals brokerage firm they relied heavily on the price of gold, silver and other precious metals to keep their brokerage firm in business. If the economy took a dive, I knew I could possibly be without a job. I hadn't been with this company three years and the bottom fell out of the price of gold and I was laid off. I was devastated and hurt. I had considered that position to be the best job I had ever had. Although I was a salaried employee who worked a minimum of nine hours a day, I loved my job. The day they gave me the bad news, I came home early from work with my spirit crushed. When I walked in the door Phyllis asked me why I was home early. When I told her I had been let go, she told me that she thought nothing could top her news of just having been told she had cancer. We both just wanted to sit down and dry.

Our family doctor had discovered a cancer spot on Phyllis's left cheek bone near her left eye and she had to have it removed. The actual procedure took a couple of hours, but we were relieved that it didn't leave a huge scar on her cheek bone. Little did we know that the cancer would reappear in that same spot 20 years later.

I was still devastated that the only job I loved so well was taken away from me. I filed for unemployment and decided to take a few weeks off to help me heal from the wounds that had been inflicted on my self-worth. During those few weeks I begun to create a self-pity party with one person at the party, ME!

Many days I didn't want to go anywhere, let alone go to church. I would occasionally go out in search of another job, but was always told that I was either too qualified, or not qualified enough for the position. I was content to just sit and collect unemployment. My only outlet was working with the praise team at the church in Castle Rock.

The only times I thought about my unemployment were during the week when I had very little to do. I found myself watching TV or taking a nap, but one day I found a TV evangelist on one of the TV channels and sat down to listen to him. At one point he asked the TV audience to place their hands on the TV screen so he could pray for them, so I decided I wanted prayer and knelt down on both knees in front of that TV and placed both of my hands right on the TV screen. As the evangelist prayed, all I could do was cry. I was now depending on a TV evangelist to pray for me, hoping that the Lord would hear my plea for help and provide me with a job. What I didn't realize was that I had been placing all my self-worth, and who I was defined by, in my position as an accountant. Why wasn't I placing all my self-worth and my identity in the Lord, who was responsible for who I was and who I might become? I am who I am through Him.

Within a few months I received a call from my old boss at the precious metals brokerage firm telling me they wanted me to come back and resume my position as assistant controller. They couldn't pay me as much as I had been making, but maybe within a few months to a year, I could be earning as much as I had before and even more. I jumped at the chance and accepted their offer. The Lord and I had a talk that evening and I told God that I was not depending on my position at a bank building to define who I was, and if I were to ever get laid-off again, I would not go back to that company and I'd ask Him for a way to be able to serve Him in some kind of a full-time music ministry.

The following week I resumed my job at the bank building in Littleton and began a whole new chapter in my life with this firm. My attitude had changed and I told myself that I wasn't going to let the possibility of my being laid-off again cloud my better judgment. I was going to totally trust in the Lord.

Within the first year of my re-employment at the brokerage firm in the bank building, I had to be rushed to the hospital for an emergency appendectomy. My appendix had become inflamed and the hospital operated to remove them. When I returned to work within a week, my boss started treating me differently and I felt we were not the team we once were. I started feeling an uneasy, empty feeling in the pit of my stomach, and my instincts were correct because the firm laid me off again. This time I was not devastated and I told them that I would not be coming back.

When I came home early from work again from being laid-off, I was flying high with much anticipation of a new direction for us. I walked with confidence and held my head up high with a constant smile on my face. The spirit within me knew that something exciting was about to happen. I just wished at that point that my spirit would have informed me what all the excitement was about!

FORTY THREE
EXPECT THE UNEXPECTED

Our condo was located in south Denver near the highway intersections of interstate highway 25 and interstate highway 235. The Cherry Creek Park and recreation area was only a few miles from us. Although I had the most wonderful job as assistant controller of a precious metals firm, and we lived in a prime location in Denver, we missed our involvement and our worship time at church.

Phyllis and I took a drive one week-end heading towards Colorado Springs. The drive south on interstate highway 25 is so picturesque with the rolling hills and a view of the Rocky Mountains to the west of us. Just to the south of us we could see the top of Pikes Peak off in the distance. Our traveling took us through the town of Castle Rock, so named because of the huge rock formation that sat on top of a hill at the edge of town, so we decided to pull over and take a tour of the town and see if we could walk up to the base of the Castle Rock.

Much of the town was a tourist trap but very quaint. We found the entrance to where we could park our car and walk up to the base of the rock formation called Castle Rock. We hiked up a weather worn path that had deep water-eroded ruts in it that we had to dodge in order for us to not trip and fall into on our way up to the base. I told Phyllis that I thought the pathway was suitable enough for us to try and drive up the

286

path in our little Volkswagon Beetle. We turned around and walked back down to where our car was parked, hopped in, and drove back up the hill, carefully straddling the ruts. I was able to drive our car around three quarters of the base of the rock formation before heading back down. If you were to try and drive or even walk up that path now, the ruts have gotten deeper and wider enough so that no car can handle the rugged terrain anymore. Walking up the path had always been a challenge.

As we drove around town we found ourselves crossing the highway, discovering a whole different area of town. This part of town was closer to the foothills and more of an industrial area. We turned down one of the side streets and noticed, what looked like a vacant strip mall, a sign that indicated a church met there. I walked up to the front door and saw they had posted their office and church hours. We decided we wanted to come back on Sunday morning and check out the church.

That next Sunday we visited the church and were excited about their praise and worship services. Everyone had been so friendly to us. We decided to start attending every Sunday.

It wasn't long before we both were asked to join their praise and worship group. For me, this was a thrill of a lifetime. I had always loved to sing, not only solos, but harmony as well. With this praise team I could do both. Singing gospel music came natural to me. When I was younger my father used to minister at nursing homes and retirement homes, and I'd tag along with him. He always carried a hymnal and would choose a song for me to lead everyone in singing. Somehow I knew exactly what the pitch was and I could sight read enough to either sing the lead part or the tenor part.

Working with this praise team became one of the highlights of my life, and I always looked forward to our rehearsals and our performances on Sundays. There were so many talented, gifted people on the praise team and I was thrilled to be a part of it. Phyllis played the piano for it.

Phyllis and I had met a widow at the church in Castle Rock who wanted to rent her basement out, and we told her we were interested. We were living in a condo in south Denver at the time, so we visited with her at her home in Castle Rock and told her that we'd like to rent her whole house, not just the basement. She agreed to rent her home to us and she moved into a local apartment building.

Frankie and Phyllis's 3700 square foot home on a hill overlooking Castle Rock, CO

This home had 3700 square feet of living space, with three fireplaces, four bedrooms, three baths, a formal dining room, and a double car garage. There was a wrap-around wooden deck on the back with a walk-out basement under the deck. From our deck we could see the Castle Rock, Devil's Head Mountain, and Pike's Peak. After moving in we held a house blessing in which we invited the praise team from the church to lead in worship. We even had a visit from what we felt were two angels whom nobody remembered seeing but us. The Lord was blessing us.

Since I had made contact with my two oldest children in New Jersey, I asked Jennifer if she would fly out to spend time with us if we bought her an airline ticket. She agreed and she flew out from New Jersey and spent about a week with us in Castle Rock, and we gave her the whole basement, which was like another apartment. I took her to Red Rocks on the west side of Denver, we drove to Colorado Springs and toured not only a cave, but the Garden of the Gods. We hadn't met my oldest son, Brian, but I was working on it.

Phyllis had been writing and arranging her own compositions for many years, whenever she felt the inspiration to do so. I was encouraging her to record some of her arrangements for posterity, so with the help of many of the praise team instrumentalists who wanted to volunteer to be a part of our recording, they helped us to step out in faith.

In 1990 I found the Fastrack Recording Studio in Denver that was available and affordable and booked studio recording time to record a cassette tape. Phyllis knew she would play all the piano parts and/or keyboards, and the instrumentalists from the church would provide our drummer, conga drum player, lead-guitarist, acoustic guitarist, saxophonist and violinist. We didn't have a bass guitar player so Phyllis decided to play all the bass notes on the keyboard. All the vocals would entirely be just the two of us, singing both lead and background vocals.

A friend of ours at the church, whose husband was a pilot, had just been given an expensive keyboard with all the bells and whistles on it, so she donated the use of it at the studio for our project. She came to the studio many times to instruct Phyllis on what button to push for the particular sound we were looking for in a song.

Each musical arrangement Phyllis had written all came from an inspiration the Lord had given to her. I remember her sitting at our baby grand piano playing and writing as she felt led. She asked me one time what she might be able to put down on paper about being a child of God and what He might say to us as the loving Father He is. I told her to write down words that sounded as if God was speaking to His children. That helped to inspire her to write "My Child." I knew that that song had to be a solo with Phyllis expressing her feelings about her personal relationship with the Lord. We included our dear friend, Corlis Preheim, who did a voice-over in an interlude for the song. When we got to the studio Phyllis told us she wanted the song to have the style of a Broadway musical.

In her bible reading one day Phyllis found herself in Habakkuk, reading chapter one, verse five, which states: "Behold ye among the heathen and regard and wonder marvelously; for I will work a work in your days, which ye will not believe though it be told to you." That inspired her to write the title song for our album, "Expect The Unexpected."

The 'all original' album project first featured only 10 songs. The first song we wanted to include was a song Phyllis had written called, "Be Patient." When we sang that song for a friend to hear, she explained, "That's where you are in your life right now." The song "Friends" was originally submitted to, and published by, Standard Publishing for their use in one of their Vacation Bible School courses. The song, "The Lord Is Exalted" is from Isaiah 3:3-5 and has a Jewish flair, and a friend from the church's praise and worship team played the violin on the interlude. "You Alone" is based on Jeremiah 17:14 and is part of a medley that also includes the song, "I Love You Lord." "Praisin' My Lord" came when Phyllis was looking for a different style for one of her compositions and gave it a Fats Domino flair. We also included the song, "Be Content Where You Are," and the lyrics themselves explain the meaning of the song. "This Wonderful Life" was written while Phyllis was driving around Denver. She sang most of the song in the car, grabbing some paper and jotting it down as she was driving, obviously without the use of a piano. The monologue, "Little Red Wagon" came when Phyllis had been left alone working on a temporary job assignment. For lack of work to do one afternoon, she wrote the monologue, then later added the original music. When we recorded that song in the studio we brought in my youngest daughter, Heather, who was twelve years old at the time, to be the little girl's voice that we needed to complete the song.

While in the studio editing one of the songs we had recorded, Phyllis kept telling us she had heard a beep go off. The engineer kept playing back the master recording tape and each time Phyllis kept saying, "There it is!" After much insisting, he narrowed down the location on the tape and finally found the beep Phyllis heard. No one else had heard it but Phyllis. We discovered that the lead-guitarist's watch had a built in alarm and it had gone off during the recording! Because the recording studio was a multi-track studio, we were able to record our lead vocals then turn around and record our own background vocals.

She has written in so many different styles. Some had a distinctive Jewish style, while others sounded like a Fats Domino hit song. One song had the sound of a movie soundtrack. She was told that if she wanted her music to sell, she needed to write in a prescribed style, but she said she wasn't writing to sell, she was writing from her heart.

In 2007 we remastered the cassette tape into a CD, which now includes 12 songs, adding Phyllis's songs "Praise Medley" and "Books

Of The Old Testament." The "Praise Medley" was comprised of two choruses, "It's A Beautiful Day" and "Praise Your Name, Lord Jesus."

Another story about one of the medleys we included on the album was when we were living in San Diego and we were driving around one Saturday afternoon enjoying the gorgeous day when Phyllis declared, "It's a beautiful day to praise the Lord." She began to sing a melody to those words and I answered back, "It's a beautiful day." When the next phrase came, I answered it again. Phyllis ended up writing that song as we drove around on that sunshiny afternoon. The second half of the medley came about a few years later when we were house-sitting for friends in Lake Havasu City, Arizona. While Phyllis was in the shower, one day she began singing the phrase, "Praise your name, Lord Jesus." Different succeeding days in the shower she added more words.

The song, "Books Of The Old Testament" came about when Phyllis's oldest daughter called her one day to see if she knew of a song about the books of the Old Testament. Phyllis wanted to help her daughter but didn't know of any song.

One night she woke up about 2:00 am and the old hymn, "Standing On The Promises" kept coming into her head, and she began thinking of the Old Testament books. When she started singing the books of the Old Testament to that song, they matched exactly, down to the last book of Malachi. We took her idea to our friend Tim Raymond, who had his own recording studio in his basement, and he provided the full musical arrangement of the adaptation Phyllis had been looking for. She wanted children to sing the song for the recording and contacted Cheryl Shellenberger, from the Sunrise Christian Academy in Wichita, who brought in her K through 5 students that provided all the children's voices for the song. Interestingly, a short time after we finished that recording, we received a note from one of the mother's stating, "Thank you for allowing my son to have this experience. He really enjoyed singing. This is all we heard about for weeks! Thank you."

FORTY FOUR
A MINISTRY WAS BORN

We made life-long friends at the church in Castle Rock. One such couple was Loren and Althea Riley, who actually owned a farm near the town of Yuma, Colorado but had moved to Castle Rock so one of their daughters could attend school there. We became instant friends, even when they moved back to their farm in Yuma. Another friend was Polly whom we had hired to come clean our home once a month, who told us, "I don't know why, but I just enjoy cleaning houses." Phyllis has always admitted to not being a very good housekeeper and she actually wrote in the dust on her baby grand piano, "Dust Me!" We sure needed Polly. We three have been the best of friends ever since.

The church in Castle Rock asked us to direct their first Easter pageant, and I was thrilled. I knew Phyllis and I could handle all the preparations it took to create a musical version of the death and resurrection of the Lord. The musical was something I could sink my teeth into and keep my thoughts away from my unemployment issues, so Phyllis and I began auditions.

We had excellent people who auditioned for parts. We not only needed solo singers and choral singing, we needed townspeople. We also needed someone to play a non-singing Jesus, and we found the perfect man to play the part.

A young slender man by the name of Wade Dye, who just happened to have long hair, had been attending the church. We approached him

Wade Dye played "Jesus" in a musical directed by Frankie and Phyllis. The play was called "The Witness" with Tony Kogan as the small boy.

one Sunday and asked him if he would be interested in playing the part of Jesus. He was delighted that we had asked him and we ended up casting him as our non-singing Jesus figure. We thought that no one would be able to look like who we thought Jesus actually looked like more than Wade.

We had been rehearsing for some time when the pastor called Phyllis and me in for a discussion. He informed us that the man we had chosen to play Jesus was living with a woman and he told us we should not cast him to play that part. We had no choice but to inform Wade that we couldn't use him unless his circumstances changed, so he and his live-in girlfriend married that same week. His wife later told us that she had a hard time sleeping with her husband after watching him perform in our musical. She kept picturing him as Jesus!

A lady told us that she had driven by our church one evening and the Lord prompted her to come into our rehearsal. She was a beautiful soprano singer that we had needed to sing a solo that no one else could sing. It wasn't us working but the Lord working through us and for us.

I started designing the backdrops we needed for the production, and volunteer carpenters from the church took over and created what I had drawn on paper. An artist in the church helped me draw and paint all the backdrops, and then helped me nail them together to look like one whole background scene. Even a small child at the church told someone that "Jesus comes to our church. I saw Him in the musical!" The whole production was a huge success. Was this the excitement that my spirit was trying to tell me?

With this musical production behind us I found myself wanting to do even more in the ministry. I told Phyllis that I'd love for us to go on the road in a full-time music ministry, but she told me that the Lord would need to do a 180 on her for her to accept being on the road full-time because she didn't like to travel.

I started calling local churches telling them about our ministry. Some churches invited us in to minister in concert. Our first concert away from

Frankie and Phyllis Valens

the Denver area was in Hays, Kansas. Phyllis had a friend who attended a church there and she invited us to come and minister. We left in the heat of the day from Denver, driving our Volkswagon Beetle that had no air-conditioning, and arriving at the church all sweaty and tired. All we could do was take a wash cloth and go into their restroom and wash up so we could be presentable to do a concert.

One of my calls to schedule a concert was a church in Syracuse, Kansas. My dad had been the pastor of the First Christian church and I so wanted to be able to come back to Syracuse and show the people that their former pastor's oldest son had become a gospel singer.

When Phyllis and I arrived at the church we noticed several people already going into the church for our concert. What we hadn't realized was that Syracuse, Kansas was in the Mountain Time Zone, not Central Time, and because of the hour difference our concert was supposed to start in only 20 minutes. We did a very fast quick change at the parsonage next door!

When I wanted to book another concert in Syracuse I chose to contact a smaller church in town and made a call to a sister church to the Christian church. When we arrived in Syracuse I followed the directions the church had given me for where their church was located, and when we pulled up and parked in front of the address the church had given us, we saw a very small white building with a circular window near the roof of the building that had been covered and a small cross had been nailed to it. We couldn't believe that this was a church building. As I kept staring at that small circular covered window with a cross over it I commented to Phyllis that this church looked like a converted bird house. I had remembered seeing bird houses shaped just like this building was, only on a much smaller scale.

After our concert at this church, Phyllis and I had to repent from what the devil was trying to deceive us with. This little church was only the depth of three pews and a place for a pulpit, with each pew filled to capacity with 49 people, but the sister church, where we had been before, had cancelled their Sunday evening service so they could attend our concert at this church, and that evening a healing took place between those two churches that had split earlier on over differences. We were so blessed to be part of God's plan.

Since I hated making cold-calls I contacted a local Christian booking agent, Tracey, who agreed to meet with us and was considering booking us for concerts. Tracey started asking me questions that I was not prepared to answer. Up until this time, I had not discussed anything with anyone about my being a former pop-singer in the late 1960s, and his prying questions led to my wanting to guard my heart even more from the exposure that I knew might be revealed. When I told him I was indeed the Frankie Valens who sang a remake of "This Magic Moment," he came unglued and wanted to know even more about my past. Up until this point Phyllis had not ever heard me talk about my Frankie Valens' days or that I had been a pop-singer. She had seen and heard my comeback album titled "Showstopper" but didn't quite put the two and two together. I told Tracey that I had been an independent artist and had never been on a major record label, and even though I sometimes traveled with some well-known artists in concert, I was still very much an unknown. Before I knew it he had contacted local newspapers in Denver, telling them my story. Since one newspaper in Denver hadn't heard of me, and there was very little publicity on record of me, they chose to make up a negative story about me, which was based on false accusations, and published a fabricated story which some pastors believed and started canceling our concerts. We chose not to use Tracey as our agent.

Phyllis and I had an opportunity to go on our first concert tour that would lead us all the way to Yuma, Arizona. We were both so excited to be able to travel such a distance for the first time in our ministry and welcomed this tour with open arms. Our tour would end with us ministering in concert at our own church in Castle Rock.

After our concert in Yuma, Arizona we received a disturbing phone call from our pastor in Castle Rock. He told me that he had to cancel our concert with them because the Holy Spirit told him to cancel. He also told me that the Holy Spirit would reveal the reasons to me.

Until we arrived back in Castle Rock and found out that a Denver newspaper had made many calls to our friends and to our church asking about us, we didn't realize that a newspaper reporter had told our pastor that Frankie Valens was a fraud, and he believed the newspaper reporter! It wasn't the Holy Spirit telling him to cancel our concert! If our own pastor would have just come directly to us and discussed the issue, we could have told him the whole story about my being an independent recording artist. Right then and there I thought our ministry was over before it had begun. I cried out to the Lord asking Him for direction. Romans 8:31 KJV says: "What shall we say to these things? If God be for us, who can be against us?" If we were in the Lord's will then it didn't matter what people and newspapers said about us, we continued the race. We were not in a ministry because of our own will and certainly not by our own works. We felt the Lord had called us into serving Him full-time by His paving the way for us, and as Zechariah 4:6 KJV says: "Not by might, nor by power, but by my spirit, saith the Lord of hosts."

After our pastor so heartlessly canceled our concert at our own church, we felt that he had not only rejected our ministry but totally rejected us as part of his flock. How could a pastor so blindly make rash decisions that would affect the lives of the members of his own flock without discussing and confronting that person first? We had no desire to go back to that church. I had to love him in the Lord and forgive him, but I had lost all respect for him as a pastor, and as a friend. There were times I wanted to have a pity party for the way I felt we were treated, but I remembered that old saying, "it's alright to sit on your pity pot every now and then, but be sure to flush when you're done!" I knew we had to move on.

Texe Marrs stated exactly what we felt: "Let the critics criticize. Let the liars sharpen their quills and open wide their mouths. Let them do their utmost to slander you in their ridiculous, vain attempt to stop you from doing God's work and from telling the truth. Be assured, they'll get nowhere with their unbecoming campaign of deception. In fact, you can take all the junk and garbage they throw at you as a blessing in disguise. What's more, you should be truly alarmed if the critics actually begin to praise and speak well of you." We should be more concerned about our character than our reputation. Our character is who we really are, while our reputation is merely what others think we are! Yes, we had to be strong and were able to bless others with our God-given talents. We learned the value of being vulnerable enough to let others be strong for us, to let others bless us by opening their homes to us and helping us to receive blessings through their giving, which turned out, was a blessing to them as well. We had to learn to receive instead of always wanting to give through our ministry.

Our friends, Loren and Althea, knew what had happened to us at our church and knew that we wanted to move out of the area, so they told us that there was a beautiful home in Yuma that belonged to a doctor that was for lease and not far from their home.

I had no job and we had no church, and we were ready to make a move out of Castle Rock. Our plans were to move a couple of days before Thanksgiving and rent a large U-Haul truck. Loren and Althea drove down from Yuma and brought their farm trucks with attached trailers, to help load everything up we owned and move us to Yuma.

On moving day a blinding blizzard struck the whole Rocky Mountain region and made it even more difficult for us to load everything. We had hired a special moving van who came by earlier and loaded up our baby grand piano to deliver it to our new home in Yuma, but Loren and Althea brought two farm trucks with trailers attached, for everything else. We were still determined to stick with our original plans and not let a blizzard stand in our way.

FORTY FIVE

THE RED HOUSE

Our caravan of cars and trucks heading out in a blinding snowstorm was not the smartest thing any of us could have planned, but we had no choice. We had already given notice to the owner of the home in Castle Rock that we were moving.

Loren knew all the back roads to Yuma as he led our caravan east on highway 86 out of Castle Rock. Highway 86 ended at interstate 70 where we picked up highway 71 north out of Limon. Highway 71 took us to highway 36 heading east where we caught highway 59 north that took us into Yuma.

Before Limon the roads seemed passable, but when we started heading north out of Limon, the roads became slick with ice and snow and were hazardous. There were times when the visibility had deteriorated so badly that I could barely make out where the vehicle in front of us was. The situation made me even more wanting to diligently pursue our goal of making it safely into Yuma.

When we arrived in Yuma it was late at night and we did not know the town of Yuma or where in Yuma Loren had led us to. Phyllis and I had not seen this home before moving to Yuma. Our caravan pulled into a circular driveway and every vehicle parked. When we pulled up into the driveway, we found ourselves parked in front of an open garage door that Loren had pulled open for us, but because it was dark, we could not see much of the house in the dark. There were many trees and bushes lining the front of the home and along the circular driveway, and everyone carried in boxes and furniture through the open garage door.

With all the help we were able to unload all the furniture and personal belongings, that night, and our bed was the first priority to set up, then get the kitchen items unloaded. Everything else had to wait till morning. We parked our van in the double car garage and closed the garage door

The "Red House" in Yuma, CO

when everyone began to realize just how tired they were from the long horrific journey with the added stress and anticipation of getting to Yuma from Castle Rock, and decided to call it a day. We too were tired and just fell into bed exhausted.

The next morning we realized that we needed a post office box, and I found the post office on Main Street easily because of the American flag that was flying in the breeze above the building. I walked in and told the clerk that we had just moved to town and we needed a post office box. When the clerk asked me the address, I told him our home was on Albany Street, and he exclaimed, "Oh, the red house!" I responded with, "the red house?" He told me that the former owner was the town doctor.

When I left the post office I saw a donut shop a few doors down and decided I'd stop and pick up a dozen donuts. I parked my van and walked up to the front door that had a posted sign on it that said that they were not open on Mondays, and this was Monday! Heading back down Main Street towards home a few cars passed by me heading into town. Each time a car passed by me the driver waved to me. Did I know them? I began to realize that we had moved to a very small rural community where everyone knows everybody and waving was their gesture of being neighborly. Although we had trouble adjusting to a small town rural life, we loved our home.

This home had a large eat-in kitchen, a formal dining room, a large living room with an over-sized fireplace, a master bedroom and three spare bedrooms which we named, the Panel Room, the Green Room, and the Heather Room (so named when my daughter Heather came for a visit). The family room had been a new addition with a cathedral ceiling and many windows that were built onto the back of the home, so we called the room our Music Room and moved our baby grand piano there with all of our music books and recordings. The whole entire floor of our new home had built-in heating that made our floor always warm and toasty. This had to be the best home we had ever lived in.

Phyllis and I decided we wanted to present a concert locally to help introduce ourselves to the community and to the surrounding towns, so we consulted with a few friends of ours in Yuma and they suggested we hold our concert at the Yuma High School auditorium. They also suggested that we might want to borrow or rent a portable sign to place on the main highway near the exit to the high school advertising our appearance. To find out where to find such a sign they told me to first consult with the local police department.

The police department was located in downtown Yuma. I walked into their main lobby and saw a short partition wall standing in front of me that helped give a division to the room. A police woman was sitting behind this partition reading something, and I simply walked up to the counter and asked her how I could find a portable sign to place on the main highway advertising a concert at the high school. She didn't look up but proceeded to make a call, and in her conversation she mentioned that there was a lady here that wanted information about renting a portable sign. She then hung up. I stood there in disbelief wondering who she was referring to. I looked around the waiting room and realized that I was the only one there. I spoke up again, but this time trying to speak using a lower tone in my voice, just in case she had been referring to me. "Ma'am," I said," what woman were you referring to?" She looked up in shock and made a hurried call back to whomever she had called previously and told him that there was a "party" here that wished to speak to him. I asked myself again, what party? When I had time to think about what she had been trying to say, I realized that my hair length made me look like over 80 per cent of all the women in that small community town. Added to the fact that my speaking and singing voice is one or two octaves above the typical male voice, I had to forgive her for her inability to show any kind of remorse in referring to me as a woman. There were no excuses given to me as she went back to whatever she had been reading, before this 'party' had interrupted her. We consulted with the high school and they approved the concert, the only fee being that we needed to pay a cleaning fee for the janitor. And yes, the police department provided us with a portable sign that we placed on the main highway to let those driving by know that there was going to be a concert at the high school.

Phyllis and I also advertised our concert by sending flyers out to various churches and organizations, and we drove to Wray, Colorado to drop off flyers. Our longest trip was to Burlington, Colorado where we hung posters and flyers in local establishments. We wanted this concert to be a success, but with all the hard work we had done to help give this community by providing a free concert, only a handful of people attended our concert.

To make matters worse, when I needed to have a pair of slacks dry-cleaned, the only dry-cleaners in town said she couldn't dry-clean them at that time because she only stoked up her oven once a week and she didn't have enough business yet to stoke the oven up!

I had called a church in Scottsbluff, Nebraska and they wanted to book us for a concert, so this would be one of the first official out-of-state concerts for us. Our concert was well received and the church packed out. Phyllis and I were excited, until the offering was given to us. We had always told ourselves that any offering would be a blessing from the Lord, but something was wrong. There had been over 300 people at the concert, and yet the pastor handed us a check for &75.00! We later found out that their treasurer had been embezzling from the church for years, and after much suspicion, he took off for parts unknown. We were wondering if traveling in a full-time music ministry was the right choice for us or not.

We were just not adjusting to this rural way of living. I still did not have a full-time job and we were living on my unemployment checks. Many days I would drive to a town nearby to apply for a position, just to be told I was over qualified. My unemployment benefits were running out and I still could not find a job. We were able to schedule a few concert dates and minister at various churches in the surrounding areas around Yuma, but I don't know how we would have survived otherwise.

We decided we needed to move back to civilization again, yet we had only lived in Yuma about four months.

Phyllis had been in touch with her sister in San Diego, and again her sister offered to help us move back to San Diego. Since we saw very few options opening up for us we decided to have a garage sale and sell as much as we could to help pay for our move back to San Diego. Why we kept accepting a false sense of support from her sister, I don't know. Her sister was just so much fun to be around, but we learned early on not to get too close to her or sparks would fly.

We threw such a big garage sale that half the people in Yuma must have visited our driveway and garage to take a peek at all we had to offer. Our biggest item was our baby grand piano. As much as we wanted to keep it, we knew it would be tough for us to take the piano all the way to San Diego, but a married couple came by and his wife saw the baby grand piano, and she wanted it. She told us that it had been her life's dream to own a baby grand piano, and being able to give them a special offer they were able to purchase our piano.

We offered many collectable Avon items at our garage sale. Phyllis had been an Avon manager and had been one of the top 10 managers in the nation, winning trips to Hawaii and Monte Carlo, so over the years she had collected quite a few Avon products. These items sold quickly at our garage sale, especially since I didn't often know their value!

Our driveway was littered with all kinds of garage sale items including chairs. I decided to sit in one of those chairs for a few minutes watching people browse when I noticed an older couple drive up and began looking over some of our items. The older man came over to me, bending over to take a closer look at me, and called me "ma'am" when he asked about a price of an item. Was my hair 'that' long, or was this guy so near-sighted he couldn't tell who he was speaking to? My hair length had been a little over my ears and I did let the back of my hair grow to my collar, but I sat there in surprise, realizing again that my hair length was the length of most of the women in this community. I yelled to Phyllis to come out and help this man, telling her that this man had ignorantly insulted me and didn't even know it.

We ended up selling most all of our furniture, and we no longer had our baby grand piano. We were able to buy an 88-key keyboard to replace Phyllis's piano, knowing that we could carry the keyboard to our concerts. I was able to rent a U-Haul truck with an attached trailer that could carry our van on, and we were ready to move.

FORTY SIX

IN THE FULLNESS OF TIME

Our mistake when we left Yuma, Colorado, for our move to San Diego was trying to drive over the Rocky Mountains. We were driving a U-Haul truck with a trailer on the back with our van secured with chains, but we should have headed the southern route which would have taken us through New Mexico, because there were fewer mountain ranges. I had chosen the northern route because my atlas had shown that it was fewer miles to travel.

We headed west on interstate 70 and traveled through the Eisenhower Memorial Tunnel in the Rocky Mountains, which is well over an altitude of 11,000 feet, and we started heading downhill. The downhill was a seven-mile trip to the town of Dillon. Because I had to keep applying my brakes so frequently, we virtually had no brakes in the U-Haul truck by the time we reached the bottom of the hill, so we exited into Dillon to get the brakes fixed before we continued the rest of our trip. We had to spend the night while a mechanic worked on the truck, and the rest of our trip to San Diego seemed a breeze after losing our brakes on that mountain side.

After a few days but when we arrived in San Diego we drove directly to Phyllis's sister's home. She had divorced her fifth husband and was living alone with just her dog. We were able to store what few personal items we had left in her garage, because the garage had not been used as a garage since most of it had been turned into a mother-in-law's wing. That became our temporary home.

I immediately started making calls to local churches in the San Diego area to schedule concert dates, and with the Lord's help I was able to schedule several concert tours. We had a concert at a church that had been meeting in a school in Del Mar, California and met Rich Palmer, who had been running the sound for the church services. We told him about our next concert at a church in El Cajon, and he came the next night and brought his wife, Gloria. They became life-long friends of ours.

Rich approached us after our concert in El Cajon and told us that he wanted to support our ministry. Rich and Gloria were direct distributors with a large multi-level company, and Rich asked us for permission to contact his upline about our ministry, his upline being just one step down from the billionaire distributor. We had no problem with his referring us to others and especially a large corporation like this one. If this muli-level company booked any concerts with us, I thought that I might be able to incorporate a concert tour that would include churches.

After our concert at the church in El Cajon we met a man who said that he knew Phyllis's father, Paul Cook. He said he used to own a tavern and Phyllis's dad kept coming into the bar to minister to him and wouldn't give up on him. He said that Phyllis's father ended up baptizing him, which was a real special serendipity.

I had originally been in contact with a record company in Virginia Beach when we still lived in Castle Rock, Colorado and decided to call them to see if we could set up a recording session to record an album.

The record company wanted us to come to their studio as soon as we could make the arrangements to come to Virginia Beach, so I decided to book a concert tour to the east coast that would include our spending time in the studio. When Rich Palmer found out we were heading to the east coast he contacted his upline, and they booked us to do a concert in Atlanta, Georgia for one of their functions. They were expecting over 10,000 people to attend this one function. I couldn't understand why this billionaire upline would want to book us in concert since we were not distributors. I told Rich I would start booking a tour that would include our stopping off in Atlanta before heading back to San Diego and he was pleased. Rich and Gloria said they were going to attend the function in Atlanta and would see us there.

We had a wonderful concert tour to the east coast that took us through Arkansas and Tennessee. When we arrived at the studio, we had already decided which songs we wanted to include on our album. The only thing we didn't have was an album title. We were already in the studio recording a few of the songs when I happened to open my bible to Galations 4:4 KJV which states: "But when the fullness of the time was come, God sent forth His Son, made of a woman, made under the law," which goes on to say "to redeem men that were under the law, that we might receive the adoption of sons." I called Phyllis over to witness this scripture and we both knew at that very moment that our new album title would be based on Galations 4:4. It became "In The Fullness Of Time."

We wanted our new album to reflect who Phyllis and I were, by including not only old hymns and concert piano numbers, but also contemporary Christian music that we had been performing in concert already. We chose to also include the three secular songs that I had recorded in the 60s and had based my testimony on. We included: "I'll

Fly Away Medley," "How Majestic Is Your Name" (Piano), "She Cried," "Smoke Gets In Your Eyes," "My Turn Now," "In The Garden Medley," "I Cry," "This Magic Moment," "Jesus Loves Me" (Piano), and "All Rise." In 1995 we re-mastered this album and added: "Midnight Cry," "People Need The Lord," "Country Church," "Home Free," "Personality," and "Healing Under Your Wings." Although we had recorded the 10 songs we needed for this album, the studio engineer had to do the final mixing and add background vocals, using local professional singers, although I had supplied my own three-part harmony on the song, "This Magic Moment." We couldn't wait around until the final mix was completed so we headed south to Atlanta, Georgia to sing at the Atlanta Civic Center where the multi-level company function was expecting over 10,000 people. Rich had already contacted his upline to let him know they would be at the meeting as well as us.

We arrived Saturday afternoon in Atlanta and attended the muli-level company function, and there were over 10,000 people in attendance. We didn't know when his upline wanted us to perform, so we sat towards the back of the auditorium with our friends Rich and Gloria Palmer, waiting for our time to be called up on stage. We were ever so glad that Rich and Gloria were there in this sea of people to help us feel comfortable.

During the function Saturday evening, the billionaire distributor got up to make a speech and during his speech he told the people in attendance that Frankie Valens, the former pop-singer, was in the audience and Frankie would be performing Sunday morning. Rich leaned over to me and said, "he never does that. You must be someone special for him to mention your name!"

We performed on Sunday morning in front of about 7,000 people. Some of the people had left after the function on Saturday evening and some had left Sunday morning to drive home to attend their own church services. Neither one of us had ever performed in front of this many people before, so we were excited and awed all at the same time.

After our ministry time at the function Sunday morning we needed to get back to San Diego. We did not have enough funds to pay for another night at the hotel, and we didn't even know if we had enough funds to even afford to drive back to San Diego.

FORTY SEVEN
RESCUED

On our drive back to San Diego from Atlanta we decided to take highway 10 west, which would take us to highway 8 leading into San Diego. We knew we couldn't afford to stay in a motel during our drive, so we slept overnight in our van for two nights. The second night on the road we must have been somewhere near the Mexican border just east of El Paso, Texas when we pulled over at a roadside park to sleep in our van.

Sometime in the wee hours of the morning, I heard a knock on the window of our van. It was the police. They were asking us if we had a small child in our van. We said no, we were driving home to San Diego. He searched our van anyway and then told us that a couple had reported to the police that they had seen a small child in our van when we had pulled over to fill up with gas at a service station several miles back. We told him that we hoped he had not let the real kidnapper's go by tracking down the wrong people—us!

By the time we reached San Diego, we were tired, broke and mentally exhausted. We had just experienced sleeping in our van for two nights and been accused of kidnapping. What else could go wrong! When we pulled up into the driveway of Phyllis's sister's home and entered into her mother-in-law's wing, we both realized that something was wrong. All of our belongings had been put into boxes and sitting on our bed. Her sister had moved us out while we were on tour. Why we kept accepting help from Phyllis's sister, I do not know. Were we gluttons for punishment? Every time her sister offered to help us, she really wasn't helping us at all and it became either a loan, or we ended up getting hurt in the process because of her backhanded behavior. Apparently while we were gone on tour Phyllis's sister's daughter, Julie, needed a place to live, so Phyllis's sister simply moved us out. We were never notified, and we felt so violated, and we hurt to the core. Phyllis sat down on our bed and cried. I didn't know what to do, so I called our friends Rich and Gloria Palmer. They had mentioned to us before that if we ever needed help to let them know, so they came over immediately and helped us move everything we owned into their garage and gave us their spare bedroom to live in for about nine months.

I continued to schedule concert tours while we began to find a more permanent place to live. Over the past few years we had gradually been scaling down and had no furniture and very few personal belongings left. At one point Phyllis told the Lord, "If you want the Tupperware, Lord, I'm willing to get rid of that too!" It was then that we also discovered that our storage unit in San Diego had leaked and destroyed many of our belongings, including our high school yearbooks and all of Phyllis's Standard Publishing VBS songbooks and recordings. I guess we were to forget the past, and were meant to be on the road full-time, traveling wherever the Lord led us and having no home! We were both aware of how much the Lord had gifted us and we wanted to use our talents for His glory. I had quite a testimony about never smoking and never taking drugs in my entire life, and although I had been in many situations where I was tempted, I chose not to get involved with either smoking or drugs.

In about 1991 we met a man in San Diego by the name of Frank Holmes, who told us he was a singer and a song writer and wanted to know if we wanted to record one of his songs. He had rewritten the gospel song "Jesus Loves Me" and added a couple more verses to it. When he found out who I was back in the late 60s he told us about a studio which belonged to friends of his called, J.C.'s Construction Company, and he offered to record some of my oldies onto a cassette.

We decided to find out more about this studio which was located in one of his friend's apartments on the ground floor, so we visited it. We set up studio time and recorded "Happy Together," "Just A Dream," "Get Ready," "My Phyllis," "We Belong Together," "The Lion Sleeps Tonight," "Summertime Blues," "Donna," "Come On, Let's Go," and "Sixteen Candles." When we needed a title for this new album Phyllis suggested we simply call my new cassette album, "Frankie's Back," indicating my return to singing.

Most of the songs I was able to record on the first try. The guys would record all the instruments and background vocals, and then invite me in to record the lead vocals. On two songs I not only sang the lead, but also a harmony as well. A lady friend of the band wanted so much to sing the high soprano background vocals to "The Lion Sleeps Tonight," but she couldn't quite reach the high notes, so the studio engineer simply slowed down the speed of the recording tape so she could sing with that pitch, and she became a part of my album.

The last song the guys recorded for me was the song "Sixteen Candles." They worked so hard making the song sound just like the original and included all the background vocals. When I came into the studio and finished laying down the final touches with my lead vocals, Frank Holmes came over and gave me a big bear hug and had tears in his eyes, and told me that my vocals helped put the finishing touches on that beautiful song. We later re-mastered the cassette in 2009 and transferred all the music onto a CD, adding five more songs, including: "Forget Him," "Silhouettes," "Oh, Boy," "Daddy's Home," and a live version of "The Lion Sleeps Tonight" that we found on an old cassette recording of my singing that song in a night club circa 1973.

I booked another tour for us all the way up the west coast to the state of Washington. In California we had concerts in Oxnard, Bakersfield, Fresno, Concord, and Redding. In Oregon we had concerts in Klamath Falls, Grants Pass, Coos Bay, and Woodburn. When we reached the state of Washington our first stop was in Olympia. The music director of the church in Olympia was Ron Newman, the former second lead-singer of the legendary singing group "The Diamonds." When he found out that we needed a place to spend the night, he and his wife offered their guest bedroom to us. What an honor to meet another former pop-singer of the 60s, and a fellow Christian. Ron Newman has since moved to Arizona.

Our last stop on this tour was at a church in Everett, Washington, and at this point we were so tired and ready to go back to San Diego. However, Pastor Dave Eggebraaten met us at his church and gave us a tour of the church before we set up for our concert, telling us that he was also a singer and a songwriter, proceeding to tell us about the studio in his home.

After our concert, we needed a place to stay during the week, so Pastor Eggebraaten offered to let us stay at their home for that week so we wouldn't have to stay in a motel during that time, which we couldn't afford to do.

When we arrived at their home the pastor's wife, JoAnn, seemed to be somewhat cold and distant, and we both started feeling a little uncomfortable, but we now know that our feelings came from the pastor's wife needing to do something and had to be busy elsewhere in their home. She did join us later in the evening and we had a wonderful visit. When we retired to the guest bedroom Phyllis started crying. When I pressed her for her reasons, she said, "I want to go home, but I have no home to go home to." I wanted to sit and cry with her. She was right. We had no home and we were living in a temporary housing situation back in San Diego.

During the week we witnessed their special time of feeding of the squirrels that came up to their sliding glass doors to grab a peanut from your hand. If the peanut had a hole in it, the squirrel would take the peanut outside and eat it. If the peanut was perfect, the squirrel would bury that peanut somewhere in the back yard. Before we left for San Diego, Pastor Dave Eggebraaten and JoAnn gave us a bread machine. They have since retired and are living in southern Missouri and have become life-long friends. Pastor Dave calls us each time he writes, sings, and produces another album.

FORTY EIGHT

CAR THIEF

During one of our many tours we were able to attend my youngest son, Mark's, high school graduation in Denver, Colorado. Now Phyllis and I were living in San Diego, California, and we wanted to do something special for Mark for his graduation, so we decided to fly him out to San Diego so I could take him to Disneyland. We had already flown his sister, Heather, out earlier when we lived in San Diego before, and I had taken her to Disneyland. Now it was Mark's turn.

After we flew Mark back home to Denver, I decided it was time to book another concert tour. This time we had offers to do concerts as far away as Albuquerque, New Mexico.

Our first stop on this tour was in Victorville, California, where the church arranged for us to stay in a bed and breakfast. When we arrived there we noticed that there was an old jeep sitting on the front lawn but we didn't realize the significance of it until we checked in. This was the original home of Roy Rogers and Dale Evans! The jeep sitting in the front yard was the famous Nelly Belle jeep that was used in some of their movies. The next day after our concert the pastor took us on a tour of Victorville and showed us Roy and Dale Evans new home. We drove up to a tall metal gate that was the entrance to their home and the gate simply read "R R." The pastor told us that Roy was just one of the townsfolk and was friendly to everyone. Although we didn't get to meet Roy and Dale, we were privileged to hear the stories that were told and see their homes and see their old jeep, Nelly Belle.

We continued our tour to Kingman, Arizona, then on to Flagstaff. We drove on to Gallup, New Mexico and then to Albuquerque. After our concert at the church in Albuquerque, we met the most wonderful couple, Rick and Susie Soto, who invited us to their home to spend the night. They opened up their hearts and their home to us and we have become life-long friends. The famous yearly balloon festival was in progress and they took us out to witness the balloons taking off into flight. Rick had a photography studio where he took a picture that we had and placed It onto a coffee mug, and we still have that coffee mug.

The next day we headed on to Farmington, New Mexico where we had a church concert. After our concert a couple offered to have us spend the night at their home, and we found out that the man owned a used car lot there in Farmington. He had asked me pertinent questions about our van as though he was interested in it, but I never gave it much thought when we left for San Diego.

The next morning we drove on up to Flagstaff for our next concert, but on our way north on interstate 17 our van broke down. The elevation goes from almost sea level in Phoenix to an altitude of almost 12,000 feet in Flagstaff. There was no cell phones back then so we just had to wait until someone stopped to help. After a few hours of sitting alongside the road, a car pulled up and a highway patrolman approached us. To us he was an angel for stopping. He told us he would drive to the next town north and have a tow truck sent back to us.

A tow truck came and hooked up our van and asked us where we needed to take it, and we told him we needed to be in Flagstaff. The tow truck driver towed us to a mechanic in Flagstaff but the mechanic in Flagstaff told us he couldn't get around to fixing our van for a couple of days, so I decided to call the family with whom we had spent the night in Farmington, New Mexico. I knew this man owned a used car lot and could possibly help us get our van fixed.

The man in Farmington sent one of his salesmen in a tow truck to tow our van all the way back to Farmington. He took our van to his shop in his used car lot, and loaned us one of his used cars to continue our tour. We drove back to San Diego to Rich and Gloria's home where we were staying at the time and continued our concert tour in our borrowed car.

In the coming weeks I kept calling the man in Farmington to ask how our van was coming along, and each time he told us he needed for us to send more funds. We started to become concerned and wondered why the money we had been sending never seemed to be enough. We decided to drive to Farmington to find out what the problem was.

We drove our borrowed car to the used car lot and asked where our van was. The owner was not in but the guy who had come to tow us was there. He said our van was in the garage across the street. When we went into the garage we noticed our van was totally taken apart and had not even been fixed yet, so Phyllis and I decided to contact the local police. We drove over to the police station to tell them we had been sending the used car owner many checks to cover his mechanics bill to repair our van, but the bills were never paid. The police said they would accompany us to the used car lot to retrieve our van, and have a tow truck meet us there.

We arrived with the police and a tow truck to get our van. The owner drove up and told the police and the tow truck that we were not allowed to take our own van, so the tow truck driver left. The police said they couldn't do anything more because our van was in his possession and we had no recourse but to leave our van with him. Unless we took this man to court, he now owned our van, a New Mexico law! We had no time, nor money to take anyone to court, because we didn't even live in Farmington or New Mexico. Our van was stolen and we had no way to leave Farmington except to fly out.

We were able to catch a flight out of Farmington to San Diego the next day, but wondered why the Lord had allowed all this to happen. We had no home, and now we had no vehicle. How could we continue our ministry touring? Over the past few years we had been scaling down and now we had very little to even call our own. We had to continue to rely totally on the Lord more now than we had ever had to do before. Maybe this is where the Lord needed us to be so He could work a new work in us. The Lord needed to get the 'things' out of the way for us to completely place all of our trust in Him.

We flew back to San Diego where Rich and Gloria picked us up to take us back to their home. Phyllis and I never felt so detached, abandoned, and helpless than we did at that very moment. It was so hard for us to keep trusting in the Lord when it seemed everything was being taken away from us.

At Rich and Gloria's home Phyllis and I walked everywhere. If we needed something from the store, we walked to it. We had very little money and no way to get to our concerts to create an income. We had no choice but to sit and wait on the Lord.

We decided to attend the church in El Cajon where we had been in concert earlier where the pastor had been so kind to us. We felt right at home. One Sunday Rich and Gloria offered to take us to the church in El Cajon and not attend their own church, and we ended up meeting Gary and Carol Kay Murrow there. Gary was on the praise team at the church. When we first met them and told them where we lived, Carol Kay said that she and Gary lived only a few blocks away from us. Phyllis and I were able to walk over to their home from Rich and Gloria's home and spend time with them. Their youngest son, Derek, lived with them and was the youth pastor at the church in El Cajon. We are still the best of friends.

After the first Sunday at the church, Gary and Carol Kay knew we had no vehicle for transportation so they offered to pick us up. During one of the church services I noticed a woman sitting in the pew in front of us that we had met earlier by the name of Shirley when we first came into the sanctuary. I told Phyllis that there was something about her that made me think of our old friend Vince. We knew that Vince's wife Mary had left him. I thought maybe we could try and have the two of them meet. We were able to find Vince in the phone book and I called him. It was so great getting back in touch with an old friend, so I told Vince about this woman we had met at church and wanted to see if he'd like to meet her.

We set up a meeting by taking Vince with us to a store where Shirley said she'd meet us. When Vince got out of our car and took one look at Shirley walking out of the store towards us, his eyes lit up as if he knew at that very instant that this was the right woman for him, so we later found out that Shirley had felt the same thing, and they married shortly afterwards. It was a great feeling knowing we had been the catalyst for this couple to meet.

When the pastor of the church heard that we had no transportation he mentioned from his pulpit that we were in need of a vehicle. A family spoke up and offered to sell us their small motorhome. We could pay them a little at a time after each concert, but when Rich and Gloria took us over to their home to see the motorhome, Phyllis and I were in shock. This small motorhome was an older model and it looked like it wasn't even drivable. We knew that we had no choice but to accept their offer however and drive the motorhome back to Rich and Gloria's. We took that small motorhome on a tour that took us all the way to Cozad, Nebraska and on the way we rain into a blizzard and the driveshaft in the motorhome failed us. We had to stay another night in a motel in Wyoming until the motorhome was fixed. After taking the motorhome on one concert tour, we decided to take it back to the owners, thanking them for the use of it.

Another couple came forward and gave us the use of their Bounder motorhome. They knew we had a concert tour to Colorado and they wanted us to license their motorhome there, because licensing their motorhome in California was going to be too expensive for them. They told us that if we liked traveling in the Bounder we could rent the motorhome from them for $450 a month. We were not too sure about renting it, but we wanted to try it out.

I set up a concert tour that would take us to Denver, Colorado where we could license the motorhome. We had been invited to appear on the TBN station in Denver on one of their programs.

One of our concert dates along the way was a church in Moab, Utah. The drive to Moab was a sight to behold. We passed the Arches National Park to get to Moab and we were hoping that maybe we could take a tour of the park sometime during our stay in the area.

We had a wonderful Sunday morning concert, and when the pastor told us he had created a special drama 'one man show' to the song "Behold The Lamb," we told him we wanted to see him perform it. Before any of us went to lunch we were privileged to witness his rendition of the song. What a Christian message this pastor had become when he created that drama.

Sunday evening in Moab, our concert was at a restaurant on top of a mesa. Just north of town was a hill with a narrow one-way winding road leading to the top, and on top of this mesa was a restaurant. I had to drive our Bounder motorhome up that very narrow one-way winding road to the parking lot in front of the restaurant, and I found myself praying all the way up. One false move and we could have driven off the jagged edge. After our concert, I had to drive that motorhome all the way down that long and winding road, in the dark. Scary!

Monday we had a free day and the pastor took us to the famous Arches National Park where we walked up close to the famous Arch and to the Balancing Rock. So many sights to see and to remember! We were realizing more of the benefits from traveling in a full-time music ministry.

Tuesday we arrived in Denver to make an appearance on a TBN program along with another guest that had been invited to speak too. We had been given only a half an hour to do an interview. When we started to go on, the host told us that their other invited guest could not make it and told us we could take the whole hour.

Phyllis and I shared a couple of our songs on the TBN TV show and then the host interviewed us. We always gave our testimony and included testimonies of our sexual abuse as children. The phones were ringing off the hook at TBN and a lady came running into the TV studio bringing with her hundreds of pieces of paper showing responses from callers who had experienced sexual abuse as children as well. The host was in shock and told us that this had been the most responses they had ever had to a TV program. She thought that perhaps Jan and Paul Crouch would invite us to their TV station in southern California to share our story to the world, but they never did. We were invited to share our talents and testimony to several other TBN stations throughout the nation but never with Jan and Paul Crouch.

While in Denver we visited my parents and headed northeast to stop and see our friends, Loren and Althea Riley who lived on a farm just outside of Yuma, Colorado, where we had recently lived. My mother knew I loved her homemade raisin pies, so she sent two wonderful pies with us. They were just out of the freezer and were topped with foil and when we arrived at the Riley's farm we placed the pies on the floor of the front seat so they wouldn't melt on the fabric of the seats, and then we cracked the windows to allow air to circulate.

We had a great visit with our special friends, but time was running out and we needed to get back on the road. However, when we opened the vehicle door, we saw the most incredible sight! The foil on top of the pies had been torn off, and both pies had been partially eaten! All we could figure out is that the farm cats had somehow smelled the raisin pies, (frozen and covered with foil) and somehow squeezed through the slightly open window, and apparently had enjoyed my mother's delicious raisin pies as much as I did! I'll bet later on there were some cats with sick tummies! We, however, had to throw away both pies, going on our journey, pie-less!!

Our next concert date was at a church in Hays, Kansas. The concert was a total success and we met up again with gospel singer Roger

Cooper, who attended the church. Roger and the pastor of the church wanted us to move to Hays and the church would sponsor us. A lady in the church offered her basement apartment to us and we decided to stay and see what the Lord had in store for us.

While living in Hays the thought came to us that we had been having problems with using our legal last name of Piper. Since I had been going by my stage name of Frankie Valens in concert, and Phyllis was going by her married name of Phyllis Piper, we had people ask if we were 'living' together, and the coquettish part of Phyllis said, "Yes," but then finished with, "but we're married!" We even had one family tell us that "No one with different last names is staying in our home!" We decided it was time to change our names legally.

While we were still living in Hays, we found an attorney and decided to legally change our names. He expedited our case by hand-carrying the papers to the judge, and we became Frankie Valens and Phyllis Valens right then and there, but when we drove over to the DMV to get new driver's licenses and the man asked Phyllis her name, she said "Phyllis Valens," he asked what her middle name was, and Phyllis said, "Middle name?" We hadn't even thought about middle names! The man said to her, "You have to have a middle name!" Phyllis said she didn't, and even showed our court papers to him, but he was really upset we didn't have middle names. We legally became Frankie Valens and Phyllis Valens, with no middle names!

Our travels have taken us from coast to coast and to Canada. We have met so many wonderful people and some have become life-long friends. We were able to visit many tourist attractions and experience so many different aspects of our beautiful country. Along the way we were able to visit with family and friends and experience people wanting to turn their lives over to the Lord. We were being blessed.

Rich Palmer called while we were on tour telling us that the billionaire from the largest multi-level company wanted to book "Frankie Valens" to do a mini-oldies concert for his function in Salt Lake City, Utah at the new Delta Center, where on the same ticket were former President Reagan and country singer, Crystal Gale. He said they were expecting at least 25,000 people at the Delta Center, and with satellite connection, another 10,000 would be in attendance at the Salt Palace. All the speakers and entertainers were to speak and sing at both venues.

Phyllis and I continued our trip that led us to the Des Moines, Iowa area in concert. I booked a round trip airline ticket from Des Moines, Iowa to Salt Lake City, Utah, leaving Phyllis in our borrowed motorhome parked at a friend's home in Creston, Iowa. I had contacted our friends Dave and Rita Nugent who live near Salt Lake City and asked them if they would pick me up at the airport and take me to the Delta Center. I invited Dave and Rita to attend the function and they were thrilled to be invited.

When we arrived at the Delta Center we entered in at a side entrance through security gates that led to the stage area where the security was incredible because of former President Reagan that had been invited to be the guest speaker. The multi-level company people had set up a display table for me in the huge corridor and provided volunteers to help me sell my albums after my performance. I left Dave and Rita so they could be seated and I was escorted backstage to a dressing room to await my appearance.

Within 30 minutes a representative from the multi-level company came to escort me to the backstage area to wait till I would be introduced. When a couple walked out onto the stage to introduce me I could tell by their voices that they were all excited that a former pop-singer was going to perform. When they introduced me I walked out onto the brightly lit stage with spot lights glaring at me that were almost blinding. As I looked around the top of the huge auditorium I noticed the name "Frankie Valens" posted in lights all around the room. As I walked nearer to the front of the stage I could barely see the hundreds of people waiting for me to perform, but when I took a closer look at them, they had given me a standing ovation before I even started to sing. I had to hold my emotions in check before they could have a chance to overwhelm me. I couldn't take a chance that my eyes might fill up with tears of joy of being recognized.

Maybe these people did remember my music and who I was, even if my stardom was so fleeting back in the late 60s. I had quit the music scene but I was hoping that my music had lived on. Was I still chasing some kind of an illusive dream of one day becoming a recognized international star? This appearance at the Delta Center seemed like it was the highlight of my singing career and maybe I was back on my way up? But somehow, what I had been dreaming for and wanting for so many years, didn't seem as important to me now. I found myself praising Jesus throughout my whole performance.

I was only asked to sing three songs at the new Delta Center. The last song I chose was a fun song I had always sung in the night clubs. I knew everyone loved, "The Lion Sleeps Tonight." As soon as I started singing, 25,000 people stood to their feet, joined hands, lifting their joined hands into the air and began to sing along with me. I have never felt more humbled than I did at that very moment. The song itself was actually composed by Solomon Linda as "Mbube" in the 1920s and Solomon recorded it at South Africa's Gallo Records in 1939 after he had moved to Johannesburg to begin work as a record packer. It was the American folk singer Pete Seeger who changed the "Mbube" to "Wimoweh." Solomon, a Zulu musician never earned a cent in royalties and died in poverty early in the 1960s. Today, his daughters remain poor in Soweto, South Africa but are fighting for their father's fair share of the profits.

After my performance I was led backstage where my friends Dave and Rita were waiting. When the three of us started walking backstage towards the corridor where my tape table was set up, we saw Crystal Gayle coming towards us. Rita went right over and gave Crystal Gayle a hug. I also walked up to Crystal Gale and gave her a hug and told her how much I had appreciated her concert, and she told me that we needed to do this again sometime.

When we finally reached my display table in the corridor, there were two ladies there already taking care of the line of people that were already lined up at my tape table wanting to purchase my albums and to meet Frankie Valens. I only had two albums on cassette to offer to the long line of people, our album "In The Fullness Of Time" and "Frankie's Back," and we had literally just received our newest venture, "In The Fullness Of Time" just before this function.

It was so exciting for me sitting there handing out cassette after cassette and some wanting my autograph. I was signing my autograph on one of my albums when a man standing right in front of me spoke my name as if it were a statement. I looked up and saw someone standing in front of me but I didn't readily recognize him, and he asked me, "Don't you recognize me? I'm your first drummer, Dennis!" As surprised as I was I really didn't have the time to sit and chat with him so I asked him to please write his address and phone number down so we could stay in touch (this was before the internet and cell phones.)

After having the opportunity to meet Dennis after my concert, our touring took us on through Tucson, Arizona, where we decided to stop and look him up. Since Dennis had not given me a phone number I had no way of calling him, but he did give me an address.

When we arrived in Tucson we picked up a city map of Tucson and located the address that Dennis had given me earlier at the Delta Center. When Phyllis and I reached the address he had given me, it was an empty lot! You had to live in the area to know that that address was an empty lot. Why didn't he want me to find him? When Phyllis and I prayed about it the Lord spoke to my spirit telling me that He didn't want me to look to the past and to leave the past behind. It wasn't until 2010, 43 years later, that I discovered a band member from my very first band in New Jersey when I just happened to find my first lead-guitarist on FaceBook. I took a trip to New Jersey in 2010 and was able to meet my first lead-guitarist, John Bowden and my first bass-guitarist, Tom Slack. My very first drummer, Bob Barone, lived near Atlantic City and I was not able to meet him, and he just recently died. The Dennis I met at the Delta Center was the first drummer in the Fragile Glass band when I was known as Frankie Valens.

Many doors were opened for us to do concerts when we got involved in a large multi-level company through our association with Rich and Gloria Palmer. Rich and Gloria were 'directs' in this company and third from the top. This multi-level company, one of the largest in the world flew me to New Orleans to perform an oldies concert where 4,000 people were in attendance. Because the ballroom was near the top floor of the hotel where the swimming pool was located, we had a problem with all the people dancing on tables and hopping around to my music, and the pool water was splashing out of the pool on top of the building because of the dancing. I later was flown to Dallas/Fort Worth to sing at a company function and to Heritage USA to perform on their main street. Heritage USA had been built on 2500 acres of land near Fort Mill, South Carolina.

Main Street at Heritage USA

After my last concert for one of their functions I was told that they would not book me into any more functions until we became direct distributors. We had become members through Rich and Gloria Palmer at the beginning of our concert touring, but when I was told this, we decided we didn't want to be members anymore. We always felt that our concert touring was not at all related to our involvement with our membership in the company, but apparently it did matter.

FORTY NINE
THE CHOO CHOO THAT COULD!

Throughout the 18-plus years we traveled in our music ministry, we have always strived to give our very best, no matter what. We were not always well-equipped with the best vehicle to travel in or the best in sound equipment, but during the early part of our touring ministry, a gospel recording artist, Roger Cooper from Hays, Kansas, had compassion on us and donated a complete sound system for our use. We still use that sound system today. As of this writing we will soon meet Roger Cooper again at the Rush County Fair in LaCrosse, Kansas where we are in concert, Haskell Cooley is in concert, and Roger Cooper as well.

We have owned vehicles that we used for our traveling, we've had friends loan us vehicles to use, and we've had vehicles given to us. We've driven cars, vans, trucks, and motorhomes. We met a wonderful couple in Cozad, Nebraska, Pastor Jim and Michelle Henry, who literally bought a motorhome so we could rent it from them by making their monthly loan payment. Phyllis and I were elated to be able to travel in a motorhome, so Pastor Jim and Michelle told us they would drive the motorhome to Hays, Kansas and we could meet them there. We had a southern California tour coming up and we sure needed that motorhome.

There are so many advantages to traveling in a motorhome. We didn't have to worry about overnight housing or having to eat in restaurants.

Phyllis knew that if she needed to use the restroom, all she had to do was walk to the back of the motorhome. We carried all of our own sound equipment and ministry information, and could cook our own meals right there in the motorhome. When we needed to park for the night we met the most wonderful people in RV parks.

For the first few thousand miles we traveled in this motorhome we had very few problems. We were able to travel to Minnesota, Michigan, and most of the mid-western states in concert. In one of our travels to the St. Louis, Missouri area, a couple in a church donated a small travel trailer that we towed behind our motorhome. It had a king-size bed in it and plenty of storage, with even a porta potty, and a man from one of our concerts volunteered to paint it to match the colors on the motorhome. When we stopped for the night we could either sleep on a bed over the cab of the motorhome, open up the sofa to a full-size bed, or sleep in the travel trailer that had the large bed.

Then the problems began!

We left Wichita in our motorhome with the travel trailer on the back, heading to southern California for a tour. I didn't notice any problems in traveling until we were driving through Oklahoma City heading west, when I felt the transmission slip. I told Phyllis we'd better stop and have someone check the dip stick for the transmission to make sure we had enough fluid. The mechanic checked the fluid and everything seemed fine. Heading west on interstate 40 I kept feeling something was wrong with the motorhome but I couldn't put my finger on it.

We had traveled west of Clines Corner on interstate 40 in New Mexico, just east of Albuquerque when I heard a high-pitched squeal coming from the back of the motorhome. I thought that the travel trailer tongue had come loose so I immediately came to a stop alongside the highway before something tragic could happen. I walked around the entire motorhome and the travel trailer and couldn't see anything wrong until I looked at the right rear wheel of the motorhome and saw a few lug nuts missing. The lug nuts were coming off as we were driving! What could we do? We had no cell phones and no way of getting in touch with anyone. I had to flag a motorist down.

After trying for what seemed like hours to flag someone down, a motorist stopped. I told them we needed a tow truck to get us to Albuquerque because we had friends there that were waiting for us. After they left I was hoping and praying that they would indeed contact someone and have a tow truck sent out to us, and within a couple of hours a tow truck did pull up alongside of us. What the motorist didn't tell the tow truck driver was that we needed two tow trucks because of the travel trailer attached. Because we needed two tow trucks, we had to wait till morning before they could come out to help us get to Albuquerque. Have you ever tried sleeping in a motorhome right next to the highway with all the 18 wheeler trucks passing by within inches of you, causing such a disturbance with the force of their breeze they create, that it causes the motorhome to rock? It was a frightful night.

Two tow trucks did come the following morning and towed us into Albuquerque, and it was at the mechanic's office that we were able to contact our dear friends, Rick and Susie Soto. It didn't seem like it took long for the mechanic to replace the missing lug nuts and we were back on the road again. We knew we had lost valuable time and didn't have time to stop and visit with the Soto family so we headed south on interstate 25.

We hadn't gone very far south out of Albuquerque when we started having problems again with the motorhome. We had to pull over into a roadside park to examine what was going on with our rear wheels. The lug nuts the mechanic placed on our rear wheel were coming off, again! Apparently the mechanic couldn't find the right size lug nuts for our wheel so he literally placed the wrong size lug nut backwards on our wheel. I flagged a motorist down who had come to take a break at the roadside park and he took me into the next town to get help. I was able to call a tow truck that was able to pick me up at the convenience store where the motorist had left me, and we rode back together to the motorhome where we had the it towed to a mechanic in Las Cruces.

The mechanic in Las Cruces told us that the lug nuts had caused a problem with the transmission and the transmission needed replacing. We had no choice but to spend the night at a motel and figure out how to get to southern California while our motorhome was being worked on.

The people at the motel told us that a shuttle bus comes to Las Cruces from El Paso, Texas everyday where we could catch a flight to San Diego. We scheduled the shuttle bus to pick us up at our motel where it took us to El Paso and we caught the flight to San Diego.

The mechanic in Las Cruces told us it may take a week to fix our van because he was already behind schedule with so many others needing help, but when I did call for the status of our motorhome, he told me the bill was over $2,000. He wouldn't take a credit card or a check. He wanted cash. The Lord not only provided the cash but gave me enough funds to fly to El Paso to take a shuttle to Las Cruces.

I left Las Cruces in the motorhome and started heading west on highway 10. From highway 10 I could take highway 8 all the way into San Diego, and before I had driven even a hundred miles west of Las Cruces, the motorhome started acting up again. The third gear on the transmission refused to work. I pulled over into a rest area and found a pay phone to call Phyllis. I had left her back in San Diego and didn't want her to have to take such a trip, so when I got her on the phone the tears just started to fall like raindrops. I just couldn't hold onto my emotions any longer. All I could see was that I just paid over $2,000 to have our motorhome fixed, and now the transmission is not working again. I started praying up a storm and told the Lord that he was pushing it with me. This was almost more than I could handle. I told Phyllis I would just spend the night at this rest stop and try and drive as far as I could the following morning.

I could only sleep for a few hours before I found myself wanting to get behind the wheel and drive up to a speed that the transmission could handle, no matter how slow I had to drive, so I could get to my wife in San Diego. All the stress of what I had been going through helped to irritate my sinuses and I started having problems breathing with coughing fits, but I was so determined that I was not going to let this problem keep me from my goal and I became very strong-willed.

The motorhome could only travel up to the speed of 45mph in second gear without giving me too much grief. It just wouldn't go into third gear. I traveled all the way in second gear through Arizona and was on highway 8 that would eventually lead me into San Diego, when I saw a mountain range coming into view. Up until that point the traveling I had to do was pretty flat with very few hills, but now there was a huge mountain range to cross over. My spirit was crushed and I started sobbing. I told the Lord that he had given me a mountain too high for me to climb.

Somehow through the blinding tears I realized that I had to have the strength and determination to drive right up over that mountain range as if it were nothing more to me than an ant hill. I had to trust in the Lord. I had nothing else! The more I thought of my wife waiting for me at the other side of that mountain range made me realize how much I loved her and missed her and I became that much more determined that I was going to make it over these mountains even if I had to walk.

As I approached the steep incline of that first mountain, my heart began to beat a hundred beats a second as I kept telling myself that this motorhome was going to be like the little Choo Choo that could. That little bit of humor coming from somewhere in my mind helped ease the tension that I was feeling.

That motorhome took the mountainous steep-graded highway as if it was nothing but a tiny ant hill. I went sailing over those rolling ant hills and coasted down every ant hill till I arrived in San Diego, driving straight to our friend's home where Phyllis was staying. Somehow I had to park the motorhome with the travel trailer attached to the back, near the front of their home that was on a cul-de-sac, but I was never so grateful to the Lord for bringing me safely to my destination.

We stayed with these friends in San Diego for almost a month. I had a sinus infection that just wouldn't let up and we had a motorhome sitting in the street with a transmission that wasn't working properly. Furthermore, we had no prospects of concert dates that would help create an income for us, and I had just paid out well over $2,000 in vehicle repair bills on a motorhome that was almost useless to us. But somehow we knew that we knew that the Lord would take care of us. We had nothing left but our faith.

During the month we were left stranded at our friend's home, I was able to make a phone call to a mechanic that told us he could fix our transmission that would help us to get back on the road again because I had told him we needed our motorhome to get to our concerts to help create an income. When the mechanic agreed to fix the motorhome I proceeded to make calls and set up a few concert dates. One concert date was in Garden Grove, California near Santa Ana in which a donation was offered that we knew would be more than enough to pay for the repair bills on the motorhome, so I had planned on sending the mechanic full payment for the repairs after our concert.

After the wonderful concert in Garden Grove we drove to highway 10 heading east where we found an RV park to spend the night. We needed the rest before heading out on our long journey to Freeport, Texas, which was located near the Gulf of Mexico. Highway 10 would take us all the way.

We awoke early from camping out in our motorhome with our attached travel trailer, and headed east on highway 10. We hadn't driven very far and our transmission decided it wasn't going to go into third gear, AGAIN! I stopped at the nearest gas station and called our mechanic in San Diego to tell him our transmission wasn't working. His wife answered the phone telling us that her husband wasn't there and proceeded to tell me that she had told him not to use some of those inferior parts he had used on our transmission, but she said he wouldn't listen. She told me she would have her husband call me right back. Within 30 minutes while I waited at the phone booth, the mechanic called me. I knew that the phone call would not be a pleasant one because I was really upset that we were left stranded again with a transmission that failed after only a couple hundred miles on it. He wanted me to turn around and come back to San Diego so he could work on the transmission again. I told him we had no time because we were due in southern Texas in a couple of days. I told him I could not honestly pay him for the shoddy work he had done and I hung up. We headed east on highway 10 in a motorhome that couldn't go above the speed of 45mph, all the way to Freeport, Texas. That was perhaps the most difficult time we had ever experienced in our ministry. The tensions that were created between us during that long, slow journey to Texas made riding with each other strenuous and nerve racking.

Just a day away from the Los Angeles area we heard on the radio that a huge earthquake had hit the area where we had just been camping overnight! Many bridges had collapsed and buildings fell. The Lord had spared us!

It took us several days to arrive in Freeport, Texas. When we arrived in town I stopped at a gas station and called the pastor to let him know we were in town, and he told us he would meet us at the church so we could set up and get a sound check.

Frankie's great-uncle Charles (Charlie) Piper, and his wife Pauline

When we pulled up into the church parking lot the pastor came out to greet us. After we introduced ourselves he told us that because of the appearance of our motorhome and travel trailer, he said "You guys look like the Beverly Hillbillies!" We were not sure that his sly remarks were called for or appropriate, but we realized that we probably could have been a representative of the folks who were from the back hills of Tennessee. When I was growing up and visited our relatives in Arkansas I knew that my great-uncle Charlie and his wife Pauline often reminded me of what living in the back hills can do to a person's psyche and appearance, but I loved them anyway.

During our concert at the church in Freeport we noticed that the children Phyllis had brought up onto the platform to sing and clap in a song she had just taught them that she had written, included hand-signing and clapping, but the children wouldn't clap. They kept looking out at their parents in the congregation. We didn't know why there was such a problem with clapping until after our concert when the pastor informed us that the church had just had a major split because of clapping and non-clapping, and we ended up with the non-clappers! Psalm 47:1 KJV clearly commands "O clap your hands, all ye people; shout unto God with the voice of triumph." This is not just a statement but a commandment from God! By creating our own set of rules and regulations in our churches we must grieve our Lord.

When we told this pastor in Freeport that our transmission wasn't working properly he recommended a local mechanic. The free-will love offering from our concert the night before was more than adequate to pay for yet another transmission. However, we decided we had had enough of replacing transmissions and decided to take this motorhome back to its owners in Cozad, Nebraska. We didn't know yet what we would do for transportation, but replacing three transmissions in one vehicle in eleven months was just too much.

Before we left Freeport, Texas we called Pastor Jim and Michelle in Cozad, Nebraska to let them know that we were bringing their motorhome back and asked them if we could meet them halfway between Cozad, Nebraska and Hays, Kansas, so we decided to meet them in Norton, Kansas. We contacted the church in Hays, Kansas to confirm our concert with them the night before we were to take the motorhome back, asking the pastor if there was someone in his church that could follow behind us to Norton, Kansas to bring us back to Hays. The pastor told us that there was a family in the church that wanted to help us and would bring us back to their home to stay until we could find other transportation.

As we drove north out of Texas and into Kansas the weather started turning ugly and the temperature dropped out of sight. When we reached Salina, Kansas to head west on interstate 70 it started to snow, the wind blowing the snow straight across the highway so we could barely see. It just seemed like the problems with this motorhome were going to dog us all the way to the end. We knew we could not afford to replace one more transmission.

We pulled into Hays, Kansas and drove straight to the home of our new gracious friend's home who wanted to help us. We unhooked the travel trailer and left it on the front lawn and we headed to Norton with our friends traveling right behind us. There were times we didn't think we were really going to make it because of the blinding snow and blowing wind, but we did make it to Norton, and Pastor Jim and Michelle were waiting for us. When we turned the keys to the motorhome over to them, we both felt such a relief. We didn't know how or where we would have transportation after leaving the motorhome, but we had enough faith in the Lord to know that if He wanted us ministering and traveling full-time on the road, He was going to provide something for us to travel in.

Our newfound friends drove us back to their home in Hays and we were so grateful to be somewhere safe and sound and out of the awful blizzard that was taking place. That family ended up helping us to purchase a Lincoln Continental by using one of their own cars for collateral. I wanted to cry. All we had to do was send our monthly payment for the car to the bank, although the loan was not in our name, but in their name. Phyllis and I had no credit because we had been paying cash for everything we owned and had not established any credit rating. We would have much preferred to have a van to carry all of our equipment in, but if a car was the only door that the Lord opened, then we knew that the Lord provided what we needed.

Our Lincoln Continental was a gift from God and we were able to travel from coast to coast ministering in concert in almost every state. Our concert touring even led us on tour to Canada twice. We took several trips to the west coast in concert, to upstate New York, and even to Florida, and although we couldn't carry as much, we were able to put our sound system in the trunk of our car and our clothes on the back seat. We put thousands of miles on the Lincoln.

FIFTY

GONE ARE THE TEARS

While we were in Wichita in 1993 on a concert tour we met a singer/songwriter, Dennis Craven. Dennis had attended one of our concerts, and after our concert he invited us to come back to his home where he also had a studio and listen to a couple of the songs he had written.

Phyllis and I had been discussing the idea of recording an original album, using not only Phyllis's compositions but also songs from other writers as well, and after listening to some of Dennis's original recordings there were at least three of his songs that I knew I wanted to record. Most of what Dennis wrote was about children. After we heard the song "Gone Are The Tears" my heart just melted into a thousand pieces. Dennis told us that his inspiration for that song came after his nephew died from placenta previa. I knew that that song was written for me. Our friend Roger Cooper was the one who had sung the demo of it for Dennis and we had met Roger in Hays, Kansas earlier, the man who had donated the sound system to us.

With much excitement we made an appointment to record at Dennis's studio, just to have him tell us that he didn't think he could do the keyboard work that he knew his songs needed for our project, and he referred us to Tim Raymond. We had never met Tim but Dennis told us that Tim had traveled with gospel singer, Carmen, and was in charge of his band on the "Coming On Strong" album. He told us that Tim had left working with Carman when they had a difference of opinion on a project and now Tim had a recording studio in his home.

We had no idea how talented Tim Raymond was when we first walked into his studio. We had already chosen nine songs ahead of time that we knew we wanted to include on this album and Tim told us he would provide all the instrumentalists and background vocalists needed. An album needed at least 10 songs but we hadn't decided what song we wanted to include as our tenth song. We already wanted to re-record a few songs from our very first album "Expect The Unexpected" and see if Tim could really make the songs shine. From that album we asked Tim to re-create: "You Alone," "Praisin' My Lord," and "My Child," and I had already decided to record three of Dennis Craven's songs: "Gone Are The Tears," "In The Eyes Of Children," and "Tiny Voices."

In one of our concert tours we had met a couple in Nevada who were singer/songwriters and had recorded an album. When they gave us one of their albums I particularly liked the song "Never Ending Love," and wanted to include it on this new project. Another song was written by a woman in Iowa, Carlene, who had gone through a separation with her husband and she felt the townspeople were saying bad things about her and about them, so she wrote the words to a song she called "Throwing Stones" that she told us came from the Holy Spirit. She had recorded her voice onto a simple cassette recorder singing the melody that she heard in her head. All I had to work with were words on a sheet of paper and a cassette recording of her voice. I wanted to add this song to our album but I needed to rewrite the order in which she had written her words down so that the words would form verses and a chorus. I knew the Lord had to help me with this proposed song because I was not taught how to arrange music, but I must say that the song "Throwing Stones" was totally Holy Spirit inspired, because it came from Carlene's personal experiences, and this became a poignant song on our album.

Another song we added was a song written by our friend, Frank Holmes that we had met in San Diego who helped me to record my album "Frankie's Back." Frank had taken the song "Jesus Loves Me" and rewrote the lyrics adding his own verses to the melody. But we still needed one more song.

While we were in Wichita on tour we had had a concert at the Pawnee Avenue Church of God and had met Pastor Moore and his wife. When they knew we were in town recording an album and needed a place to stay, they offered us a guest bedroom in their basement, so we stayed with them during our recording, Pastor Moore's home was only a few blocks away from Tim Raymond's studio, which was a "God" thing!

Late one evening after we had returned from the studio, Phyllis wrote our tenth song sometime during the night at Pastor Moore's home. She says she remembered that she had heard a song that had the style and progressions she was wanting in a song, so she thought about writing her own song, and the idea began coming to her. Everyone had gone to bed, including me, and she didn't know where any paper was to write her ideas down on and there was no piano, so she quietly got out of bed in the dark and began fumbling around for some paper and a pencil on a desk nearby. She said she felt like a thief, stealthily searching through things that were not hers! But she finally found the paper and pencil, started drawing five staff lines, proceeding to write the melody to the song and adding in the chords she said she "heard" in her mind.

The next day she took the song into the studio and gave the "scratchings" to Tim. He looked at it and asked Phyllis what style she wanted him to play it in—Jewish, contemporary, or what? She told him she wanted it to be more contemporary, so Tim immediately played an intro that exactly fit what she had wanted, and then took the melody, and played the modulations as if he had practiced them. Tim had not even heard this song before but played it as if he knew it already. Phyllis and I were totally amazed and realized that Tim made a wonderful song out of her scratchings, and the song "Give Him Praise" was born.

The next day when we played the song for Pastor Moore, mentioning that this had been written in his home, he asked her if there was any way to include him, to which she quickly responded, "Ok, we'll call it, 'Give Him 'MOORE' Praise!'"

While we were at the studio, Tim took the taped recording of "Gone Are The Tears" that Dennis Craven had recorded in his studio, and gave the song a contemporary feel. Tim had found an album of the sound tracks from the movie Grease, and listened to a bass progression in one of those songs that gave him the inspiration to re-create the song. I told Tim I also wanted the music to sound celestial, like music being played in Heaven. After all, the song was about a little boy who had died and gone to Heaven, and was speaking to his mother from heaven. True to form, Tim provided all the background vocals, except where I decided to add a little harmonizing with myself.

What was so interesting is the fact that when I recorded Dennis's song "In The Eyes Of Children," that I had taken from his vocal demo, he mentioned on the tape at the end of the song, "The rest is up to you!" So I spoke it at the end of the recording, too. I thought Dennis meant that he wanted me to speak that quote at the end of my song. Wrong!

What he meant was that he wanted me to take liberties in whatever I wanted to do from that point on. We still laugh about it, but ironically the meaning does fit.

When Tim Raymond realized that I was a former pop-singer from the late 60s he offered to record an album of oldies, featuring songs I had sung during that era and for the first time we had two recording projects going at the same time. Financially we could not afford to pay his full fee for two recordings all at the same time, but he let us pay as we recorded and the Lord provided our funds through our concert touring.

I wanted to title my oldies album "Unchained Melody" because of what the song meant to me. I had auditioned with that song back in 1967 in New Jersey to become the lead singer of my first band the "Eminent Domain." This new album I recorded not only included "Unchained Melody" but also: "Stupid Cupid," "Hello, Mary Lou," "Rockin' Robin," "My Girl," "Pretty Woman," "At The Hop," "Johnny B. Goode," and "Will You Still Love Me Tomorrow." For the tenth song Phyllis persuaded me to also record "Only You," a song originally made popular by the Platters.

William Stirrat, better known as Hy Zaret, wrote the lyrics to "Unchained Melody" when he was only 16 years of age about the prettiest girl in his neighborhood, Mary Louise "Cookie" Pierce. The lyrics were inspired by Stirrat's young, un-requited love at an age when "time goes by so slowly, and time can do so much." Alex North wrote the music. The song emerged with the release of the movie "Unchained" in January, 1955 as a prison movie theme song that featured life in the California Institute for Men. Hardly a romantic film! The movie sank into obscurity, but the song is still one of the most requested songs of all time.

FIFTY ONE
THE ANGEL WAS A PATROLMAN

Brent Luck, a singer from Lake Havasu City, Arizona whom we met earlier, called us to tell us he was the music director at a church in Kingman, Arizona, which was about 59 miles north of Lake Havasu City and he wanted us to move to Kingman to help him in the music department at the church. He told us that he would help us book concerts in the area and maybe record a music video with him. Brent had quite a history in music and had worked with such notables as evangelist Benny Hinn, and singer Jeff Fenholt, who had a TV show on the Trinity Network in Los Angeles. We knew we were in good hands with Brent and welcomed the opportunity for a change.

Phyllis and I packed our bags in our Lincoln Continental and rented a U-Haul trailer to carry all of our belongings and headed to Arizona. Once again the Continental started giving us problems in New Mexico just west of Santa Rosa. The motor made some strange sounds and then completely gave out and we were stranded, again, about four o'clock in the afternoon on interstate 40 westbound. As many times as I stood out next to the highway trying to flag someone down, no one would stop. When it started to grow dark outside and colder, it became more difficult for me to try and persuade someone to stop for us. When darkness fell, I knew that no one would see me standing next to our car so I decided that I'd better try and grab our coats out of the U-Haul trailer and bundle up for the night while we slept in our car. We had no cell phone at the time but realized before falling asleep that maybe we ought to purchase one!

There were many times when we both thought that this must be the end. Snow had started falling and the wind had picked up and we were stuck in our car with no way of providing heat. I just thought for sure we were going to freeze to death before help came. Phyllis kept insisting that we pray for the Lord to give us mercy and send us help, but I was in a state of not believing that the Lord was taking care of us at all, so I was hesitant at first to ask the Lord for help. After praying, I was mad at God but started to relax and we both fell asleep.

About three o'clock in the morning I awoke after seeing a bright light shining through the passenger's side of our car. Our windows had fogged over and had frozen during the night with ice an inch thick on the 'inside' so that it was hard to see in or out of our windows, so I poked Phyllis to tell her about the light. I thought for sure we had died and this was the end, but it was a highway patrolman who had been driving by and happened to notice our U-Haul trailer out of the corner of his eye, and pulled his patrol car up to the right side of our car to check and see if someone was in the car. He found us. I'm not sure if we would have made it through the night if it were not for this angel of light. When the officer offered us the warmth of his squad car, we told him that it seemed like he was an angel sent to help us. He told us that he'd been called worse, and we all laughed.

When the patrolman called our friends Rick and Susie Soto in Albuquerque they were relieved to know that we were ok. After the tow truck arrived and informed us that we needed a new motor, we both fell apart, because we knew we couldn't afford the expense. However when Rick and Susie heard about it, they said they would loan us the money to pay for the new motor. We let the tow truck driver tow our continental east to Santa Rosa, and the patrolman took us west to Rick and Susie's home in Albuquerque. Our U-Haul trailer had to be towed to yet another place, we had no idea where at the time.

We stayed a few days with Rick and Susie until our car was ready and then we headed on to Kingman, Arizona without our trailer. The mechanic told us that they thought it would be best on our new engine not to pull a heavy load on the back of the Lincoln. After we arrived in Kingman, men from the church drove back to pick up our U-Haul trailer, and after several months we were able to repay Rick and Susie Soto the full amount of the loan for the cost of the motor. We were then able to travel on to Kingman, Arizona.

Phyllis and I were not comfortable at all with the situation we had to deal with at the church in Kingman and with Brent, but we knew we had made the decision to come to Kingman in 1996 and would continue our concert touring. Through a referral from someone in the church we found a small two-bedroom home to rent on the east side of Kingman. Although we continued attending the church and became part of their worship team, we were non-paid volunteers helping out in the music department. We made life-long friends at this church who we stay in touch with even today, and one such couple, Cliff and Carolyn Goodwin became very good friends. Cliff was like a brother to me, and Carolyn had a voice like Patsy Cline, having recorded several cassettes.

While we lived in Kingman and even when we moved to Lake Havasu City, we often met Cliff and Carolyn and played card games. Through Cliff and Carolyn we met Jack and Joylene Hurley. I miss Jack and Joylene and the fun we had as a close knit group that became more of a family to us before we moved away. Cliff had a major heart attack after we moved away and through the nursing of his wife, Carolyn, who was a registered nurse, Cliff is still with us. They have since moved to the Kansas City area. The Hurleys have family in Oklahoma and when they visit them they drive on up to Wichita to spend a few hours with us.

Brent made plans to have a music video made of his music, and a video of me singing "Gone Are The Tears," and "This Magic Moment." It was my very first music video and I was thrilled. Most of the filming and camera work had been donated to us by a local cable company.

An old school bus was donated to the church and the church turned the bus over to Brent to use in his ministry. Brent wanted to use it for not only himself, but for Phyllis and me to travel with him. We took one look at that bus and realized that the bus was not equipped well enough for a group of people to travel on a ministry tour to anywhere. The bus was old and had not been taken care of. Phyllis and I were not even sure we wanted to travel with Brent. We knew he had a ministry and a beautiful voice, but his plans were too sketchy and not too well planned, and we were left in the dark most of the time. He talked about our traveling and appearing on TBN an\d making guest appearances on various gospel radio stations and on TV shows. He wanted to use the "Frankie Valens" image to catch the attention of unbelievers and then tell them about Jesus. His ideas seemed fine, but the more we heard of his plans, we knew that we were not comfortable joining another 'ministry.'

Brent had recorded an album called "Be Still" and had used the famous singer, Jeff Fenholt, on his album as a background vocalist on a couple of songs that Brent had written. Over the years Brent had worked with such evangelists as Benny Hinn, and had made guest appearances on TBN. We became instant friends. The two of us were able to make a music video together on the shore of Lake Havasu, and I later recorded the title song of his album, "Be Still." Phyllis and I wanted to make a 'live' album or a video on the Lake Havasu beach, but never did.

We were invited to do a concert at Chubby's, a 50s diner in Lake Havasu City. I had driven over to the restaurant to meet the owner and to make plans for an outdoors concert in the parking lot. When I walked in the door, a man by the name of Lee Harrison walked over to me and asked me if I remembered him. I told him no, but that he looked a little familiar. Phyllis and I had met Lee and his wife Kay a few years earlier when we traveled through Arizona and had stopped at their small restaurant to eat. When they found out who I was they wanted me to sign my name on their wall of fame. These were those same people! They had moved to Lake Havasu after selling their restaurant and had started an industrial cleaning company, and one of their jobs was cleaning Chubby's 50's diner. After our concert Lee and Kay took Phyllis and me on a ride in their speed boat on Lake Havasu. It was about 120 degrees that day, but on the lake it seemed like it was only 90 degrees, and we rode that boat all the way up the Colorado river to where interstate 40 crosses over the river.

We loved our little home in Kingman. It had a one-car garage, two bedrooms, and a concrete patio in the back. I used one of our bedrooms as an office and we had a desk there where I could make calls to book concert dates. One church I called was a church in Anchorage, Alaska, and they wanted to book us for a concert. The church could not afford to pay for our airline flight but offered to house us at an apartment in Anchorage that the church rented for special speakers. I really wanted to go, but I knew we could not afford two airline tickets to Alaska, so after calling airlines in Las Vegas we decided I would go alone. Brent drove me to the Las Vegas airport to catch a plane to Seattle with a connecting flight to Anchorage.

I saw the most beautiful sights flying from Seattle to Anchorage. There were also hundreds of snow-capped mountain peaks. The rest of the mountain itself was invisible and dark, and when we flew over the ocean I saw thousands of small icebergs floating. I had never seen such sights!

When I arrived in Anchorage the pastor and his family came to pick me up at the airport. They took me directly to their home to have dinner and then took me on a tour of Anchorage to see an actual glacier near an inlet of water. In the inlet were large chunks of ice floating about. The pastor told me that I had not seen anything yet until I'd seen moose pellet wreaths. A lady in his church made Christmas wreaths, earrings, and various other items from moose pellets. Moose pellets are made odorless by shellacing and then they are made into jewelry and such. When we visited her at her home she showed us a picture album of everything she had ever made using moose pellets. It was most interesting.

While I was in Alaska Phyllis told she me heard a knock on her door on Sunday morning about 7:30am. When she answered the door a little girl was standing there, and her mother was sitting in a car in front of our home. This little girl wanted to know if Frankie was home because she wanted his autograph!

When we got word from the owners of the little house we were renting in Kingman that they needed to move back to their home, we had no idea what to do or where we were going to live. We knew we had friends in Lake Havasu City and decided to drive there to see if there was a home we could rent, and we found a home through a church we had visited in Lake Havasu City. The pastor told us that this family from their church was going on the road in a full-time music ministry and needed a couple to house-sit for them while they were gone. This seemed to be the perfect solution to our housing problem, so we immediately moved to Lake Havasu City.

FIFTY TWO
LAKE HAVASU

The home we moved to in Lake Havasu City, Arizona was a furnished two-bedroom older home with a formal dining room, a large kitchen, and a breeze-way to the carport. We had a fenced in backyard with palm trees and fruit trees, both orange and lemon. The home had central air but only a wood burning stove in the living room for heat. We started attending the church that had recommended our house-siting this home, and I used our guest bedroom as an office and continued making cold calls to schedule concerts. Many times we would pick lemons and oranges off the trees and use our juicer to make wonderful home-made lemonade and orange juice. We often invited Cliff and Caroline or Jack and Joylene from Kingman over for home-made lemonade and to play games.

I contacted the Lakeview Community Church in Lake Havasu City asking them if we could record a "live" album at their church. They loved the idea and invited us to perform in concert, advertising that we were recording a 'live' album. Phyllis and I met with the sound engineers a day in advance and practiced with them, however the night of our concert was a disaster when it came to the sound engineers. It was almost like they didn't know what they were doing and made all kinds of mistakes, and even though they taped our concert, we found only one song we could even salvage. We were able to use "Rejoice In The Lord

Always," featuring Phyllis's various musical piano stylings that led us

Frankie and Phyllis in concert

down through the ages from very early Christian music to Dino, which is now on her piano CD, "Piano Joy."

One morning I came out to our carport to get into our Lincoln Continental and noticed a pool of water under our car. I decided to check with a local mechanic to see what could be done. He told me that the radiator was made of plastic and needed to be replaced, and because it was a plastic radiator he couldn't repair it. The cost of a new radiator was not in our budget. We had already paid for a new motor and now the radiator was leaking, so we decided to sell the Lincoln. I posted an ad on the Post Office bulletin board and a few people came to look at our Lincoln, but no buyers yet. I was afraid to drive the Lincoln very far and would always fill up the radiator before heading out to do any errands.

A man answered our ad and wanted to buy the Continental, especially after he found out that I was the former pop-singer Frankie Valens. He came to our home and took it for a test drive, telling him we had just bought a new motor for it, so we ended up selling our car to this man for the price we had paid for the new motor. We were now without any transportation whatsoever, again.

I didn't know how we would be able to fulfill our obligations to minister in concert and earn a living ministering in concert without a vehicle. I had already booked concerts for us not only in town but also in Page, Arizona.

A couple from our church came forward and offered to loan us their second vehicle, a van. They warned us that the van really smoked awfully bad, but it would get us from point "A" to point "B." We borrowed their van and headed to Page, Arizona to do a concert. Yes, the van smoked up such a cloud that we were afraid we would be stopped by the highway patrol. The smoking van got us all the way to Page but I feel that we polluted the whole air space between Lake Havasu City and Page. Anyone traveling behind us would have needed to wear a gas mask!

At our concert at the church in Page we mentioned that we had no vehicle to travel in and we had to borrow a van to get to their church. A couple met us after our concert and took us out to the church parking lot and showed us their Silverado dual-wheel truck with a camper top covering the bed of the truck, which would be great for carrying our sound equipment and suitcases. They told us they wanted to loan it to us. I wanted to cry in disbelief. On the way back to Lake Havasu City I drove the truck while Phyllis drove the van. We were so thankful to have the use of the van, but now we had the use of a much better vehicle.

Just when we had a vehicle to travel in, the owners of the house we were house-sitting for decided to rent their home out to a single lady that needed a place to live. We were again going to be without a home, so we loaded everything we owned in the back of that truck, heading out on the road again, living on faith, and trusting the Lord to provide all of our needs.

While we were in Lake Havasu City I had already started booking an extended concert tour that would take us up the west coast to

Washington and then east to Idaho, Montana, Wyoming and then on to Colorado. We had contacted several T-shirt manufacturers in Oregon to sell their T-shirts on consignment at our concerts, as well as ball caps, ties, and mouse pads. We loaded up the back of our Silverado truck with all of our belongings, along with boxes of products, our cassettes, and our keyboard, and left for this extended tour.

We headed south out of Lake Havasu City, without any place to call home, to Parker, Arizona to sing at a church. From there we headed west to Joshua Tree, California for a concert at an outdoor church amphitheater. We headed to Barstow and then west on a highway that led us to interstate highway 5 and further west to Ukiah, California for another church concert. From Ukiah we headed back to interstate 5 through Sacramento and then north to Redding.

After our concert at the church in Redding we decided to tour the famous Redwood Forest and the huge tree that you can drive through. From the Redwood Forest we drove north into Oregon so we could visit one of the t-shirt manufacturers we had been ordering our t-shirts from in Klamath Falls. When we arrived at the factory the owner asked us to do a mini-concert for them. What fun! We sang to all the workers there.

From Klamath Falls we headed west to Coos Bay, which is on the coast near the Pacific Ocean. Everywhere we ministered in concert became a blessing to us. The Lord blessed us in offerings and an opportunity to meet wonderful Christian people and to witness God's beauty in His creation that was all around us as we traveled.

I must say that when we headed north from Coos Bay and away from the coast, I noticed balls of snow hitting our windshield as we headed into the mountains. Apparently we were so high up in the mountains that hail didn't have time to freeze and came down as soft, billowy snowballs. Oregon is so beautiful and it was the first time I had ever been to Oregon.

We headed on north through Portland and into the state of Washington where I had lined up concerts in Olympia, Aberdeen and Everett. We had a wonderful concert in Olympia and met the music director who just happened to be one of the lead-singers of the famous Diamonds from the 60s. After our concert he invited us to have dinner with him and his wife and also stay overnight. They have since moved to Arizona.

We were scheduled for two concerts in Aberdeen. The first church had provided Phyllis and me with overnight housing at a motel, and after our concert we were in our room when the phone rang. The church we were supposed to have had a concert at the following evening told us they were cancelling our concert with them. Apparently they had sent someone from their church to our concert at another church and didn't like something they heard or saw and chose to pay us $500 not to do a concert at their church! We were not upset about the change in our itinerary. We knew God didn't want us there, and He blessed us in the process.

We headed on up to Everett to the church where we had been the year before with Pastor Eggebraaten and his wife JoAnn. We had extra time to spend with them this time and Pastor Eggebraaten offered to transfer all of our cassette music tracks onto CDs. The pastor spent hours and hours in his studio making those transfers, and we surely could never thank him enough. We had finally arrived in the twentieth century!

When we left Everett, we started heading east on interstate 90. It had been foggy that day and the visibility was not good, but the pastor had told us that we should be able to see Mount Rainier as we headed south to interstate 90. I kept looking for the mountain and just couldn't see it. Phyllis was reading something and wasn't paying any attention when all of a sudden, the clouds cleared just enough for us to see the snow-covered peak of Mt Rainier in all its beauty. We only caught a glimpse of its beauty before the clouds and the fog took over and it disappeared. The locals say that doesn't happen that often.

Our next stop on this tour was Coeur d'Alene, Idaho, just across the border from Spokane, Washington. As we drove through this wonderful, beautifully wooded area we were told that the author, Frank Peretti, lived here and used this valley as the setting for his novel, "This Present Darkness."

The church in Coeur d'Alene provided overnight housing in one of their member's home. They lived several miles up in the mountains that had dangerous curves on a narrow road, and when we followed them home after our concert, they showed us where some cars simply didn't make a turn and had gone down in the ravine. We were not impressed.

The next stop on our tour was to Kalispell, Montana. We learned that the actor, Jim Nabors, lived in the area. Although we never got a chance to meet him, we heard that he was well-respected in the area. As we headed towards Kalispell we had to turn off of interstate 90 and take highway 28 north, and as we drove north and came to the top of a hill, straight ahead of us was the large Flathead Lake. At the far end of it was a mountain and in front of the lake was a low hanging fog. I had never in my entire life had ever seen such beauty in nature before as I did right then. This was truly "God's" country. Before we left for our next concert date the pastor and his wife took us to the Glacier National Park for a tour. We almost hated to leave.

The next day we drove south to interstate 90 and headed to Butte for our last concert in Montana. We truly experienced why it is called "Big Sky Country!" Then we headed east to Billings where we resumed our tour that led us south into Wyoming. When we stopped for gas I phoned the Pawnee Avenue Church of God in Wichita to confirm our concert with them. When Pastor Moore answered, he asked me if we wanted to come off the road to be their music pastors, and we told him we were interested and would talk with him further when we arrived.

FIFTY THREE
MUSIC PASTORS

In 1999 we came off the road to become the music pastors of the Pawnee Avenue Church of God. When we met with Pastor Moore he told us that the church could not afford to pay us but the church could get sponsors to support us through a Faith Promise every week. We would still be able to schedule an occasional concert but our main thrust was working with every aspect of the music at the church, which included the choir, three hand bell choirs, drama, puppet ministry, praise team, special music, scheduling of special speakers and singers, and head of the building and grounds committee. The church also had a school and we were able to work with the youth, helping them with their drama and music.

Phyllis and I found a furnished studio apartment on west Pawnee Avenue in Wichita. Our drive to the church would not take us long and we often found ourselves working 10 to 12 hours a day or more at the church because we loved our jobs. Phyllis directed the choir, praise team and three hand bell choirs. I worked with the drama, puppets and the building and grounds committee. I also sang in the choir and praise team, and played in one of Phyllis's hand bell choirs. We put our own ministry on the back burner and tried to help nourish other people to grow in their own talents.

For Easter, Phyllis and I wanted to create a musical presentation for the church that would include live animals, special biblical costumes, special lighting, and painted backdrops to help create the feeling of actually being in Jerusalem. We knew that the church had no budget for such a project but that didn't stop us. I went searching through the church and adjoining buildings to try and find anything we could use for this big production. I found wooden office dividers stashed away and not being used and I drug them one by one over to the church sanctuary and found a way to create life-like buildings and street scenes. Every day I would be in the sanctuary finding ways to build this make-believe setting. After I arranged all the room dividers and nailed them together for effect, I started drawing make-believe stones on them and then I painted each area a stone color. The doorways I painted in 3-D with shadowing. I wanted to make them look like someone could walk right through the door. A lady in the church worked for a nursery and she brought in shrubs and bushes for me to place around the scenery to make it come alive. Men in the church who could do carpentry came in and built a platform for the temple, while I painted the 3-D temple in the background. They also made a life-size cross. I had originally planned on using a special motor with a cable attached to Jesus to have him ascend up into Heaven, but that didn't work out.

Phyllis worked with the choir and soloists as well as with each individual, helping them create a drama scene around each scenario. A week before our pageant we had teams of volunteers go out into the neighborhood door to door all around the church, letting each family know that we were holding a pageant and they were invited.

The Easter pageant was a huge success and over 400 people came to the presentation. Ten years later we had people tell us that they were still talking about that pageant.

We received a call from the owners of the Silverado Truck we were driving and they asked us if we would bring back their truck so they could give us a motorhome to use. We were both excited. We had just finished the Easter Pageant and needed to take a break, so we hopped into our truck and drove straight out to Page, Arizona.

When we arrived in Page the owners told us that they were still working on getting the motorhome ready for us. They were replacing the carpet and fixing everything that needed repairing, so we waited the whole night and couldn't leave in the motorhome till morning.

When we drove over to pick up this motorhome, we were both in shock. It was an old, old motorhome that was barely able to stay on the road and nobody had driven it in years! We had no choice but to accept this motorhome because we had no other form of transportation. All I wanted to do was to get this motorhome back to Wichita and park it, but we had one last concert to do in Yuma, Arizona, our farewell concert. The motorhome seemed to drive fairly well during our trip from Page to Yuma, and even though it was old, we had the comforts of living on the road without having to stay in a motel or someone's home.

The next morning after our concert we headed east on highway 8. The drive to Wichita from Yuma, Arizona was the most horrendous, nerve wracking drive I had ever taken in my entire life. It wasn't until after we left Yuma the next morning when the trouble began with the motorhome.

We had just driven a few miles east of Yuma when the motor started sputtering, and the engine died. We didn't know what to do. I got out and tried flagging down a motorist for help. A few cars drove on by and I was becoming a little frustrated, when a pickup truck pulled over and parked behind our motorhome. This couple from California offered to help us by stopping at the next gas station and call for help, but while we were talking they asked us where we were heading, and we told them Wichita. The lady said she had a sister there. We told them that we were coming off the road, and were going to be the music pastors at the Pawnee Avenue Church of God. She said, 'My sister attends that church!' Her sister was Madeline Rosenbaum! Madeline had told her that if she ever got a chance to hear Frankie and Phyllis in concert, she would be thrilled. For this couple from California to stop and help us in Arizona, and this lady's sister from Kansas was the sister that attended the church where we were headed to, had to be a huge 'God' thing.

We traveled over 1,280 miles and had spent two days in a motorhome that had no heat and took more oil than gas to drive, and still had parts in it that were not working right. We never turned the engine off the whole trip, even to get gas, because we weren't sure it would start again. We knew we could not drive this motorhome around town as a form of transportation, so we parked it in an RV park between Wichita and Derby on highway K15 and lived in the motorhome. For transportation we could not keep unhooking all the hoses and electricity to go to the church daily, so we still needed a car.

When Pastor Moore heard that we were in need of a car, he made an announcement from the pulpit asking if someone had a car they could donate for our use. A family did have an old Chevy they donated to us, and we gratefully thanked them. We licensed it and drove it for a while.

Then a call came from the owners of this old motorhome from Page, Arizona, asking us to bring their motorhome back. We both thought that they had given us this motorhome! We told them we were not able to bring it back but we would park it in our friend's Keith and Gail's driveway and they could send someone to pick it up there, which they did, sometime later.

About a year after we had been at the church, one of the other pastors called us into his office to discuss with us about the Faith Promise that the church had worked out with us. He told us that some of the Faith Promise people had left the church and the church was picking up the slack by taking from the church's funds to pay the difference in our salary that was lost when these people left. We reiterated to the pastor the fact that when we first decided to be their music pastors we told him that if at some time there weren't enough funds to pay us, we would leave. Due to circumstances when we left the position, we also felt that we needed to leave the church as well. We felt that this was the Lord's way of telling us to move on and go back into our ministry.

We started attending a small church in Haysville and became involved in their music. The pastor approached us one day and told us that he and his wife had just bought a home and wanted to know if we wanted to rent the home where they had been living. We had been living in a studio apartment and had very little furniture but yes, we were interested. We drove over to south Wichita to take a look at this cute two-bedroom home with a one-car garage, and a chain-link fence all around the property. We were not sure we could afford to rent this home but placed our total trust in the Lord that if He wanted us to have this home, He would open the doors. We took a step of faith and stepped out of the boat and paid our first month's rent and moved in. Friends from the church in Haysville came to help us move. There had been an ice storm, and Phyllis and I were both sick and were hardly able to help at all, but we made the move anyway.

When we moved into the home we didn't have a refrigerator, so the owners of the home left theirs for our use. We also didn't own a washer or dryer, but the pastor's wife left her green dryer because it wasn't going to match her new washer. We didn't care about matching. We were just glad to have a dryer. Friends told us about a slightly dented washer they had seen at Sam's Club that was reduced in price, so we drove to Sam's and purchased it. When we didn't have the deposit needed to start our electric, the pastor/previous renter, gave us a check to cover the cost. Someone commented to us that it was as though we were being fed by the ravens.

We had been driving around in the old Chevy and decided we needed a more reliable vehicle to travel in, so we found an ad for a van that seemed very reasonable in price. When we drove out to test drive the van we noticed it had a horrible cigarette smell in the van, but the van itself seemed fine. We purchased it, but even though we had it professionally cleaned inside, we never got rid of that smell.

Before we left Pawnee Avenue Church of God we had been invited to attend the Nazarene's annual meeting held at the Central Community Church. We were so blessed by the music and the ministry, and after the meeting we met the pastor's wife of the First Church of the Nazarene. She invited us to come visit their church, so the following Sunday we attended their morning service. Talk about God's timing~! The church was in need of a church pianist and when we came that Sunday morning, the music pastor met with us, taking us out to lunch, and asking Phyllis if she would be the church pianist. She accepted.

When we came to church that evening Pastor Leonard approached us and told us that this was indeed the Lord's timing that we started coming to First Church.

FIFTY FOUR
ON THE ROAD AGAIN

We started attending the First Church of the Nazarene in Wichita. Phyllis was the church's pianist and I joined the church choir. At last we had found a church home, and we loved our pastor, Larry Leonard. We were often moved to tears by his sermons, and felt he was very anointed.

Working with Jody in the music department was such a joy. He asked me if I would help in trying to book the gospel singer, Larnelle Harris, to come to First Church to perform, because it had always been Jody's dream to have his choir back Larnelle in concert. After I made a few phone calls I found Larnelle's booking agency, and we booked him for Easter Sunday. Jody's dream had come true. We were however disappointed in the lack of attendance at the concert but realized that many gospel singers had been experiencing the same problem and many have had to team up and perform together in concert.

Our friend, Mark Johnson, who ran the El Dorado Dinner Theatre, called to tell us he had invited the legendary Mickey Rooney to come and perform at his dinner theatre, so we made our reservations for November 18th. We so enjoyed the show and I had mentioned to Phyllis during the show that Mickey Rooney was 82 years of age, the age of my father. The next morning after I had gone to the store, my mother called

our home and told Phyllis that my dad had died in his sleep during the
night on November 19th. By my calculations my dad died shortly after
we had attended Mickey Rooney's show. Since my dad had gone to a
nursing home in Grand Junction, Colorado just a few days before he
died, his body had to be flown back to Denver for burial, and he was
buried at the Fort Logan military cemetery with full honors befitting a
war veteran.

We started rehearsing for the upcoming Christmas pageant at First
Church. The pageant was called "The Christmas Gift." Phyllis and I
had volunteered to help decorate the gymnasium as well as sing in the
choir, and while decorating the gym, we met Gloria Cline who had also
volunteered. She became like a second mother to me. The pageant was a
total success and we were honored to be a part of it.

We became busy in our own ministry and started resuming our
concert touring. Phyllis had to give up her position as the church's
pianist, because I started booking concert tours and one of the first tours
was to Iowa. We received a call to sing for a benefit at the De Jardin
Hall at the Community College in Marshalltown, Iowa, and I had also
booked a concert at a local Christian Church.

Just a week before our touring was to begin to Iowa, I received
a call from the pastor from the Christian Church in Marshalltown
in which we were scheduled in concert. He said to me that he had
made a mistake and had double-booked, and since he had scheduled
another group first, he needed to cancel our concert with them, but
he recommended a pastor at a church located in Laurel, Iowa, just nine
miles south of Marshalltown. That church in Laurel wanted to have us
come and minister in concert.

What I realized later was that we had been to this Christian Church in Marshalltown the year before and were so well-received, but just minutes before our concert was to begin, the pastor called me into his office to answer a phone call. The call was from another pastor in western Pennsylvania where we had a successful concert a few months earlier. That church had advertised well and even made special church fans with the engraving "I Am A Frankie Valens Fan" for people, which they could take home with them. That same pastor somehow realized that I was not the original artist that recorded "The Lion Sleeps Tonight" and accused me of misrepresenting myself. I tried to reiterate to him that I never, ever said that I was the original recording artist that sang that song, and that I had helped make it popular when I was out there singing as a pop-singer. I told him again that I was an independent recording artist and never had a major recording contract, but was promoted through independent record companies that helped book concerts and supplied the marketing tools that helped me to become a household name back in the late 1960s and early 1970s. Many songs are often re-recorded by other artists and that same song becomes a hit all over again. It's done all the time in the music industry, so why was it different for me? Because I was now in the 'ministry,' which like most ministries, is usually held up with a powerful microscope for intense examination and scrutiny. We have been attacked many times in our ministry over the years by well-meaning, misinformed pastors who don't come to us first, but choose to believe whatever rumors that land on their ears.

That whole phone call scenario helped to destroy my spirit just minutes before we were to minister in concert, but it did not destroy the reason the Lord had sent us there. What that pastor in Pennsylvania might have already said to this pastor in Marshalltown, even before I got on the phone, is beyond what I might even consider decent accusations in the ministry field. The thought came to me, "God wants spiritual fruit, not religious nuts," and that's what I felt the pastor in Pennsylvania was being at that time. The trouble is, the pastor in Marshalltown believed the slander from the pastor in Pennsylvania and didn't want to book us again. The best answer he could give us was that he had double-booked the concert date. We were not hurt for we knew that the Lord did not want us to go back there. I wish pastors and preachers could be more honest with their flock and with their dealings with other people in the ministry.

Our concert at the De Hardin Hall that following year was a total success, and unbeknownst to us, the sound man had recorded the whole concert. Friends that we had just met invited us to their home for dinner and the sound man brought the CD recording of our concert. As we were all in the kitchen fellowshipping we heard our music being played in another room. We asked them what that was and they told us it was our concert. Dare I dream that this could be salvageable to use for a 'live' album? After we arrived back in Wichita we took that CD to the Crimson River Studio in McPherson, Kansas and made it into our "Live! At de Jardin" CD album. (de Jardin—pronounced "day Hardeen" is Spanish for "the garden.")

The sound man captured us singing "Salvation Medley," "You Alone Are Worthy," "Sorry, I Ran All The Way Home," "To Know Him Is To Love Him," "Goodnight My Love," "Going To The Chapel," "Unchained Melody," and "Go Rest High On That Mountain." He recorded four of Phyllis's piano numbers: "How Great Thou Art," "Battle Hymn," the "Hallelujah Chorus," and "I Want A Girl," a ragtime number. We had performed oldies and gospel, along with concert piano numbers, a perfect combination for a 'live' album! The evening had been a benefit for the youth for a trip they had planned, and at the end of the concert, one of the young men had publicly thanked us for doing the concert, and we chose to leave that small speech on the CD as a memento to the event.

We met the most wonderful pastor and his wife in Laurel, Iowa who are still friends of ours, Pastor Neil and Debbie Montz, and their two adopted sons. After our concert at their church Neil and Debbie had planned on taking a vacation, so we offered to house-sit while they were gone. Pastor Neil told us that their van had no air-conditioning and it would be uncomfortable for them to go on their trip. At one point in our concert, Phyllis stopped and told the congregation that Neil and Debbie needed air-conditioning for their car, because they couldn't afford to get it fixed, so she asked anyone who had a $10 dollar bill to hold it up and someone would come get it. We raised $400 for their repair, and they had air-conditioning for their trip! It was also sweet corn season so we foundered on the peaches and cream corn for the whole week! The Lord chose to bless us in Laurel and to meet Neil and Debbie, who have become our life-long friends.

When we returned to Wichita I booked another concert tour that took us all the way to the east coast. This tour took us to Tennessee, Kentucky, West Virginia, Virginia, North and South Carolina, and Georgia. Our concert touring was going fine but I kept receiving phone calls from a booking agent in Wisconsin after every concert, always asking me how our concert went. This agent was Rick Skelton, third cousin to the famous Red Skelton, the comedian. When I told him we had a standing ovation, he seemed to get excited and wanted to set up a concert tour for us in Wisconsin. Rick was talking to me about a guest appearance on Oprah and other TV appearances, but we were a little apprehensive about him and felt he was leaning more towards the secular side of our ministry than our ministry concerts, but we continued our tour.

As we were getting ready to perform in concert at a high school auditorium in Virginia, Phyllis had gone out to our van and was heading back into the auditorium when she fell in the loose gravel in the parking lot. When she came in there was blood all over her white blouse. The school personnel called the EMT and they arrived within minutes. At the time we had no idea that Phyllis had dislocated her shoulder. We just knew that she had damaged her shoulder and would not be able to play any special piano numbers during our concert.

After that concert we had to drive late into the night to arrive at our next concert. During our travel time Phyllis knew that if she didn't exercise her arm she could lose the use of it and it might freeze up on her. I had called ahead to make sure someone could meet us at the church.

We arrived around 11:30 pm, and Linda from the church met us and said, "And we rented a grand piano for you to play on!" Phyllis didn't think she'd be able to play, but God came through for her, and she was able to play some, although I knew it was pushing it for her to play. After the concert we headed north to Roanoke on highway 81 where we had to cross over a mountain range with a steep uphill grade. As we neared the top of the hill we heard a loud pop and our engine started smoking, so we pulled over and stopped. Our cell phone had no reception in the area so I flagged down a motorist. Their cell phone worked and we called for a tow truck that towed us all the way to the church parking lot in Roanoke. The tow truck driver was talking about the problem with "cell tars" in the area, and Phyllis said she knows she is somewhat technically challenged in this area, but had never heard of "cell tars." In actually, the dialect was so strong, the man was really saying "cell towers."

The church secretary, Linda, met us at the church and we unloaded our equipment and set up our sound equipment. She let the pastor know that we had had trouble with our van and we needed another vehicle. He told her that he thought someone in his church was selling a van, so we talked with the pastor and told him we were interested.

The next morning after our concert the lady brought us the vehicle we told her we wanted to buy from her, but it was not a van! It was a Ford Taurus station wagon! We had no choice now but to accept her offer to buy her car and I didn't even know if all of our belongings and sound equipment would even fit in it. We were in a time crunch because we had a concert that evening, so we rushed into Roanoke to purchase a car-top carrier and went back and, in a hurry, transferred as much as would fit into the smaller car and the carrier, left our old van in the church parking lot, along with quite a few items that just wouldn't fit, and headed for South Carolina.

Our last concert date was in Statesville, South Carolina and we didn't know if we even had the time to drive to Statesville and be there in time for this concert. We called Pastor Frank in Statesville and told him that our van had broken down and we had to purchase another car and we were just leaving Roanoke, Virginia. He told us that it was impossible for us to be there in time for our concert so he said he would have someone from their congregation entertain the people until we arrived! All we can say is that we traveled the speed limit the whole drive from Roanoke, Virginia to Statesville, South Carolina and we arrived 10 minutes before our concert was to begin. There was no conceivable way we should have arrived when we did except that it was truly a miracle! Even the pastor was flabbergasted! Was this "time travel" or what? Only God knows.

On our long drive back to Wichita, Phyllis and I had discussed the idea of recording a Christmas CD. She continued to exercise her arm so that she wouldn't lose the use of it, and she could play the piano fairly well in spite of her fall, although there still was considerable pain. When we arrived back in Wichita we decided to go back to the Crimson River Studio in McPherson to record our Christmas CD. Our dear friend Celeste took a picture of us at her home and we included that picture as the front cover of our new project.

Since Phyllis still felt she couldn't play piano very well yet, we decided to record all of our vocal songs first. We recorded: "Winter Medley," "This World," "I'll Be Home For Christmas/White Christmas medley," "The Noel Medley," "Jingle Bell Rock," "Come On, Ring Those Bells," "Peace, Peace/Silent Night medley," "Most Wonderful Time Of The Year," and "The Christmas Song."

Our last drive to McPherson was to record Phyllis's two Christmas piano numbers. Her right shoulder and arm were still not functioning well and she didn't know for sure if she could even record the two songs she had chosen. She hadn't been able to practice her two piano numbers well enough and was very apprehensive about what the outcome might be, but we prayed before going into the studio and Phyllis told me she prayed again just before the studio engineer started recording her. She recorded both "Noel, Sing We Noel," and "Oh, Holy Night" each in one take! It was truly a miracle! She told me later that when she was playing "Oh, Holy Night" there were a couple of times she had forgotten where in the piano piece she was, but she told me that the Holy Spirit just took her hands and her fingers, guiding her through the song. Every time I listen to those two piano numbers, I still get emotional because I know what it took for her to record those two songs. Interestingly, she was never able to play them again during the whole Christmas season. It was a true miracle!

Phyllis still had problems with her right shoulder so we made an appointment with our chiropractor. When Phyllis told him that she had fallen while we were on tour, he took one look at her shoulder and told her that one shoulder was lower than the other and it looked like her shoulder was out of the socket. When he grabbed ahold of her shoulder and pushed her arm back into the socket, Phyllis said that she had had two children and never felt such pain, but about five minutes later she said she could have hugged the doctor. Her arm will never be the same but it hasn't stopped her from doing what she likes to do most, play the piano. We simply called our Christmas CD "Christmas with the Valens."

While out driving one day near the Towne West Mall in Wichita we stopped by a gift shop and met Debra Lee. She asked us if she could display some of our CDs in her shop, so we gave her our business card and she suggested to us that we needed an album that included 'the best of' all of our CDs. We told her that it sounded like a good idea, so we headed back to the Crimson River Studio in McPherson and recorded a six-album compilation CD, containing the best of all six of our CDs that we had recorded up to that time. Debra has become a life-long friend of ours and we may try and help her write a book.

We decided to call the new CD "Give Him Praise," from a song Phyllis had written. We included: "Give Him Praise," from our "Gone Are The Tears" CD; Jesus Loves Me" (piano), from our "In The Fullness Of Time" CD; "To Know Him Is To Love Him," from our "Live! At De Jardin" CD; "Oh, Holy Night" (piano) from our "Christmas with the Valens" CD; "You Alone," a song Phyllis had written, taken from our "Gone Are The Tears" CD; "That's When The Angels Rejoice," an added bonus; "God Bless America Medley," another added bonus; "Sixteen Candles," "The Lion Sleeps Tonight," and "Rockin' Robin" all taken from the "Frankie's Back" CD; "I Can't Help Falling In Love," an added bonus; "This Magic Moment," taken from our "In The Fullness Of Time" CD; "I Want A Girl," (piano), taken from our "Frankie & Phyllis Valens Live! At De Jardin" CD; "Heaven Medley," an added bonus; and "Praise You," another added bonus.

Although we were driving our Ford Taurus station wagon we didn't have a lot of room to carry all our luggage and equipment. We didn't realize how inadequate our station wagon was until we received a call from a pastor friend of ours in Craig, Colorado that wanted us to come do an outdoor concert for his church. We knew that we did not have enough room for all we needed to take for such a tour, and Phyllis was enough concerned about how small the car was, having to go up those mountain roads that she simply told the Lord she wasn't going to Colorado in that car. And guess what? A ministry friend from First Church bought a red mini-van for us and donated it to our ministry. We left our station wagon at Trinity Auto in Wichita, (Phyllis's cousin), and they were able to sell our car to someone else from our church. Small world!

FIFTY FIVE
AMONG THE STARS

In the year 2000, most of our concert touring was in Kansas, except for a short tour to Iowa and Oklahoma which transpired during the latter part of the year. We had concerts in churches, country clubs, an appearance in a parade, an auto show, a KAKE-TV appearance for the Kansas Literacy Telethon, the performing arts center, a diabetes telethon held at the Hyatt Regency Hotel in Wichita, a grand opening of a bible book store, Derby Days, the Kansas Association of Massage Therapists held at the Broadview Hotel, wedding anniversaries, an EMS regional meeting in Meade, the Orpheum Theatre in downtown Wichita, class reunions, the very private Candle Club, the Public Accountants Association of Kansas meeting held at the Hyatt Regency Hotel, a performance at the famous Boathouse in Wichita, a revival, Christmas parties, 'Valens-tine' banquets, Sunday school class parties, and a 'Night With The Stars' held at the Minneola School Gymnasium in Minneola, Kansas.

Most of these concerts were booked through Kirby Horn, who just happened to attend one of our concerts in Wichita along with his fiancé Kathy. Kirby took such a heart for not only my vocal ability but also my life story. When he heard me sing "Go Rest High On That Mountain" he came unglued and excited about the possibilities of what he might be able to do to help get the "Frankie Valens' name back in circulation again. He became like a brother' to me and we tried to accept him as our representative, but his direction was for the secular side. Even though he opened many doors for us, we decided that our direction was not his direction because we were gospel singers now who occasional sang in the secular arena. Kirby was a smoker and it was hard for me to be around him because of it. We later found out that Kirby had developed a tumor in his lungs and had to be operated on. Even though we didn't want him to represent us anymore, we still love him.

We received a call from Karen, the music teacher at a school in Minneola, Kansas who said she had seen us in concert at an EMS banquet in Meade, Kansas. She told us she was planning a "Night With The Stars" banquet and concert where all the kids would impersonate stars and they wanted to bring me in as the 'real thing!' We thought it was a fun idea and booked the event. Karen wanted us to send music ahead of time so she could teach her students to sing and dance behind a couple of the songs I planned to perform. She suggested that maybe Phyllis could come as the famous Joan Castle from the old Lawrence Welk show, and she wanted to keep our identity a secret until we were introduced.

We arrived early the night of March 25th and met with Karen who whisked us off to the backstage area where the dressing rooms were. She wanted to make sure we were not seen and were not dressed in stage clothes. She then showed us a basement area where she said that the city had planned to bury a space capsule with various items from the year 2000. We donated one of our CDs to her to place in that capsule. The capsule would not be opened for a 100 years! We didn't think anything more about it.

The lasagna and garlic toast dinner started at 5:30 and we sat at a table with everyone else but remained incognito. After we ate we disappeared to the backstage area and changed into our concert clothes. Phyllis wore a blue sequins gown, and I wore a special fancy shirt and slacks that had a kick-pleat in them. We both wore black patent-leather shiny shoes. We only wore these clothes for special occasions.

The concert itself was fun and exciting. I was introduced as "Frankie Valens" and came out to sing some of the old hits and songs from the era. The kids had a blast dressing like Elvis and other pop stars and singing along with me. Phyllis was introduced as Joan Castle and she played a couple of Joan Castle piano arrangements. We were literally singing among the stars! The children stole the show.

At the break a lady sat down next to Phyllis and asked her how her back was. Phyllis didn't know what she was talking about at first, but then remembered that we had just been in Branson about four months before and had seen Joan Castle in concert. She did not come out after her performance to greet and sign autographs because she had just had surgery on her back. Phyllis told the lady she was not Joan Castle, and the lady said, "Yes you are!" Phyllis again told the lady that she wasn't, but the lady insisted, telling Phyllis, "Yes you are, my mother told me you are. You look like her and you play just like her!" That lady was not easily convinced that Phyllis was not Joan Castle, so if they had had a contest for the best impersonator, I think Phyllis won, hands down.

When we packed up to leave the gymnasium we hadn't noticed if we had gathered all of our clothes, at least I thought I packed everything. It wasn't until a few months later when we were planning our wardrobe for our concert at the famous Orpheum Theatre in downtown Wichita that we found our concert clothes missing. What happened to our clothes? My speculation is that someone from Minneola, Kansas wanted to place our concert clothes in that time-capsule they told us about that they were preparing that wouldn't be opened for over 50 years, but we never found out for sure if maybe our concert clothes ended up in that time-capsule! Maybe our friends or our family can be there in 50 years when that time capsule is opened to witness whether or not our concert clothes were included? It would be interesting! We two won't be around but maybe our family will be blessed by the unfolding events of a time capsule and its contents.

Our best concert clothes were now missing but that didn't mean we didn't have other concert clothes available. We shopped all across the nation for our concert clothes, and we probably had more concert clothes than casual. We wanted to look our very best for our concert at the famous Orpheum Theatre in Wichita that Kirby Horn had booked for us. Many famous people had appeared there including Red Skelton. We invited the church choir from First Church of the Nazarene in Wichita to join us, and the Impact Players from Central Community Church. We invited Helen Galloway to be our host. Helen was very well known in social circles in the Wichita area and was very well respected. Since the Orpheum had no decent piano we rented a baby grand piano for Phyllis to play her special concert piano numbers on.

Before our show began the lights in the theatre were dimmed. The piano was situated center stage. Phyllis and I took center stage in front of the piano and started singing an upbeat version of the song "Jericho." The Impact Players started marching from the back coming forward through the audience holding candles. The only thing we could see out in the audience was the candles, as the Impact Players and choir marched through each aisle heading up to the front of the stage. When they reached the stage area, the choir proceeded to march behind us and stood in line on the risers, while the Impact Players carrying large colorful banners marched to the front of the stage and stood in line with their banners held high. At the very end of our song we sang the lyrics, "And the walls came tumbling down!" And at that precise moment, all the Impact Players lowered their banners to the floor and stood there silent and still. It was quiet for just a few pregnant moments while people had time to engulf what they had just witnessed before there was a roar of applause and a standing ovation. We were told later that evening that we had received three standing ovations, although we couldn't see any of them because of the bright lights. Our whole plan was to present a concert for the city of Wichita to introduce ourselves, and I think we accomplished what we set out to do. It was definitely a night with the stars.

FIFTY SIX
A CARNIVAL CRUISE

Our biggest concert tour came in March 2001 when we were booked to do a concert for a Carnival Cruise on the ship Sensation for a Caribbean cruise. We had a referral for this cruise from our friend, gospel singer Larry Dodds who lives in Iowa. He was already booked on this cruise and suggested that we call Pastor Pearson, who was in charge of the cruise, to see if we could be included. The pastor set up all the arrangements and told us that he had booked us a private room and a concert time in the Plaza Lounge for us to entertain. We were both thrilled since neither one of us had been on a cruise before. A few days before our concert tour begun, I came down with an awful sinus infection. That problem dogged me the whole tour.

I booked our first concert for this tour in Tulsa, Oklahoma. We then drove to Bentonville, Arkansas, followed by New Albany, Mississippi. From New Albany we drove to Smyrna, Georgia, which was just north of Atlanta. Our longest drive was from Smyrna, Georgia to Lakeland, Florida. That drive took us over seven hours, and the pastor in the church in Lakeland was our former pastor from the First Church of the Nazarene in Wichita, Kansas. Lakeland is a town just east of Tampa, where we were to catch our ship to go on our cruise. But, we had a few more concert dates in the area before boarding the ship. We were booked in Dunnellon, Florida, about 91 miles north of Lakeland and then our last stop was in Brooksville, about 39 miles south of Dunnellon. After our last concert Pastor Pearson suggested we drive back up to Dunnellon and leave our red van. He told us that they would bring our van back to us after our cruise, so we drove back up to Dunnellon and Pastor Pearson drove us to Jacksonville where we boarded the ship Sensation.

We checked into our room and scouted around the ship to try and discover what all was available for us. Our room was on the main level of the ship with a window. We didn't have any cell phones with us and there was no TV in our room. We came back to our room to get more settled in when I leaned over my bed that was next to the window and I told Phyllis that I saw logs floating by. When I took a closer look, those logs were not moving! We were!

We left Tampa on the first day of our cruise on Sunday, March 25th about 4:00pm. The meals were wonderful and we could walk to the informal dining area on a different level and snack between meals. There was always an assortment of fruit and drinks available. The first evening we had been invited to sit at the captain's table, which is an honor. We don't know why he picked us to sit at his table but I was assuming it was because of my name, but I don't know for sure, but Phyllis sat right next to the captain. Every evening when we walked the corridors we could hear music playing loudly in the bar and disco areas. There wasn't much entertainment for people like us that don't frequent the bar scene and don't drink, but one evening we did attend a Las Vegas style show with all the feathers and plumes that we thought was entertaining.

Day Two of our cruise we just had fun walking the outside decks and getting to know our way around the ship. We met with our friends Larry and Mary Dodds who were the couple that referred us to the pastor to take this cruise. We often walked to shops looking for something to bring back home. Day Three the ship stopped at the Grand Cayman Islands and we were able to disembark and spend time on the main island shopping, eating and walking around town. That evening on the ship we performed a concert in the Plaza Lounge. We were surprised at the lack of attendance, and when we left we noticed that there was a sign outside the closed door that said, "Reserved for Private Party!" No wonder very few people came to our concert.

Day Four our ship stopped at Playa del Carmen and Cozumel, so we disembarked and took a bus ride north to tour the Mayan ruins. When the bus stopped for a bathroom break we purchased clothes to bring back to our grandkids.

The old Mayan ruins in Mexico during our cruise

On Day Five we were heading back north in the Gulf of Mexico, heading to New Orleans, and that night while we slept, the sea was rough and the boat rocked back and forth. Day Six the boat docked and we left the ship to walk around New Orleans and do more shopping. Day Seven we had fun all day walking around the ship and eating great food. That evening we had another concert in the Plaza Lounge. Day eight, April 1st, we arrived back in Tampa about 8 o'clock A.M. We had to rush off the ship because we had a concert in Macon, Georgia at 7 o'clock P.M. When I had originally made calls to book this tour, I can still remember my conversation with the pastor in Macon, Georgia, because his name was "Johnny Mathis." When I told Pastor Mathis who I was, he wasn't sure at first if the call wasn't a joke. After all, Frankie Valens was calling Johnny Mathis on April Fools Day to book a concert! Pastor Mathis reiterated to me that he was not the famous singer and he actually could not even sing, but he wanted to book the former nightclub performer, Frankie Valens, to do a concert in his church. He was part of the Bellevue/Hillcrest Ministerial Association in Georgia, and we had a great concert there.

We had to quickly drive back to Wichita so we could leave for our next tour that started on April 4th with a concert tour that started in Burlington, Colorado. We were heading to Denver for my youngest daughter's wedding on the 7th at the Meadow Wood Free Methodist Church, and after Heather's wedding we drove to Castle Rock for a concert on April 8th.

After spending a couple of days in Smith Center, Kansas ministering for the Ministerial Alliance of Smith Center we continued touring throughout Kansas, Oklahoma, Indiana, Iowa, Missouri, and Nebraska. We had radio interviews at KOMA radio and KCDL-FM radio in Oklahoma City in August.

By December we scheduled several Christmas concert dates and a Christmas concert at the El Dorado Dinner Theater including some of our grandkids as part of our show. We were booked for Thursday, Friday and Saturday, December 20th, 21st and 22nd. We had people come up to us after the show who said, "You were great, but your grandkids stole the show!"

FIFTY SEVEN
RICK SKELTON, NOT RED!

Early in January of 2002 I was booked at the Century II auditorium in Wichita, Kansas for a Quixtar two-day function. One of their diamonds, John and Jodi Meyers, had given me a call asking me if I would include their function in our concert touring. They were expecting over 4,000 people in attendance, and they had invited B.J. Thomas to entertain on Friday evening and invited me to entertain on Saturday. I didn't get the opportunity to meet B.J. Thomas but when B.J. heard I was coming he told them to tell me 'hi.' After my concert a pastor came running backstage to meet me and invited me to come out to Meade, Kansas and do a concert, and he said he wanted to book a concert soon. We booked a concert at his church on January 20th, and we had a great time.

In February we performed at many Valens-tine banquets including Hays, Salina, Hutchinson, Wichita, McPherson and Burdett, Kansas. We also performed for a D.A.R.E. graduation in Mulvane, and at the grand opening of a Walmart Super Center in east Wichita.

I booked a tour in March and April that took us to Iowa and various towns in Kansas. In May I booked an oldies show at the El Dorado dinner theater and then we headed to Oklahoma to sing not only at churches but at a letter carriers food drive held at the Hutchins Memorial Auditorium in Ponca City, Oklahoma. From there we drove to

Harrisonville, Missouri to sing for a Walmart Super Center Lube Rodeo, and on our way back home I was asked to sing the national anthem for the Mulvane High School at their sports complex.

In June we had a concert in Independence, Missouri but also performed a concert at the Grandview Assembly of God in Grandview, Missouri. During our concert Phyllis mentioned that I used to be 'Frank Piper,' and after our concert while we were standing at our tape table in the foyer, a lady came up to me and asked me if I had relatives who used to live in Belton, Missouri and I told her yes. She then said, "Were they Roy and Marie Miller?" And I told her, "Yes." Then she asked me if I had visited there one summer and I told her yes again, to which she queried, "Do you remember coming over to the house next door and kissing a girl on her front porch?" And again I said yes. She was that girl! Also at this concert was my friend, Phillip Seaton, whom I knew in the seventh grade at the Rosedale High School in Kansas City! I always envied Phillip because he played in the school band, and now he was the choir director of a church in Kansas City. I truly enjoyed reminiscing with these friends from my past.

We met a lady who told me that she had come to one of my concerts in New Jersey many years ago when I was a pop-singer, and the Lord had placed me on her heart to pray for. She told us that it was such a blessing to her to know that her prayers had been answered after all those years of praying.

July proved to be a very busy month for us starting with an outdoor concert in the park in Wamego, Kansas and then traveling to Nebraska and Iowa on tour. July 6th and 7th we were invited to sing for the Fremont Church of the Nazarene in Fremont, Nebraska. I initially had called from the church directory and talked with Pastor Tom Shaw. At first Pastor Shaw wanted me to send our ministry information, but when I told him those dates could be filled by the time he receives our packet, he almost immediately called us back and booked us. We ministered in concert for his church in a tent on July 6, 2002 that had been constructed in their parking lot on Saturday evening, and then Sunday morning the 7th we ministered at 10:00 AM for their morning worship.

It was just after the morning service when Phyllis and I retired to the foyer to stand behind our product table and be available for people wanting to fellowship with us or wanting to purchase our ministry products, when an elder of the church brought over a young man to meet us. The elder asked the young man to tell us what he had told the elder about why he had decided to come to the morning service. Apparently this young man had seen an ad showing that Frankie Valens was appearing in concert at the church and out of curiosity he came. He didn't know what to expect, but when he came he was so ministered to that he gave his life over to the Lord and was saved that morning. We thank the Lord for using us in a mighty way for His glory.

From Fremont, Nebraska we traveled to Sioux City, Iowa and then on to York, Nebraska and met Pastor Will Haworth, Jr. whose dad was the pastor of a Nazarene Church in Hays, Kansas where we had ministered before. Pastor Will is now a missionary in Brazil. From there we traveled on to Omaha, Nebraska where the church had no pastor at the time.

On July 12th we sang on the main street at the Henoween Festival/Chicken Days in Wayne, Nebraska and shared the spotlight with the "For The Master" quartet. July 13th we headed to Concordia, Kansas to sing to a packed house at the famous Brown Grande Theatre. In August we were asked to sing in Cottonwood Falls for the 4-H County Fair, after which we headed to Colorado.

When we returned home we received a call from Trayce Warner who wanted us to sing at the Florence Labor Day Celebration at the old high school auditorium. Florence is the town where my dad was born. During the concert I mentioned that my dad was born and raised in Florence, and someone came up to me and told me that there is still a farm house in the area called the "Piper" place.

From early March we had been receiving calls from Rick Skelton from Wisconsin wanting to book "Frankie Valens" in concert. Rick was a third cousin of Rick Skelton, the comedian. He wasn't interested in the gospel part of our concert touring as much as he wanted the oldies and promoting the former pop-singer, so he asked me to send him pictures, videos, promo and anything else to help him advertise. I ended up sending him one-of-a-kind videos and pictures, assuming he would send them back to us.

Rick booked a Wisconsin tour for us in September and we headed north from Kansas early in September to meet him and perform at all the venues he had booked me at. I booked churches on the way starting in Sedalia and then O'Fallon, Missouri. Heading north we had a TV appearance on the WWHO-TV (TBN) for the Praise The Lord program at 10:30am and then on to Wisconsin. Dinner at the Meade Hotel in Wisconsin Rapids was at 6:00pm and then I started singing at 7:30pm at the dinner theater they had set up specifically for my appearance. Tickets were selling at $45 per person or $49.95 after a certain date. Stage-side seating cost $55 per person, and they nearly sold out to a very enthusiastic audience.

Rick had provided us with a long white stretch limo during our concert touring, and a free massage. Saturday, September 21st he booked me to sing oldies on a cruise of the Clear Lake Harbor near Waupaca,

Wisconsin, and that evening I was to do an oldies concert at the Waupaca High School Performing Arts Center. When he saw our gospel brochures on our tape table he came over and flipped them over so no one could see them, telling us this was an oldies venue. This however became an early red flag. One of our last bookings by Rick was autograph signing and a short concert at the Rapids Mall in Wisconsin Rapids before we headed on to Indiana and Michigan to finish our tour.

When we left Wisconsin Rick sent us to Chicago to spend the night using his credit card number that he had written on a piece of paper for us. After going through the problem of parking our car at the hotel with a valet in downtown Chicago, the hotel would not accept Rick's scribbled message giving us permission to use his credit card, so we had to forego the free nights lodging and we left Chicago, heading south towards Nashville where Rick had booked us to sing at the Christian Country Music Association's Eighth Annual Convention And Award Show.

When we arrived at the convention center in Nashville there were hundreds of people already there and the hallways were lined with vendors and artists that had product tables set up to display their music and ministry information. We met Paul and Susie Luchsinger and had our picture taken with them. Susie is Reba McIntire's sister. We then ran into LaVern Tripp who appears on TBN frequently and we had our picture taken with him. I was told to take my CD music tracks to the sound man and wait in the audience until I was called up to sing.

During the whole program I kept wondering when they were going to call me up. I was never called up, but after the program ended when I went to the sound man and asked for my CD music tracks back, he looked like he was in shock that they had totally forgotten to call me up to sing. He asked me where I had been and I told him I was sitting in the audience where they told me to sit. It was just one more disaster that Rick Skelton had set up. We knew we were finished with Rick.

We felt Rick had his focus in the wrong direction. He wanted to play up the secular side of our ministry, which in and of itself would have been all right, but apparently to the exclusion of our gospel side, and that was not acceptable to us. When he didn't receive financially what he had expected, he paid us considerably less than he had said he would. It was a case of greed and fame, and God couldn't honor it. We were glad to be released from him.

Months later when I tried contacting Rick to get my one-of-a-kind videos and pictures back, he never returned my calls. Then one of his relatives contacted us to tell us that Rick's ex-wife found Rick dead in his garage. Apparently he committed suicide a few days before being found. We know that Rick was hoping that his booking Frankie Valens in concert would reap him a big profit, but when it didn't, not only had he lost considerable money, but he had lost all hope and apparently didn't want to live. It was a very sad ending. I never received my one-of-a-kind videos back from Rick.

FIFTY EIGHT
PIANO JOY

When we were looking for someone to record an all-piano CD, we knew it had to be someone who could record digitally, because Phyllis says she was not comfortable in the studio in the first place, and secondly, she really couldn't handle playing a piano number, making mistakes, (yes, she said, she does make mistakes!) and then having to redo the entire song all over again. When we found Mark Mazur she was delighted because he recorded digitally and knew that at least this way she could possibly make the recording happen. Mark was expensive but he was good, so we proceeded. We had no idea when we started this project that we would be moving out of state, and to finish this project we would need to take several trips back to Wichita over a several month period to finish the project.

Phyllis's uncomfortableness (is this even a word?) was always present. Nearly every time Mark would say 'record' she would clutch, oftentimes causing her to have to re-do passages, but at least it was only passages and not the whole piano piece.

She chose mostly songs she knew pretty well and had ministered with in concert, but she also added a few other songs for variety. The "Invocation/Sweet Hour of Prayer" piece was a song that she and I used as a background to a skit we used to do about the prodigal son. She had used portions of it from a Dino arrangement.

The "American Anthem" was its own challenge. The song was originally written as a piano duo, meaning two pianos, four hands, so she recorded the Piano One part, then, using that as a track, recorded the Piano Two part. She was pleased with the final product, and she could say that she played both parts!

"Bach To The Future" was a Dino arrangement that added a classical touch to her CD.

The "Somewhere Out There/Over The Rainbow" selection added a warmth to her list of numbers, from the secular field. As with most numbers included on this CD, she often added her own touches along the way, including this song.

"The Battle Hymn Of The Republic" had already been included on our "Live! At De Jardin" CD, but since this song was often requested, it wasn't the best quality performance on that CD, so she decided to re-do the song and add it to this collection.

Phyllis allowed me to help sing a duet with her on the piano piece "Can He? Could He?" my token participation in the project.

Phyllis said she had always enjoyed playing the arrangement she had of "I Will Call Upon the Lord," partly because it was such a different style, so it became a member of the collection of piano numbers on her CD. Since it was just piano, she decided she'd add a bit of a 'beat' to the number, so she requested a drum part. Mark found a great drummer and he improvised a part. He made the drum track for her, but she could not quite put the two together, and because the piano and the drum were recorded separately, and the drum track was so unique, she couldn't feel the beats enough and never could play the song with the track.

Her arrangement of "Rejoice In The Lord Always" was a fun composition. Phyllis had had cataract surgery in 1994 and her doctor would not let her go out of town for 30 days, so I had to go on tour by myself for a month without her. She told me she really didn't know how she did it, but she did because the Lord gave her the strength. Her idea for this piano piece came when she was asked to do a piano concert, which she had never done before, and she wanted to work on an original composition so she could add it to her concert.

She said she was staying in the home of a dear friend who fortunately had a piano, and she had heard of, and played, classical compositions with a theme and variations, and decided to try her own hand at it. Each variation of this song reflects a part of her musical career and interest. The first part is from the very early church music in the style of an old hymn. The second part is in a ragtime style, which is one of her favorite styles she loves to play. The third part she incorporated into a 50s style rendition of "Unchained Melody," which was the song I had auditioned with to become a pop singer, thus reflecting her love for me as her husband in this variation. The fourth variation was a Dino arrangement, of course in tribute to that famous piano player, an all-time favorite of hers! She did present the piano concert and included this number in the program, and has presented this number in many of our concerts and it's always been very well received.

On the song "I Exalt Thee," Mark, the producer, added some very beautiful keyboard sounds to it. "This Little Light Of Mine" was originally written as a piano duet—two people at one piano, so once again she recorded Part One, and using that as the track, she then recorded Part Two. That, too, became a real favorite with the audiences and often generated singing along to that very old children's song.

Towards the end of all the recording, she still hadn't recorded "Higher Ground" yet. However, she mentioned to Mark that whereas she didn't feel that she was ready to record it yet, she asked him to play the track so she could get the length time on the song so she would know how long the CD would run, but she told him she would just play along with the track for practice. Mark played the track and she played right along with it. When she finished, she realized that she had played her part probably the best she'd ever played it before, and she was so disappointed that he didn't record it, to which he calmly replied, "I did!" Phyllis was flabbergasted, but his "I did!" was so incredible to her she almost cried. He knew how she would 'clutch' when he said 'record,' and the pressure was off since she didn't think she was recording. Her best came through at the end. She's still in awe of that day at the studio and how the Lord worked. She said she could have hugged him because of what he did.

The beginning of "Higher Ground" was supposed to be a voice-over and she wanted to do that herself, so we set up a different part of the studio so she could record her speaking the verses. She tried two or three times and each time Mark would say, "No, that wasn't it." She was getting a bit frustrated with how or what to do when I said to her, "Pretend you're speaking to your heavenly Father." Bingo! She did just that, and that 'take' was perfect. She has thanked me ever since.

Many, many, many hours were spent in the editing, but the wonders of digital were really working for her. There were all kinds of ways to 'fix' errors, and Mark knew just what to do and how to make everything right. Then, since we had recorded everything digitally, Mark took the

CD to an electric piano, gave it a 'grand piano' sound, and most do not know that she did not record this CD on a grand piano. She will be forever grateful to him for his expertise.

The cover picture to Phyllis's "Piano Joy" CD was taken by Ken Austin, music pastor of the church where we were attending in Duncan, at the church's gorgeous concert grand piano, which she was blessed to be able to play several times.

The piano CD was the most expensive project that we had ever recorded, and with Phyllis's lack of being comfortable in the studio, it made this the only piano project that she will ever do. She has since recorded a few more piano numbers on other CDs, but she has said she will never go through any of that again. That's her "Piano Joy!"

FIFTY NINE
OUR DUNCAN DAYS

In January of 2002 John and Jodi Myers from the Quixtar Flying Eagles booked me into the Century II Auditorium in Wichita, Kansas to perform an oldies show for one of their functions. They were expecting over 4,000 people. In Februarys we always have been booked to entertain for Valens-tine Banquets at churches, but our main thrust for the next several months was to rehearse with the First Church of the Nazarene choir to present their Easter pageant.

After one of the dress rehearsals we had no time to change clothes and headed home to south Wichita in our red van when unbeknownst to us a young guy driving 80mph hit us from behind. All of our back windows imploded. Feeling a sudden jolt to our vehicle, we pulled over to the side of the road, while the car that hit us had flipped over onto its roof and was skidding to a stop on the opposite side of the road behind us. Phyllis and I were still dressed in our biblical costumes and dark makeup. When the police arrived to assess the damage, they were a little surprised to see two people dressed in biblical garb standing next to the van.

Our van was totaled. We were able to drive it home but with much difficulty, and we both just wanted to cry. That red van had been donated to us and now it was totaled. We didn't know what to do. However, when we told our friends at church what happened, someone from there donated another van to us to use in our ministry, and we are still using that van today.

Phyllis and I wanted to record a duet CD of old 50's tunes and songs from the big band era, and we finally decided we'd call it "Vintage Duets." Then one day we went to a Sam's Club in Wichita and right inside the front door was a display set up that said "Vintage Photography!" Another God-thing! They had vintage clothes for people to wear and a vintage background setting. We were so excited that we made an appointment right then, and a few days later we had the cover for our new "Vintage Duets" CD.

We called the Crimson River studio in McPherson and made plans to record this new CD, and we recorded 18 songs: "Catch A Falling Star," "Love Is Strange," "Que Sera Sera," "Muddy Holly and the Cricket" (parodies of Buddy Holly songs), "I've Told Every Little Star," "Mockingbird Hill," "I Got You, Babe," "Three Coins In the Fountain," "Put Your Hand In the Hand," "Lipstick On Your Collar," "Hey, Paula," "Two Lost Souls," "Doggie In The Window," "It Had To Be You, Lord," (a gospel parody of "It Had To Be You,") "TV Themes," (which were theme songs from nine old TV programs,) "Tennessee Waltz," and "Unforgettable."

We received a call from Beverly Shaner. She told us that she and her husband, George used to be in our Sunday school class at the First Church of the Nazarene in Wichita, Kansas but they had moved to Duncan, Oklahoma to be near her family. Although we did not know them personally while we attended First Church, we did remember seeing them in our Sunday school class of over 150 people. Beverly told us that she and her husband were attending the Immanuel Baptist

Church in Duncan, Oklahoma now and she was in charge of their Sunday school class's Valentine's banquet and wanted us to come and entertain. We decided to book the 'Valens-tine' banquet on February the 11th and then they also requested a regular concert for the whole church the following evening.

Driving to Duncan, Oklahoma from Wichita was about a four and a half hour drive. Beverly had given us directions to their home to spend the night, and when we arrived at the Shaner's home we were amazed at how beautiful it was. They told us how the Lord had opened many doors for them to have their home, down to the smallest details. The Lord had richly blessed them, and they were giving Him the glory.

We had a wonderful, fun-filled evening entertaining about 250 people at Immanuel Baptist on Tuesday evening, and after our concert we followed George and Beverly to their home to spend the night. We had time to fellowship with them and discovered that they wanted to know if we would be interested in moving to Duncan. We hadn't even thought of such an idea, but being in ministry, we could actually live anywhere, and living in a new area of the country might open up more doors for church concert tours.

Phyllis and I had become members of many different denominations over the years, wherever the Lord planted us, and we always felt that it didn't matter where we worshipped, the Lord was looking at our hearts. The Lord doesn't look at a man's outward appearance, He looks at the heart.

We had been members of Christian Churches, Baptist Churches, Assembly of God churches, Church of God churches and Nazarene churches. I found it interesting over the years when I tried scheduling concerts in various denominations that the 'spirit-filled' churches were more acceptable about inviting us in to minister in concert, knowing that we may not be spirit-filled, but the non-spirit-filled churches, who, if they knew we were 'spirit-filled,' might not invite us in to minister. Phyllis and I decided during the early part of our ministry that 'if the Lord wanted us there to minister in concert, He would open the doors!' After all, the Holy Spirit does the drawing! The Lord works 'through' us to accomplish His work. We are only His vessels.

We knew that part of our ministry calling was to reach the unsaved, and another part was to help strengthen the faith of our fellow Christians. I had never smoked or taken drugs in my entire life, even though I had many opportunities and had been tempted over the years to do so, but in my profession, I still chose not to. On a couple of occasions when I was singing in bands I tried drinking, but I could not handle it and most of the time didn't even like the taste of it. The Lord already had His hand on me, knowing the direction He had for me to take. I didn't think the Lord could use me because of all the mistakes I had made and the wrong choices I had made over my life-time, but the Lord is in the forgiving business! All He wanted me to do was to ask Him.

The next night at Immanuel Baptist Church the Lord worked in us and we felt His anointing on us throughout the entire concert. We met Lynn Parr and we found out that Lynn not only taught Sunday school, but was also a real estate broker and played piano. After the concert Pastor Jack came up to us and wanted to pray over our ministry. The choir had a meeting in the choir room the next morning and the pastor called us into the choir room so the choir could pray over us as well. Phyllis and I were very emotional and felt the love that was coming from this church and wanted to be a part of it, so Pastor Jack asked us what it would take for us to move to Duncan and be a part of their church.

We had struggled over the years at almost every church we had ever been a part of with non-support of our ministry efforts or lack of interest. Sometimes jealousy would rear its ugly head and try to create problems with church pianists that maybe felt a little threatened by Phyllis's piano skills. All we were looking for in a church home was to be supported and loved. We wanted a pastor who would show an interest in our ministry and send us out with prayer. We were on the front lines of the battle field when traveling, and we often felt so alone. Before we left for home Lynn referred us to another Baptist church in Duncan that would be interested in having us come and minister in concert. His close friends, John and Debbie Croy, were the pastors, so we booked a concert with Graceway Fellowship Baptist Church in May. We left for home truly knowing that there was indeed a church out there that cared about us and had a genuine concern for our ministry.

We returned to Duncan on May 25th to minister in concert at the Graceway Baptist Church for their evening service. The church was a very small church but had so many friendly, loving people. Pastor John Croy had invited Lynn Parr to come to our concert, and after our concert Lynn invited us to a special fellowship that several of the church people had been invited to attend north of Duncan. We accepted and followed the group to the fellowship meeting. When we arrived we saw Pastor Jack there also. All these special friends had found out that Phyllis's birthday was just a few days away and had planned this surprise meeting for her benefit. They had a special t-shirt made for her and gave it to her for a gift.

At the meeting Pastor Jack asked us again what it might take for us to move to Duncan. We told him that we needed to pray about it and secondly we didn't have the funds to move. He gestured with an out-reached open palm hand, as if he were handing us a check and said, "if money wasn't the problem, would you pray about it and ask the Lord's guidance in making such a decision?" Phyllis and I walked into another room and held hands in prayer, and we felt the Lord was telling us that He would bless our decision, whatever our decision would be. What was so prevalent in my mind was the over-whelming love and support I knew we both were feeling, caused by this group of believers who earnestly were wanting us to come and be a part of their church. We knew that Pastor Jack would support us and pray for us. Lynn, being in real estate, told us that he would find several homes for us to look at before we left and we could choose the one we wanted to move to. He would make all the arrangements and get the help we needed in getting us settled. Pastor Jack told us that we could present a concert at Immanuel that would help defray the cost of our moving. We decided to move to Duncan on Friday, June 20th.

Monday morning Lynn drove us around Duncan and showed us three prospective homes. After touring through all three we chose a home on a corner lot that had an eat-in kitchen, a master bedroom with a master bath, a family room, a two-car insulated garage, and a wonderfully landscaped yard. Lynn told us that men from the church would drive up to Wichita and load up their church vans and trucks and move us to Duncan on June 20th.

After we arrived back in Wichita we had been considering becoming a part of Central Christian Church, one of the largest churches in Wichita, and had met with Pastor Joe Wright and their music pastor Peter Abood. Peter had invited us to sing a special song for both of their morning services on Sunday, June 15th. When we had met with Peter he asked us if we'd sing the song "People Need The Lord." We knew of the song but had never sung it. Peter told us that Pastor Gene Williams' wife, Joyce, had written a skit about a woman in hell and wanted us to sing

"People Need The Lord" in response to the skit. We knew Pastor Gene and Joyce. Pastor Gene had been the pastor of the First Church of the Nazarene in Wichita before we had started attending but we met them when they came for a visit, and we became instant friends. They have both written several books and were a part of the Billy Graham crusade, and were now attending Central Christian Church.

I was very torn as to what to do! I knew that the Central Christian Church was looking forward to working with us and our being a part of their church, but now we had an opportunity to be a part of a church we knew was going out of their way to move us to Duncan so we could be a part of their growing church.

Sunday morning, June 15th we sang "People Need The Lord," and the very evangelistic skit about a woman in hell came to fruition. After we sang our last note, we heard a woman screaming and running towards the platform. If you didn't know what was going on, it could have been frightening. She was dressed in rags with dirt all over her face and skin, as she proceeded to tell of not being told about hell, even from her Sunday school teachers. She said that friends often passed by her home and didn't tell her about Jesus and that there was a literal hell. She said "Now it was too late! Why didn't someone tell me? Why? Why?" And then she ran off the platform in another direction. The congregation was stunned and I'm sure felt a little guilty in not telling others about heaven and hell. It certainly gave one food for thought. Phyllis and I were able to get permission from Joyce to use that skit as an evangelistic tool in our ministry, and Phyllis presented it several times in our concerts.

What do we do? We had already made plans with Pastor Jack and our new friend, Lynn Parr, to move us to Duncan, Oklahoma. Were we making the right decision? Maybe the Lord was testing us to see if we would be obedient? A part of me wanted to stay in Wichita to be a part of a large church that had a wonderful choir, orchestra and music department.

We ultimately knew that we were to move to Duncan, so on Friday afternoon, June 20th several vans and trucks from the Immanuel Baptist church in Duncan pulled up in front of our home in Wichita. We had been packing for several days getting ready for this move and now the day of our moving was here.

It took us several hours to pack all of our belongings into the vans and trucks, and then we caravanned to Oklahoma. We arrived late at night in Duncan and another group of people from Immanuel were there to greet us and help us get unloaded. It was a wonderful sight! And I'm sure the men that had helped us load up in Wichita were glad to have the extra help upon our arrival.

We didn't have much time to get settled in when we ministered at Immanuel on Sunday evening, June 22nd. This concert was to help pay for the cost of our move. The church kept our offering and disbursed the funds to pay for our rent, etc. Five days later we had to leave for Iowa to resume a concert tour I had set up before our move to Oklahoma.

One of our first Iowa concerts was at the Val Air Ballroom in West Des Moines. We had agreed to do a benefit concert for the Mayberry Shelter and Recovery Home. We then traveled to Marshalltown to entertain at a high school reunion for the Marshalltown class reunion of 1958, held at the Elmwood Country Club. From there we traveled to Muscatine, State Center, and then to Nevada, Iowa where we entertained at the Camelot Theatre.

Many people have wondered why we had often entertained at secular events such as county fairs, car shows, dinner theatres, state fairs, class reunions and outdoor amphitheaters, when we were professed Christians, serving the Lord full-time.

When the Lord called us into a full-time music ministry I had a testimony to tell. I had been a former nightclub performer and had a recognizable name. When we held secular concerts we drew many unsaved people to these events, and in doing so we were able to minister to these audiences, telling them that we were not ashamed of the gospel and professing that we were Christians. We planted many seeds in our ministry but the Lord did the watering. Even our Lord didn't spend all of his time ministering to the Christians of His day, He spent much of his time ministering to unbelievers. When the Pharisees saw Jesus sitting with publicans and sinners they asked the disciples why Jesus ate with such people, but Jesus overheard them and told them in Matthew 9:13 KJV: "for I am not come to call the righteous, but sinners to repentance." We had always felt that our calling was for the lost. Not everyone agreed with how the Lord used us to further His Kingdom on earth, but we were not concerned over man's opinions, we had a higher calling. As Peter said, "We ought to obey God rather than men." Acts 5:29 KJV

In August I booked a concert tour to Colorado. I booked Longmont, Boulder, Denver, Thornton, Louisville, Ft. Morgan, Craig, and Cheyenne, Wyoming. In Denver we had family and were able to visit with many of them, and we spent our nights at the home of our friends, Pastor Lowell and Pam Pearson in Sedalia, Colorado.

Our last concert was an outdoor concert in Craig, Colorado. We met Pastor Bob and Karen Snavely when they were pastoring at a church in Denver. They had invited us to Craig to represent their church's outreach program to the community and to try and reach the unsaved. Our concert went really well except when it started raining. We had set up speakers on speaker stands and now it started to rain, so folks scrambled around to find plastic bags to place over our speakers, and we continued our concert. No one sitting at the park benches seemed to mind that it had started raining.

Pastor Snavely made arrangements for Phyllis and me to stay overnight in the church basement, and there was a special room just for their guests. There were no windows and when we turned the lights off, it was completely pitch black in the room. We didn't know it was morning until someone came knocking on our door, wondering where we were. We both awoke with the knocking at the door and I was so disoriented because of the blackness of the room that I got dizzy and felt sick the rest of the day. To this day I cannot sleep in a totally darkened room and need a nightlight.

The drive of our 950 miles back to Duncan from Craig, Colorado was a long one. We were needing to get back in Duncan because we were scheduled to appear on Duncan's DTV-10 TV that was being televised live at the Chisholm Mall.

By September I had booked tours that led us to Missouri, Illinois, Indiana, Michigan and Wisconsin. In Wisconsin we were booked at the McComb Bruchs Performing Arts Center. They booked Frankie Valens for two oldie shows and were bringing busloads of people in. The concert was a huge success. Our concert tour ended in St. Johns, Michigan with Pastor Bob and Nancy Besemer.

We had met Pastor Bob several years ago when we first booked a concert tour to Michigan. I met him when friends of ours had taken me to breakfast at a local restaurant in Lansing. Our friend happened to tell one of the waitresses who I was and word got all around the restaurant that "Frankie Valens" was eating at the restaurant.

Before we knew it, a lady walked up to our table to tell us that she was at the restaurant with her pastor and told me that her pastor had been considering whether to leave the ministry and seemed very discouraged and she asked me if I would talk to her pastor. I told her of course I would, and she invited him over so I could meet him. She wasn't gone long when she returned with him, and Pastor Bob told us that he had been very discouraged and wanted to do something for his congregation and community but wasn't sure what the plan would be. I immediately told him that Phyllis and I would love to come and minister in concert either at his church or an outdoors concert. Pastor Bob said, "You'd do that? You would come to our small community?" I reassured him that we would love to. We did schedule an outdoor concert for Pastor Bob's church and we felt that this was the catalyst that helped Pastor Bob stay in the ministry.

At our outdoor concert for Pastor Bob a couple of ladies surprised me when I started singing "Pretty Woman," by coming on stage, dressed up in cow outfits, complete with udders. My face must have turned every shade of red! The audience loved it!

It took us over 16 hours to drive from Lansing, Michigan back home to Duncan, Oklahoma, or about 1,083 miles. The rest of the year we chose to book concerts closer to our home in Duncan.

In the beginning of 2004 our concert dates were in and around our home in Duncan, even though it had been difficult for me to book any concerts in Oklahoma. Most of the churches that wanted us in concert were located in other states. We ended up traveling to Tennessee, Texas, Missouri, Georgia and Iowa on tour during the year.

At a church in Burlington, Iowa it was obvious that not every church wants an outreach program, although they say they do. At the Saturday night concert very few people attended. The next morning we were visiting one of the Sunday school classes and some of the people were talking about wanting and needing an outreach program for their church. One person pointed to a couple of empty chairs, stating that we need to try and fill these chairs. Phyllis, as outgoing as she is, asked the Sunday school class how many people in the class had been to our concert on Saturday evening. No one held their hand up, so she went on to tell them that our concert on Saturday evening was a perfect example of an outreach program. That concert was supposed to be the church's outreach program for their community, but no one in the Sunday school class had even come out to support the church's efforts. What we do or even don't do, sometimes must grieve our Lord.

In September we were booked at the Kansas State Fair on the Dodge Stage in Hutchinson, and our friends Richard and Barbara McKee came to hear my oldies show. I always use pre-recorded tracks to sing from in all of our concerts, and the fair was no different. I am sometimes such a perfectionist when it comes to my singing that sometimes people can mistake me for lip-syncing, although I have never done that, but while I was singing, a couple stood up and left quickly and I couldn't understand why. They had been sitting near to Richard and Barbara, who heard them saying that they thought I was lip-synching and had stormed out!

We drove from a concert in Leavenworth, Kansas to Metropolis, Illinois. The town of Metropolis has a large stone statue of Superman with a museum of Superman movie items that people can purchase. We enjoyed the side trip. As we started driving south to our next concert engagement we heard on the radio that a hurricane had hit the gulf coast and was headed up through the states and would hit in Georgia about the same time we would be there in concert. We didn't know what to do but pray, but after our prayer the Lord showed us that we were to continue our tour and not be afraid, because He would take care of us, so we continued our drive. Our first stop was in Winchester, Tennessee and then on to Dalton, Georgia where we had a concert at the First Church of the Nazarene. We drove straight to the church to set up our sound equipment and then headed on to our motel room. When we arrived back at the church, a heavy, heavy wind hit the back of the church. The remnant of the winds of the hurricane hit, but fortunately there was no damage to the church building. The next night we had a concert at the famous Wink Theatre in Dalton. The Lord had protected us and had taken us through the storm.

On the way to Loganville we noticed many fallen trees from the hurricane that had just passed through, and we thought for sure that our outdoor concert in Loganville would be cancelled. We drove on to Loganville anyway where the pastor had us sing outdoors in the church's parking lot, starting at noon and then performing again in the evening. A car show was going on all day as well as all kinds of crafts being displayed and various types of fast food items. It was a fun day.

The next day we drove home to Duncan, which was about a 415 mile drive. We then drove to St. George, Kansas to surprise our friend Carlene Kaiser for her birthday and sang an oldies concert for her and for all their friends. From St. George we drove to Wamego for a church concert and then on to Peabody to sing for the Summer Concert Series in the Santa Fe Park.

When our pastor from Immanuel Baptist gave his notice that he was leaving the church we were in shock. Pastor Jack had been at this church for so many years and we wondered if the church would continue to support our ministry with Pastor Jack gone.

We were traveling a lot throughout the year, including an oldies concert at the West Plains Civic Center in West Plains, Missouri, and had an interview on a radio station with Myra Ohloff. Our concert touring carried over into 2005 with a concert for the Lost Cherokee Nation in Ada, Oklahoma. This tribe was trying to be recognized by the U.S. government so they could become a true Cherokee Nation and receive benefits.

The first time I was asked to perform a concert for the Cherokee Tribe I developed such a heart for these people. I had heard rumors over the years that there was Cherokee in our family tree, so I went into the Haskell Cooley Sound Studio and recorded the song "Cherokee Nation" that was first recorded by Paul Revere and the Raiders, along with the song "Spirit In The Sky." I made a special CD of those two songs and they were used as a fundraiser for the cause at that concert.

At the end of May and the end of this concert tour we were heading back home to Duncan from Smith Center, Kansas when we decided to stop in Wichita to visit our friends Larry and Celeste Munsinger. When we arrived at their home, Celeste handed Phyllis the want-ads from the Wichita newspaper and had circled a few homes for rent, obviously suggesting for us to move back to the Wichita area. Phyllis made calls to three of the homes for rent and none were available, but when she called the fourth number, the man said he could meet us in Derby in 15 minutes. Larry and Celeste drove us to Derby to look at the home.

The home available was a duplex with a double car garage with wall-to-wall carpeting, three bedrooms and two baths. The kitchen was an eat-in kitchen and there was a very large living room.. The only thing that bothered me was the smell of smoke throughout the home. I am allergic to cigarette smoke, and its smell stuffs me up. The landlord told us he would get rid of that smell before we moved in. There was no garage door opener, so Celeste piped up and asked him if he would install one, and he said he would. The rent sounded reasonable but we told him we didn't come prepared to pay it, however, to make sure all this went through, Celeste wrote him a check and told us that we could pay her back later. I guess we were moving back to the Wichita area. And that's how we ended up in Derby, Kansas!

SIXTY

OUR STORMY ENTRANCE

Before we moved back from Kansas in 2005 our last concert in Oklahoma was a concert for KTLR 890 AM radio located in Oklahoma City for a program called "Carol's Christian Joy." The beginning of June was devoted to packing our belongings and having a garage sale to help pay for our expenses for the move back to Kansas. A couple from the City Heights Baptist Church came over to help us move, along with Lynn Parr and his brother. We were surprised that no one from our own church came out to help us even after I had attended one of their prayer breakfasts with a plea for help. Larry and Celeste drove all the way down from Wichita to also help us move, and Larry ended up driving the U-Haul truck all the way back to Derby, Kansas on June 11th. The U-Haul truck and both of our vans were full, and whereas we had made precious friends while living in Duncan, we were ready to move closer to our family.

Larry drove the truck, while Celeste drove their van. Phyllis and I rode in our own van, and as we headed north on interstate 35 towards Wichita we noticed a very dark thunderous cloud hanging over the Wichita region. We were having a very stormy entrance back into Kansas! Phyllis and I immediately went to prayer. We did not need to run into a storm and have to unload our vehicles in the rain. The further we drove into Kansas we ran into rain, and as soon as we parked in the driveway of our home, the rain stopped. We started unloading but because it was late and we didn't want to be unloading in the dark, we told everyone we would resume unloading the next morning, and as soon as we stopped unloading, the rain hit. The next day the same thing happened. All the time we were unloading the U-Haul truck it didn't rain, but as soon as we were finished it started raining again. As I drove the truck over to the far side of Derby to return it—the rain stopped, but the minute I left the truck and hopped into a waiting car to go back to our home, it started raining again.

As we were getting settled into our home in Derby we were asked to sing at several county fairs. Our first county fair was on July 14, 2005 at the Howard/Elk County Fair in Howard, Kansas, about 77 miles east of Derby. Oh, my, it was hot out there! Then, on July 20th we were invited to sing at the Marion County Fair in Knoxville, Iowa, at the famous Knoxville Speedway race car track, and it was so hot then that they brought in huge fans to give us some relief! In September we entertained for the 1960 class reunion of the Webb City High School in Joplin, Missouri. On September 28th we sang at the Blankenship Stadium for the Fredonia West Park Rodeo, and in October we sang for the Blackwell High School Class reunion of 1955 in Blackwell, Oklahoma.

We returned again to Wellston, Oklahoma on October 9th where we had been in concert for an outreach and revival the year before. It was always such an honor to return to the church that my dad had preached at. I remember when my first wife and I were traveling to New Jersey from Las Vegas, we had stopped in Wellston to visit my parents, and my daughter Jennifer was only about a year old at the time. My dad has since passed away, but my mother still attends this same church in Wellston.

In August we received a call from Pastor Bob Gilpin in Sawyer, Kansas. He told us that someone from his church had seen Phyllis and me in concert at Medicine Lodge and wanted to invite us to minister at his church in November. That one concert at Pastor Gilpin's church has led to a wonderful friendship with him and his wife Loree. We performed an oldies concert on a Saturday evening and ministered in concert Sunday morning, and went back in concert a couple more times later.

Another large church in the Wichita area is the Central Community Church. We were asked to do a concert for their senior adult Christmas program. We had already ministered at this church in February, 2001 for their 'Valens-tine' banquet where we received a standing ovation from the 250 people in attendance.

On December 31st a severe blizzard struck the mid-west as we were traveling to a New Year's Eve concert at a church in Maryville, Missouri. Phyllis and I went to immediate prayer and we felt the Lord was telling us to turn around and go back home. The Lord knew we were not comfortable traveling all the way to Maryville with such a blizzard, and underneath the snow was a solid sheet of ice. It was so bad that we had to call the church to cancel our concert with them. The pastor was so irate that he told us we would never be invited back to his church again, but I think the Lord already knew about the attitude of this pastor and He didn't want us there.

Living in Derby was a perfect launching pad for us to branch out in all directions, and be able to travel to various cities and travel to different states. Most of the time we loved visiting small towns where the churches normally could not afford to bring in a 'big' name because the fees were too high. When we came to do a concert we only asked for a donation or a love-offering. We would always have our CDs and cassettes available but they were never for 'sale,' they were always advertised as a donation. We often gave away more CDs than were purchased.

We had heard horror stories of churches that had invited in a Christian artist who demanded to have special water to drink, special snacks available, or a limo at their disposal, and the list goes on and on. When we came in to sing we were immediately asked what we required, and we told them we didn't require anything, and then they proceeded to tell us about some of the artists they had had to deal with in the past, and then we were in shock. I just feel that sometimes Christian artists must be prostituting their talent for money. One of my former pop-singer friends had become a Christian and had started touring, performing concerts in churches, but he told me that he couldn't afford to sing in churches anymore and went back to sing in the secular arena again. He told us that that was where the money was. Where was his heart?

SIXY ONE
WE STAND IN AWE

The year of 2006 was a banner year for concert touring. So many memorable moments, from entertaining for many 'Valens-tine' banquets, to being invited to sing for the YMCA of the Rockies, located in Estes Park, Colorado. And when we weren't busy touring we recorded an album, "We Stand In Awe."

For each concert we always requested that the church or organization provide us with an eight foot table so we could display our CDs and cassettes, plus pictures of us that were free with a donation. We also displayed the Frankie Valens story, business cards, and a sign-up sheet for people who wanted to start receiving our newsletter. For many years Phyllis would work at putting a newsletter together and then we would mail all of them out. When the list got too long, we often let our grandkids help us fold the newsletters and stuff them into envelopes. We later started using the computer to e-mail our newsletter.

Joyce and Carl Bastion in Perkins, Oklahoma had been receiving our newsletter and called us to come do a concert at their Oak Park Gospel Jubilee that they held every Saturday night. This Oak Park was a large complex with cabins, a building which was used as a cafeteria, and a place for people to park their motorhomes and trailers. Joyce told us they would provide a cabin for us for the night, and after our concert Joyce and Carl became some of our dearest friends.

Our former pastor, Pastor Jack, from Duncan, Oklahoma had moved to Lafayette, Indiana and became head of the mission board, so he invited us to minister to the churches in his district. In April we decided to make it a tour. We ministered in Mt. Vernon, Illinois, and then in Lafayette, Indiana, Crawfordsville, Fowler, and finally Clifton, Illinois. From Illinois we extended our tour to include Michigan.

When we received a call to come minister at the Community Christian Church in Moore, Oklahoma I had no idea who I would be meeting when we got there. I knew that Phyllis knew Danny and Jeanie Cavett that attended this church, because both Danny and Jeanie had been part of a youth group where Phyllis and her former husband Sam, were pastoring a church in Canton, Oklahoma in the early 60s, and the church had an active youth group. You know, the kind that tee-peed their home! They developed a very close relationship with the youth the three years they were in Canton. And, as is often the case, after they left, they lost track of the kids. But, when Phyllis advertised on the website of the Christian College she had attended, that we were going to be in concert in the Oklahoma City area and wanted to let the alumni know, she knew that many lived in or near that area. Jeanie saw the notice and when she began to think about the name, she wondered if it just might be the same "Phyl" she had known back in Canton, Jeanie's home town. When she checked our web site, and determined that it must be one and the same, she e-mailed Phyllis. There had been no contact in over 40 years, and Phyllis almost screamed when she received the e-mail from Jeanie! They began e-mailing lots of 'remember when's' back and forth, and Phyllis learned that Jeanie had married a young man from the same youth group, Danny. The two of them had been going together during the time that Phyllis and Sam were there.

I too met a couple I had not seen or talked to in over 44 years! After our concert in Moore a couple came up to me and asked me if I remembered Pastor Vernal Johnson from Tonganoxie, Kansas. They were also members of this church. Yes, I remembered them. Vernal and my dad were the best of friends back when I was a senior in high school in Winchester, Kansas. Dad was pastoring a church in Winchester, Kansas. I used to date their daughter, Margaret. I was dating Margaret even after I graduated from high school and was living in Kansas City, Missouri with my cousin Tharen, just prior to when I started attending Nebraska Christian College in Norfolk, Nebraska. Margaret was wearing my class ring at the time, and I was also dating another Margaret in Kansas City at the same time, but the two of them met and I lost both of them. Yes, I remembered the Johnsons. Then, Vernal's wife turned to me and asked me if I remembered their daughter, Margaret and I told her yes. She then handed me her cell phone. She had already called Margaret and wanted me to talk with her. I hadn't spoken to Margaret since 1962. That was over 44 years ago.

In July we were invited to sing at the La Harpe Christian Church in La Harpe, Kansas. This was the last church my dad pastored before he retired. It was here where Phyllis and I had driven to years before to visit with my parents when we met the Peggy Johnson that I had gone to high school with in Winchester, Kansas. When Peggy found out we were coming for a visit she waited at my parent's parsonage for us. Peggy and her husband lived in the town of Gas, just a few miles away, and I got to re-connect with her. Traveling in our ministry we were able to come in contact with many long lost relatives and friends.

In July we were invited to sing at the Palmer Inn and Lamplight Dinner Theater in Holdenville, Oklahoma. The next night we sang at the Agee/Williamson Family Reunion in Henryetta. Donny Williamson was the owner of the Crystal Theatre in Okemah where we had our last concert in the area.

When Danny and Jeanie Cavett asked us to come and minister to his staff at the Camp Cavett in Kingston, Oklahoma we had no idea about the full extent of what this camp was for, until we got there. Camp Cavett is a camp for youth who are terminally ill. We arrived the day before all the kids arrived. All the staff was there preparing for the youth to come for a week of enjoyment and fun. We were so pleased to be able to entertain the staff, but I don't know how Phyllis and I could have emotionally handled seeing children suffering from any kind of a terminal illness.

Phyllis had been playing a piano piece in our concerts called "I Stand In Awe," which started to become a favorite, and we talked about having that song on an album, titling the album after the song. When we called the publishers to get permission to use the song, they told us we could record the song but we could not call our project, "I Stand In Awe." That didn't stop us! We decided to call our project "We Stand In Awe," which really meant more to us.

A friend had recommended that we contact the Mark Winston Sound Studios in Wichita to record our new CD. We had heard that artists who came to Wichita chose to record with Mark, so we took their advice and visited his studio. Mark had a grand piano sitting in his studio! The piano was perfect for Phyllis to record several piano numbers for our CD.

We wanted this new CD to include more southern gospel and reflect who we were in our ministry. We had started singing songs that we hadn't yet recorded onto a CD, and since we thought that this could very well be the last album we would record, we wanted to add as many different styles of music as we could.

One song we chose was a song that Phyllis's dad, Paul Cook, who had recorded a long playing 33 1/3 album in 1967 sang. He was a minister/missionary, but he was also a gifted singer, and probably his most favorite song he sang was "When They Ring Those Golden Bells." In Oklahoma City, with funds provided by his sister, he recorded an album of the songs he had often sung. Phyllis played for her father on the original album, and with other family members, she also sang on the album. Her dad went to his reward in 1981, and those Golden Bells are ringing for him now, so we decided to include this song on our album with her dad's original recording, but adding an extra harmony with Phyllis, in the style of Natalie/Nat King Cole venture some years ago. When I heard his song I added the sound of church bells and a heavenly choir. You will hear the 'hiss' from the original album, giving it more 'presence' and authenticity from 1967.

Another song I included was a song that our friend, gospel singer and songwriter, Jack Smith had written called "I Wonder." It had the sound of a 50's country rock. I included the song "Praise The Lamb Of Calvary," which has a 50s sound, after I heard our friend John Croy sing this song in Duncan, Oklahoma. I contacted the writer and singer, David Petete to get permission to use it, and we included it. It is always very well received in concert due to its wonderful music style and "my testimony" message.

Phyllis not only recorded the piano number of "I Stand In Awe," but she also recorded "Praise And Thanksgiving," "You Are My All In All," "Power And Glory," and "Lily Of The Valley." Another style of a song we sang was the southern gospel song called "What God's Gonna Do." Other songs we included were: "This World Is Not My Home," "Leaning On The Everlasting Arms," "Down At The Cross," "His Eye Is On The Sparrow," "Come On Home," "Let My Words Be Few," "Shoutin' Time In Heaven," and "Worship Medley."

In July we were invited to perform an oldies concert at the Marion County Fair in the famous Knoxville Speedway in Knoxville, Iowa. Our friends, Pastor Neil and Debbie Montz, whom we had originally met in Laurel, Iowa had moved to Knoxville where Pastor Neil had been sent to preach at a large Methodist church. It was because of them that we had been invited to sing at the county fair. The following year when we were invited back to sing at the fair, it had gotten so beastly hot out that the fairground representatives asked Pastor Neil if he would hold the concert at his church, which we did. Not as many attended because it was in a church, but it was certainly much more comfortable for us in the air conditioning.

From Knoxville, Iowa we drove to Oshkosh, Wisconsin to sing for the Oshkosh Senior Center. When we arrived at the senior center there was much excitement in the air, and it seemed from what they said, that it was the fact that they could bring in a former pop-singer with a small fee. For them it was like bringing a little bit of "Branson" to them. The crowd was very responsive, and we were told a good time was had by all.

SIXTY TWO
YMCA OF THE ROCKIES

In the fall of 2006 we received a call from Bob Ruesch, chaplain of the YMCA of the Rockies in Estes Park, Colorado, asking us if we would consider coming to Estes Park to perform two concerts, a gospel concert on Sunday, August 13th and an oldies concert on Monday, August 14th. They had seen us in concert at the Valley Baptist Retreat in Mission, Texas. We accepted his offer and I immediately started making calls to churches in Colorado to set up a concert tour. I was always trying to schedule concerts in and around Denver because we have family living there. My youngest daughter Heather, and her then husband Matt had moved to Colorado Springs, and I found myself calling churches in the 'Springs' area to set up concert dates.

We left Derby, Kansas on Friday, August 4th for Colorado. It was about 541 miles, or about an eight hour drive. When we arrived in Denver we had been invited to spend the night at our friend, Marsha Preheim's home. Our first concert was in Broomfield and then we drove to Colorado Springs to minister at a couple of churches. While there we visited with my daughter Heather, whom we found at her mother-in-law's home. We drove back to the Denver area and had a concert in Arvada before we headed into the mountains.

On Saturday we headed to Estes Park. It is the most beautiful drive and is truly God's country. The YMCA of the Rockies is situated on the southwest side of Estes Park, and we had to drive through the town to get to the park. Estes Park is a tourist trap and there is always traffic there, so it was such a relief when we arrived at the YMCA welcome center to check in and away from the traffic we had encountered in downtown Estes Park.

Bob Ruesch had arranged for Phyllis and me to have a room in one of the lodges, and they provided all of our meals in the cafeteria as well. We set up our sound equipment and Bob set up a table so we could display our ministry information. We had a wonderful concert on Sunday morning in the chapel, and that evening we had a concert at a local church that was situated on the east side of Estes Park. Monday evening we had yet another concert at the YMCA, but this time they had requested oldies. It was an exciting evening because many people want to hear the 'oldies,' and we had a large crowd that night. It was hard for us to leave the next day but we had a concert planned for Burlington, Colorado, which is near the Kansas border, and we had a four-hour drive ahead of us. My cousin, Tonda Scott, was living in Burlington at the time and she came to our concert. She is from my mother's side of the family, her mother Marie my mother's sister. We then drove back to Derby, Kansas the next day.

Soon after we had arrived back home, Bob called us to invite us back to the YMCA of the Rockies to sing the following year, but we declined. However, after much coaching, we did go back in 2008.

SIXTY THREE
THOSE CHICKEN DAYS

Later in August we were asked by the chairman of the Constantine Arts Council to sing for a fundraiser at the Constantine Theatre in Pawhuska, Oklahoma, right in the middle of the Osage Indian Reservation. We had a full house at the theatre that evening and received a standing ovation. We could feel the excitement in the air.

Then in September we made plans to attend Phyllis' 50th high school class reunion of 1956 in Wayne, Nebraska. When Phyllis's class heard we were coming, they asked us to do a concert for the closing night of the reunion.

Her class reunion just happened to be the same weekend as Wayne's yearly famous Chicken Days, with a whole weekend of celebrating 'chickens!' Everything about anything was about chickens! There was a parade on Saturday, and all the floats had something to do with chickens. It was a riot! Phyllis got to ride with her class on a float, and we bought t-shirts that had chicken slogans on them, one saying, "Higher 'Egg'ucation." We actually performed in an outdoor concert for the whole town of Wayne after the parade, and then we had a concert for Phyllis's class that night. We spent part of the day "jamming" with a local men's gospel quartet, and then we sang at the outdoor concert as well.

Phyllis hadn't been back in Wayne for many years so she took me sightseeing to places where she had lived and worked in her high school years. She showed me the hospital where her youngest sister was born, and the auditorium where she had played a piano solo with the high school band. The house her family had lived in during that time had been torn down and was now a used car lot. She said that the church building her father preached in was so much smaller than she had remembered, and it was still there. We stayed in a bed and breakfast that was now run by a woman who had been the lead cheerleader when she was in school. And of course, people were wowed by the fact that a local girl had married a pop-singer! It was definitely a weekend to remember.

After making many calls to book another concert tour I booked a concert at the Canton Christian Church in Canton, Oklahoma. This is the same church where Phyllis's former husband pastored, and where she had played the piano and led the church choir. This is also the same church where Danny and Jeanie Cavett had been part of the youth group, who now live in Moore, Oklahoma. There were still a few people there who had been there when she lived there, and she enjoyed the memories.

We then drove to Blackwell to sing for the Blackwell High School class reunion of 1956. This reunion had requested us to sing the "Chicken Dance" song, and Phyllis and I had heard of it but we hadn't sung it before, so we found the music tracks for the song and rehearsed it beforehand. When we sang it at the reunion, all the people got out on the dance floor and danced to the 'chicken' song. First it was Phyllis's 1956 class reunion in Wayne, Nebraska with the 'Chicken Days' festival, and now a 1956 class reunion for a school in Blackwell, Oklahoma who wanted the 'chicken' song. What was all the 'hoopla' about back in 1956 with the obsession with 'chickens?' It's all a mystery to me, but we sure had a 'clucking' good time! Egg-xactly! I think I received my egg-ucation!

Now the yolks on you!

SIXTY FOUR

MAGNANIMOUS YEAR OF EVENTS!

We so enjoyed living in Derby, Kansas, formerly known as "El Paso," and a suburb of Wichita. As of 2008 the population was estimated at 22,517, making it the 17th largest city in the state of Kansas, and Family Circle magazine named it one of the 10 best towns for families. In 1869 the area, which is now the town of Derby, had been best described as the 'garden spot of Kansas' by a trader named MacWilliams who had made this statement to the Garrett family who had stopped for a while in their covered wagon on the Spring Creek bank. Even though the Garrett family had arrived first, the town wasn't established until July 11, 1871 by Mr. Minnich and John Hufbauer who had come from El Paso, Illinois and decided that this plat of land should bear the same name. In 1878 a disastrous fire consumed half of the business district and many residents decided to leave. When the railroad pushed further south and was delivering mail to El Paso, Kansas and El Paso, Texas, there was constant confusion, so to help fix the problem the railroad depot was named after a railroad official, C. F. Derby. It was not until 1957, almost 80 years later, that the name of "Derby" became official. It has been easy for me to book concerts here in Derby. It is a smaller town but right next to the bustling city of Wichita where all the shopping malls and stores are located.

In November of 2006 we had received a call from Pastor Bill McCary whom we had met in Cunningham, Kansas in 2001 when we were recording our "live' album. He had taken pictures of us that we used for the cover of that CD. He and his wife had moved to Slaton, Texas and wanted us to come and minister in concert at their church in January 2007 and also appear with him on a TV show in Midland, Texas. We booked a concert at the Trinity Evangelical Methodist Church in Slaton, Texas for Saturday evening, January 13th and Sunday morning, January 14th.

The weather in January in the mid-west is not always favorable, and in January of 2007 the weather turned ugly, just when we were about to take a tour to Slaton, Texas. An ice storm hit the region and our first concert on Thursday, January 11th on this tour took us to Mangum, Oklahoma, which is located in the southwestern region of Oklahoma. It had gotten colder when we left Derby and the wind picked up, blowing snow and freezing rain that covered all the roads with a coating of ice. We were not sure we wanted to tackle such a trip but we knew that the Lord had been providing for us financially through our concerts. Dare we cancel this tour? When we prayed, the Lord showed us that He would take us through the storm, again!

By the time we arrived in Mangum, Oklahoma, the front of our van was covered with a thick coat of ice. I had had to stop many times on the way to scrape the ice from our windshield wipers so they would continue to work properly, but the next day we continued on to Slaton, Texas for our next concert date.

The weather had not changed during the night and I had to battle the weather, and drive on the back roads on Friday all the way to Slaton. At least in Slaton we had Saturday afternoon off before our first concert, but when we arrived at the home of Pastor Bill and Norma, the front of our van was a solid sheet of ice.

We had a wonderful visit with Pastor Bill and his wife Norma, and during our conversation Bill mentioned to us that Buddy Holly's cousin, Kay Reed, attended his church. We couldn't wait to meet her, and we found out that she was anxious to meet us. Pastor Bill told us that there was a museum and statue of Buddy Holly in Lubbock, and asked us if he could take us there to see the statue. Even though the weather had subsided we were not sure if we should try and drive to Lubbock, but the pastor seemed ok with it and took us on a tour of Lubbock.

We had two wonderful concerts at Pastor Bill's church in spite of the ice storm, and there were only a few daring souls who came Sunday morning, but we did minister in concert anyway. The Holy Spirit was present and the 'chosen few' were blessed. On Monday morning we had to leave early and car-pool to Odessa, Texas where we were to appear on "God's Learning Channel" satellite—Web TV. The show was to start at 8:00am. On the way to Odessa, Pastor Bill's car started acting up and he had to pull over and stop at the nearest gas station for repairs. He told us to go on and they would join us as soon as they could, and we were not sure at that time if he would make it or not. Pastor Bill and Norma did make it and we were interviewed and sang a couple of songs for Web-TV.

On our drive back to Kansas we had concerts in western Kansas at Rolla and Elkhart, Kansas and then Felt, Oklahoma. After returning to Derby we had concerts throughout the coming months and in June I had booked a week's concert tour to Iowa. Our tour began in Moravia, Iowa on Wednesday, June 13th. Thursday we were in Bussey, Friday in Lacy, Saturday in Beacon, Sunday morning in Knoxville and Sunday evening in Edyville. Monday we had a day off and then Tuesday we were in Des Moines, Wednesday at 4:00pm we were at the Cedars Assisted Living and then at 7:00pm at a church in Madrid.

In February we received a call from a concert promoter, Kathleen Kachulis who represented the East Side Christian Church in Council Bluffs, Iowa. She wanted to book us for June 30th and July 1st at her church. We were more than thrilled to drive to Council Bluffs. The woman I had dated briefly at bible college in Nebraska was from Council Bluffs. I had wondered if she and her family might come to our concert, but then I thought she wouldn't know the stage name I had taken as my legal name.

When we arrived at the East Side Christian Church in Council Bluffs, there was so much excitement in the air. They had advertised the event as "From Rock 'n Roll to The Rock of Ages Concert, featuring pop singing legend Frankie Valens and his pianist wife Phyllis." Kathleen told us that when she started advertising there was a lot of interest by the media and people from other states. One of the local television stations invited Kathleen to appear on their community news to talk about "Frankie" and the event the church was hosting. The TV program was televised in Omaha, and our friends Jim and Michelle Henry, whom we had met in Cozad, Nebraska, where Jim was the pastor of a church, and were also the ones who loaned us a motorhome for our touring, saw the advertisement on TV and came to our concert that evening.

The evening began about 4:00pm with a "Dinner with Frankie & Phyllis," with reservations taken for the dinner. There had been such an overwhelming response with dinner reservations that they had to open the gym to accommodate everyone, and they decorated it in the 50's style. They provided the wise-cracking, gum-snapping, 50's waitresses in vintage clothes that served the food and bussed the tables. There were old records being played not only in the gym but also in the fellowship hall, on vintage record players. The food included the classic Maid Rite sandwiches and other popular classic 50's foods. There were 50's trivia games with prizes donated by the community merchants and 50's pictures were posted throughout the church, along with original 50's records, pictures and posters. They held a nifty-fifties costume contest and provided a photographer to snap everyone's photo, and a vintage car show that everyone enjoyed.

There was standing room only during our concert. I could see people lining the hallway at the main entrance to the sanctuary straining their ears to hear the concert and maybe being able to take a glimpse inside. There was just not enough room for everyone to sit. Among the 'filled to capacity' audience were three separate Red Hat Lady Society clubs who said they absolutely loved Frankie. It was times like these that made our travels very enjoyable because of the excitement and pleasure it gave to others, knowing that a former pop-singer could still share some of the oldies from the past and was now serving the Lord, giving Him all the glory.

When we arrived back on Derby I had set up a tour that would take us all the way to South Carolina. I e-mailed my two oldest kids, Jennifer and Brian, in New Jersey asking them if they had the time they might want to drive to South Carolina to be at our concert. Now remember, I had spent time with Jennifer when we flew her out to Denver to spend a week with us, but I had not seen my oldest son since he was about the age of six, so I was hoping they would come.

Our South Carolina tour began after I received a call from Cliff Bishop from the "Lost Cherokee Nation" in Marshall, Arkansas asking if we would come back to do another concert for their cause. Apparently the government still had not recognized them as a legal tribe and they were still fighting to be a legally recognized Cherokee tribe to receive benefits. This was the second time we had come to help the cause but the attendance was so poor, I just felt like they were starting to give up on their fight.

From Marshall, Arkansas we headed to Memphis, Tennessee to do a concert at the Longstreet United Methodist Church. It was at this concert that Phyllis did a glissando down the black keys of the piano and one of the black keys came off! What does one do when you are standing there holding a black key from the piano, and the music tracks are still playing? Phyllis was laughing, and I didn't know what was going on yet. But the track finished, she was holding the key, knowing full well she couldn't go on very well. However, the music chairman and the pastor rushed out, and came back with double stick tape. Would you believe they stuck that key right back on, and Phyllis was able to continue playing, but without any more glissandos!

They were providing a pot-luck meal at 6:30pm followed by our concert. On the way to the church I received a call on my cell phone from my youngest daughter, Heather, who lives in the Denver area. She asked me for Brian and Jennifer's phone numbers, and I wondered why she was asking but didn't think anything more about it. Heather had only met her half-sister, Jennifer, once, and that was when we had flown Jennifer out from New Jersey to spend time with us. Heather had not met Brian, her half-brother yet. While we were in Memphis I told Phyllis that I really wanted to visit Elvis's mansion and estate, but we decided that we had more time on our way back to Kansas at the end of our tour.

From Memphis we drove on to Knoxville, Tennessee for a church concert, and then drove 116 miles to our next concert in Asheville, North Carolina. The next day we when we were heading to Statesville, North Carolina to minister in concert, I received a call from Jennifer on my cell phone telling me that she and Brian were on their way to South Carolina to meet with us. I was ecstatic! I had not yet met my son face to face in nearly 35 years, and now they were on their way.

It was so hard trying to concentrate during our concert in Statesville, North Carolina. I knew my two oldest children were on their way, but we still had a wonderful concert with Pastor Frank and Ovella Turner. Some years before, we had donated one of our vans to them when it had broken down on our way to Roanoke, Virginia. Pastor Frank had driven up to Roanoke to drive it back, and they were still using that van for their church. I think the van was like the Energizer Bunny—it just kept going and going!

On Saturday we headed to Phyllis's sister, Joyce's home near where our next concert was. Joyce had moved to South Carolina from San Diego because of a job offer. She lived in a double-wide modular home and because my youngest daughter Heather had given us a portable GPS system for Christmas last year, we were able to locate Joyce's home and drive straight to it.

Jennifer called me on my cell phone and told us that they were staying at a motel in Anderson and would like to meet us at a local park. When we told Joyce about the park, Joyce took us to the wrong park. I talked with Jennifer again and asked her if we could just meet them in the lobby of their motel. Phyllis wanted this meeting to be special between me and my kids so she stayed behind with Joyce while I took off for the motel.

On my solo drive to the motel in Anderson my heart was pounding so hard with the excitement I felt about meeting my children again, and especially Brian, whom I hadn't seen for so many years. Upon arriving at the motel I kept looking for signs of my kids but saw no one that looked familiar. I waited in the lobby for what seemed like an eternity when my cell phone rang again. It was Jennifer, telling me they had to go do an errand and were heading back to the motel. I decided to wait outside the main entrance so my children could see me.

Several cars had come into the parking lot but none were my children. Would I even recognize them? Just about the time I was ready to go back into the lobby I saw a small car drive by the front entrance and noticed a man's arm reaching above the car to wave to me. That must be my son! I waited a few moments and then I saw two people emerge from that car. It was my daughter Jennifer and her brother, my son, Brian. I met them half way across the parking lot in anticipation. Brian gave me a big bear hug, and I wanted to pinch myself! These were my children that I had not been able to spend any time with at all with for so many years, and now here they were! We walked back into the lobby to sit down and chat so we could get to know each other.

As the three of us sat at a table in the foyer of the motel chatting, a young lady walked up beside me and asked me if I had a pen. Without looking up I started fumbling in my pockets for a pen and realized that I hardly ever carried a pen or a pencil, and I told her that I was sorry but no, I had no pen. When I looked up to take a look at the woman, it was my youngest daughter Heather! She had flown out, along with her husband, Mikee, to South Carolina from Denver to surprise me because she wanted to be a part of this reunion. Heather had never met Brian either, until now. That was why she had called me on my cell phone when we were in Memphis, asking for their phone numbers. She had been making plans to fly out for this reunion! What a wonderful surprise!

The five of us were able to spend the afternoon together, bowling and having dinner together, getting to know one another and bonding. By Sunday Heather and Mikee had to fly back to Denver but Jennifer and Brian wanted to attend our gospel concert at the Lake Bowen Baptist Church in Inman Sunday evening.

Sunday the weather turned ugly and it started raining. From Anderson it was about a 60 mile drive to Inman and I knew we would probably have to drive in the rain. Jennifer and Brian decided to follow behind us, and I was totally depending on my GPS system to get us all to the church. Sometimes the rain was so bad that we had to pull over and stop, until it subsided and we could go on.

The Lake Bowen Baptist Church is a large church and they are able to bring in many known Christian recording artists. The pastor had called us in May asking us to come and perform a concert for his church. He told me that he knew his congregation would love the music and our testimonies, so it was because of this pastor that I booked this eastern tour, not knowing at the time that my two oldest children would be driving down to South Carolina from New Jersey just to spend time with their father.

We set up our ministry information in the church foyer and did a sound check in the sanctuary. When people started coming in Brian asked Phyllis, "Are all these people here to hear you guys sing?" Phyllis told him yes. Then he asked her, "Would some of these people have come anyway?" She told him, "Maybe! But they are here mainly to hear your dad sing." I don't think Brian realized the full impact his dad had made over the years as a nightclub performer and recording artist. After all, Brian only knew his me when I was just starting out in the music industry as an unknown, and he was quite young when I had a band rehearsing in our basement. He did tell me that he would sneak downstairs while I was at work and play around on the drums, while Jennifer would grab the tambourine and toss it about. Brian told me his love of music came from his being able to play around on the band instruments. Now Brian can play almost any instrument, from guitar to drums, and he has his own band. He told me he didn't sing and didn't inherit that gift from me, but he did inherit the love of music.

It was hard on us when my children had to leave and drive back to New Jersey, but we had to also leave to continue our concert tour. We had to drive to Little Rock, Arkansas for our next concert, which would be about a 12 hour drive or 644 miles, but we had till Wednesday to arrive in Little Rock, Arkansas, and I had mentioned to Phyllis that I wanted to stop in Memphis and visit Graceland, Elvis's home.

When we arrived in Memphis it was difficult trying to find Elvis Presley Boulevard and the Graceland Estates. All the signs for Elvis Presley Boulevard are always taken by souvenir seekers and there are no markers for this boulevard, but we ultimately did find it.

To purchase tickets for our tour of Graceland we had to drive to a building across the street from Graceland. From there we could see the famous music gates at the front entrance to the estate that Elvis had installed in April of 1957. He had purchased Graceland in March of 1957. The Graceland property was originally established as a 500 acre farm during the American Civil war, so says publisher Stephen C. Toof, owner of the Memphis Daily Appeal. Mr. Toof named the property after his daughter, Grace Toof.

We enjoyed our tour of the mansion and surrounding buildings where most of Elvis's costumes and records are on display. In 1965 Elvis added a meditation garden complete with a pool. When he died in 1977 he was first buried at the Forest Hill Cemetery, but because of problems they moved his burial plot to the south side of the pool at the meditation garden. Also buried there is Elvis's mother, Gladys, his father Vernon, and his grandmother Minnie May Presley, as well as Elvis's still-born twin brother Jesse Garon who has a marker there as well.

We then drove on to Little Rock, Arkansas for our concert date at a church there. After our concert in Little Rock we had a few days between concert dates and decided to spend time with Phyllis's mother in Heavener, Oklahoma. From Heavener we drove home to Derby, Kansas and celebrated our 22nd wedding anniversary.

Our next tour took us to Minnesota and the town of Elysian where we met Pastor Steven Hultegren who not only was a preacher but also had a prison ministry. Our next concert date was in Eagle Lake before heading to Iowa for five concert dates. One of those concerts took us to the Midwest Christian Children's Home in Peterson, Iowa, a home for abused young men. My heart went out to those boys. I too had been abused as a young boy and knew what some of them may have gone through. I was not only sexually abused as a young man but felt an overwhelming feeling of rejection, starting with my own father. Although as a child I didn't understand why I had such feelings of rejection, it wasn't until I got older that I started putting all the missing pieces to the puzzle together.

Shortly after my mother and father were married, and mom was pregnant with me, dad enlisted in the army to fight in WWII. About three years later when my dad came home after the war, my brother was born, so my dad bonded with my brother. He had not had time to bond with his firstborn son, because I was about three years old when he came home. Even though I had a 'father' around and he provided for us, I really didn't have a father. Dad was not the kind of man that showed much emotion, and he wasn't the kind of man who showed any affection! He probably learned all that from his dad who when his dad got angry he threw a two-by-four at his wife. Thank the Lord she ducked and didn't get hit. Grandpa also got so angry that he put his fist into the back of a hay wagon and moved the hay wagon two inches. Yes, dad learned well from his father. I wanted to show much more affection with my own kids to let them know that, no matter what happened, they knew I loved them.

In June we had received a call from Michael Price who ran the AmeriKids Christian Center in O'Fallon, Missouri, a Christian Day Care. I think the Lord was trying to get my attention about dealing with my own problems and turning those hurts over to Him so I could heal from the wounds.

When we arrived at the North High School auditorium where our concert was to be held for the AmeriKids, we met Michael and Cheri Price who educated us in what they were doing for the children and some of the problems they had to deal with. One particular young man was Dakota

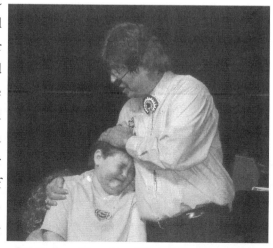

Dakota Fravel from AmeriKids with Frankie in 2007.

Fravell, and his birthday was the same day as our concert, September 13th. While his parents had been having marital problems and were talking about divorce, Dakota's dad died. Phyllis and I wanted to do something special for Dakota and wanted to recognize his birthday, so during our concert we called Dakota up onto the stage. When I put my arms around him to sing 'happy birthday,' he started to cry. We did not know at the time that his father had just passed away only five months before. Mike told me that when he started promoting our concert with AmeriKids, Dakota was the one who was the most excited, and he told Mike days and days after our concert that Frankie and Phyllis had sung 'happy birthday' to him. Michael told us that we made a life-long memory for Dakota.

From O'Fallon, Missouri we traveled to Farmington, Illinois to sing at the Farmington Music Theater. We had sung at this theater in 2006 and by popular demand we were asked to come back. Our friend, Lynn Parr, who we met in Duncan, Oklahoma, had referred this theater to us because his cousin, Gordon, lived in Farmington as well as Lynn's widowed mother. When Lynn told Gordon that we had a concert nearby, Gordon and his mother came to our concert. Gordon told Lynn that of all the songs we sang, his favorite song was "You Alone." Lynn told him that that was his favorite song as well. Without either one of them knowing ahead of time, they both loved the same song.

SIXTY FIVE
FORCED RETIREMENT

Because Phyllis and I had to carry much of our own equipment most of the time during our 18-year ministry, Phyllis developed a bulging disk in her lower back, and my chiropractor told me not to lift anything heavier than my underwear! Of course neither one of us had much choice in our travels to always have help when we needed it. Although Phyllis always sent a "Schedule Confirmation" along with an advertising packet ahead of time to each place where we had a concert, asking for help when we arrived, we oftentimes didn't get the help we needed. I always brought along a four-wheeler and a two-wheeler dolly in our van to help carry our sound equipment and CDs into the church or auditorium, but we still had some lifting to do in order to set up. We were beginning to realize that if things didn't change we would need to stop touring.

Most of our concert touring at the beginning of 2008 was local concerts in and around Wichita and we wanted to take time to record a gospel CD. We wanted to record a gospel album that would include quasi gospel tunes from the 50s that were a cross-over to pop music, and also gospel songs sung by Elvis. We decided to call our new CD "Looking Back" and included on the front cover our graduation pictures from high school and then a current picture of us. We contacted Haskell Cooley, who had produced several of our albums, and told him what we wanted to do. Haskell said he could record anything we wanted to record, and when we told him one of the songs was "I Asked The Lord," he told us he had already recorded that song and we could use those tracks for our new project. We also recorded: "Where Could I Go?," "Swing Down, Sweet Chariot," "One Day At A Time," "Somebody Bigger Than You And I," "Wonderful Time Up There," "I Believe," "Crying In The Chapel," "Put Your Hand In The Hand," "His Hand In Mine," "Lead Me, Guide Me," "He," "Let Us Pray," "Precious Lord, Take My Hand," "Let There Be Peace On Earth," "Mansion Over The Hilltop," "You'll Never Walk Alone," "Count Your Blessings," and "May The Good Lord Bless And Keep You."

During one of our earlier concert tours we met a wonderful friend, Marie Kugler, from Red Cloud, Nebraska, who became one of our 'roadies.' She wanted us to come to Red Cloud in concert so she wouldn't have to drive so far to come hear us, so she contacted the Red Cloud Opera House who booked us right on the spot. Then, Marie contacted her church in Riverton, Nebraska and they too booked a concert with us. All the churches and the theater that Marie contacted, booked a concert with us.

When we arrived at the Red Cloud Opera House there was so much excitement in the air. We were told that the theater sold out 30 minutes prior to our concert and they had to start turning people away. They told us that when some of the locals had arrived at the theater a few minutes before show time thinking they would have no problem getting in, had to be turned away. The volunteers who could usually sit at the back of the auditorium during the concerts, had no place to sit either. Phyllis actually got to play on a Steinway grand piano, the Rolls Royce of pianos, during our concert.

Back in February we had received a call from Ron Chronister, the choral director of the Halstead High School in Halstead, Kansas. He was planning their Spring Choral Pops concert in May and wanted to bring in "Frankie Valens" and have his choral group back me up, especially when he learned through another teacher there that Frankie Valens lived just 47 miles away in Derby, Kansas. Never having included a 'celebrity' in his concerts, he was fascinated by the idea. We booked the concert, and it turned out to be one of the highlights of our 18 years of ministry! We sent music and tracks to Ron ahead of time so his choral group could learn them before the concert.

When we arrived at the Halstead High School Ron met us and introduced us to his choral group. He told us that he was hoping to have a large crowd because of us, and because there had been a lack of interest in the community for his group's efforts in the past. The evening turned out so fantastic with 350 plus in attendance! The students not only backed me up vocally but Ron had taught them choreography to go along with each song, and Ron told us later that that crowd was the largest he had ever had for one of his Spring Coral Pop concerts. At one point I turned around to face the students and shouted, "You kids rock!" and the place erupted. We were thrilled to be a part of it, and after the concert and while at our product table, a woman came up and said, "You guys are Christians, aren't you? I could tell." Praise God for the "silent witness!" Many of the students wrote us 'thank yous' for coming.

During rehearsal his select group called "Bel Canto" had performed an 'artsy' piece written in 1558 for a music contest and received a '1' rating. It was a story about a Phyllis. So the group brought Phyllis to the stage and while standing in a semi-circle, they sang the song to her. What fun! It was an evening we'll never forget. Here are just a few notes we received from some of the students: "Thank you so much for a great

444

concert. You guys are really talented. I hope you guys come back and perform with the choir again. That was the best concert ever. My family couldn't stop talking about it. I hope sometime you come to the school and see us all again! We really appreciate you taking time and singing with us! Your friend!" Another student wrote: "Thank you so much for coming to our Pops concert. It was really fun and we really enjoyed you coming and singing with us. I hope you can come back again soon." "I just loved the concert that you presented at Halstead High School in May. Wow! I sat on the 2nd row right in front of Frankie and took a lot of pictures!! I talked with Frankie during intermission and got my picture taken with you both. I told Frankie that I was the elementary music teacher at Halstead/ Bentley and have been here 41 years. All of Ron's students once were mine! Thanks so much for coming."

Frankie singing on stage with the Halstead High School choir in 2008

Ron told us afterward, "You'll never know what you have done for the kids, for the school, and for the community. These are kids that sang at Carnegie Hall a couple of years ago, and are going again next year—that's the caliber of young people we're talking about. I think the highest compliment of all, however, came from some people who came up to us after the concert and said, "You're believers, aren't you?" The light of our Lord and His testimony did indeed shine through and God was glorified. We do praise His holy name! What a wonderful memory! Thank you!"

In July I booked a concert tour that took us to the YMCA of the Rockies again. I had contacted my children in New Jersey and they were making plans to fly out to Denver and attend our concerts, but they also wanted to have the first ever reunion with all my children in Denver. When I contacted Chaplain Bill Huth at the YMCA office, he was thrilled that all of my kids were going to get together for the first time ever, and he invited my whole family up to the YMCA facilities and provided everyone housing and meals. What a treat! Thank you Mr. Huth.

Our Colorado tour started in Cozad, Nebraska at a church where Pastor Jim and Michelle Henry had been pastors. Jim and Michelle were the family that provided us with a motorhome to tour in, but we returned it to them when we had to replace three transmissions in eleven months. Jim and Michelle have since moved away and now own an Italian restaurant in Omaha, Nebraska.

From Cozad we drove to a church in Fort Morgan, Colorado before heading into Denver to meet up with my children. My son and daughter from New Jersey had flown in to Denver and were already at my youngest daughter's home in Parker, Colorado. I was getting anxious to join them and be a part of the first ever reunion of all my children.

We drove to Parker and joined up with all five of my children at Heather and Mikee's home. I had contacted Heather in advance to tell her I

Frankie's children united for the first time in 2009

wanted to celebrate Jennifer's birthday and asked her if she wouldn't mind picking up a birthday cake. Jennifer's birthday was on the first of July and we were there on the third, so when all of us had eaten, Heather brought out Jennifer's birthday cake all lit up. I wanted a group picture taken of all my children together but it was hard trying to get all five in one location. Jeff was at his mother's home and couldn't join us so we drove into Denver to his mother's home where I was able to take pictures of all five of my children together for the very first time.

On Saturday Phyllis and I headed to Estes Park to check in and get a sound check for our concerts at the YMCA of the Rockies, and my children drove up on Sunday afternoon to join us.

Sunday morning we were scheduled to sing special music only at the Hyde Park Chapel service. Sunday evening we had a concert at the Estes Park Baptist Church. During our concert I had turned off our cell phones, and little did I know that my children wanted to come hear us, but they didn't know where we were and had tried calling our cell phones all evening. They had checked in on Sunday evening while we were in concert at the church. By Monday morning while heading to the cafeteria to eat breakfast, Brian got a hold of me on my cell phone and we all were able to meet for breakfast. We toured during the day and then drove out to a camp site where my youngest son Mark, was camping. All my kids were somewhere in the park except Jeff.

Monday evening the YMCA of the Rockies wanted an oldies concert, and Tuesday evening a gospel concert. I didn't know it at the time that that would be the last time that my kids would hear us in concert. Phyllis was starting to have problems with pain in her legs, which were an early sign of diabetic neuritis, and would be one of the reasons we needed to retire from touring. Jennifer and Brian were not able to stay for our

Tuesday night performance because they had to fly back home to New Jersey, and Heather needed to take them to the airport.

We knew that we needed to retire soon because of our health and decided to have our last concert at the Louisburg Baptist Temple in Louisburg, Kansas. I informed our dear friend, Jack Smith, who was the worship leader at the church, letting him know that our concert at his church would be our farewell concert. I had earlier recorded one of his songs that he had written called "I Wonder" and wanted to debut it at his church.

Our farewell concert to retire from traveling in 2008 in Louisburg, KS

On Saturday, September 27th we drove to Louisburg for an outdoors concert on the church lawn. Many of our friends, when they found out that we were retiring, drove many miles to be at our farewell concert. My second cousin Milton Piper and his wife Glenda drove in from Independence, Missouri to be there for the occasion as did my cousin Gary and Deborah Piper, who is my dad's brother Billie's son, and his family. Roger and Robert Lee, my high school friends from Fontana High School, came with their families. Keith and Gail Johnson from Wichita also came. It was a concert that we will never forget and we had our family and friends there to help us with the transition. Jack Smith presented us with a special framed plague containing memorabilia from the many years of our ministry, and church people gave Phyllis a corsage and a basket of goodies.

Sunday morning we did a mini-concert, and when we sang our last song, both of us started to get very emotional because we knew that this was our last song at our last concert! While heading home after this last concert of our 18-year ministry, and we had just turned east onto 63rd street from K15, heading to Derby, Phyllis burst into uncontrollable tears. The realization that we wouldn't have to travel any more finally hit her. She had often joked about the fact that when I had wanted to go on the road to do a ministry, she had said that she didn't like to travel, but God did a 180 on her and we went on the road. She had not realized how deeply ingrained that was a part of her nature, and she really didn't enjoy travelling, but she let God use her for His glory. When our traveling ministry was coming to a close, and her supposed extreme relief of not having to 'fight' her true nature was over, she just burst out in crying that just could not seem to stop. And, somehow, I too was relieved that we didn't have to travel extensively anymore.

What we both had forgotten was that we still had a concert at the Downtown Senior Center in Wichita in October. Before I could cancel the concert we received a donation check in the mail from the senior center for our concert date with them, so I couldn't very well cancel now. But it went well, and several of our local friends came and could say their good-bye this way.

With no other means of support now, we signed up for social security, so we spent time at the Wichita Social Security Office giving them all the information they needed so we could start receiving our social security checks. When people asked us what it was like to retire, we simply told them that we had not retired from the 'ministry,' we only took another direction. Some even asked us if we missed the concert touring. No, we didn't miss the traveling but we sometimes missed our opportunities to use our talents for His glory in concert and see our wonderful friends. We've decided that we would continue ministering in concert whenever we would receive a call to do so.

SIXTY SIX
A BUMPY YEAR

When Phyllis's lower back started to give her more problems she visited our chiropractor near Derby. He told her she had a bulging disk and needed to be very careful lifting anything. And, if having lower back problems wasn't enough, she started having extreme pain in her legs, which oftentimes kept her up most of the night. We had no idea what was causing her pain but knew we had to do something soon. Phyllis had been struggling with diabetes for several years. She consulted with over 10 doctors, including a kinesiologist, our family doctor, various chiropractors, and a Chinese acupuncturist who sometimes left her legs bleeding. A naturopathy doctor suggested that she go on a very strict diet which her body could not handle, and she often felt dizzy and faint. One chiropractor worked only on her lower back, placing her on a machine that stretched her body to help relieve the stress on her bulging disk. Still, there was very little relief in sight for her.

The biggest help came from the kinesiologist who identified Phyllis's pain as being diabetic neuritis. At least we had identified what was causing the problem and we could work on trying to lower her blood sugar by diet, exercise, and medicines to help in the healing, and our family doctor prescribed some diabetes medications.

I had booked 'Valens-tine' banquets back in 2008 for the following February 2009 year that I knew we needed to either cancel or try and fulfill. I wasn't sure that we could handle doing any more concerts with all of our physical problems starting to surface, but we went ahead and fulfilled all five concerts.

With no more concerts lined up I decided I wanted to record one last oldies CD, and we called my new project "Rock 'n' Roldies." I contacted the Haskell Cooley Sound Studio in Wichita and he was more than thrilled to help me produce the project. I wanted this album to sound like it had been recorded 'live,' even though it hadn't been. Haskell, with all his expertise, found all the special sound effects I needed and even provided a third vocal part and played piano where I needed it. I asked Mark Johnson to come in and harmonize with me on "Bye, Bye, Love." All the music included renditions of songs that 50's and 60's artists sang, such as Buddy Holly, The Drifters, Bobby Rydell, Brian Hyland, Bobby Vinton, Bobby Darin, Bobby Helms, Bill Haley and the Comets, The Carpenters, Sheb Wooley, The Casinos, Chubby Checker, Elvis, The Cordettes, The Beatles, Buddy Knox, and Fats Domino. I included one song that did not fit the category of 'rock and roll,' the country song, "I Love You This Much" which was originally sung by Jimmy Wayne, telling a wonderful story that hits very close to home for me, but I had to include this song on the project. Mark Johnson not only sang a duet with me but he also designed the art work for the CD.

It wasn't long before I started having pain in my left heel and couldn't figure out what was wrong. When I made an appointment with our family doctor he put me in touch with a podiatrist. When the podiatrist X-rayed my foot he found a bone spur, and gave me a special boot to wear 24 hours a day. Because of my bone spur I qualified to have a handicap placard. I now not only had lower back problems but now I was struggling with a bone spur. During the day I wore a special walking boot, and at night, a different kind of foot support to sleep with.

And if all this was not enough, our family doctor had noticed a growth on Phyllis's left cheek and sent her to the Moeller dermatologist. They discovered that Phyllis's cancer had reappeared from 20 years ago, and she needed immediate surgery to remove it. She had had cancer removed from that same spot while we lived in Castle Rock, Colorado, and that doctor did not tell her that the cancer had a 40 per cent chance of returning, in five years. The dermatologist removed a portion of her left check about the size of a half dollar, and then she had reconstructive surgery performed by another physician who stretched her skin to cover the area, and because they had to stretch her skin, the stretching pulled her left earlobe up and it had to be cut and reshaped, thus closing her pierced ear. She didn't mind having her ears re-pierced, because at least the cancer was gone.

Our faith over the years has been stretched to the max, and there were many times we wanted to give up and became discouraged, but we never lost sight of who our heavenly Father is. Even though we sometimes complained and told Him that we couldn't handle any more, He still had his hand on our shoulders. We oftentimes wondered what we did to deserve this, and wondered why God allowed these things to happen to us! Then someone sent us a wonderful story that helped to explain why. A daughter was telling her mother how everything was going wrong with her. She was failing algebra, her boyfriend had broken up with her, and her best friend was moving away. Meanwhile, her mother was baking a cake and asked her daughter if she wanted a snack, and the daughter says, 'Absolutely mom, I love your cake.' Her mother asked her if she wanted some cooking oil, and her daughter says, 'yuck.' Then her mother offers her a couple of raw eggs. Her daughter was grossed out by even the thought of it. As a last result her mother offered her some flour and some baking soda, to which her daughter says 'yuck' again. The mother then replies, "Yes, all of these things seem bad by themselves, but when they are all mixed together in the right way, they make a wonderfully, delicious cake!" God works in the same way. Many times we wonder why He would let us go through such bad and difficult times, but God knows that when He puts these things all in His plan and order for our lives, they always work for our good! We just have to trust Him and eventually, all the circumstances will make something wonderful! Whenever we talk to God, He listens. God can live anywhere in the universe, but He chose to live in our hearts. I would much rather live my life as if there is a God, and die to find out that there isn't, than to live my life as if there isn't a God, and die to find out that there is. Hebrew 10:31 KJV says "It is a fearful thing to fall into the hands of the living God."

We have seven children between us and only one of them is actively serving the Lord. Some are agnostic, while some are living lives that I know are not pleasing to the Lord. One of my sons told me once that 'if I can't see it, I don't believe in it.' Apparently he doesn't believe in the oxygen that he breathes. He can't see it, therefore it doesn't exist. He doesn't believe in gravity because he can't see gravity. He cannot believe in radio waves and TV communications or even cell phones, because those airwaves don't exist and he can't see them. All these unseen things are real and do exist. I believe because I have read His word. James 1:5 KJV says, "If any of you lack wisdom, let him ask of God, and it shall be given him." Sometimes we just make too many desperate calculations in our worldly beliefs that we know in our hearts are not true, but are forced into a belief system that the majority holds onto, and we tag along and join in their scam because we're too afraid to believe in something unseen and hard to prove. If only we would just let go and let God!

We were created in God's image with a body, soul and spirit. No other living creature has a spirit! When our heart stops, our spirit is released and is taken where you have chosen it to go. If you believe in the Lord and have asked for forgiveness, you will join Him in heaven, but if you have never made a conscious decision to accept God's only begotten Son, no matter how giving and how good you were before you died, you get hell by default. That's why we live with hope, and the promise that we will someday join other believing family members in heaven. Now 'that' will be a reunion. Maybe I should have written lyrics about a reunion in the sky. I did re-record a pop song that says just that, the song is "Spirit In The Sky." James 2:26 KJV says "For as the body without the spirit is dead, so faith without works is dead also."

Over the years I have probably written the lyrics to about five songs, and only one song, "Lord Ivy," appeared on my album. The lyrics I wrote were: "In the year that Lord Ivy lived, people shook at his beck and call, he said, I am a man of unclean lips, for my eyes have seen and that ain't all. My house is filled with smoke and ash, for I am lost in my guilt and shame. I have heard a voice saying here am I, but is it me that is really to blame. How good it is living lifted and high, above a world full of smoke and ash. With two covered feet to flee away fast, into a world full of dirty old cash. Lord Ivy lived a life full of wit, and elbowed his way through the rushing crowd. And into the heart of all mankind, came the legend of Ivy to read out loud. How good it is to read about you, lord Ivy, dear lord Ivy."

I also wrote the lyrics to "I Am Set Free," which goes something like this: "Just the time I think I am lost, I'm reminded of the terrible cost. Lord, you paid it all to set me free, free in you Lord is where I will be. I lift up your name Lord and cast out my net. I'll be a fisher of men and men I will get. Please send me to nations that you feel are lost, and we will sip from your merciful cup. I am set free, yes free as can be. Because I am free Lord, now I can see. I am set free Lord, I sing praises to Thee. You set me free and free I will be."

Another song I wrote was called "God Loves Us Chicken Hawks." "Sitting regal on a fence, I wonder where my love has gone. She's flown away and I don't know where. I sit and wonder, or do I care? Sometimes she acts more like a dove, and dives to me from far up above. She thinks she's being funny just chirping away. I'm so gullible, what can I say? We need to spend more time in God's word, learning scripture as we cook. She flies away more often than not, and that's not the way that we have been taught. God loves us little chicken hawks, He spent much time in creating us. I'm not a dove and never will be, look at my feathers, what do you see? In unity is where we should be, flying together as far as the sea. Don't let Satan tear us apart, our God is real and He has a real heart."

The lyrics to "Change Me, Oh Lord" are: "I'll sit and bask in the glory of Your love. Your mercy surrounds me like a glove. I am a child of the King and I glorify Your name. I honor and adore You, Your love remains the same. I will not fear, though I have many tears. Your word is so clear, how could I have fears? For you are my God, and I am your son, for You stay the same Lord, and I am not done." The lyrics all had a good message, but they never made it into songs.

Early in 2010 Sierra Scott from TV channel 8 Public television in Wichita contacted us about an interview for her Sunday evening program called "All Things Good." We were delighted that she wanted to hear our story. She came and interviewed us and then wanted to capture a 'live' performance of us and sent her camerawoman to our August 27th concert held at the Civic Center in El Dorado, Kansas to film our performance for the Gold Wing Road Riders Association Rally. The show was aired on Sunday, November 28, 2010, and we have permission to have it also on YouTube.

In July of 2010 I was asked to be the emcee and perform oldies, and we were asked to sing gospel music at the Summerville Arena and Conference Center in Summerville, Virginia. We had been in contact with Pastor Butch Paugh who initially set up the conference called "Broken Arrow: A cry for deliverance." Pastor Paugh made all our arrangements for housing and meals while we made arrangements for our flight, but Pastor Paugh made sure all our travel expenses were paid.

Since our retirement late in 2008 we have accepted some concert dates and have had to turn down a few. In June, 2010 we made a decision for me to fly out to New Jersey and spend time with my two oldest children and their families. It was a wonderful trip and I enjoyed every minute of it. While in New Jersey I got to meet my very first bass-guitarist from the Eminent Domain band, Tom Slack. My son, Brian, drove me out to Tom and Karen's home so I could surprise Tom. I did not realize that Tom had started work the same year at the same company my daughter has been working at for 27 years, and neither one of them knew about each other, nor the relationship to me.

I had found my first lead-guitarist on FaceBook when I typed in the name, John Bowden. I contacted him and told him I was coming to New Jersey. Shortly after I arrived in New Jersey my children took me to surprise John at the place where he worked. He had gone to lunch before we had arrived so we drove to the restaurant where he and his boss were and surprised him there. We talked about a band reunion but before we could set a date, my first drummer, Bob Barone, died. Bob's wife had died about a year ago and he took it very hard. He had been playing drums at a local church when he died, so when I contacted the church he attended, asking about his memorial service, they asked me to send them a song for them to play for the service. I never got to meet Bob or to even talk with him before he died. John, Tom and I have talked about a possible band reunion in 2011 using my son Brian, as the drummer and dedicate the reunion to Bob Barone but only time will tell if that indeed happens.

In September 2010 we performed two concerts, one in Udall, Kansas and the other in Manhattan, Kansas. In October our pastor friend Steve Brecheisen contacted us to see if we would fill his pulpit on Sunday morning, October 17th while he and his family were on vacation. We had first met Pastor Steve when he was the pastor of a church in Pratt, Kansas. In November we performed in concert at the First Baptist Church in El Dorado, Kansas for a prison ministry outreach.

We are staying busy and enjoy being asked to come do a concert now and then. Besides being sued by family members over false accusations and having to hire an attorney to represent us with money we don't have, we are still trusting in the Lord, for He sees the whole picture. These family members are suing God's people. They will have to answer to Him on judgment day.

Over the last 18 years of our ministry we have met and encountered many pastors and church leaders who either treated us like children of God, or totally had very little regard for our welfare. I believe that America's basic problem and why our nation is collapsing from within is because our pastors are sitting idly on the sidelines and refusing to educate their own flock about important issues. Most are more interested in receiving their weekly paycheck and keeping their jobs. No duty or responsibility is greater than being God's watchman! Isaiah 58:1 KJV says, "Cry aloud, spare not, lift up thy voice like a trumpet, and show my people their transgression, and the house of Jacob their sins."

We were always thrilled when we arrived in town to present a concert and checked into our motel room just to find a basket full of goodies and/or flowers waiting for us from the church. It always made us feel so special.

Some people attend church every week-end. Some sit and listen to a sermon that sounds like the sermon they heard last week-end, and the week-end before. The preacher frequently seems to address the same issues such as how to conduct yourself, how to raise your family, how to manage problems in your marriage, how much you should tithe, or how to be saved. Granted, these things are all important but why is everything done in such a regimented fashion? How can the Holy Spirit work freely in such an atmosphere? The church has their opening prayer, followed by announcements and then about 15 minutes of music and then greetings. The preacher gets up to preach, followed by an offering, an altar call sometimes, and then a closing prayer.

One pastor quoted to me "Render unto Caesar what is Caesar's." We are not the Roman Empire, and there is a big difference in our government, which is supposed to be "We the people," not some dictator or emperor. Our government, according to our constitution is you and me, but somehow the perception of this has changed over the years and we are led to believe that the federal government is the supreme entity in the land. It's time that we demand our church leaders to begin addressing issues like these that threaten us the most. They should be the leaders that God intended for them to be. They should be outspoken, brave, firm, and putting on the whole armor of God. Don't worry about offending a few pew warmers, or back row tithers, or the ACLU, or the

Devil himself. It's time we started having church rather than just 'playing' church.

Since our retirement I have been able to go back into the studio and record four songs that do not appear on any of our CDs. They can only be found on our web site. I recorded "Cherokee Nation," "Spirit In The Sky," "Part Time Applications," and "Be Still." In order to find these songs, along with many others, go into "http://ipod.frankie-valens-music-ipod.com" http://ipod.frankie-valens-music-ipod.com and scroll down to the songs you want to hear. Our Christmas CD can be found at: "http://christmas.frankie-valens-music-ipod.com" http:// christmas.frankie-valens-music-ipod.com This world is not my home. I am just passing through. Watch for my new album titled "Chasing An Illusive Dream-the CD." This CD will include rare studio recordings from circa 1967 to present with bands I had been the lead-singer of such as: The Eminent Domain, Fragile Glass, Iron Mule, The Ivy Museum, and Showstopper.

SIXTY SEVEN
COLLECTANEA OF TWENTY YEARS

This chapter has been reserved for special events that occurred over a twenty year period in our ministry that didn't make it into my storyline but deserve attention.

A LIZARD SURPRISE!

Most of my friends who know me really well know that I startle easily and am afraid of spiders and bugs and anything else that crawls, flies, or moves. One of those startling times happened when we were spending time with Helen, Phyllis's 90 year old mother, between concert tours. Helen was living in a small apartment at the back of a garage owned by a real estate firm, and we were just sitting with her chatting when something moving caught my eye. It was a lizard! I gasped! A lizard had gotten into Helen's apartment and of course I came unglued and panicked. Phyllis told me to go find something to hit it with. Helen found a flyswatter, but she's so slow (only 88 years of age at the time) and didn't get it in time before it headed under a piece of furniture. I'm moving things, trying to find the blasted thing and couldn't find it. Each time I moved something, I was almost afraid I would find it and go into hysterical 'afraidness,' but also hoping that the lizard had found its way back outside.

Just when I was trying to move a delicate piece of furniture, something dropped and I jumped, and my heart stopped~! Phyllis had moved something and it scared me so badly that I burst into tears. She came over and gave me a hug, realizing how badly the whole ordeal had affected me. Apparently the lizard did find its way back outside because we never saw it again.

'ETHEL'S' HOME TOWN

One September we had been invited to do a concert in the park in Cherryvale, Kansas, and the church that sponsored our concert made arrangements for us to stay in a local motel. We noticed pictures and articles about Vivian Vance, Lucille Ball's nosey neighbor, Ethel, on the "I Love Lucy" show posted all over the walls. Vivian Vance was from Cherryvale, Kansas! She was involved in the local theater but later moved to Albuquerque, New Mexico and had wanted to launch her career, when the city paid for her trip to Hollywood. Desi Arnaz spotted her and cast her in the "I Love Lucy" show. These are just some of the perks we were able to experience while traveling.

THE ROYAL THEATER

We were invited to perform at the famous Royal Theater in Archer City, Texas. The town is very small, but the theater has historic roots. The Royal Theater was a fixture in Peter Bogdonovich's movie, "The Last Picture Show," generally on everyone's top 100 movies of all time. That black and white classic movie about small town America helped spawn the careers of Jeff Bridges, Randy Quaid, and Cybil Sheppard, among others. Archer City, for a long time, went by the monikor 'The smallest small town in America,' or something to that effect. The area is also famous regarding the infamous Jesse James.

IT WAS GAPOSIS!

While having breakfast at a hotel one Sunday morning before our concert, I noticed that some women at the next table were snickering and looking in my direction. Phyllis and I were both dressed in our Sunday-best concert clothes, so why were they snickering? My suit was a three piece suit that had the fancy long jacket with thousands of buttons on it that made it very fashionable. However, when we arrived at the church and we sat down in the front pew waiting to go on, I crossed my legs and when I crossed them, I noticed my pants were not zipped! I had gaposis! No wonder the girls were staring and snickering! If I had the slightest hint of being proud of how I was dressed, that experience really brought me back to earth!

THE SHORTEST PARADE IN HISTORY

One summer Phyllis and I were asked to be the Grand Marshalls of a parade in Oklahoma. It turned out to be the shortest parade in history, just two blocks long! We had purchased a bag of candy and didn't even have time to throw the whole bag of candy out for the children.

THE WIG WAS ASKEW!

We were often asked to entertain at Valens-tine banquets every February, sometimes being booked a year or two in advance. We changed the spelling of the holiday to reflect our last name, or didn't you notice? During this musical program we also always included a skit about two famous lovers, Samson and Delilah, where I don an awful, scraggly long black wig. During one of these times, in Phyllis's words, "After I had played a ragtime number, I spent a little time introducing us and our ministry while Frankie could go make a costume change in preparation for the skit. This one particular time had to be a first!"

She continued, "After I finished the piano number Frankie left to get into costume. As I was talking, a very loud sound burst forth, and I thought there was something wrong with the church's sound system, so I continued talking. Then came another blast that continued on and on. Panicked, I looked over at the sound man, and he motioned that it was coming from Frankie's microphone. I couldn't understand that except to comment, 'It's all about Frankie.' As I tried finishing the introduction, Frankie came out of the dressing room looking haggard and frazzled." Now, let me tell you in my own words what was going on in the dressing room.

When I went into the dressing room to change, I immediately turned out the light so no one could see me changing, but I left the door slightly ajar so some light could come into the room. I tried muting my cordless microphone in the dark, but when I did, the battery pack and microphone fell to the floor, still not muted. I tried putting the battery pack back on my belt loop when it fell again, thus causing more noise out in the other room. I finally was able to get the microphone muted but now I was in a hurry to get dressed. I took an old shirt out of a bag I had brought in and put it on to hide the gorgeous Valens-tine shirt, and then tried to put that gosh-awful long black wig on for effect. When I flipped the wig up to go on my head, strands of that wig got caught in the dangling string attached to the light above me, turning the light on. I immediately pulled at the string to turn the light back off for fear that someone would see me through the slit in the door. Now it's almost pitch black in the room and I realized that the door had drifted shut and there was no light coming into the room at all now, so I reached up and was able to pull the string to turn the light back on, but saw strands of that wig still caught in the cord.

There I was, standing with my microphone ON and struggling, and trying to get that awful strand of hair out of the entanglement of the string hanging from the light on the ceiling. In doing so, I yanked on the hair again and turned the light back off! There I was standing in the pitch black again.

Now I'm panicking because I'm hearing Phyllis summing up her introduction and preparing for my entrance, and I'm not nearly ready! I did manage to turn the light back on and get that strand of hair out of the light cord but had trouble adjusting my shirt and that long hair hanging down my back. I was able to attach my cordless microphone to my belt loop but I couldn't see enough to know if my battery pack was on or off, but I knew I had to make my grand entrance, ready or not!

When I walked out of that dressing room my wig was on sideways, and I had no sound coming from my microphone. Phyllis was riotously laughing! I must have still been muted, but when I checked it, the battery pack was on. What I didn't notice was that the microphone cord had come loose from the battery pack and was hanging down my backside unattached. The skit was a success in spite of me! One just never knows what goes on behind nearly-closed doors!

IT HAPPENED AT APPLEBEES!

After our morning concert at a church the pastor and his wife took us out to eat at Applebee's, and there were several of us in a corner booth. When the server came to ask us what we wanted to drink I ordered a large sweet tea. It was then that the waiter commented on how beautiful my tie was, and he went on and on about how much he liked my tie. When the server came back with our drinks he reached over to hand me a menu and when he did he tipped the huge glass of sweet tea into my lap, ice cubes and all. The tea splattered all over my shirt, tie and slacks and I was sitting there with sweet tea and ice cubes in my lap! The waiter was beside himself and offered to have my clothes dry-cleaned, but we told him it wasn't necessary. The pastor told the server, "Do you know who this is?" When the server found out, he was even more in shock and apologetic. Phyllis was laughing and laughing at me, saying, "This couldn't have happened to a nicer guy!" I spent the rest of the meal "out in the cold!" The rest of the group had a hard time concentrating on eating, too, the whole episode regaling all of us.

'ELVIS SLEPT HERE'

One of our tours took us to Clinton, Oklahoma, and the church provided us with overnight housing in the Best Western Tradewinds Inn there in Clinton. When we arrived at the Inn and the owner found out who I was, he decided to give us a very special room. Apparently Elvis and his entourage often came through Clinton and stayed at this motel, and they had a special Elvis guest suite that was preserved and dedicated to Elvis and had never had been changed since Elvis's last visit. We were assigned his room and then presented with a certificate that verified that we had indeed slept where Elvis slept.

WE SENT A WOMAN INTO LABOR

We were invited to sing at a small church in Custer, South Dakota. The town of Custer is just south of Rapid City and near Mount Rushmore, and is situated in the Black Hills National Forest. We made plans to tour the area while we were in Custer after our concert.

There were only about 12 people who attended, and during the concert a pregnant lady apparently went into labor and had to leave. When she left, someone went with her, then another, until hardly anyone was left for us to finish the concert. I must admit that this was the smallest crowd we had ever ministered to in concert in our 18 years of touring. The pastor and his family lived in a parsonage not far away from the church and they invited Phyllis and me to spend the night. When we woke up in the morning there was a flat tire on our van. I had no ready cash on hand to pay for our tire to be repaired, so I asked the pastor if he could cash a check for me. He assured me he would and told me that he was the town sheriff and would come looking for me if the check was no good!

The next day Phyllis and I drove to the famous Mount Rushmore and toured the museum. The day we tried looking at the busts of the presidents it had rained and it looked like all of them had been crying. As we left, we then traveled down the famous pigtail road leading through the Black Hills National Forest. It was quite an experience.

YOU DO BABYSIT, DON'T YOU?

In Iowa a family had volunteered to provide housing for us after our church concert, so we followed them home after our concert ended. They lived in a cute double-wide modular home just outside of town. When we arrived they told us that they needed to go to a class reunion and asked us if we would babysit their children. We were a little in shock, but realized that we had no choice in the matter, because they took off and we were left with three children we did not know. No plans had been made for us to eat dinner and though the kitchen was full of dirty dishes, as was the large kitchen table, the children had to create something for all of us to eat. There was only one bathroom and the stool didn't work. Downstairs in the furnace room was a stool that did work. Although we did return to that church the next year, needless to say, we didn't go back to that home.

COW TIPPING

Another church in Iowa in another small town invited us to sing in their town square where there was an open pavilion with a stage. All we can remember was that it was a very hot day with no trees to shade us and Phyllis's make-up was running down her face. While we were in concert a man on a horse rode by and wanted to give to our ministry. After our concert a couple of the guys who had come to hear us sing, asked me if I wanted to go 'cow tipping.' At first I didn't know what they were talking about, but then they explained that at midnight the cows go to sleep standing up, and all anyone has to do is go push them and they fall over. Gullible and naïve that I am, I considered it, but after much thought, I decided against it. I finally figured out that this was like going snipe hunting.

THE GOD OF SMALL THINGS!

When we left for dinner one evening the price of gas was at $3.36/gallon. However, on the way home we began seeing that the price of gas had jumped to $3.49/gallon, and we were somewhat distressed that we were going to have to pay a higher price to fill up our van before we left on our tour of Texas the next day.

We anxiously drove to Derby and to our local Kwik Shop to fill up. On the way to Derby we were seeing $3.49/gallon, although one Kwik Shop on the way was still at $3.37/gallon. It didn't occur to us to stop there because we were heading to our regular station. The QT station was already showing the $3.49/gallon and we were becoming a little disappointed that we may not get the lower price.

When we arrived at our local Kwik Shop for gas, the prices were still posted at $3.37/gallon, and all the bays were full with people waiting in line to fill up. I pulled up behind one of the cars to be the next in line. When that car left, I pulled up to the pump, and as I did so, the price outside changed to $3.49. I threw my hands up in the air and said 'oh well!' When I started to fill up with gas, the gas pump still read $3.37/

gallon! Wow! The price 'should' have changed when the car ahead of us left, but God kept it from changing, taking care of His servants, and let it hold for us. Right after I filled up, the price changed to $3.49/gallon! Now is that an amazing, wonderful, caring God, or what?

Phyllis and I had learned a skit called "Senior Scrabble" and we used an actual Scrabble game as a prop for the skit, but when we were asked to do that skit again and needed to use that Scrabble game, we couldn't find it anywhere, but as we were walking through Dillons Marketplace in Derby, we noticed a display of board games marked "Buy One, Get One Free" and guess what—the Scrabble game was right there!

Well, the game was marked at $14.99, but we didn't want two Scrabble games, so we thought we'd just take the one. But neither did we want to pay $14.99 for it. However, in fine print, the ticket said the product would scan at 50 per cent, so we grabbed the game and decided that if the one game did scan at 50 per cent, we'd take it. If not, we wouldn't!

When we checked out, we asked the cashier if the game scanned at 50 per cent off. Yes, it did! Hallelujah!, but as she rang it up, she pulled the receipt off and looked further at it, and we wondered why she was looking at it. She said, "There is an additional 30 percent off. You got the Scrabble game for $5.24~!!! The receipt said something about plush toys and games being 30 per cent off—apparently an additional 30 per cent off—so we got the NEW Scrabble game for 80 per cent off!!!!! Is our God again awesome, or what?

THE MAN WITH THE TILTED HEAD

One of our concert tours took us to western Kansas. I had called ahead of time asking if the church would provide help for us when we arrived, to assist us in carrying our sound equipment into the church. When we drove up in front of the church, there was a long walkway leading to the front entrance. We sat for a while waiting to see if another car would arrive with help, and in just a few minutes, the front door of the church opened and an older man appeared. His head was tilted to the left, almost to his shoulder. When he approached our van I at first thought he was joking, especially after he told us he had come to help us unload. I thought we were on Candid Camera and I started looking for the cameras hidden in bushes, but this guy was serious and apparently had trouble with his neck and he did walk like that. He indeed was able to help us, and I later had to repent.

THE DAY THE LINCOLN DIED

On our way to Benkelman, Nebraska to sing at a 'Friends' church we were driving our Lincoln Continental. In Nebraska I had the choice of filling up our car with ethanol, which I didn't know at the time that our Lincoln could not handle that kind of gas. As we approached the small town of Max on our way to Benkelman our car started sputtering and just stopped. At least we had pulled over into a gas station that was closed and there was a pay phone. I called the pastor at the Friends church in Benkelman and told him we were having a problem. He drove the few miles east to meet us, and when he realized we were driving a Lincoln, he told us that Lincolns cannot handle the ethanol grade of gas. He followed us into town where we could fill up with enough gas that would help thin the ethanol out so we couldn't have any more problems, and our problems did clear up then.

WHAT WAS THE ADDRESS AGAIN?

When we approached the town where we had been invited to do a church concert, I drove directly to the motel where the church had made arrangements for us to spend the night. We called the music pastor and he told us he would meet me at the church to get set up and have a sound check. Phyllis told me she would stay at the motel.

I drove to the street where the church was located and found the church. Then I drove around to the back and parked, waiting for the sound man. It seemed like I was there for over an hour and no one came. I decided to walk around to the front of the church to see if there might be a car parked out front, and when I did and read the church sign, I realized that I WAS AT THE WRONG CHURCH! I quickly got in my car and drove further up the street and there I found the church I was supposed to be at in the first place, and the sound man was just getting in his car to leave. When he saw me he told me that my wife had called asking why it was taking so long and when I told her you weren't here yet, she told me that she would call the police to try and find me. Phyllis did call the police. She knew that I had trouble with directions and often got lost. I wasn't lost. I just happened to drive to the wrong church!

THE GOD OF A WISE CHOICE

For a couple of years after we retired, Phyllis could only wear her trusty white shorts everywhere, even in the bitter, cold weather, because of the problems her diabetic neuritis caused in her legs that created sensitivity, and anything rubbing against her legs would cause irritation.

When we were visiting our daughter and her family in Wichita for our Christmas celebration, she had tried to wear long pants, but it just didn't work, and the pants were hurting her legs, so our granddaughter let her wear a pair of her black soccer shorts while we were there. Hmmmmmmmmmm! She hadn't thought of black! The next day we went looking for a pair of black shorts in a sporting goods store. We found a store that was going out of business, and would you guess what we found—a black pair of shorts! We weren't sure we could afford them, but we decided we could handle the $1.00 they cost us! Voila! A whole new wardrobe! Now is God awesome, or what?

WHO IS YOUR DADDY?

While touring in southern California one winter we were invited to be a part of the Christmas parade in San Diego, their only parade that started after dark. Someone had donated a convertible for me to ride in and my name was in big letters on both sides of the car. While we waited to begin, I sat on the top of the back seat so everyone could see me. I wore a beautiful blue sequins long sleeved shirt, appropriate for a former pop-singer, when all of a sudden a woman came running up to the car and gushed, "I thought you were dead!" Apparently she must have mistaken me for Richie Valens, who died in a plane crash in 1959.

As the parade began moving and we were heading to downtown San Diego, I saw people lining the streets and some were sitting on the curbs as we drove by. Phyllis was riding in the front seat of the convertible and said she was a bit afraid of all the people because she had never done this before. On my left, sitting on the curb was a young man who yelled out, "Holy Toledo, Frankie Valens!" When we entered the main street at a major intersection, there were announcers sitting up high that announced over the loud speakers what each float and car represented. When we drove by, we heard the announcer whisper, "Who is this?" after which he exclaimed, "Here comes Frankie Valens, son of Richie Valens!"

WE MET MARY AND JOSEPH

At one of our concerts in Illinois we met Mary and Joseph! Joseph was 91 and was in a rest home, and a lady from the church where we were to present the concert, told us about him, and how he had been such a pillar in their church, and had always been a very 'up' type person. However, he had broken a bone in one of his legs recently, then he broke another bone in that same leg, and he was getting a bit discouraged. I think so! She told us this just before our concert, because he and his wife, Mary, really wanted to come to our concert, so we asked if we could go see him—take the concert to him! She said, 'You'd do that?' We said, yes, we had the time. So, it was only about a five minute drive to the rest home, and his wife was there with him. His eyes absolutely lit up when we walked in the door. I sang a portion of "This Magic Moment" and we sang an old gospel hymn, prayed with him, and then we left. It was a wonderful experience. His wife did come to our concert and she was really blessed. People asked us, "You went to see Joe?" We sure did!

ALL TEN GOT SAVED!

Pastor Steven Hultengren from Elysian, Minnesota invited us to come and minister at his church for a morning and an evening service. We spent the day with him and his wife at their home and during the afternoon he was going to do his jail ministry, so he asked if we would autograph a few of our small pictures for the inmates. We autographed ten pictures, and when we returned for the evening concert, the pastor told us that the men were so touched that we would take the time to do this small thing for them, that several had tears in their eyes. And the best news—ALL TEN GOT SAVED! Isn't it amazing what God can do with a picture! We were told later that the inmates are still talking about those pictures they were blessed with. Some have served their time and have been released. Some keep the picture of us in their cell, while others keep them in their Bible. The testimony of these black and white pictures reminds them that God loves them and so do others, even Christians who are known for their music, past and present. God bless you!

IT'S 'SHOW-AND-TELL' TIME

Six cheerleaders from the Chase High School attended our concert, and they had their picture taken with me before the concert. Afterwards, they asked me to sing an oldies song, so I offered to do a short afterglow for them, and that was the hit for the evening. I joked with them, saying they probably wanted to take me for their Show-and-Tell, and they quickly responded with, "Could we?" The evening was truly a witness to them because they heard the gospel story, they saw that Christians indeed can have a good time in the Lord in a church, and seeds were planted. God will do the watering.

THE CHECK WAS STILL THERE

We were in a revival at the Poteau, Oklahoma Church of the Nazarene, and Pastor David Gordon had given me a check for food allowance, which I promptly folded up and placed in my pants pocket. The next morning I looked for the check but couldn't find it. I think I moved around every moveable piece of furniture in the motel, scoured the van, and still couldn't find it. We were not a little concerned!

About noon we drove over to meet the pastor at the church to have lunch with him, and when we arrived at the church, I parked next to the spot I had always parked in because the lines on the ground weren't clear enough. When Phyllis got out of the van, there was that folded-up check on the ground! It had probably fallen out of my pocket the previous night and had been in the lot all night, obviously had not blown away, and if I had parked in my regular spot, we might not have found the check because I would have driven over it! Is our God beyond awesome, or what?

THE HOUSE BELONGED TO THE RACOONS

While we were in concert at a church in Iowa a lawyer from the church told us about a house that was going to be blown up for a movie that was going to be filmed in the area called "Twister," filmed by Warner Brothers, and the executive producer was Steven Spielberg. When we told him we had been looking for an old house to have our picture taken in front of for a new CD we were planning on recording, he took us out to the house. The old farm house was built in the late 1800's—no one had lived there for many years. Whoever had built the house must have been very wealthy because there were fancy faucets, and a dumb waiter, and an inside bathroom, which in those days was almost unheard of. When we took a tour of the house and walked up to the top floor, or was it the attic, the house had been taken over by raccoons! We took pictures of the home but the pictures didn't work out for our CD cover. If you see the movie "Twister" look for the last scene where a farm house is involved. We toured that home a year before the film crew arrived to film it in their movie.

"OK, GOD! I'LL ASK!"

Throughout most of our ministry our main means of travel was a car, or a van. We did have a couple of motorhomes loaned to us for short periods of time, and one you read about earlier that we had to return to the owners because of the expense involved. So, in between concerts we would either have to stay in motels, which was very costly, or sometimes we had to request housing with church people. This began to wear on Phyllis after several years of this, and she felt humiliated at times to have to continually ask people to let us stay with them.

This all came to a head for her in a concert in Iowa, and she had just had it! She told God that He was just going to have to provide the place for us, that she was not going to ask again. However, during the whole concert He was dealing with her, saying to her, "Won't you let me bless someone?" Finally towards the end of the concert she gave in, and in her frustrated spirit she said, "Ok God! I'll ask!"

When the concert was over, she mentioned that we would need housing for the following week—and FIVE families offered! Then we had to pray and see which one God wanted us to choose and He told us to choose the Howard Johnson family.

The Johnsons had a most gorgeous home with a swimming pool, and we had a good week with them, but after we left there we had lost contact with them. Then, several years later, lo and behold, we were watching TV and there was a commercial for the Howard Johnson restaurants, and we recognized this family we had stayed with—the Howard Johnson family—was swimming in their pool, having a great time! They told us that the Howard Johnson people were choosing families with their name, of which there were over 150, and we just happened to have known these people. What fun that was! And, all because she submitted her will and frustration to the Lord and let Him lead.

A PAPER BATH MAT

Very early in our ministry we needed to find a motel near Gallup, New Mexico. I saw a sign at a motel that stated one night for $14.95, and I liked the price, and even though Phyllis cautioned me that "You get what you pay for," the price was too tempting. I checked us in. We were afraid to take our shoes off, and when we turned down the sheets, there were holes in the sheets. I got undressed and went into the bathroom, and I let out a yelp!! The distance between the sink and the wall was a body's width, and my naked body touched the cold sink! When I reared back, there was no space to rear back to, and the now challenged body hit the cold wall! We took showers carefully and had a paper bath mat for our feet, and we even questioned whether this room rented by the hour! I think I got a lesson about truly getting what you pay for!

THE DISAPPEARING OFFERING

After our morning concert at a church in Derby, Kansas the pastor gave us the cash of our offering in an envelope, and we thanked him greatly because it was quite a large sum of money. We left to join our daughter and her family for dinner at her in-laws, and upon arriving, decided we didn't want that much cash in our van, in case someone recognized our van. We asked our grandson to put the envelope in their van for safe keeping, locking their van.

Later that evening we were at our daughter's house and Phyllis asked our grandson if he would go get our offering for us. He came back somewhat terrified, saying he couldn't find it! The whole family took their van apart—it was not to be found! We double checked our van, thinking there might have been some error somewhere—not there either. We called the pastor, thinking maybe we had just not remembered taking it with us. We were quite distressed because this was several hundred dollars, and that was no small amount for us to have. But, after a lot of frustration, Phyllis told me that we had to turn this over to the

Lord because He knew what happened and this had to be totally in His hands, and a peace came over Phyllis when she determined to do this.

In the middle of the morning the next day, we got a call from the pastor, and guess what? He said he found the envelope of cash in a magazine rack in the church! We have no answers for what happened in between, but God knows! We call it a miracle!

THE SURF BALLROOM

We were asked to do a concert at a church in Clear Lake, Iowa. When I booked the concert I had no idea the history that this town held. This is the town where the Big Bopper, Richie Valens, and Buddy Holly all appeared at the Surf Ballroom before their plane crashed just outside of town. Ricky Nelson was supposed to be on that plane but he didn't board with the rest. While in Clear Lake we visited the ballroom where the pop-singers made their last appearance and got to visit the dressing room where the owner asked us to autograph the celebrity wall right next to a Richie Valens family member. In the foyer the original pay phone that these pop-singers used to call home before leaving on that fatal plane crash, is still there. The owner also asked me to come back and perform an oldies show, but I turned him down because there was drinking and smoking allowed in that ballroom, and I just didn't feel that was the right venue for me.

THE CHURCH MOVED AND DIDN'T TELL US!

Towards the middle of our ministry touring we developed what we called a "Schedule Confirmation" that we included in our advertising concert packets, and this was requesting confirmation of the date, time, address, directions, etc . . . for our concerts. The following incident was a perfect example of 'why' we needed the Schedule Confirmation, but at the time we did not have it, so as you will see, proved why we needed it.

We drove to Texas for our concert, checked into the motel, then left at the time we would need to arrive at the church. When we drove up to the address we had been given, there was a church building, but it was vacant, and there was a fence around the vacant parking lot. We were stymied and we sure didn't know what to do, or where to go. We called a pastor friend of ours in Wichita from that same denomination, but they couldn't help us, so we just headed back to the hotel. Phyllis was crying from complete frustration. Upon arriving at the hotel the manager told us that someone was trying to get ahold of us, and told us to come back to the vacant church building, so we headed back. As we drove up in front of the vacant lot, a woman was standing outside the locked gates, and when we stopped, she said, "Are you the Valens?" Phyllis said, yes. Then she told us that she had forgotten to tell us that their church had moved! Oh my goodness! By this time it was time for our concert to start, and we weren't even there yet, but she said they had moved the time down one hour to allow for our late arrival, and to follow her over to the new building. That night we had one of the best children's ministry times we had ever had! God is the best maker of lemonade there is!

WAS IT A CAROL BURNETT SKETCH?

While Phyllis and I were on tour in Northern California and were staying at a pastor's home in Ukiah between concerts, we were invited to participate in a church's Singspiration in a town just north of Ukiah. When we arrived at the church we noticed that it was a small, quaint, old church building and many cars had already arrived, the gravel parking lot already full. We entered into the church and decided to sit towards the back and wait till we were called up to sing.

The song leader got up and asked if anyone wanted to sing, and several hands went up. She chose someone and they told her a hymn number from the church's hymnal and we all proceeded to sing all the verses, no matter how many verses the song had. This went on several times, but no one had yet to come up to the platform to sing, but when the song leader asked for one more request, a lady jumped up and said yes, and then proceeded to ask for other volunteers to join her on stage, including a guitarist, then she joyfully, and almost with a hop, walked up to the stage. The way this lady acted made both Phyllis and me think that she was putting on a skit for our entertainment, and we almost started to laugh out loud, but realized that this lady was not doing a Carol Burnett sketch! She was for real! She bounded up to the podium, then asked three volunteers to join her to help sing all 20 verses of a song straight out of the church's hymnal! We were so glad we didn't laugh out loud. We realized these were very precious people who truly loved the Lord, and their way of praising him was just different from ours.

The song leader then announced that there were special guests in the audience and asked for us to come up. Phyllis wanted to play a piano number but the stage area was so small that her piano bench was flush with the wall behind her and she had very little room to sit in front of the piano to play. She almost had to bend her arms even more so to be able to play the piano, but it worked out in the long run. We both left there knowing that it was ok to participate in simple old hymn singing and the fellowship of special people.

BAD AXE!

The first time we were invited to Michigan to do a concert was from a pastor in Bad Axe, Michigan. We had never heard of the town, but when we questioned the pastor, he told us that the town was located in the center of the 'thumb.' You almost have to live in Michigan, or have knowledge of Michigan to know what they mean by the 'thumb.'

We had a wonderful concert at the church, which was located just outside of Bad Axe and was told the history of how the town got its name. The story goes that when the first settlers arrived in the area from Lake Huron they decided to call their new town, "Axe," and threw an axe into a tree, but when the axe hit the tree, it broke. One of the settlers stated, "Bad Axe!" Thus, the name of the town was created and it's our understanding that that broken axe is in the local museum in Bad Axe, even though the tree is no longer there.

MY DESSERT SHELF

We were having dinner at our daughter's home in Wichita one evening and our eight-year-old grandson, the picky eater, commented that he was full, to which his mother responded, "Well, I guess you don't have room for dessert then." His very quick reply was, "But my dessert shelf is empty!"

THE GOATS ARE SINGING!

Our three-year-old grandson made the astounding comment to his mother one October day and said, "Mom, the goats are on the mountain, and they're telling about Jesus!" His mother calmly queried, "Did you learn a new song at Awanas today?" "Yes," he replied. "Well, why don't you sing it for me," answered his mother, to which he began singing, "Goats tell it on the mountain," to the tune of "Go Tell It On The Mountain." At least that's his story and we're sticking to it.

AN OVERLY ENTHUSIASTIC FAN

When Phyllis and I moved to Derby, Kansas we decided to have our mail delivered to our local UPS store, to not only have protection for our mail, but also for us. That turned out to be an even bigger blessing recently when of one of our overly enthusiastic fans tried to contact us again. He had been bothering us in the past, calling and writing to us frequently, wanting autographed pictures to give to his friends, but we chose to ignore him for many reasons. He found our mailing address, probably thinking it was our home address, and showed up at the UPS store looking for us. We received a call from UPS asking us if it was ok for her to give our fan our phone number, to which we emphatically said NO!! UPS told us that our fan hung around in his car in front of the store for quite some time, probably thinking we'd come and get our mail, but the UPS lady said he looked really angry! Another clue for a red flag! We were being stalked!!

"DON'T SCRATCH YOUR NOSE!"

During one of our concert tours to a church in Goodland, Kansas we had asked the church to provide us with overnight housing, in which an older couple from his church that owned a farm southeast of Goodland offered their guest bedroom to us. After our concert we followed the couple to their farm out in the country. When we arrived the couple told us the history of their home and that it had been two old school houses that had been transported to this location and attached together to make their home. When they showed us where we were to sleep for the night we noticed that the guest bedroom was right off the kitchen. When we retired for the evening and when I sat on the side of the bed, it squeaked! The bed was just an old box spring and mattress. We got undressed and with much squeaking, got into bed. While lying there quietly side by side on our backs, the bed started squeaking in rapid successions. I looked over and Phyllis was scratching her nose. I asked her to please stop because that squeaking sure sounded like we were in the middle of a heated love-making session. I told her I didn't want to be guilty of something I wasn't actually even doing!

BEAR SAUSAGES

In southwestern Kansas we were invited to minister in concert at a church, and after the concert a couple invited us to spend the night at their country home. When we entered their family room we noticed many deer heads with antlers mounted on the wall, plus a bear. The man told us many stories of his hunting escapades and when we ate dinner that evening his wife served us venison. When we got up in the morning the lady had cooked a complete breakfast with biscuits and gravy and sausages patties. We noticed that the sausage patties were rather dark and greasy but didn't say anything. After breakfast the man told us that we had just eaten bear meat sausages. Although they were probably used to eating wild animal meat, it was rather new to us. As much as we were in shock we had to 'bear' it and just enjoy our wonderful breakfast.

IT WAS AN HONOR TO BE ASKED

Several years ago a church in Florida contacted us, asking Phyllis to consider being their church pianist. We don't close any doors, so we agreed to fly there to check out the situation. The church offered to pay Phyllis $100.00 a month, plus all the piano students she wanted to have, and since this was a rather large congregation, there seemed to be no end to those possibilities. They also offered to help us with housing, should we decide to come, and they even loaned us a car to use while we were scouting around the area.

The music pastor and associate took us to witness the most beautiful white sand beaches that we had ever experienced, and took us on a tour of their town. The next day we had a free day and a car at our disposal so we decided to drive on over to Pensacola to see if we could meet up with Dr. Kent Hovind and his Creation Science ministry facilities. What an experience that was! Some years later we heard that he was in prison because of some "irregularities" (translation: persecution) and actually he is still in prison.

While in Pensacola we then decided we'd check out the large church where we had seen and heard about strange and unusual goings-on with people barking like dogs and rolling on the floor. It was during the day when we arrived at the church and there was no activity going on in the huge parking lot that was large enough to handle the thousands of people who were coming from all over the world to stand in line for hours just waiting to get in. We noticed a sign at the front door, and Phyllis got out of our car so she could read it. The sign was a disclaimer that told everyone that they could not charge any money if they were going to be on TV, because their services were telecast. What a statement! As Phyllis stood there she began weeping, and the Lord showed her that she was feeling His grief at what was going on there. It definitely was not of Him, which we already felt, and the Lord confirmed it to us.

After driving back to the church that had invited us to check them out, we decided to decline their offer. We would not have been able to continue our ministry touring that we felt God had called us into, and whereas for Phyllis, it was an honor to assist in their worship, but that was not where God wanted us at that time.

CAT HEAVEN

One day Phyllis and I received a disturbing phone call from a pastor friend of ours in Overland Park, Kansas. He could hardly speak to us as he was sobbing so hard on the phone. He told us that his cat Isaiah died in his lap while he was on the way to the vet for help. He told us that he wanted to hold a memorial service for Isaiah and bury him in his back yard, and asked if Phyllis and I would come and sing for the service. We had never sung at a cat's funeral before but knew that we needed to be there to support our friend.

We knew that we did not have funds to travel from Wichita to the Kansas City area because we were in between concert dates and all we had were a few rolled up coins we had been saving for a rainy day. Well, this was that rainy day! We cashed in all of our coins for gas and took off for Overland Park.

When we arrived at the pastor's home, he took us with him to shop for memorial markers for Isaiah. He had placed the cat in cold storage and picked the cat up for the service. He invited all his neighbors to attend and had placed a few fold-up chairs in his back yard for the people to sit on. During the service he asked everyone to say a few words during the eulogy on how Isaiah affected their lives, and then he had me sing "Go Rest High On That Mountain," with Phyllis hand-singing the song with white gloves on, and "Gone Are The Tears." Through tears and sometimes sobbing he buried Isaiah in a beautiful wooded area beside his garage. After the service everyone was invited into the house for snacks he had prepared ahead of time.

Isaiah was not the only animal our pastor friend owned. He also had another cat and a dog. I must say that this was the first time we had ever been asked to sing for a cat's funeral! Do you think I can put this on my resume?

SIXTY EIGHT
MINISTRY BOUQUETS

Through the years people would send us letters, notes, e-mails, or tell us after our concerts how they were blessed. The following is a small portion of how our wonderful friends expressed their feelings to us. And, this is no glory to us—"TO GOD BE THE GLORY ONLY!"

- "The evening was spectacular, and I have been to lots of concerts!"
- "Thanks for the wonderful evening of singing, playing and conversation!! You guys are just so wonderful!!! I enjoy your concerts so much and I can always feel the Holy Spirit's presence, so I know you are doing this from the bottom of your hearts and for the glory of God."
- "Thank you so much for your wonderful performance at the Red Cloud Opera House at the Cather Center! We are still receiving rave reviews from our audience! You are both a joy to work with. Thank you for sharing your gifts."
- "Reading your newsletter this morning I just needed to tell you once again what a blessing you both gave to me here in Waynesville, Missouri. I was led to tell you I had to stop and "Be Still and know that I am God" came to me. I too can be a blessing to God even in such a tiny way as to tell you, you are

loved even in this tiny town so far from you . . . Thank you so much for being a part of my life even for a fleeting moment. Keep up your spirit and your works for God."

- "As far as the FVM news, [our ministry newsletter] I am proud of you two and how you've taken the trials and tribulations you have endured in the ministry. One man's trial is another man's education. Thanks for sharing with others so we can all grow in Christ together."

- "You don't know me but I wanted to let you know how much I enjoy receiving your newsletter. The diet drink information is really interesting. My brother-in-law has lupus but I am not sure if he drinks diet drinks . . . I will find out."

- "I have your pictures on my dresser under the glass top. I touch it and pray for you guys every day. I want to add that God is so good. I am still glad that God put you two in my path. Your pictures constantly remind me that this is God's world and we are in it and His eye is on us. Meeting you guys was no accident. My friends that do not go to church anymore because of some dumb reason or another are in awe that I ran into you guys in 'church' one night. Well, you guys are like dessert after a good meal. God is a rewarder of them that diligently seek Him. I can also remember a guy named Thomas that skipped church one day and Jesus visited their little group behind closed doors. You never know who is going to be there, just be there yourself . . . I hope to meet again someday here in Minnesota and for sure up in heaven. Bet you two will sing a few together with King David . . . God bless and keep you both very well and anointed. Love you in Jesus."

- "Thanks so much for coming to Fredonia, Kansas and sharing your personal witness of the power of Jesus on Saturday evening. We enjoyed you and appreciated the concert."

- "Once again, I would like to thank you so much for coming to Memorial Baptist Church tonight! You were truly a blessing. I believe we had at least five decisions for Jesus, and that was those who came forward. I'm sure there were others who did come forward as well. Praise God! I can just imagine the crown you will have in Heaven to place at our Master's feet! I will treasure this night for eternity, and I am looking forward to the time in Heaven when we can all sit down and just 'jam' and sing, and reminisce!"

- "You all were at Memorial Baptist last night and I want to let you know that God truly blessed me with being able to see the realness in your love for each other and for Him. Thank you ever so much for being open to His direction in your personal lives so that your ministry rings so true."

- "You gave me goose bumps!"

- After a concert, a woman told us, "If I'd have known you guys were this good, I'd have invited my mother!"

- "The grace of God shines on you two. "

- "We are still so grateful to you two for ministering on Sunday ... even though the attendance was small that day, it carried on to others as we are still sharing about it! Many people I talk to are touched by the fact that you gave of your time that Sunday to a tiny new church."

- At an assisted living place, one of the residents, through tears, said "It's a great blessing when you're here. We appreciate you." At another time, one of the residents followed us out the door, pleading, "Please come back!"

- "A pastor admitted to us that he had 'checked us out' by calling a church where we had previously ministered, and he said, "They gave you rave reviews!"

- "You brought me back. I've been 'gone' for six months (from the Lord) and the Holy Spirit, working through you, brought me back."

- "Where else would you have "Unchained Melody," "Battle Hymn of the Republic," and praise and worship all in one concert?"

- At the end of a concert, a pastor said to his congregation, "I'm speechless!" There was a long pause, and then he said, "I'm still speechless."

- "A pastor said that they had had the most visitors that night than they've ever had for any event."

- "This was the first time the hairs on my arm stood up for a long time. It was all about Jesus."

- "Thanks so much for your special concert at Pleasant Hill Baptist Church last night. The Lord used your music ministry to minister to us. We've had some rough times most recently. Thanks again for your concert—it was such a blessing to us. We hope to attend more concerts in the future and in the meantime we'll enjoy your CDs."

- "There was a true worship experience opportunity at PHBC last night. We were truly blessed as a congregation of believers and also Maureen and I as well. God always has a plan A."

- "My daughter, (the praise leader) and I were standing in the sanctuary after most everyone had left after your concert, shutting things down, and in the silence I looked at her and told her, "Can you feel that? There is such a sweet spirit in this place." She could feel it too. And even though we don't go by feelings in the Christian walk, still, when the feelings come, it is wonderful! I didn't even want to leave. I wanted to sit down and bask in it."

- And in response to our article in last month's e-newsletter about Frankie and the Samson wig episode came the following: "I am with the little yellow man rolling in the isle (a cartoon character laughing!" Wish there could have been a camera in that room! We could send it in to the Funniest video program and win big bucks!" And another response was—"Maybe you should hire a stage hand to help Frankie do his quick (or not so quick) changes!!! What a HOOOOT! I can just see this happening!"

- From a pastor: "Thank you so much for your heartfelt and Spirit-led ministry. You have both been a wonderful encouragement to our entire church fellowship. May God richly bless you as you continue to serve our Lord."

- "I knew that your concert was going to be good, but you surpassed anything that I could ever have imagined!"

- "I observed you as you and Frankie were singing, and you looked like you were on your first date."

- "I've been going to this church for 22 years and you're the best we've ever had."

- "Praying with and for you both that the Holy Spirit will continue to make the message you both carry a plain one: specifically, that God has to do with All of life. Therefore, it's perfectly okay to sing a love song while representing the Author of all real love. We do not try to keep God in any box, room, locker, or church, in order to somehow keep Him from interfering with 'real' life at work or at play. God is God, and His opinions (cleverly disguised as commands) as outlined in His Word, extend to every facet of the human experience including worship, work, play and leisure. Carry on; carry on!"

- "Thank you so much for the time and effort that you put into your newsletters. I am so thrilled that Jerry and I have had the opportunity to enjoy fellowship with you. We continue to keep you in prayer in your travels and ministry that you are doing for God's kingdom."

- "I want to thank you for the two wonderful concerts you both performed in Estes Park. One of our guests was a Methodist woman and her non-practicing Jewish husband. Both really enjoyed Monday night's concert. I appreciated the ways you thanked God for your musical talents and praised Him for guiding your lives—all in a mostly secular concert. May God continue to bless your lives and your music ministry. My husband and I look forward to seeing you again in Estes Park. Blessings!"

- "You were great last night. One man got saved! Praise the Lord. Kelly and I will always be missing you both. Thank you for your service to the Lord and I'm so glad we met you that day in LaCygne, Kansas at the Christian church."

- "On behalf of all at AmeriKids Christian Center, we are going to miss the chance of you ever coming to St. Louis again for a concert. On the other hand—HAPPY RETIREMENT! God bless you both. We love you."

- "I just received your awesome e-newsletter. Yes, I said awesome . . . your newsletters are the best around, anywhere! It's like eating a great meal . . . a good square meal, comprising of everything that's good for you. Oh, by the way, please, please continue sending me the e-newsletter by snail mail."

- "You folks were great! You had the audience in the palm of your hands. God bless!"

- We received the following note that a friend of ours received when she had forwarded our e-newsletter to her: "This is absolutely FANTASTIC! ! ! Can you PLEASE put me on this e-mailing list to them (the Valens)? It's the Greatest Thing . . . next to the Bible . . . I'll read today! ! ! ! How the Lord has used their lives . . . and is using them for His GLORY! ! ! It is

THRILLING . . . "Hollywood's loss is truly Heaven's gain" . . . Glory to God and Praise God that we're blessed on earth to share in it until He comes for us ALL! !"

- "Thank you for singing-'This Magic Moment.' I used to hear that song on the radio in high school. I cried when you sang 'His Eye Is On The Sparrow.' That is one of my mother's favorite songs. She is 90 and failing fast. I had just left her bedside for a couple of hours. I needed perking up so I came to hear your program. I always sit at the back for a fast exit. I am a cancer survivor and am always exhausted, and have to be in bed by 8pm at the latest. I don't get up until around 9am every day. I was able to take my mind off of mom for a while. Thank-you"

SIXTY NINE

HAZEL AND THE BUTTS FAMILY

My great-great grandpa on my mother's dad's side of the family was Charles Cornett Day, who was born on May 17, 1833. He married my great-great grandma Matilda Willemina Washburn who was born on August 23, 1842. Great-great grandpa Day died on January 13, 1909 at the age of 75, and great-great grandma Matilda Willemina (Washburn) Day died on April 29, 1922 at the age of 79. Matilda's parents were Thomas Horton Washburn (1814-1891) and Harriet Louisa (Austin) Washburn (1819-1889). Charles and Matilda are buried at the Milford Cemetery, Milford, Geary County, Kansas.

One of Charles and Matilda's sons was my great-grandfather, Frank Charles Day, born on December 11, 1861 in Keokuk, Lee County, Iowa. He married my great-grandmother Margaret (Maggie) Jane Harris, who was born on August 11, 1865 in Junction City, Kansas and is also the mother of Laura Patrick and Walter, who is buried in Oregon. Maggie's parents were George W. Harris, who was born in 1841 and died in 1911, and her mother Ida A. (McClellan) Harris, and she was born in 1845 and died in 1870.

When my great-grandfather Frank Charles Day died in 1902 Margaret married Charles E. Rupp, who was born in 1890 and died in 1959. Great grandpa Frank Day died on April 7, 1902 at the age of 41. Great grandma Maggie died on December 27, 1932 at the age of 67. They are buried at the Milford Cemetery, Milford, Geary County, Kansas.

They had nine children and I have listed them in the order of their birth: Laura Ida Day was born in 1885 and died in 1965 at the age of 80; Mamie Belle (Day) Taylor was born on May, 28, 1887 and married Burton Gwinett Taylor. They had at least one child, Carroll Taylor, who was born in 1913 and died in 1934. Mamie died on June 9, 1919 at the age of 32 and is buried at the Milford Cemetery, Geary County, Kansas. Charles Franklin Day, the third child born was my grandpa. He was born on September 13, 1888 in Wakefield, Kansas and died on February 21, 1959 at the age of 71 in Junction City, Kansas. Grandpa Charles's registration card for the service was dated June 5, 1917. He was 29 years of age. His reason for registering was support for his family. Walter Harold Day was born in 1890 and died in 1955 at the age of 65. Grace Gertrude Day was born in 1892 and died in 1976 at the age of 84; Lottie Pearl Day was born on July 4, 1898 and died on September 10, 1905 at the age of 7; George Walter Day (some records show George's middle name as Washington), was born in 1895 and married Edith S. and died in 1980 at the age of 85 and both are buried in Junction City, Kansas. George used to own a cheese factory in Herington, Kansas, and there is a street named "Day" in his honor. Harry Amos Day was born in 1899 and died in 1967 at the age of 68. Harry used to own a motel and gas station in Chapman, Kansas; Cora Myrtle Day was born in 1901 and died in 1992 at the age of 91.

My grandpa, Charles Franklin Day, was the third child born to Frank and Maggie Day. He was born on September 13, 1888 and married my grandma Ida Hazel Fern Nickell on March 6, 1909 in Junction City, Geary County, Kansas. Grandpa was 21 and grandma was 18.

Frankie's grandpa Charles Franklin Day Ida Hazel Fern Nickell was born on

November 1, 1890 in Council Grove, Kansas. Charles and Hazel had 10

children and I have listed them in the order of their birth: Frank Amos Day was born on September 11, 1909 and married a Louise. Frank had adopted two Korean children. Frank was left-handed. He died on August 28, 1962 and is buried at the Fort Riley Post Cemetery in Fort Riley, Kansas, plot number F 558. Helen Mabel (Day)

Frankie's grandma Hazel Fern
(Nickell) Day

(Spradlin) Settgast was born in 1912 and first married Robert Spradlin and then

Clifford (Kip) Settgast. Helen died of a massage heart attack in 1973 when she and Kip had just arrived at a Safeway Store. She stepped out of the passenger side of their car, stood up and fell dead on the concrete parking lot; Marie Elnora (Day) Miller married Roy Miller and she later died of stomach cancer; Their children were: Betty Jane Miller who died after seven months of age with double pneumonia, and is buried in Fort Riley, Kansas. My mother Pauline remembers Betty Jane as a beautiful baby girl with reddish hair, and mom said that she cried when she heard of Betty Jane dying.

Marie and Roy's other children were Shirley Marie (Miller) Herl who married Curly Herl and their children were: Terry, Tony, Jimmy, Ted, Tyler, Todd, Rex and Charlett; Roy B. Miller, Jr. who married Hilda Ortega and their children are: Roy B. Miller III, Iris Nadine

Frank Day, my mother's brother, and
his wife Louise

Miller, and Michael Lee Miller. Roy's wife Hilda died. Another child of Marie and Roy was Elnora Faye (Miller) (Williman) Cash, and her children were: Veronica (Williaman) Brackenbery, Patti (Williman) Laverntz, Susan Williman, Sheila (Cash) Carver, and Amy Cash; Tonda Lee (Miller) (Rush) Scott first married Charles Rush and their children were: Robert Dean Rush, and Leslie Danial Rush. Marie and Roy's other child was: Charles F. Miller who first married Kathy Albers, and

their children were: Charlene (Miller) Jeffries, Bonnie Miller, Connie (Miller) Wasserman, (Bonnie and Connie are twins), and Jamie Miller. They divorced and Charles married Bonnie White and their children included: Barbara Miller, Jessica Miller, and Charles F. Miller Jr. When Charles and Bonnie divorced he married Samantha and they had two children, Ronnie Miller, and Tara Miller. Ronnie is now deceased.

My mother's sister, Marie, and her husband Roy

I've been in touch through FaceBook with Sheila Cash, who is Faye (Miller) (Williman) Cash's daughter. She told me that her daughter Britany Michelle Carver is a singer in the Salina Children's Choir and plays the violin in the Salina Youth Symphony. Her son Dustin Michael Carver plays the viola and sings in the Salina Children's Choir. Sheila herself told me that she sang with the Choraliers at Salina Central High School, and was in "The Sound Of Music" play at the high school as well. She also told me that Roy B. Miller the third owns Millers Shotokan Karate in Salina, Kansas. He is an instructor there as well.

My grandparents Charles Franklin and Hazel Day's son Charles (Charlie) Edward Day was born on August 4, 1916 and married Thelma

Charles Day, my mother's brother, and his wife Thelma

Leona Bogart. Thelma was born on April 3, 1920 and died on January 4, 2000 at the age of 79 and both are buried at the Highland Cemetery, Junction City, Geary County, Kansas. Charles died in October, 1960 at the age of 44. Charles and Thelma's children included: Ida Lee (Day) Darby who married Donald Darby and their children included: Michael Edward, Gregory Allen, Debra Lyn, Curtis, and Trease Ethel. Ida died in 2010 at the age of 72. Charles (Speedy) Kenneth Day married Anna Belgrade in 1960 and they had three children that included: Steven, Patty and Ronnie and they divorced in 1989. Speedy died in 2009 at the age of 68. Sharon Sue (Day) (DeMott) Titus was born in 1943 and first married Ronald DeMott. When Ronald died she married Rick Titus and they are now divorced. Sharon and Ronald had one natural child, Kathleen Elaine DeMott, and with Rick Titus they adopted their son Anthony David Titus. Diane Darlene (Day) Monroe married Tommy Monroe and they had two children, Randall and Corey Monroe and they live in Reno, Nevada. Juanita (Jeannie) (Jean) (Day) Yoho married Chuck Yoho and they had two children, Jason (Day) Yoho and Joshua Yoho who is deceased. Another child of Charles and Thelma was Bonnie June (Day) (Christensen) Bix who first married Perry Christensen in 1960. They had two children, Barbara Ann and Lauri Kay Christensen. Bonnie and Perry divorced in 1970. Bonnie then married Larry Gene Bix in 1972 and they had one child, Anthony (Andy) Gene Bix.

Another child of my grandparents Charles and Hazel Day was Clifford (Cliff) Kenneth Day who was born in 1919 and first married Jackie and they divorced. Their children were Mary Beth Day and Patricia Day. Clifford's second wife was Georgia. Clifford died in 1967 of stomach cancer and is buried at the Newton Burial Park, Nevada, Vernon County, Missouri; Pauline Evelyn (Day) Piper, my mother, was born on November 29, 1921, and she married Bernard Hobert Piper and their children are

Clifford Day, my mother's brother

LeRoy Day, my mother's brother

Frankie, Douglas, and Debi (Piper) Garner. LeRoy Joseph Day married Dawn and they moved to Kentucky; Vernon Paul Day was born on October 19, 1926 and served as SGT 85th Air Police SQDN Depot U S A F Munich, Germany and died of a brain tumor on December 1, 1950 while he was serving his country in the military. Vernon loved to play the drums. He is buried at the Fort Riley Post Cemetery in Geary County, Kansas. My mother can still remember the taps that was played during his funeral, and to this day she cannot stand to hear taps being played. His grave memorial is

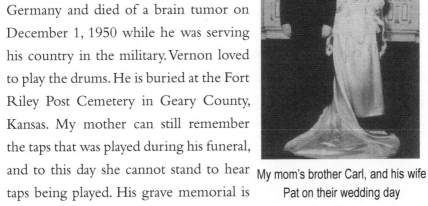
My mom's brother Carl, and his wife Pat on their wedding day

number 72909684. Carl (Willy) William Day was born on April 11, 1929 and married Patricia (Pat) A. and their children included Michael, Patrick and Carol Ann (Day) Fielder. Carl died on November 19, 1997 and Pat died on August 15, 1982 and both are buried at a Catholic Cemetery in Junction City, Kansas. Robert (Bobby) Frederick Day married Joy and their children included Robert, Tina, Tony, Vera Ann, Elizabeth Rae, and Vernon. I have no record of most of their birth dates or when any of them may have died.

My mom's brother Bobby, and his wife Joy

My mother, Pauline Evelyn (Day) Piper was born on November 29, 1921 in Junction City, Kansas. She was the sixth child born to Charles Franklin and Ida Hazel Fern (Nickell) Day and is now 89 years of age.

My mother is left-handed, and I am my mother's first child, and I am left-handed. My first child, Jennifer Sue (Piper) (Cunningham) Biondo is also left-handed, and our first grandchild, Haley Ann Piper is left-handed as well. She is the daughter of my youngest daughter Heather Ann (Piper) (Sherman) Allen.

Trying to piece together my grandma Ida Hazel Fern (Nickell) Day's heritage has been the most difficult part I have ever tried to research for my book. There have been so many conflicting stories from family members about grandma's name and where she was born. My mother said she thought her mother told her she was born in Enid, Oklahoma. According to my mother, when her mother, Ida Hazel Fern Nickell, was about three years of age, her mother died and her dad remarried shortly after. My grandma Hazel, as she was called, grew up with a step-mother and at least one step-brother and was moved around from family to family. A birth certificate of grandma Hazel's son, LeRoy Joseph Day, shows that his mother, my grandma, was born in Council Grove, Kansas.

When I checked with the Kansas Historical Society in Topeka, the only records they could find for my grandma was from a census that was taken on June 28th and 29th, 1900 showing that a Hazel Nickell lived in the household as a boarder of a John and Abbie Butts, along with Forney Alexander Nickell, age 35, and his wife Alice, age 26. Alice was the daughter of John and Abbie Butts. Was Forney my grandma's father, and Alice her step-mother? An 1880 census showed an F. Nickell age 18 and a Louisa Kickstern age 22 as servants living in the household of Charles and Maria Grover with Charles's mother Martha Grover age 76 living with them as well. Did F. Nickell and Louisa Kickstern (the spelling of Kickstern is so difficult to read on the census) have an affair and had to marry, or decided to get married because Addie, my grandma Hazel's sister, was born in 1881? All speculation! My grandma Hazel's brother Charles was born in 1887 and then Hazel was born in 1890. By 1894 Louisa died and by the 1900 census Forney has remarried to an Alice Butts and they're all living with Alice's parents. When I tried researching the surname of "Kickstern" all I found was a German rock group with a group member called Jorg Bohm Kickstern. We do know that Forney had a brother, Charles Luther Nickell. One family tree posted online shows that Forney's parents were James A. Nickell and Sarah Mildred (Mitt) (Jones) Nickell, but I cannot verify that.

I have done much research trying to find out if this is indeed my grandma Hazel living with the Butts family. I talked with my mother and told her that her mother, Hazel, lived with the family of John and Abbie Butts, and my mother told me that she remembers her mother Hazel talking to her about family members by the last name of Butts. This gave me some hope. I knew that I was on the right track.

According to a census taken in the Smokey Hill district of Kansas on June 28th and 29th in the year 1900, there was a combined household of 11 people living under one roof and my grandma Hazel may have been one of them. The 1900 census showed a John Butts, born in 1837 in New York, age 62 and was married to Abbie Butts, age 42, who was born in 1858 in Vermont. Also living in that same household were a daughter Cora E. Butts, born in 1876, age 20, and a son Larry E. Butts, born in 1883, age 16. William Boyd was listed as a servant, born in 1874 and was age 26, and Forney A. Nickell born in Virginia in 1862, was age 35 and a farmer. His wife was Alice M. (Butts) Nickell, born in 1874 and was age 26. They were married on January 23, 1896 by the justice of the peace in Jackson County, Missouri, which is where Independence, Missouri is located.

As boarders listed living at the Butts family home was a Charles Nickell, born in 1887 and was age 13, probably Hazel's brother. My grandmother Hazel Nickell was born on November 1, 1890, was also listed as a boarder, and she was nine years of age at the time of the census. Last listed was Addie Nickell, who was born in 1889, who was Hazel's older sister. She was 19 years old and listed as a boarder. My mother remembers her Aunt Addie and Uncle Charles. Were Charles, Hazel, and Addie, living with their father Forney and their step-mother Alice (Butts) Nickell, who were living with Alice (Butts) Nickell's father and mother and Alice's siblings? Was Forney A. Nickell my grandma Hazel's dad, or was he her uncle, and Alice (Butts) Nickell her step-mom? According to Alice's age she would have been too young to have had a daughter, Addie. Alice would have to have been only seven when she gave birth to Addie. Definitely, this is not possible. On the 1900 census of this household of 11 people, everyone had a title but Charles, Hazel and Addie. They were only listed as boarders.

My mother had always told me how much her mother had been moved from one family member to another as a young girl after her mother died, and my mother stuck with the fact of what her mother told her, and that was that Hazel's mother died when Hazel was about three years of age. If Hazel was born on November 1, 1890 and the census was taken in June, 1900, my grandma Hazel would have been around 9 or 10 years of age. I have a small picture of my great-grandma holding her daughter, my grandma Ida Hazel Fern Nickell on her lap. Grandma's dad remarried but I haven't found any records of his second marriage, but Alice is probably Forney's second wife. A family tree was found for Forney A. Nickell and it posted his parents as being James A. Nickell, born in 1842 in Virginia and died in 1918, and Sarah Mildred (Mitt) (Jones) Nickell, born in 1840 at sea and died in 1890.

My mother's grandmother, Louisa Nickell, holding my mother's mother Hazel on her lap

I have been in contact with Lin Fredericksen, who is the reference archivist for the State Archives and Library for the Kansas Historical Society in Topeka, Kansas. She has found a Louisa (Kickstern) Nickell who was born in Indiana on June 7, 1857 and died on December 11, 1894 at the age of 37, and is buried at the Polly Creek Cemetery in Pottawatamie County. Pottawatamie County is right next to Riley County and Geary County, which is where Junction City is located. Louisa's father was from New Jersey and her mother was from Ohio. We are not sure of the spelling of her maiden name of Kickstern. The census that was taken was not clear enough for me to know if Kickstern was indeed the correct spelling of her maiden name.

The picture I have hanging on my wall of my great-grandmother was taken in Junction City just before she died. Is this lady that's buried at the Polly Creek Cemetery my great-grandmother? If so then Forney A. Nickell could be my grandma Hazel's dad, and Alice Nickell was grandma's stepmother at the time the 1900 census was taken, and Hazel's birth mother is Louisa (Kickstern) Nickell, who had died in December of 1894 when Hazel had just turned four years of age that November.

My grandma, Ida Hazel Fern (Nickell) Day, died on October 26, 1971 with complications with her diabetes and is buried at the Highland Cemetery, Geary County, Junction City, Kansas.

SEVENTY

JULIUS'S FAMILY

My great-great grandpa Julius Piper

My great-great grandfather, August Julius Edward Piper, (better known as Julius) was born in Callies, West Prussia, Germany, which is now Kalisz, Poland, on July 7, 1846. Kalisz is a city that is situated on the Prosna River in the south-eastern part of Wielkopolskie Voivodeship (Province). The city received city rights and location privileges according to the German Magdeburg Law between the years of 1253 and 1260. The bombardments and arsoning of the city by German troops commanded by Major Herman Preusker almost completely destroyed the city during World War 1, and during World War II, Kalisz was incorporated in the Third Reich and became part of the Warta Country. The years following the war brought about rapid industrialization and development to the city's infrastructure and cultural growth. In the middle to late 1800's Prussia included Germany, Poland, part of Eastern Russia and several smaller countries. This was a Federation of States, which united in 1872 into a single country of Germany.

Between WW 1 and WW II Pomerania, Germany added several counties, but after WW 1 the province of Brandenburg, Netzekreis, Schneidemuhl, DeutschKrone, Flatow and Schlochau were given over to Poland, but after a few years Netzekreis and Schneidemuhl, being mostly German populations, were allowed to rejoin Germany and were made part of the province of Pomerania. In 1938, after Germany invaded Poland, some areas were incorporated into Germany and made part of Pomerania as well. Are you confused yet? Callies (or Kalisz) Germany where my great-great grandfather Julius was from was also in the south part of Pomerania, which is now in Poland.

Julius was christened, or was it a baptism, in the German Lutheran Church on October 14, 1860 at the age of 14. According to my cousin Betty Criss's research she found that in 1869 at the age of 23 Julius sailed to America on the German ship Tripoli, and became a U.S. citizen on April 3, 1876 at the age of 30, denouncing all allegiance to William, King of Prussia and Emperor of Germany, and first settled in Iroquois County, Illinois. At that time Julius's naturalization papers showed his last name spelled as Peiper! His brother Herman, who came over about a year later was naturalized on the same day as Julius, and Herman spelled his last name as Peiper! Both were naturalized in Marshall County, Lacon, Illinois at the courthouse. Herman later spelled his last name as Pieper on legal documents when he was applying for homestead papers.

Was there so much hatred for the Germans since before WW I that carried well into the 80s that our family had to develop a disguise that would help protect them and their children by telling everyone that they were from Prussia instead of Germany, or that they were of Dutch descent, or even English descent? We have no idea what prejudice existed when they arrived in America. All we know is that through the years the spelling of their last name changed and showed up on documents they had signed, such as Pieper, Peiper, Pipper, Peper, Pifer, Piper, Piepper, Pieper, and Paper in German with two dots over the 'a.' Herman's homestead papers, which are legal documents, showed Herman's correct spelling of his last name as Pieper. One record that was sent to Washington said that Herman was a hard-headed Dutchman who couldn't understand anything explained in English!

Julius's older brother Herman William Piper, or his German name, Hermann Wilhelm Pieper, at least according to legal documents he signed to purchase land from the government, was born on January 16, 1840 in Germany, and migrated to America around 1868. A family tree posted by Stacey Carpenter shows Herman's name as Wilhelm Herman Piper and his wife's name as Minerva Wilhelmine (Marquardt) Piper. The German Lutheran Church's death records showed Herman's real name as Johann G. Pieper! His wife, Wilhelmine (Minnie) (Marquardt) Piper, age 28, also came to America around 1870, according to ship records coming out of Hamburg, Germany, bringing with her their daughter Bertha age 6, and their son William (or Wilhelm in German) age 4. The ship records showed that they were from the town of Adolphshof, county of Greifenberg, in the German province of Pommern. Adolphshof was not far from the town of Plathe. These ship records showed their last name as Pieper. When they reached New York their last name was spelled Piper! There is a theory that Herman applied for an emergency passport back to Germany in 1896 when his mother died. Their son William was born on April 1, 1865 in Germany. Another theory is that Herman was a stow-away aboard the ship and was caught and arrested in 1868 in the New York harbor and was on his way back to England first, but as the ship was leaving the harbor, he threw his trunk overboard and jumped in himself, and was picked up by a fishing vessel that took him to shore. Was he arrested for being a stow-away? Or was it because he was the thief that stole money in his homeland to come to America? All speculation!

Herman and Wilhelmine (Minnie) first settled in Iroquois County, Illinois. Wilhelmine was born on February 2, 1842 in Germany. Wilhelmine's parents were Friedrich Marquardt and Carolyn (Piper) Marquardt. Herman's daughter Rosalie (Sarah) O. Piper married her cousin Will Marquardt, son of John and Carolyn (Piper) Marquardt who was a nephew of August F. Marquardt who was born in 1853 and died in 1923 and was Wilhelmine's brother. Was Carolyn (Piper) Marquardt Julius's sister, or could she have been a cousin? Records show that Caroline (Piper) Marquardt was a native of Wangerin in Kreis (Kreis, meaning 'county')

A rare photo of Caroline (Piper) Marquardt

Dramburg, Pommern (called Wegorzyno, Poland since about 1945). She was born in 1817 and died in 1907. The Marquardts were from about twenty miles east of there and near Dramburg (Drawsko). Caroline (Piper) Marquardt had married in 1840 and widowed in 1870. As a widow she came to America in 1873 with three of her children. A census showed that Caroline first settled in Douglas Township, Illinois, and then three of her children came with her and settled in Chase County, Kansas while some may have gone to Nebraska and Oklahoma. An 1880 census showed a Caroline, age 62, the mother, and William Marquardt age 31, with a brother August age 26, a sister Augusta age 25, and a servant Joseph Benley age 17. William was born on November 22, 1884 and died in March, 1964.

While visiting the old Elk Cemetery in Chase County, Kansas we came across the tombstone of Fritz Piper who was born May 26, 1879 in Chase County and died on January 1, 1881. Fritz was the son of Herman and Wilhelmine that must have been born in Chase County but was not listed in the 1880 census. Maybe the son Frederick on the 1880 census was actually Fritz?

Also buried at the old Elk Cemetery are Michael and Augusta Wilhelmine Fritz. Their tombstones are right behind Herman and Minnie's, plus Herman and Minnie's son William. Michael and Augusta's tombstones are right beside where Julius and Minna Piper are buried. Was Augusta related to the Piper's? At the time of William's death his probate records mentioned that Augusta Fritz was his aunt. Was Augusta a sister to Herman or to Minnie? When a tornado destroyed the home of John and Amelia Mau, they moved in with the Fritz family at Wildcreek. John and Amelia survived the tornado by staying in their basement!

By the 1880 census it showed that my great-great uncle Herman and Wilhelmine (Minnie) had moved to Diamond Creek Township in Chase County, Kansas, and the children living with them at that time were William age 15, Albert age nine, Sarah age three, and Frederick age one. Was Frederick really their son Fritz who was born in 1879 and died in 1881? Herman and Minnie had moved to the area sometime in 1879, before his brother Julius and Minna came. Herman's daughter Bertha had already married Gustave Hahn and was living in the area.

A large family photo (taken in Florence, KS)

Rumor was that there was a Range War going on because of the land that the railroads owned, and the section of land that Herman and Minnie were living on was supposedly railroad property, section number 20 of township 19 in the south range 6 east. When railroad agents came to try and take the land away from some of the homesteaders, the German community of about 150 people rose up and hung a few railroad agents! The homesteaders were so afraid to leave their land for fear that they wouldn't have it when they returned!

Herman and Minnie had placed an application for homesteading 160 acres of land on April 7, 1879 and paid a $9.00 fee. By May 30, 1885 Herman signed a homestead proof of purchase. Three years later, in 1888, it was approved for patent, and he was granted a patent deed on April 12, 1889. We don't know why it took almost 10 years to accomplish owning his property but some of the reasons could have been because of the language barrier, and another could have been because Herman had filed two different applications.

When Herman was first refused his first application for homestead papers for 160 acres of land, he applied for 80 acres, which was allowed, but the commissioner said he was entitled to 160 acres of land. But a notation was made that said that Pieper was a Dutchman with a thick skull which made it difficult to make him understand anything said to him in the English language!

Herman's property was located in the southeast quarter of section 20 in township 19, south range 6 east in Chase County. His stone house was 18x24 with a shingle roof and was one and a half stories. He had built a stone stable

Remnants of my great-great uncle Herman's first stone foundation in Chase County, KS

measuring 20x40 with a corral and planted 54 peach trees, 86 apple trees and 5 cherry trees. He also dug a well that was 30 feet deep.

My great-great uncle Herman was born on January 16, 1840 in Germany. According to the Chase County Leader News dated May 18,

My great-great uncle Herman and aunt Minnie's 50th wedding anniversary in Chase County

1911 from Cottonwood Falls, Kansas, Herman and Minnie had celebrated their Golden Wedding anniversary at the new home of their son William Piper in Chase County with between one and two hundred friends and family present. The aged couple stood beneath a floral arch and the background was of lace draperies. A dinner was served continuously all afternoon with different kinds of meats, vegetables, fine pickles, fifty pies and about thirty cakes. The bride's cake was not only large but decorated to perfection. Wilhelmine (Minnie) Piper was born on Feb 2, 1842 in Germany and died on February 23, 1917 in Chase County, Kansas. Their son William Piper, or his German full name of Wilhelm Hermann Heinrich Theador Pieper, was born April 1, 1865 and had come over from Germany with Minnie, and their daughter Bertha must have come with Minnie as well. Herman and Minnie, along with their son William and daughter Bertha, lived in what was known back then as the German settlement in Chase County.

Herman and Minnie's daughter Bertha had come to the U.S. around 1870 with her mother and Bertha's brother William. She later married

Gustave Valentine Hahn in Middle Creek Township, Chase County, Kansas, on October 20, 1879 by Reverend C. H. Sueker. Bertha was born in 1863 in Germany and was two years older than her brother William. Bertha's husband Gustave's father was Johann Heinrich Hahn who was born on November 2, 1812 in Ingersleben, Germany and was a farmer. Gustave's mother was Johanna Margaret Fredericke (Reckschwardt) Hahn who was born on December 19, 1819 in Germany and died on June 16, 1876 in Chase County. We know that Gustave and Bertha lived on Bertha's dad's old property in Chase County before moving to Oklahoma. I found no

Bertha and Gustave Hahn

other information about Bertha (Piper) Hahn except that their family had moved to Guthrie, Oklahoma about 1909. They used the Homestead Act to purchase 160 acres of land in Ellis County on the west half of the southeast quarter and the south half of the southwest quarter of section nine in township eighteen of range twenty one west of the Indian Meridian, Oklahoma, containing one hundred sixty acres. I do know that Gustave and Bertha had a daughter Louisa K. (Hahn) Buck who married James Alvin Buck. Louisa (Hahn) Buck and James had a daughter Mamee Viola (Buck) Belt who married William C. Belt and Mamee (Buck) Belt, and William had a daughter Louise F. (Belt) Karther who married Richard Carl Karther. Bertha (Piper) Hahn died on August 30, 1918 and is buried in Arnett, Oklahoma while her husband Gustave is buried in Cortez, Colorado. The Buck and Belt families became involved with mining in Cortez, Colorado, Jarbridge, Nevada and Gem County, Idaho where there were active mines.

My great-great uncle Herman and Wilhelmine also had a son Albert Otto Piper who married Wilheminia (Minnie) Giffler, Aunt Minnie as she was called, on March 14, 1895. The clerk spelled Albert's last name as Pipper four times on the marriage license! This was a legal document according to the probate court in the state of Kansas! Wilheminia (Minnie) was born on February 11, 1876 in Albany, New York. Albert was born in Illinois on November 27, 1870 and was a cousin to August and Henry Piper. Albert and Minnie are buried in Florence, Kansas. Minnie died of a cerebral hemorrhage at the Conklin Rest Home in Strong City on March 16, 1952 at the age of 76, according to the Chase County Leader News dated March 19, 1952, and her certification of death had her last name spelled as Pipper! She became a member of the Christian Church during the Evans revival and was an active member till her death. Her honorary pallbearers included Gerald Carpenter, Robert

Albert and Minnie Piper

Piper, Gary Piper, Morris Gene Carpenter and Gus Carpenter, Jr.! Albert Otto Piper (or was it Pipper?), died on January 12, 1931.

The 1910 Chase County, Kansas census showed my great uncle Albert and his wife Minnie's children listed as Mary age 14, Herman W. age 12, Ida age 10, Mable age

An early picture of Herman, Ida, and Minnie Piper

8, Arthur (Art) T. age 5, and Evelyn age 15 months. According to the Chase County Leader News dated March 31, 1920, Albert and Minnie's son Herman age 22 married Jessie Byrne age 18 by the judge, and they were living in Florence, Kansas at the time. According to a tombstone we found at a cemetery in Florence, Kansas, Albert and Minnie's daughter Mary Amelia (Piper) Flowers was born on March 25, 1896 and married Lester C. Flowers, who was born on June 27, 1894. Lester died on May 18, 1982 and Mary died on November 5, 1982 in Augusta, Kansas. Mary and Lester's daughter Evelyn (Flowers) White was born on February 19, 1915 and married Glenn White, who was born on November 14, 1912. Evelyn died on July 7, 2006 and Glenn died on May 31, 1967. Herman and Minnie's daughter Evelyn L. (Piper) Hill was born in 1909 and married William G. Hill. Evelyn died in 1967 and her husband William was born in 1905 and has died, but is buried in another state. Albert and Minnie's son Arthur (Art) T. Piper was born on September 13, 1904 in Florence and died on September 4, 1973 in Topeka, Kansas.

Albert and Minnie's daughter Ida (Piper) Carpenter married Gustav (Gus) Thomas Carpenter on April 18, 1920 in Cottonwood Falls, Chase County, Kansas. Gus's parents were Jerome and Carolina C. (Uppenkamp) Carpenter. 1110 Gus's father Jerome was born on July 29, 1868 in Illinois and died on July 24, 1941 in Fredonia, Kansas. He had married Carolina on August 5, 1980. Carolina was born on April 27, 1871 in Wullen, Borken, Nordrhein-Westfalen, Germany and died on February 9, 1932 in Florence, Kansas at the age of 61. Carolina had a twin sister Anna Uppenkamp who never married and lived in Burns, Kansas. (my parents, Bernard and Pauline Piper, were married in Burns, Kansas in 1942.) Anna died in 1933 at the age of 62 and is buried at the Burns Catholic Cemetery in Burns, Kansas.

Jerome Carpenter's father was Joseph and he was born in September, 1820 in French Quebec, Canada and married Susannah (Susan) Wilcox Holden in 1846. Susan was born on June 29, 1831 in Stockbridge, Windsor County, Vermont and the daughter of Abel Edgell and Diadama (Amy) (Cole) Holden from Vermont. Jerome's wife Carolina's parents were Joseph from Pruessen, (the official German name was Das Pruessen Kaiserreich—the Empire of Prussia), and Margareta (Lueka) Uppenkamp was from Germany. The Carpentier family came to the USA around 1840 from Canada. The Uppenkamp family came to the USA around 1884 from Prussia.

Joseph Uppenkamp was from the old Empire of Prussia that was officially called Das Pruessen Kaiserreich. The Kaiserreich of Prussia was an ancient nation with its roots imbedded deeply in pride, and consisted of powerful nomatic tribes of both Germania and the Kingdom of Old Prussia, a Polish-Germanian ruled nation that lasted for centuries. Its current incarnation was formed in 1541 and has preserved through the years by strength of will and military might. The Kaiserreich was once a ruler of the known world, holding colonies in Asia, Africa and Pacificia, the foundation of the German Empire, and is the survivor of that great time of the German people. Their official motto was Fur Gott und Vaterland, which means For God and Fatherland. Though it has now fallen on darker times and trials of faith, no doubt it will survive with the same discipline that held back the armies of Napoleon.

In 1847 Joseph and Susan had their first daughter Susan Delilah in New York. Sometime between 1847 and 1849 they moved from New York to Green Garden, Will County, Illinois where they had 7 more children, Louisa in 1849, Joseph J. in 1852, Levi in 1855, Louis Henry in 1857, Sardinia (Sarah) D. in 1860, Able August in 1863, and Jerome on July 29, 1868.

Jerome was Stacey's great-grandfather who moved with his family to Texas but was adopted by the Hurt family sometime before 1880 as he shows up on a census as their adopted son. He had come to Kansas about 60 years ago, first living in Marion County and then Chase County near Cedar Point. Jerome was killed in a tragic horse and wagon accident at the age of 72. He was attempting to stop a runaway team of horses at the home of a neighbor, Charles Stewart, near Fredonia, Kansas. Jerome had only lived in the Fredonia area about two years and owned a farm. He had borrowed a hayrack and had driven through the gate at the Stewart home when the accident occurred. The horses got spooked and began to run. Jerome tried to quiet them by grasping their reins, and in doing so he was dragged several hundred yards and was crushed against a tree. When he fell he was thrown under the wheel of the wide-tired wagon which crushed his chest. He died before he could be taken to a hospital. His funeral was held at the high school auditorium at Cedar Point.

Between 1868 and 1870 Joseph and Susan moved from Illinois to Pawnee, Bourbon County, Kansas where they had their last 2 children, Josephine Viend in 1870 (who married at the age of 12), and Charlotte (Lottie) May in 1874. Sometime between 1874 and 1880 Joseph and Susan moved for the last time from Kansas to Jacksboro, Jack County, Texas. Susan died sometime around 1900 and Joseph died on January 26, 1903.

Ida (Piper) Carpenter

Gus was born on March 18, 1894 in Chase County and died on November 19, 1982 and is buried at the Cedar Point Cemetery, Chase County, Kansas, alongside his wife Ida who died on Monday, July 26, 1982 at the St. Francis Regional Hospital Medical Center in Wichita from a cerebral hemorrhage (according to the El Dorado Times dated Wednesday, July 28, 1982.) She was 82 years of age at the time of her death. Her grandson Stacey remembers it well because he was only 11 at the time.

Stacey says that he was with his grandparents at their house in Cedar Point when his grandmother Ida started complaining of a headache. She had been sitting in her old green rocking chair with her back to the TV since she couldn't see it but would listen to it, when all of a sudden she jumped up complaining of a headache and needing to go to the restroom. Stacey's grandpa, age 88 at the time, tried to help her but no one could help much. Stacey said he called for an ambulance to come from Florence, which was about 7 miles away, and they arrived in less than 10 minutes!

As the ambulance was leaving town with his grandma Ida, Stacey says that his dad Gerald and brothers were just about ready to turn off of highway 50 in Gerald's wrecker and they were able to block the highway so the ambulance could get out onto the highway. Gerald didn't know at the time that the ambulance was for his own mother! She died 3 days later at the St. Francis Regional Hospital in Wichita. When his grandpa was told that his wife had died, Stacey said that that was the only time in his 11 years that he witnessed his grandpa cry. His grandpa died 4 months later in November, 1982. To this day, Stacey says that his grandpa died of a broken heart! His grandparents had not been separated from 1920 to 1982 and slept in the same house and same bed until that fateful day in July, 1982!

Ida and Gus had been members of the Cedar Point Methodist Church. Ida was known to be a very good cook! In her later years she became blind from glaucoma but remained a good cook. Her grandson Stacey told me that she would bake pies but wouldn't take them out of the oven for fear of getting burned, and would call her grandsons to come take her pies out of the oven. She warned them that if they didn't come to get her pies out of the oven, she wouldn't bake any more pies! Needless to say, they would drop anything they were doing when she called. Gus had built their home in 1929 onto the auto garage, which was originally called the Trail Garage, he had built in 1920 in Cedar Point, Kansas because he was constantly being robbed when they lived elsewhere. Most of Gus and Ida's children had been born in that home. That garage and home is still there today!

Ida and Gus's children included (in the order of their birth): Morris Gene Carpenter who was born on May 27, 1922 and married Mary Anna Louis. He divorced Mary and married Nancy Strassburg. Morris Gene told Stacey about the story of how Joseph Carpenter changed the spelling of his last name from the French-Canadian spelling of Carpentier to an Americanized spelling of Carpenter shortly after their arrival in the USA in 1840. Morris died on April 11, 2001. He was cremated in Arizona but has a marker at the foot of Gus and Ida in Cedar Point, Kansas.

Gus and Ida's other children were Juanita June (Carpenter) Pierce who was born on January 1, 1924 and married Dale Pierce and she died on October 18, 2008; Yvonne Lenora (Carpenter) Allen was born on May 20, 1929 and married Lee Allen who died on August 11, 1999; Cleta Mae (Carpenter) Scott was born on June 26, 1931 and married Vernon Lee Scott who died on September 26, 1981; Anna Margaret (Carpenter) Starnes was born on May 17, 1933 and married Jackie Wayne Starnes who died on November 11, 2001; Gustave (Gus) Carpenter, Jr. was born on October 29, 1934 and married Romana Bland and divorced; Janet Jo (Carpenter) Swanson was born on May 13, 1937 and married Donald

Swanson and he died; Janet Jo died on February 8, 2004; Gerald Lee Carpenter was born on December 18, 1938 and married Sharon White and divorced; Richard Jay Carpenter was born on October 12, 1943 and married Mary Ann Butcher. Their father, Gustav (Gus) Thomas Carpenter was a Christian and read his bible often. Wherever his bible opened up to, those were the pages he would study.

Gus and three of his sons, Morris Gene, Gus Jr. and Gerald, Stacey's father, were all Kansas State Champion trap shooters. Gus tied for third at the 1947 Grand American, and Morris Gene was recruited to become a pro shooter for Winchester in the late 40's and early 50's. At the local shoots Gus was nicknamed '100 Straight Gus' because he was so notorious for shooting 100 out of 100 targets during the final rounds to win.

After meeting recently with Yvonne Lenora (Carpenter) Allen and Cleta Mae (Carpenter) Scott in Cottonwood Falls, Kansas, which are two of my great-aunt Ida's daughters and my second cousins, they told me about the 'dirty thirties' there in Cedar Point, Kansas where the dust storms were so bad at times that no one could see the grocery store right across the street from them. Their mother, Ida, would soak towels and sheets to hang them on their windows to help keep the dust out. They said the dust storms came about 1930, just after the crash of 1929. Their grandparents were Albert and Minnie Piper.

My great-great uncle Herman died on January 13, 1912 at the age of 72 and his service was held at

The old Elk cemetery in Chase County

Elk, conducted by a German preacher. The Chase County Leader News dated January 18, 1912 announced his death. Herman and Wilhelmine (Minnie) are buried at the old Elk cemetery on Middle Creek Road in Chase County, Kansas.

Herman and Wilhelmine Piper's son William was listed in the 1910 Census as head of the household and his parents, Herman and Minnie, lived with him. In the 1920 census it showed William's sister Sarah living there, as well as Richard Piper. Was Richard the adopted son of Albert, or the son of Sarah, or the son of William? The census only showed the letters "AL Son." What did "AL" stand for? Did "AL" mean Albert? William died on April 20, 1915 at his adjoining farm at the age of 50 years and 19 days, according to the Chase County Header news. Funeral services were held at the German Lutheran Church and he was buried at the old Elk cemetery. Friends and family said that he was a good and honest neighbor and a true friend. It was a virtue of his to be hospitable, and nothing was too good for those found under his roof. He had become disabled by illness and pain, yet he was a true Christian and a member of the German Lutheran Church till his death.

My great-uncle William Piper's old stone foundation in Chase County. Frankie is standing on top

Herman died on January 13, 1912 at the age of 72, and five years later Wilhelmine died on February 23, 1917 at the age of 75 and both are buried at the old Elk Cemetery. Herman and Wilhelmine were living with their son William in 1910, but in 1912 Herman died at William's home. By 1915 William died, leaving his mother Wilhelmine behind, and then in 1917 Wilhelmine died. Legal homestead documents showed many spellings of Julius and Herman Piper. Some were spelled Piper, Pipper, and Pieper, but their tombstones all say Piper.

To confuse the matter even more so, there is also an emigration record of an Albert Julius Otto Piper from Brandenburg, Prussia, Germany that came to America. Was he a shirt-tail relative? The Germans named their male offspring using four names. The first name indicated who the father or grandfather was or someone of honor in the family. The second name given could be a favorite uncle or a person of honor in the family. The third name usually was a pet name or someone famous or simply because the parents liked that name, and the last name of course was the family surname. In my research I have found many documents that indicated that our family surname in Germany could very well have been spelled Pieper!

In my research I also found that the earliest German names were single names. It was not a first or a last name, it was just a name with generally two syllables with each 'root' having a specific meaning. All that this person represented was in that name. Surnames were chosen by either their profession, by physical traits, or by their location or environment. The name Piper means "Fifer." A Fifer was someone who played or performed on a Fife, a small-high-pitched, transverse flute that usually accompanied drums in the military or a marching band. The "Fife" part of the name was the person's profession, and the 'ER' on the end meant that that person played the Fife and/or was an owner of a farm. Were my relatives Fife players who owned a farm?

Rumor has it that the main reason for Julius Piper and his brother Herman sailing to America was because Germany was starting to draft all the young men into the Army to fight Russia. Many Germans were leaving their home country and sailing to other countries. It was our understanding that it was a criminal offense to not show up for the military draft and active duty. Germany had previously been at war with Russia for many years, and perhaps my great-great grandfather and his brother did not want to be drafted. Another rumor has it that one of them had stolen the city's money and had hid on a ship bound for America. Was my great-great grandpa a thief, or maybe his older brother Herman? But again, it has been nothing but a rumor and may not even be so. I have to remember that only one of them may have actually stolen the money, if it ever happened.

Many Germans were moving from Germany to Pomerania because land was being given to the Germans to get them to come live there. The Germans brought with them their knowledge and helped establish banks, helped create industry and improve the educational system. They helped build canals and railroads. In the end though the polish people turned on the Germans and wanted them to leave Poland and made life harder for the Germans in the late 1700s. Millions of German and Polish fled Poland after WW II for a better life. When Russia took Poland after WW II they punished the Germans by moving them to East Germany and gave their homes away to the Polish, and in doing so they destroyed many records of the Germans or took the records back to Russia.

Many of our early ancestors came to America and were able to acquire land, something they weren't able to do in the old country because most of the land was owned by the lords, or priced out of reach. Germans could not buy land without the permission of the Polish government in the mid to late 1800s.

There was a William Piper from Macoupin County, Illinois who came to the town of Belleville, Republic County, Kansas around 1870 and erected the Belleville Hotel on the north side of the public square in September 1870. The original building was 16 by 32 feet, 14 feet in height and had a board floor and a shingle roof. When completed he received a bonus for building this hotel on two choice lots on the public square and an excellent residence lot three blocks away. In good weather the people seated at the tables enjoyed a fine perspective through the openings between the boards of the farm lands of Freedom and Liberty townships, and the fertile plains of Thayer County, Nebraska. In rainy, cold or stormy weather some of the guests would take their meals and gather around the kitchen stove, while others retired to the parlor. The entire upper story was used for six sleeping apartments and a bridal chamber. The other rooms were occupied by William Piper and his family, the cook and waiters.

This William Piper was also the proprietor of a less pretentious building which stood near his hotel but remembered by the early settlers as the Cottonwood Saloon, which has a history all its own. In the spring of 1871 Mr. Piper sold his hotel to Mr. Vantrump, who enlarged, refitted, and refurnished the hotel, and for the first time in history made it a desirable stopping place, spreading a table which has not to this day been surpassed in Belleville.

By the 1900 census of the Diamond Creek Township in Chase County, it showed a William Piper and his wife Sarah. Sarah was born Rosalie O., but was called Sarah. Is this the same William Piper that had lived in Republic County in 1871?

There was also a William Pieper who was a farmer and raised thoroughbred stock near Mechanicsville, Indiana. This William was born

525

in Germany in 1817 and came to this country in 1840 and settled in Ohio and worked for $6.00 a month. He later moved to Indiana and remained there until 1854. He married Augusta Schwalbe in 1868. Augusta was born in Prussia and came to America in 1855. They had nine children, seven being from a former marriage: Henry, Lizetta, William, Lewis, Minnie, August, Hannah, Augusta and Alvina. Was this the same William Piper that moved to Belleville, Kansas, and is he a shirttail relative? He owned 275 acres of land and was a school director for four years.

We also know that my great-great grandfather August Julius Edward Piper had at least one sister, Amelia (Emilie) Christiana Pieper, who came to America from Germany around 1875 at about the age of 28, heading to Wisconsin. Her tombstone at the old Elk Cemetery showed the spelling of her first name as Amela, which could have been the German spelling of her name. She was born in Pomerania, Germany (part of which was formerly Prussia) on December 20, 1849. Church records in Chase County showed her father was Johann Pieper. If so then my great-great-great grandfather was Johann Pieper! When Amelia first came to America she settled in Wisconsin where in 1876 she wed John Mau, and in 1879 they moved to Illinois, and in 1887 came by covered wagon to Chase County where they lived nearly 40 years near the community of Elk in the Elmdale and Cottonwood Falls area.

Amelia's husband John Mau was born on March 1, 1846 and died on January 18, 1929. Their children included William Mau who was born on July 4, 1880 and died on June 25, 1908; Henry Mau, who was born April 14, 1889 in Chase County but died on July 26, 1905 when a sudden bolt of lightning struck him. His tombstone showed his name as J.E. Mau and he was born on April 14, 1889 and died on June 26, 1905. Amelia and John are buried at the old Elk Cemetery. John and Amelia's other children were Frank Mau who lived near Herington, Mrs. Matilde

(Mau) Kirth, Mrs. Ida (Mau) Kauffman, Mrs. Angus Kegebehn in Chase County, and Mrs. Emma (Mau) Mauderly in Marion County. Amelia died on October 23, 1925 at the age of 77 and had a Christian burial given on October 27th at the old Elk Cemetery by Pastor J. Jacob with a brief German and English service held at the Immanuel Evangelical Lutheran Church five miles southeast of Elk, Kansas (according to the Chase County Leader News of Cottonwood Falls dated October 24, 1925).

Julius's sister Amelia (Piper) Mau died in the community of Elk, Kansas on October 24, 1925 at the age of 78. Her services were held at the German Immanuel Evangelical Lutheran Church, which was five miles southeast of Elk. The service was held with a brief English and German ceremony. She had married John Mau in 1879 in Illinois, who also was from Germany, and moved to the Elk community, Chase County, Kansas in a covered wagon from Madison County, Highland, Illinois in September of 1887 along with the families of Claus Koegeboehn, and the Frank and Wilhelmina Mauderly families. Some of the Koegeboehn cousins who had the same first names were having problems with their mail getting mixed up, so they took the 'o's' out of their last name and became Kegebehn! Frank Mauderly was born on August 17, 1856 and died on December 20, 1926. Wilhelmina was born on November 19, 1859 and died on November 3, 1920. They are both buried at the old Elk Cemetery.

The Koegeboehn family from Hamburg, Prussia, Germany first entered the US through Louisiana. They migrated north to Madison County, Highland, Illinois and then to Chase, County, Kansas. I've been in contact with the granddaughter of John Louis Koegeboehn who was born on February 2, 1867 in Madison County, Highland, Illinois, and Emma Clara (Weichold) Koegeboehn who was born on January 10, 1874 in Dresden, Germany. Their granddaughter Clarendene (Koegeboehn) Deatrick presently lives in Herington, Kansas and is married to Dick Deatrick. Dick was a music teacher for 34 years! Their three children are Stephanie, Angela and Brent. Stephanie graduated from Kansas State University as a piano major and plays the piano and flute. Their daughter Angela plays piano and clarinet but also studied engineering at KSU and became an industrial engineer. Their youngest son Brent, plays the trumpet and piano and joined the drum and bugle corp. during his bootcamp in the Air Force. Clarendene's great-grandparents were Henrich (Henry) Weichold who was born on December 19, 1836 in Germany and Agnes Florentina Weichold who was born on May 3, 1842 in Germany.

John Louis Koegeboehn's parents were Detlef (David) Koegeboehn who was born on September 15, 1844 in Prussia, Hamburg, Germany, and died on January 5, 1908, and Katherina (Moll) Koegeboehn who was born on April 15, 1846 and migrated from Germany in 1875. She died on July 5, 1934. Detlef and Chris were brothers, and it was Chris Koegeboehn who had married Augusta Mau. Augusta's parents were John and Amelia (Piper) Mau. Amelia was my great-great grandpa Julius's sister. Detlef and Chris's father was Johann Ludwig Koegeboehn.

A group picture of the Koegeboehn family

The Weichold family was from the area of Germany where Dresden is located and migrated to the US about 1881. While still in Germany, nes and Henrich purchased tickets for the family to have passage on a ship to the New York harbor, and tickets that would take them on to Lincolnville, Kansas by train. Ellis Island at that time was a US Navy ammunitions depot from 1876 to 1890. It was not until 1890 that Ellis Island became an immigration depot. Henrich's younger brother was a stowaway on the ship and jumped overboard when the ship landed at, what is now called Ellis Island, and swam to shore. When Henrich checked his family into customs, he checked to make sure his brother had reached shore and then Henrich and his family had to leave Henrich's brother behind in New York while they traveled by train to Kansas. As far as the family is concerned they don't know if his younger brother was ever heard from again, and no one remembers what his name was.

Clarendene said that her great-grandpa Henrich worked for the railroad and every Monday morning he would walk all the way into Elmdale, Kansas, which was about a 10 mile hike, to go to work where he stayed at a local hotel, and then every Friday evening he would carry either a bag of flour or sugar on his shoulder, or whatever his wife needed for staples, and walk back home. Their homestead was located about 3 miles east of the Marion County line on highway 150 on the north side of the highway. Agnes Florentina Weichold died on June 10, 1932 and her husband Henrich died on August 21, 1900. Emma Clara (Weichold) Koegeboehn died on June 26, 1959 and her husband John died on April 1, 1948.

John Mau, Amelia's husband had come to America from Germany around 1869. John died on January 18, 1929. Amelia and John are buried at the old Elk Cemetery, but according to the Chase County Leader News, Cottonwood Falls, Kansas, dated October 24, 1925, Amelia was buried at the Middle Creek Cemetery (which is another name for the Elk Cemetery).

In 1889 stormy weather ripped through the area in Chase County where John and Amelia lived, destroying John and Amelia's home. They survived by staying in their basement and no one was hurt, and the family had to live in their covered wagon for a while, or at least until they were able to move in with the Fritz family in Wildcat Creek until they could rebuild their home. John and Amelia (Piper) Mau had eight children: Matilda (Mau) (Kruger) Kurth who first married William Kruger, and their children were Emma (Kruger) Dean, Rosa (Kruger) Carr, Minnie (Kruger) Huth, and William Kruger, Jr. William Kruger senior died on October 17, 1912 and Matilda married husband number two, Godfred Kurth but had no children with him. Godfred died on July 2, 1939 and Matilda died on October 23, 1950 at the age of 75.

The other children of John and Amelia (Piper) Mau were: Henry Mau, who was born on April 14, 1889 in Chase County, died on July 26, 1905 at age 16. Henry was out in the pasture when a sudden bolt of lightning came down and killed him instantly, along with a team of horses. William (Bill) Mau, Jr. never married and died on June 25, 1908. Lena (Mau) Pufahl married Phinnie Pufahl and they adopted a little girl, Gertrude. Lena died on October 24, 1919. Frank Mau married Emma Koone and their children were, Freddie and Willie Mau. Frank Mau died on February 8, 1947. Augusta Mau married Chris Koegeboehn and two of their girls died in infancy. But they had Emil Koegeboehn who died on June 10, 1918 at age 19, and Fred Koegeboehn who was born on March 21, 1906 and died on August 5, 1972. Ida and Emma Mau were twins born on August 22, 1891. Ida (Mau) Kaufman married Louis Kaufman. Ida's children were, Clara, Mary and Edward. Ida died on February 11, 1960. Emma Mau was born on August 22, 1891. Emma married Carl William Mauderly on March 13, 1921 at the Immanuel Lutheran Church. Carl, Emma's husband, was born on July 14, 1895 in Antelope, Kansas but lived most of his life in Chase County, Kansas.

Emma and Carl had a daughter who died in infancy. They also had a son John Henry and then a daughter Martha Velma (Mauderly) Brown, who was born in the community of Elk on September 25, 1923. Martha was named after her cousin Martha (Weichold) Evans, Elvin's daughter. On December 8, 1942 Martha Velma Mauderly and Dorman D. Brown were married in Cottonwood Falls by the Justice of the Peace. We met Martha on August 18, 1990 when we attended a Piper reunion, held at the Chase County Senior Center in Cottonwood Falls, Kansas. We recently met one of Martha's sons, Ron, while entertaining for Alice Miller's birthday party out on Middle Creek Road at the Miller Ranch in Chase County.

Martha's dad, Carl, died on October 12, 1949 at the age of 54 at the Veterans Hospital in Wichita, Kansas. Her mother, Emma (Mau) Mauderly, passed away at the Chase County Nursing Home on May 6, 1977 at the age of 84. They had both been life members of the Lutheran Church and lived in the Middle Creek Community that was mainly a German settlement, and German was often spoken in the homes, churches and schools until after WWII. Both are buried at the old Elk Cemetery. Martha Brown is currently at the Salem Nursing Home in Hillsboro, Kansas.

August, Julius, Otto, and Fred Piper. Also a Joe Daily

An early picture taken in 1904 of my great-great grandfather, August Julius Edward Piper (better known as Julius) along with his sons, August (my great-grandfather), Otto and Fred Piper, also shows a Joe Daily. Was Joe Daily a cousin to the brothers, Otto, August and Fred Piper, and the son of Amelia (Piper) Mau?

Amelia was my great-great grandpa Julius's sister who came to America when she was about 28 years of age. She could have been married when she still lived in Germany. Her name could have been Amelia Christiana (Piper) Daily. Joe Daily would have been my great-great grandfather's nephew. No one knows for sure who Joe Daily was. In this picture Julius was age 58, his son August was 32, his son Otto was 30, and his son Fred was age 24. I have no idea how old Joe Dailey was.

August Julius Edward Piper, better known as Julius, met my great-great grandmother, Wilhelminna (Minna) Ponto, or was it Pontow, better known as Minna Ponto, but sometimes called Mary, or in German, Maria, in Marshall County, Illinois and they were married on January 22, 1871. Minna was born on November 21, 1840 in Germany. A copy of their Certificate of Record of Marriage, dated January 22, 1871 shows his name as "Julius Pieper," and his new wife's name as "Mina Ponto." Did the minister, J. M. Johannes, of the state of Illinois make a mistake

My great-great grandma Minna (Ponto) Piper

on the spelling of their names, or did "August Julius Edward Piper" (better known as Julius) purposely give a wrong spelling of their names because maybe (rumored) that he was indeed the thief who stole money in Callies, Germany so he could get to America? Or was it because it was a German felony to dodge the draft? Was the last name of 'Pieper' the actual German spelling of his name, or maybe Peiper? Some of my family is convinced that our given surname had been spelled differently in Germany. But remember, Julius and Minna spoke fluent German and probably spoke in a broken English accent when they came to America. When I did an online research into German surnames, I found hundreds of people with the last name of Pieper, but only a handful that were called Piper! Piper was probably the Amerianized verson of their German surname.

Before Julius and Minna were married an 1870 census showed a Julius Piper age 24 living and assumed working as a farm laborer for an August Meetzkie in the township of Roberts in Marshall County, Illinois. And, it showed a Minna Ponto age 28 working as a domestic servant in the household of William Dean, a dentist, and Sara Dean his wife in the city of Lacon in Marshall County (north of Peoria.) Julius and Minna had not married until January 22, 1871. The towns of Robert and Lacon were ninety three miles apart.

My cousin Rena in her research of Marshall County, Illinois for the surname of Ponto came across many interesting discoveries for the year of 1880. In the township of Hopewell in Marshall County, Illinois it showed an Augusta Ponto who was born in Prussia about 1835 and was the wife of a Chantaff Ponto who was born in Prussia about 1821. It showed their children as Gulaff Ponto, a son who was born in Prussia about 1864. It also showed another son Albert Ponto, who was born in Illinois about 1869, a daughter Elvina Ponto born in Illinois about 1873, and another daughter Minnie Ponto that was born in Illinois about 1876.

For the year of 1870 her research came across four Minnie Pontos. One Minnie was living in Lacon, Marshall County, Illinois and was born about 1842 in Prussia. Another Minnie was living in Waupun North Ward, Fond Du Lac, Wisconsin and was born about 1851 in Prussia. Then there was a Minnie living in Mecan, Marquette, Wisconsin and was born about 1827 in Prussia, while another Minnie was living in Niles, Floyd County, Iowa and was born about 1867 in Wisconsin. A

Louis Ponto was living in Roberts, Marshall County, Illinois and was born about 1832 in Prussia. Rena stated that she was wondering if any of these could be related since three of them were living in the county of Marshall in Illinois.

My great-great grandmother Minna, holding her children, Fred C. and Alvena Piper

According to the June, 1880 Iroquois County, Douglas Township census, it showed a Julius and Minna Piper. Children living with them were August age eight, Otto age six, Henry age four, and Liennie age one. Was Liennie the same person as Alvena Emma Piper who married Moritz Bruno Weichold or was Liennie a twin brother to Alvena that had died at birth? Alvena could have probably just been called Emma? It listed Julius as a farmer who was from Prussia, Germany. The Iroquois County is located in the northeast part of Illinois, near the Indiana border. Since Julius had been working in the town of Roberts we are assuming that when Julius and Minna married they may have lived in or near Roberts. Just nine miles north of Roberts was the town of Piper City. Piper City actually was founded in 1867, so I know the town was there at the time they lived in the area. Otto was born in Streator, Illinois on February 8, 1874. The town of Streator is about 10 miles from Roberts Township in Marshall County, Illinois.

According to family history that has been passed down from generation to generation was the story of when Minna had sewn all of their money into her corset for safe keeping when she and Julius were heading from Illinois to Kansas, or were they heading to Wisconsin, with a brother to buy land. Rumor was that Minna was a very wealthy woman back in Germany. Why she left most of her wealth there we don't know but a family member was supposed to bring it to America for her. Rumor has it that this family member squandered away her money in different countries before arriving in America.

Before Julius and Minna traveled very far, probably on their way to Kansas, or maybe Wisconsin, and were in Iowa they were robbed. The men who robbed them made them take off all their clothes while the men were looking for money and valuables. The robbers didn't make the ladies take off their corsets and never found the money Minna had been carrying in her corset! The men made off with their horses and whatever money the men had on them, and left naked people and a couple of broken down horses instead! Julius, along with their families, was forced to spend the winter in Iowa. We believe that the brother who had been traveling with them decided to stay in Iowa and didn't continue on to Kansas. Who was this brother? After buying a new horse the families didn't have enough funds to buy land. Were they originally heading to see Louis (Ludwig) Ponto, who we believe may have been Minna's brother who lived in Wisconsin? How did they become aware of the homestead land that was available in Kansas?

In May, 1854 Congress passed the Kansas-Nebraska Act which opened Kansas up for settlement. Then in 1861 Kansas became a state, and in 1862 the Homestead Act took effect. My great-great grandparents, Julius and Minna moved to Kansas around 1883, and on September 23, 1884 Julius signed a homestead pre-emption contract to purchase 160 acres of land just west of Elmdale, Kansas, near the community of Elk in the Prairie Grove area in Chase County! According to one document Julius had bought the land from Gus Weihouse. According to a land office record in Chase County dated October 1, 1889 at 12:00pm Julius bought the land from the U.S. Government. Had Gus Weihouse been squatting on this land and really didn't own it?

It is speculated that there could have been some structures on that land when Julius decided to purchase the property. He had to live on the land for five years to complete the transaction and own the land. I have a copy of the warranty deed Julius signed dated September 23, 1889 showing that Julius purchased the 160 acres and paid the remaining fees owed in the amount of $8.00 as a final processing fee. Normally to finalize a trust deed to purchase land the new owner would have to ride a horse all the way into Salina, but if you signed a hardship case form you could file with the clerk at the courthouse in the county he lived in, and in this case, Chase County at Cottonwood Falls, the county seat. Witnessing his homestead contract were David Keogeboehn age 48 of Clements, Frederick Anndefeldt age 29 of Clements, August Houke of Elk, and Samuel Harrison of Elk.

According to the homestead affidavit Julius signed on September 20, 1889 it stated that Julius had come from Iowa and was a farmer and had lived on the land he was purchasing in Chase County since February 1884. It was mainly prairie grazing land but he had planted a 300 acre orchard valued at $500.00, a vineyard valued at $40.00, and placed a fence around his 160 acres worth about $150.00. He built a wooden home 16X14 with two windows above with one door, one window and one door below in the stone basement, and a shingle roof that was eight feet high, a board floor on the main level, valued at $125.00, and at that time one stable worth $100.00. He later built at least one shed, two stables made of stone, and one barn worth $60.00 during the five years he lived on the land. He had planted corn, oats, wheat, millet, and potatoes. In the first year he raised crops on 10 acres of his land, in two years he had 17 acres planted, in three years 20, and in five years he had raised crops on 25 acres of his land. In 1889 he owned one wagon, one breaker, one plow, one rake, two stoves, one cupboard, one table, two beds, and one set of chairs. He had eleven head of cattle and four head of oxen. His land was worth $6.00 an acre in 1884. On this land he had a well and natural springs for fresh water.

According to the final Certificate of Naturalization dated April 3, 1876 Julius's name was spelled Julius Peiper! What was the true and correct spelling of his surname? All of our research records indicate that our German surname was spelled Pieper.

Where did Julius and his family live before purchasing his land when they came to Chase County in 1883? Probably on the land he was going to purchase, at least according to the Homestead Act they signed on January 24, 1884, but they had been living on that land for six years when Julius signed his homestead deed on May 23, 1889! And yet another answer on the Homestead Affidavit showed that Julius stated that they had lived on that land since the Spring of 1884, or five years. Then, did Julius and Minna live with Herman in 1883? Julius's brother Herman, and his wife Wilhelmine (Minnie) had already settled on a homestead nearby, and in the 1940s in their later years they moved to Dunlap, Kansas. When Milton and I recently

My great-great uncle Herman Piper's cornerstone in Chase, County

measured an old foundation where Herman lived in Chase County that was located on the northwest corner of plot number 28, the old stone foundation measured 21X26. We found the original 'corner stone' that held up the house which had a large hole in it that the main corner post sat in.

Julius and Ada (Julius's second wife) sold their 160 acres on November 5, 1914 to Jesse and Blanch Allen for $5,600.00. Ada died on January 17, 1917, and Julius lived with his son Emil and Emil's family until his death on March 22, 1920, three years after Ada's death, and six years after selling his property. Julius and Minna are both buried at the old Elk Cemetery together on Middle Creek Road. Ada, Julius's second wife is buried close by.

According to ship records that my cousin Betty found, they showed that my great-great grandmother Wilhelminna (Minna) Ponto and Frederick Ponto came to America on July 26, 1866. Were Minna and Frederick cousins? They were born around November, 1840 in Bramberg, Prussia, Bydgoszcz, Poland within a month of each other, according to ship records. They sailed out of Bremen, Germany on the German ship Ferdinand with their destination as Wisconsin, America. The ship records showed both Minna and Frederick Ponto as age 23 but a month apart in birth. The Ponto family tree records show that Frederick died at age 93. Minna Ponto died on December 13, 1907 at the age of 67. One of their daughters, or a cousin, Antonia, was only 2 years of age when they came to America one year later on June 11, 1867. That was almost a year later than when Minna and Frederick came to America. Was Antonia a daughter or a cousin? Antonia grew up in St. Marie, Wisconsin. Her family moved to Spring Valley, Minnesota, and she married in 1886. She and her husband moved to Stewartville, Minnesota, and in 1912 they bought the Sage Hotel in Stewartville, now called the Sage House. The census records list many Ponto families who came to America and most settled in Wisconsin. Another record shows that Albert Ponto was Minna's brother who lived in Clorinda, Iowa and Albert had a daughter Edna.

According to the researched records of my cousin Milton it showed a Wilhelmina Pontow sailing from Hamburg, Germany on July 6, 1865 for America aboard the ship Virginia with captain Delamis, and the ship was headed to New York. Wilhelmina was heading to Wisconsin and her name can be found on page 486 on the ship's passenger list. The next line shows a 19 year old female Julianna Pontow traveling with Wilhelmina. The 1870 census shows a Wilhelmina and an August Ponto born in 1843 a month apart in Germany and living in Oshkosh, Wisconsin. Also in Milton's research it showed a Julius Piper leaving Hamburg, Germany aboard the Gypsy Queen ship heading to New York via Liverpool, England, with Captain Nash, arriving in the port of Boston, Massachusetts aboard the SS Tripoli, with Captain W. H. P. Haines out of Liverpool. There are just so many speculations as to which Ponto was actually my great-great grandmother. According to a newspaper article announcing Minna's death, she was born in Bromberg Province, Germany and came to America in 1879? Yet further research may prove that Minna's brother could have been Ludwig, who was about one and a half years older than Minna. Minna's funeral was held at the German Lutheran Church in the community of Elk and she's buried in the Elk cemetery.

And, according to Milton's research, my great-great grandpa Julius Piper left Hamburg, Germany aboard the ship Gypsy Queen and was headed to New York via Liverpool, England with Captain Nash at the helm. The ship's passenger list, which can be found in the Hamburg's indirect list for 1869, showed Julius's birthplace as Thuringen, Germany. Julius arrived at a port in Boston, Massachusetts aboard the SS Tripoli from Liverpool, England. Was this Julius my great-great grandpa?

An 'indirect' passenger list for a ship only meant that that ship was going to a port other than an American port first. The ship would either end its journey at that port or go on to other ports before coming to an American port. Many emigrants from Germany took the indirect route because it was less expensive. Some emigrants would find their way to England and take a train from one side of England to Liverpool to catch a ship headed for America. It was not uncommon for passengers to change ships in Liverpool if the other ship would get them there faster or was less expensive.

A Charles Piper, age 58 and his wife Terrisa (Wrigund) Piper, age 52 came over from Prussia and first settled in Newellton, Louisiana, taken from the 1880 census of Wilson Township, Marion County, Kansas. They must have come through a port in New Orleans or maybe Boston because there are no ship records for them in New York. They also had a son, August Piper, who died on November 5, 1919 in Newton, Kansas but was buried in St. Louis, Missouri (this information is on his death certificate) that Henry Piper (probably a son) provided. This August was age 22 and probably was Julius's cousin, and Charles and Terrisa were his uncle and aunt. Charles and Terrisa's other children were: John, age 21, Mary, age 19, and Henry, age 16—all born in Louisiana. This August Piper was listed as being single and his occupation as a farmer when he died. Henry Piper of Louisiana provided the information and place of burial as St. Louis, Missouri, and said that he was living in Marion, Kansas when chronic hepatitis caused him to be in the hospital.

When my great-great grandma Minna Piper died on December 13, 1907, my great-great grandpa Julius married widow Ada (Adah) Rocelia (Brundage) Butter on June 21, 1909, in Cottonwood Falls, Kansas. Julius was age 62 and Ada was 47. Ada was born in 1862 to Stephen and Elizabeth (Newton) Brundage. Through Ada (Adah) Rocelia

(Brundage) (Butter) Piper I am related to Wild Bill Hickok through her family tree leading back to Abraham Brundage. Abraham Brundage was born somewhere between 1760 and 1765 either in Germany or possibly England. He was a German battalion soldier but fought for the British Army. The Brundage name was more prevalent in England than it was in Germany.

The legends of James (Wild Bill) Hickok are widespread with some being true and some just tales. His birthplace was at Troy Grove, LaSalle County, Illinois, but at the time of his birth the area was generally referred to as Homer. His parents were William A. Hickok and Polly (Butler) Hickok. Our 41st President, George Bush, is a descendent of Hickok's mother.

Wild Bill had driven a stagecoach on the famous Santa Fe Trail. He was also a Civil War scout and a spy for Captain Richard Bentley Owen, Quartermaster. He worked for General Custer during the Indian Wars and often was mistaken for each other. In his later years he was going blind from glaucoma and accidently shot his deputy Mike Williams. In 1876 while Wild Bill sat down to play poker, Jack McCall shot him in the back of the neck, killing him instantly. Wild Bill had been holding two black aces and two black eights, which are now known as a Dead Man's Hand. The fifth card has been held up for speculation but was probably the queen of diamonds!

How did his name "Wild Bill" come to be? The name is attributed to a lady watching Bill Hickok stop a lynching and she made the statement, "My God, ain't he wild!" There was a rumor that he had been romancing Martha Jane Cannary (Calamity Jane), but the truth is that they hardly knew each other. When she died in 1903 she asked to be buried next to

Wild Bill on Mount Moriah in Deadwood. This is where the two are buried today.

My great-great grandma Ada had been married to Carl Hermann Butter who was born in 1856 and died in 1893 at the age of 37. Ada was born in 1862 and died on January 9, 1917 at the age of 55 and both are buried in the old Elk cemetery in Chase County, Kansas. Both of my great-great grandpa's wives have stone markers, but I could not find my great-great grandpa Julius Piper's stone marking his grave. Did a flood carry away Julius's tombstone? Records show that Julius and Minna are buried together, one could be buried on top of the other, or maybe beside each other. Ada (Butter) Piper's daughter, Anna (Anne) Augusta Butter, married my great-great grandpa August Julius Edward Piper's son, my great uncle Emil William Piper on February 10, 1909. Julius and Ada had married on June 21, 1909 in the same year.

SEVENTY ONE
THE GIFFLER FAMILY

My great-grandma, Mary (Mamie) Catherine (Giffler) Piper's mother was my great-great grandma Mary Van Patten (Paddock) Giffler. She was the widow of William Paddock, from Albany, New York. He died on September 27, 1914. Mary's family history started in Bommenede, Zeeland, Holland. Her second husband, William Giffler, (or his Dutch name, Willem Keuvelaar) was born on June 28, 1832 in Bommenede, probably in the Zeeland Province of Holland, and migrated to Zonnemaire, Zeeland and then to New York about 1868. Also, he was a French Huguenot (Protestant/Calvinist), or was it that he was just from that area? His family was originally from France. With his first wife, Johanna Van Strien, or Van Strieijen, they had two children. Johanna

William Giffler

(Big Johanna) died on December 2, 1862 in Bommendede, Holland. His second wife, Josina (Rosa) or (Josephine) (Ganzeman) Schraver died after 1870. It was told that Josina (Rosa) was 12 years older than William and it was hinted that there was a scandal because of it and a divorce, which required them to leave Holland. Josina's daughter Johanna (Josephine) Schraver was born in 1850 and married Ernest Euler in Albany, New

York. Johanna's name appears as Johanna Serier in the census of Dutch households. It would be interesting to know if she had breast cancer because her half-sister Nettie (Giffler) Close (age 46), and her daughter Agnes (Close) Smith (age 69), and her daughter Tony (Smith) Thorpe (age 83) all died of breast cancer.

Antoinette (Nettie) (Giffler) Close, my great-great grandpa Giffler's 2nd wife–a Harvey Girl.

Another child of Josina was Antoinette (Nettie) (Giffler) Close who was born on November 11, 1865 in Holland, Netherlands, probably the Province of Zeeland, a place where Huguenot refugees made it to after leaving France, a historical gathering place for Protestants during the Netherlands war with Spain. Antoinette Nettie, according to Heather (Giffler) Strickland's grandmother, was a Harvey Girl and she worked in railroad diners and restaurants.

Antoinette (Nettie) (Giffler) Close had a daughter, Agnes Nora (Close) Smith that was born on April 28, 1889 and died on April 17, 1911. A son of Josina was John Giffler who was born in 1858 in Holland, according to the Dutch census, and according to the 1880 census in the U.S. he was living with Peter Ten Eych at Schodack Landing, Rensselaer, New York, and he was age 21. Jacob Giffler was born in 1860 and died young and only appeared in the Dutch census. Josina's husband Ernest lived to be age 79 and died on July 29, 1933.

Mary (Mamie) Ada (Van Patten) (Paddock) Giffler, my great-grandmother, was William Giffler's third wife. Mary was born on

April 1, 1841 in the Netherland, Holland and died on April 10, 1889 in Florence, Kansas. Mary played the organ and was a talented free-hand artist. She is buried beside her husband in Florence, Kansas.

My great-aunt Minnie and her sister, my great-grandma Mary (Giffler) Piper

According to an 1880 census taken in Albany, New York, William Giffler was 46 years of age, his third wife widow Mary (Van Patten) (Paddock) Giffler was 38 and four of their children living there included Johanna age six, Minnie age four, Mary age two, and a step-son C. (Ed) Edward Paddock age thirteen, all born in Albany, New York. Was the step-son's real name, Charles Edward Paddock? Mary was the widow of William Paddock and they had had two children, Edward and Martha Ann. Martha is not listed in the 1880 census but, on the 1885 Kansas census she is the wife of Henry Dornbush and she is 21 years of age. William and Mary's daughter Maggie is not listed yet because she wasn't born until later in 1885. Margaret (Maggie) Giffler was the Indian child left on the Giffler's doorstep in Kansas, or was this only a rumor created by an angry relative who had it in for this family?

When my great-great grandpa Willem Keuvelaar and his family came to America from the port of Rotterdam, the immigration man spelled the Dutch name the way it sounded to him, so Willem Keuvelaar became William Giffler. The Dutch people readily adopted Americanized names. William was a tile maker (pannenbakker), or actually a tile painter (pannenschilder) in Holland, and was very artistic.

Great-great grandpa William Giffler's parents were my great-great-great grandpa Johannes Keuvelaar who was born on

March 27, 1804 in Zonnemaire, Zelland, the Netherlands, and his wife Johanna Augusta (Van Diest) Keuvelaar who was born in 1801 in the Netherlands and died in 1862. Johannes Keuvelaar's parents were my great-great-great-great grandpa Andries Keuvelaar, who was born around 1766 or 1767, and his wife Jannetje (Koorman) Keuvelaar, who was born in 1773. Andries died in 1828 and Jannetje (Kooreman) Keuvelaar died in 1852. Andries parents were Jan Keuvelaar, who was born around 1697, and his wife Cornelia (Weyerman) Keuvelaar. Jan died on October 28, 1828 in Zonnemaire, Zeeland and Cornelia died in 1828. Jan and his wife Cornelia and their son Andries all died in 1828. What happened?

Johannes's siblings were, Jan Keuvelaar who was born in 1792 and died in 1837. He lived in Bommenede and married Pieternella Johanisse Van Diest (probably the sister to Johanna Van Diest who was the mother of my great-grandfather Willem). Pieternella was born in 1800. Another sibling of Johannes was Maria, and no further information was available for her. Adriaan married Anna (Schraver) Keuvelaar; Arnout married Anna (Stoutjesdijk) Keuvelaar; Issak was born in 1798 and married Neeltje (Daalbout) Keuvelaar; Cornelia (Keuvelaar) Van Popering was born on January 3, 1801 and married Sarel Van Popering; Jacomina Keuvelaar had no information; and Pieter was born in 1817 and married Levina (Filee) Keuvelaar.

Willem Keuvelaar had four siblings, Andries Keuvelaar, Jr. who was born and died in 1831, Aarout Keuvelaar was born in 1836 and died in 1837, Andries (Andrew) Keuvelaar was born in 1837 and died in 1918 in America, and Jan Keuvelar who was born in 1840 and died in 1842. In 1872 Willem's brother Andries (Andrew) (Andy) Kiefler emigrated from Zonnemaire, Zeeland to America with his wife Andriana (Anna) (Stoutjesdijk) Keuvellar and their four children. Andries (Andrew)(Andy) and Anna had gotten married on December 9, 1862 in Niuewerkerk, and after coming to America their last names became Kiefler and they moved to Cincinnati, Ohio. Some of Willem's descendants moved to Michigan. Andy and his family remained in upstate New York. William Giffler as he was now called, first lived in Albany, New York where other Dutch families lived, and may have lived in Bethlehem, New York prior to Albany. After coming to Kansas about 1884 William worked for the AT&SF Railroad as a track walker from Florence to Cedar Point. Did he leave New York because of an economic depression, or did the Euler family lead him to his new job in Kansas? The Eulers in Albany were railroad men.

William's step-daughter Johanna Schraver, daughter of his second wife, Josina (Ganzeman) Schraver was born in 1853 in Holland and came with them to America. She married Ernest Euler who worked on the railroad, and she died on August 12, 1903 at the age of 50 and is buried in the Albany Rural Cemetery, in Albany, New York. The Eulers were still living in the Albany area in the 1970s.

After the loss of his third wife Mary (Van Patten) (Paddock) Giffler, William lived with the Peter Kropp family of Florence, Kansas. William's wife Mary and his mother both died in 1862. In his later years he lived with each of his four daughters and their families till the time of his death on September 27, 1914 at the age of 81 (a copy of his obituary was posted in The Bulletin in Florence, Kansas on October 1, 1914.) His funeral was held at the home of August Julius's home and he was buried at the Florence cemetery, lot 32 in the old part of the cemetery. It was reported to Heather Strickland's mother, Tony Thorpe, and the story was repeated, that grandpa Giffler surprised everyone in his old age by regaining his vision. William had visited Heather's grandmother Agnes (before Heather's mother was born, and when Agnes and George were first married), William had lost his glasses and could read his small New

Testament Bible without his glasses, and from that day on he never wore them again. He often read his bible daily.

When the Gifflers came to Kansas about 1884 they chose to live where other Dutch families lived, between Florence and Cedar Point, Kansas. One of their daughters, Mary (Mamie) Ada (Giffler) Piper, my great grandmother, was born on April 29, 1878 in Albany, New York. She married my great grandfather, August Julius Piper, in 1885 in Florence, Kansas. She died on August 1, 1950. Three of the four daughters of my great-great grandpa William Giffler with his third wife, my great-great grandma Mary (Mamie) Ada (Giffler) Piper, all married Piper brothers. Wilheminia (Minnie) (Giffler) Piper married my great-uncle Albert Piper, Mary Ada (Giffler) Piper married my great-grandpa August Julius Piper, and Margaret (Maggie) (Giffler) Piper married my great-uncle Henry Gusman Piper. The fourth daughter, Johanna (Hanna) (Giffler) Cloverdyke, married Martin Albert Cloverdyke. Martin was born in 1869 and died in 1947. Hanna was born in 1873 and died in 1948, according to the dates on their tombstones.

Now here is where the Indian lineage rumor in my family comes into view: Henry Gusman Piper, my great uncle, was born on October 14, 1875 in Illinois, and married Margaret (Maggie) Giffler. She was born on March 3, 1885 in Florence, Kansas. Now remember, Henry Gusman Piper was one of my great-great grandpa's sons, and my great uncle. Henry's children were: William Edward Piper who married Lela Martin; Paul Henry Piper married Pauline Buick; Beulah (Minnie) (Piper) Davis married Orla Davis; Hazel Marie (Piper) Zang married Bernard R. Zang; Andrew Frankie Piper married Ruby Star; and Mamie Dorothy (Piper) Hirst married James (Jimmy) Hirst. Mamie Dorothy (Piper) Hirst and James (Jimmy) Hirst moved to Noel, Missouri where their son Ken was a Pharmacist and ran a drugstore. Jimmy owned a recreation hall and a soda fountain. A cousin to Mamie Dorothy was Paul Piper who ran the grocery store in Noel. I remember as a child when my parents and grandparents drove together from Kansas City to Decatur, Arkansas to visit Grandpa Piper's brother, my great-uncle Charlie and his wife Pauline Piper, and we stopped in Noel to spend the night in adjoining cabins. The next morning we stopped by a speedboat rental place in Noel and paid for a speedboat ride down the river. Little did I know that our own relatives owned that business too!

A Piper family member owned this Speedboat Rides in Noel, MO

My cousin Milton has traced down where the story may have originated from about Maggie being an Indian child. This story could have come from a daughter of Jimmy Hirst by another marriage. The story was supposedly told to her by a half-brother from yet another marriage. Jimmy was married twice before he married Mammie Dorothy Piper, Maggie and Henry's daughter. It was told that this half-brother by the first marriage met Maggie a few months before she passed away, and it was during this meeting that Maggie supposedly told him this story. Did this unnamed person make up this story to get back at Jimmy Hirst for leaving his mother and him? Did the woman writing this story to my cousin Lorena make this all up to get back at Jimmy Hirst for leaving her mother and her behind? And, why would Maggie tell someone else in confidence and not her own children! Maggie's family has had trouble trying to accept this story, and I don't blame them.

I had been told for many years that I had Indian blood in me, and when confronted, my own dad told me that we were part Cherokee Indian, but I could never find the connection. My second cousin, Lorena (Rena) Linder, in California, sent me this story about her great uncle and aunt, Henry and Margaret (Maggie) (Giffler) Piper, who is also my great aunt and uncle. Rena Linder says that the story could be just a rumor, but goes on to say that a group of nomadic Native Americans who were migrating, or being driven from their homes. Rena doesn't know if it was an entire tribe, or just a family unit. One was a young female who was pregnant. She was being pulled behind a horse on some kind of a sled or sling, because she was about to give birth, the family unit had to stop for her to give birth. She left her newborn baby on the doorstep of a nearby home of a pioneer family by the name of William Giffler, (German spelling, Willem Keuvelaar), and his third wife, my great-grandma, Mary Van Patten (Paddock) Giffler. The Native American group then continued on their journey. That baby was Margaret (Maggie) (Giffler) Piper, who married Henry Gussman Piper, my great uncle. The Indians may have been Potawatomie Indians, Cherokee Indians, or maybe even Wichita Indians, we're not sure. Henry Gusman Piper died on March 5, 1940. Maggie died on October 2, 1965 and both are buried at Sunset Lawns cemetery in El Dorado, Kansas. There is no direct Indian lineage to my branch of the Piper lineage. Margaret (Maggie) (Giffler) Piper's daughter, Mary Ada (Giffler) Piper, was Rena Linder's aunt, by marriage. Margaret (Maggie) (Giffler) Piper, was my great aunt. This story of her being Indian has been a rumor and cannot be proved.

Another son of my great-great grandfather Julius was great uncle Frederick (Fritz) C. Piper, who was born on March 25, 1881 in Streator, Illinois, and on February 13, 1908 at the age of 27, he married Rosalie Lee Jackson, age 18, in Cottonwood Falls, Kansas, and at that time they were both from Elmdale, Kansas. Rosa Lee (Jackson) Piper was born in

1890 and died in 1940. On their marriage certificate they had spelled their last name as Pieper! My cousin Milton found a land grant for Frederick C. Piper for 160 acres of land in Chase County on section 22 in the northwest area that was dated July 5, 1910. This parcel of land was straight east of where his father Julius lived. A 1920 census taken in Chase County, Toledo Township, showed Fred was age 38 and his wife Rosalie age 29 with daughter Thelma age 10, and Fred Jr. age 7. I did not see any other children listed at that time. Maybe I had only copied one page of the census.

What was Frederick C. Piper's middle name? Speculation has it that his middle name could have been Conrad since he named a son Conrad. Or maybe the "C" stood for Calvin, a middle name he gave to his son Dick who was born in 1928?

Five years later a census showed Fred age 43 and Rosalee age 38 and living with them were their children, Thelma age 16, Frederick Jr. age 12, Conrad age 10, Bernard L. age 8, Kenneth R. age 5, and Betty age 2. Sometime later he and Rosalie moved to Ogden, Kansas where they lived for about 15 years on a farm, and Fred was employed at the Fort Riley Quartermaster department for the Kansas State University in Fort Riley. Fred's wife Rosalie died of a brain aneurysm in 1940 and their

A recent picture of my great-aunt Anna Piper's home in Junction City, KS

daughter Thelma, whom they called "Punk," took over the mothering roll in the family. Fred lived with his daughter Thelma in his later years. Fred's daughter Betty (Piper) Lee, who had married Thomas Lee, lived nearby in Manhattan. Betty and Thomas Lee's son Neil owns Street Rods located at 1425 N. Washington

Street in Junction City, Kansas. For about two and a half years Fred and his family were living in Manhattan at 917 Colorado before he died, and he had been working with the Kansas Hybrid Association at Kansas State College. Fred and Rosalee's daughter Betty presently lives with her son Neil and his family in Manhattan, Kansas. She's had a stroke and gets around with a walker but is very much alert and has a sharp mind. She confirmed to Milton that Julius, Herman and Amelia's father's name was Johann! Kenneth R. Piper was born in 1920 and died in 1936, Thelma Piper was born on February 11, 1909 and died on January 2, 1976, and Dick Calvin Piper was born on October 2, 1928 and married Joanne Stout and he died on February 15, 2010. Kenneth and Thelma are buried at the Ogden Cemetery along with their parents Fred and Rosalie.

Dick Calvin and Joanne (Stout) Piper's son David C. Piper was born on July 9, 1953 in Manhattan, Kansas and married Heidi and their children included, Calvin, Brett, Lori (Piper) Stalker, and Paulette (Piper) Alvarez. David died on May 7, 2011 at his home in Randolph, Kansas from a terminal illness at the age of 57.

David C. Piper

My cousin Betty (Piper) Criss in El Dorado, Kansas remembers when she was age four or five when her uncle Frederick (Fred) C. Piper and his daughter Betty came to visit them. It struck her as being odd because Betty's dad was called Fred Edward Piper, and her uncle Frederick Conrad had a daughter Betty, age 15 or 16 at that time. It might have been the first and last time that two Fred Piper's with their two daughter's called Betty, got together.

Fred died unexpectedly on January 2, 1947 at his home at 917 Colorado, Manhattan, after he had shoveled snow in front of his home and had gone inside to warm up, according to the Conroy Funeral Home. Fred was 65 years of age. His funeral service was conducted by Rev. B. A. Rogers of Manhattan at the Ogden Union Church and he was buried at the Ogden public cemetery. The newspaper article that announced his death stated that he had three daughters and four sons: Thelma Piper and Twila Piper were still living at home, Mrs. Thomas F. Lee living at 1312 Colorado, Manhattan (was this his daughter Betty or was it Thelma?), Frederick Piper, Jr. of St. George, Conrad (Joe) Piper still at home, Bernard L. Piper living at 426 Kearney, and Dick C. Piper living at 300 Osage Street. The article also mentioned that he left two brothers, Emil Piper of Junction City, Otto Piper of Bushong, and one sister, Mrs. Alvena (Piper) Weichold of Marion, Kansas. Fred's wife Rosalie (Jackson) Piper died on January 13, 1940. Conrad (Joe) Piper could play any stringed instrument including the piano. He also played drums for his church.

An employee recognition ceremony dated January 14, 1947 for the Kansas State University in Manhattan, Kansas for the Years of Service Awards, January—December 2008 for Thirty Years Of Service: Annette E. Boddy, Bonnie J. Cravens, Eric L. Danielson, Jerry D. Elliott Jr., Sheila Fuhrmann, Patrick G. Gardner, Patricia Geier, Elaine A. Heller, Dixie L. Jones, Ronald F. Katz, Delaine K. Kleiner, Stephen A. Kramer, Gregory C. LeValley, Mary L. Lough, Debra McClain Williams, Arlon L. Meek, James C. Nelson, Nova E. Nickerson, Jane L. Peterson, Frederick C. Piper, Michael D. Reasoner, Charlene E. Redman, Marsha Reece, Ronald D. Stevenson, LuAnn Ward, Mary J. Winnie, and Randy L. Wisehart. Fred was also hired as a translator for German POW's at Ft. Riley. German was spoken a lot of the time but he did not allow German to be spoken in his home. He would often teach other family members how to count in German. Fred told his family of the time he lived in a

A man-made cave in Chase County that a family member built to live in and then store food in

man-made cave near Council Grove/Cottonwood Falls area but had no idea where. If Fred had lived in a man-made cave in his youth, that meant that my great-great grandpa Julius might have at some time lived in a cave? Maybe a 'cave' was built first before even a home was built?

Julius and Minna's other children were: great-uncle Linnie, who was born in 1879 in Illinois, and no other records were found. Could the name Linnie have been a nickname for Alvena? In Milton's research it is his belief that Linnie could have been Alvena, because in the 1900 census it states that Julius had six children living at the time when the census was taken. Then Linnie was not a son but a daughter? Census takers often made mistakes in spelling and genders. Or it could have been that Alvena had a twin brother, and Linnie died at birth?

Alvena was born on March 22, 1879 in Douglas Township, Iroquois County, Illinois and married Moritz Bruno Weichold. Moritz Bruno was born on August 12, 1872 and died on July 12, 1946 in Chase County, Kansas. Bruno's parents were Henrich (Henry) and Agnes Florentina (Launch)

Bruno and Alvena (Piper) Weichold

Weichold who had emigrated from Germany to New York, then using train tickets they had purchased that took them to Lincolnville, Marion County, Kansas. From there they moved to Chase County. The Chase County Leader News of Cottonwood Falls, Kansas dated June 15, 1932 said that when Agnes died she was survived by seven children: Mrs. John Koegeboehn, Bruno of Elmdale, Mrs. Clara (Weichold) Viet of Cedar Point (her husband's name was Bill Viet), Mrs. Augusta (Weichold) Galletly of Topeka, Kansas, Carl of Tonganoxie, Kansas, Will of Marion, Kansas and Gustavus of Everton, Missouri. Alvena (Piper) Weichold died on March 13, 1917 and is buried at the old Elk Cemetery in Chase County, Kansas next to her husband. The Carl Piper that my cousin Betty Criss mentioned to me, could this Carl Piper I found buried at the East Templin Cemetery in Alta Vista, Kansas be the missing Carl? He was born on February 16, 1851 and died on November 24, 1877. The listing showed that he had a sister Alvina. Otherwise, there were no records for my great-great grandparent's son Carl Piper, and I'll mention their sons Otto and Emil later in this chapter. Was there ever a Carl Piper? Did he die at birth?

Records show that my great-great-grandfather, August Julius Edward Piper, better known as Julius, died after a long illness on Monday afternoon, March 21, 1920 at the home of his son Emil Piper who lived north of Cedar Point, according to the March 29, 1920 Chase County Leader News in Cottonwood Falls. Emil had been working as a blacksmith in Cedar Point as

Emil and Anna Piper with their sons, Clyde, Gilbert, Roy, Bernie and baby Junior. Homer wasn't born yet.

late as 1926 (according to the Chase County Historical Sketches, Volume II, dated 1948.) A probate record showed that Julius owned Emil's

property, lots eight, nine and ten in section three in Cedar Point. According to my cousin Milton's research, after Julius died his estate was sold to pay his medical bills and the rest of his estate was given to his children, which amounted to about $25 each. And, according to Clyde, Emil's son, the court

Emil Piper's old home in Cedar Point, KS

gave them about a week to move out of the home. Clyde also stated that Otto and his dad had had many heated arguments because Otto was being forced to move so soon and almost landed Emil's family out in the street!

Julius's funeral service was held at the M.E. church at Cedar Point on Wednesday, March 24th, 1920 and he was buried at the Elk Cemetery. A newspaper article also stated that Mr. Piper was well known and liked by everyone in the west part of Chase County. My great-great grandfather's occupation had been listed as a farmer, but he was also a blacksmith, along with two of his sons. After a flood in 1951 with the Cedar Creek, Elk Cemetery was flooded and in the process Minna's tombstone fell over and had to be placed upright again, and to this day it is tilted to the east. We don't know if Julius indeed had a tombstone marker, and if he did, it could have been washed away by the flood, or maybe the funds ran out and he was buried without a marker?

A Dawn Hirst family tree that was posted online showed an August Julius Edward Piper that was born on July 7, 1846 in Callies, Germany (same name, birth date and place as my great-great grandfather.) Also listed were a brother Albert C. Piper, born on July 5, 1839, a Julius Piper born on July 23, 1843 and a Frederick Aaron Piper, born on May 3, 1851. All these were born to the parents of Fred William Piper, born in 1800 in Germany, who married Louise Johanna Waldeck, who was born on November 2, 1812. If this information is correct then Frederick William and Louise Johanna (Waldeck) Piper would have been my great-great-great grandparents. Did they come to America but chose to live in the San Antonio, Texas area?

According to the Dawn Hirst family tree Frederick died in 1858 and Louise died on December, 9, 1871 in San Antonio, Texas. If these records are correct then my great-great-great grandma Louise Johanna (Waldeck) Piper's parents were my great-great-great-great grandpa Friederick Arnold Waldeck, born on December 8, 1782 and died on January 7, 1850, and my great-great-great-great grandma Christiane Elisabeth (Burgener) Waldeck was born on October 31, 1782 and died on January 25, 1855. Did Dawn Hirst by chance accidentally connect my great-great grandpa August Julius Edward Piper to the wrong family tree online? How did she come up with this connection? To find out more would be another whole book I could write and maybe call it "Chasing An Illusive Piper!" In my research I did find a Pearl Cochran Pieper who was born on May 24, 1908 and died on February 13, 1988 and is buried at the Mt. Olivet Cemetery in Fort Worth, Texas. Also in this same cemetery were many Pipers buried.

My great-great grandparents Julius and Minna had been living near the community of Elk, Kansas on a 160 acre farm when my great-great grandma Minna (Ponto) Piper died. One day while going about her household duties, she had a sudden heart attack, and she died on a simple straw mattress on the dirt floor of their basement on December 13, 1907. She had been suffering from heart disease for a number of years, and she is buried at the old Elk cemetery, which is about eight miles northwest of Elmdale, Kansas on Middle Creek Road. My great-great grandpa then married widow Ada Rocelia (Brundage) Butter on June 21, 1909 in Cottonwood Falls, Chase County, Kansas. Ada was born in 1862 and was raised in the Elk vicinity. She had first married Carl Butter whose death occurred around 1893.

Great-great grandma Ada (my step-grandmother) and Carl Butter's children were: Flora Elisabeth (Butter) Sykes who was born on March 25, 1883 and married William Lee Sykes and died on September 23, 1967. Emma Elvira (Butter) Butler was born on January 29, 1887 and married Carl Butler. She died on March 3, 1973. William Henry (Bill) Butter was born on December 20, 1888 and married Mable Lee Brundage. He died on December 3, 1975. Anna (Butter) Piper was born on March 28, 1893 and married my great-uncle Emil Piper. She died on October 23, 1980. Oscar Albert Butter was born on March 20, 1891 and married Pearl Rose Berry. He died on February 2, 1960. My great-great grandma Ada passed away on January 9, 1917 and is buried at the old Elk cemetery with a tombstone marking her grave.

I was very interested in the early Piper family after they had traveled from Illinois to Iowa and then to Chase County, Kansas in the late 1800s. I wanted to know how they lived, so I decided to take a drive to Chase County and visit as many places and towns where my great-great grandparents lived or did business. In doing so I not only was able to visit the cemeteries where most of the Pipers and other family members are buried, but also I visited nearby towns and some that are ghost towns that existed during the time they lived in the area.

SEVENTY TWO
THE COMMUNITY OF ELK

When my cousin Betty Criss sent information to me about the Piper background, she mentioned a community called Elk in Chase County. The community of Elk no longer exists, although at one time it had a post office, a school, a blacksmith shop, a creamery, and a general store up until about 1923, but remnants of the town lasted into the early 1930s. The old community of Elk was located in Diamond Creek Township, Chase County, Kansas, and the only evidence of that community now is the old one-room school house that is still standing, an old stone fence where a newer school had been built and now plowed under, and the old Elk cemetery. Elk had a single westward running road that followed Middle Creek before splitting off north and south to follow two polar-trending small tributaries, the Stribby and Wildcat creeks. The area around Elk was mostly pasturage and tall prairie grass and because if it's isolation and low population, much of Elk's history has never been passed along much.

There seemed to be a village of Elk for about 50 years, or at least the seeds of one right on the county line of Marion. Henry Collett's general merchandise and post office sat in Chase County, but the blacksmith shop sat across the road in Marion County. This split was not good for the affairs of Elk and there were never more than a dozen buildings in Elk at any given time, and many of those went up in flames, one fire burned on New Year's Eve in 1930. All you'll see today as you walk around the area are maybe the remnants of an old well, metal scraps, and tall brush and trees. When I visited the area recently I met the new owners of the land where Elk sat and he took me on a tour of the area. All I found were a few metal objects from the old blacksmith shop and an old abandoned well. The new owner who lived only a field away had an original sign hanging on his porch from the store in Elk that said "Elk Store and Service Station." I so wanted that sign but knew I dare not ask if it was for sale.

The General Store in the community of Elk, KS   Inside the old Elk general store

My great-great grandparents probably did most of their business in Elk since Elk was so much closer to their farm, and according to the 1915 census my great-great grandpa listed his occupation as a blacksmith. If they needed other household supplies they probably then went into Elmdale or Cedar Point. Elmdale at that time had a doctor, two grocery stores, two livery stables, a hardware store, and a post office, but two floods rippled through Elmdale and Cedar Point that damaged once-stately homes and closed businesses. Elmdale and Cedar Point cannot be considered ghost towns because people still live there, even though most of the businesses have closed.

An early picture of Elmdale, KS

Southwest of Elmdale is the town of Cedar Point, which was named in 1857 by O. H. Drinkwater who was appointed postmaster when he established a post office there. Drinkwater had come to the area in 1857 along with a few other settlers and built a log cabin with cedar posts. It was then that he suggested calling the yet unnamed creek the Cedar Creek, which still bears that name. His log cabin became Fort Drinkwater and was used as a gathering place for settlers, and protection from Indians as late as 1868.

This nearby town of Cedar Point supplied most of the lumber for local settlers and farmers to build their homes from the mill that had been built around 1867. In the fall of that same year an awful drought hit the area and no rain fell for four months. The mill was first used for sawing lumber and had a wooden log dam, but the wooden dam was destroyed by a flood in 1871. In 1884 a stone dam replaced

The Old Mill in Cedar Point, KS

the wooden dam and the mill was rebuilt using the native limestone, and the mill began milling grain. Today the mill is in poor condition with several structural cracks, but the building still remains much as it did back in 1903.

Cedar Point had several blacksmiths including, S. L. Roberts, whose shop was on the present site of the telephone office. The other blacksmiths

Cedar Point, KS flood

were James Osman, Harry Holmes, A. L. Bartimus, Frank Long, Emil Piper, and Martin Self, who did blacksmithing in the Self Garage as late as 1926, and was evidently Cedar Point's last blacksmith.

Frankie is standing near his great-great grandpa Julius's old stone foundation

When Julius Piper moved to Chase County back around 1883 from Iowa, he homesteaded on 160 acres of land by 1884, and by 1889 he purchased it. His older brother Herman and his family had already settled on land they had purchased nearby in 1880. Later, Herman's son William lived on the land just west of Herman's. The county had been divided into eight townships: Bazaar, Cedar, Cottonwood, Diamond Creek, Falls, Matfield, Strong and Toledo. There were 11 post offices: Cottonwood Falls, Bazaar, Cedar Point, Clements, Elk, Elmdale, Homestead, Hymer, Matfield Green, Saffordville, and Strong City. Chase County had been named after Salmon P. Chase, governor and U.S. Senator from Ohio who later became Chief Justice of the U.S. Supreme Court. Chase County is famous for the airplane crash that killed famed Notre Dame football coach Knute Rockne in 1933, and in 1980 a TV film was made on the life of Julia Breese and titled "Blessed, Blessed, Mama."

The children of Julius, the children of William (Herman's son), the children of Herman Piper, and the children of the Koegeboehn family attended school district number 47. The school building was located about a quarter of mile southwest of Herman's home and just across Herman's property line. Other families of ours whose children may have attended this school and were living in the same area were the Weichold family, which was my great-aunt Alvena (Piper) Weichold (Julius and Minna's daughter), and the Koegeboehn family, which was my great-aunt Augusta (Mau) Koegeboehn. Augusta was Amelia (Piper) Mau's daughter (Amelia was my great-great grandpa Julius's sister). A school report that had been published in the Chase County Leader News dated February 6, 1896 for the month of January showed a total enrollment of 15 students with Nella Campbell as teacher. Those making a grade of 90 percent and over showed a Fred Piper, Emil Piper, Karl Weichold and Willie Koegeboehn. Emil was about the age of 13 and Fred Piper was age 16. Those making a grade of 85 percent included a Richard Piper. In the 1910 census it showed Richard Piper as age 14 as a son living with Herman. Herman is age 60 and Minnie age 58. Was Richard Piper an adopted son?

The community of Elk was founded in 1874 by Henry Collett of London, England along the banks of Middle Creek next to Marion County. He had come to Chase County in 1865 with his parents while he was still in his teens and claimed land in Middle Creek. At that time there were no roads, no fences and the land had not been surveyed, so he didn't even know what county he was in, but he loved the scenery. Henry Collett was not a farmer, instead he created a town. In 1874 the post office was established at Elk with Henry Collett as postmaster. Mr. Collett chose the name of Elk for the community because no name had been provided by the government, and since he had to write the name all the time, he chose a short name. Also in 1874 an invasion of grasshoppers came in the millions to the area, and was so high in the air that the sun looked hazy. These grasshoppers ate everything in sight and stayed for about three days. In 1882 a blacksmith shop was started, and in 1884 the blacksmith shop had a 500 pound huge grindstone installed. A store carrying groceries and dry goods was built, and in 1897 a creamery was established. An old fashioned windmill on top of the shop furnished power for the machinery in the shop, and the mill that was located on the upper floor.

Mr. Collett built a community ice house down by the creek in which people who so wished could help put up the ice with the privilege of withdrawing 50 pounds of ice daily during the summer months, and occasionally enjoyed the luxury of ice cream. He built a headquarters for his freighting lines, a lime kiln, and homes for the workmen. He ran a freight service south to El Dorado and north to Junction City. With his lime kiln the local settlers who were building stone houses and foundations and barns needed mortar and plaster. In 1897 he created a creamery that was operated by steam and it helped supply the Beatrice Creamery Company in Beatrice, Nebraska. As the whole milk was brought in to the station to be skimmed, it took some time to take care of it and the station brought a large volume of business to the community of Elk. The tools that were used in that creamery are in the Marion Museum.

The most exciting and entertaining enterprise of the community of Elk was the race track and trotting horses. This enterprise was developed, owned, and operated by Lewis E. Riggs and started around 1891. The original track lay just south of where the present farm house stands, between the creek and the public road. Some famous horses on this track were Lady Kelso, Fox Winnie, Stocking Legs, Eli and Lady. These trotting horses were all trained by the famous horse trainer George Rambo (a son of Mr. Rambo is now the director of a bank in Chicago.) There were no banks in the area so Mr. Collett issued his own 'chips of credit' and no doubt the farmers banked these in cigar boxes for the long winters when the 'hens quit laying and the cows went dry.' The first telephone was installed about 1905 from Marion to Elk by the Bell Telephone Company, and the first automobile appeared in the area about 1906 roaring down the road from Marion on two cylinders and traveling about 20 miles per hour.

SEVENTY THREE
FLINT HILLS

Until Julius and Minna could build a home, they had to live in their covered wagon. The basement of their home was built with stones they gathered from the hillsides or creek banks nearby. They could have made their own lime that would hold the stones together for their basements by digging a hole in the side of a hill, and burning wood in it for about 95 hours, which was sufficient to burn the stone into lime. After a few days the lime would cool off, removed, and stored in a dry place until they could use it for the basement stones. Along with the lime they would add sand and gravel which they collected along the river banks. Back then their homes were built from the natural limestone rock with wood that was nailed on with square nails. If that form of making lime didn't work, they could always go to the lime kiln in Elk that helped supply lime and mortar for foundations and stone structures. Could they have built a made-made stone cave to live in while building their home?

They always lived in fear of prairie fires, drought, blizzards and snakes. The land was infested with snakes that had not had much threat from any other creature until man moved into the plains. People kept snake poles under their homes for protection, and before retiring for the night they would quickly survey the night skies around their home looking for any sign of a brush fire.

Most of the land was grazing land with a few wild horses and buffalo roaming around, and the area was popularly known as the Flint Hills and better known for its big and little bluestem grasses that were so rich in the area. The rocks that cover the rolling hills in the area do contain flint and you can rub two stones together and create a fire! This part of the land possessed rich, fertile valleys with many creeks that were being fed by natural spring water. About 15 per cent of the county was valley land; 50 per cent good tillable, undulating prairie, and 35 per cent of a wild grass character. Good well water could be obtained at a depth of about 25 feet. The streams were skirted with trees, and forest land of the county was estimated at five per cent. Cottonwood, hackberry, sycamore, hickory, walnut, and burr oak were the prevailing kinds of timber in the area. The soil was generally quite strongly impregnated with lime; the subsoil was of a clayish cast, a good county for raising and fattening cattle. The winters were and are generally short, the spring opens early, and the autumn days are balmy.

Unfriendly Indians never seriously bothered any of Chase County residents, but a hostile tribe did annoy the county's first surveyors near Wonsevu. The Indian chief, Whistler, asked the men to leave, but the men went on working. When the men had finished an area the Indians followed them and destroyed each corner as soon as it was established. One of the surveyors telegraphed the Surveyor-General asking for military protection, and after the arrival of a company of soldiers, the Indians didn't cause any more problems. Even then, on Osage Hill, just west of Elmdale was an old Indian telegraph station where constant smoke signals were being made. In spite of the Kinkaid Homestead Law in 1862, it was more than 10 years before the Indians cleared out of Chase County sufficiently enough for homesteaders to settle safely.

Earlier in 1860 an excessive drought hit Kansas and caused crops to fail, and then myriads of grasshoppers completed the destruction of the vegetation. Springs and wells dried up and families suffered from malarial fever in some form or another, some resulting in death. By the winter of 1860-1861 a severe winter hit the region and snow fell to a depth of two feet, remaining on the ground for six weeks. Nothing but charity and starvation stood between many of the people. The severe storms drove the buffalo further east and though they were thin in flesh, they were gladly killed and eaten by many of the early settlers.

Around 1864 there was a general uprising of the Indians of the plains and lasted for six years. These Indian wars cost Kansas more than a thousand lives, and a million dollars to individuals, retarding settlement, and continued from time to time till 1878 when the Indians became comparatively at peace.

The first arrival of white men were the cattlemen, who took land near rivers and creeks and brought in thousands of white-faced cattle, but blizzards often killed the cattle. Soon the homesteaders started arriving around 1883 through 1885 in covered wagons, despite the resistance by the cattlemen. By 1886 there were many sod houses, dugouts, man-made stone caves and permanent settlements created. My great-great grandpa Julius had moved to this area in Chase County around 1883 and by early 1884 homesteaded 160 acres of land. With homesteading he had to live on that land for at least five years and make improvements before he could truly own that land. In 1889 that land became his. Julius's son Fred Conrad Piper had remembered that his family lived in a cave while homesteading his land. The cave he was referring to were the man-made stone caves families used to store their food in that protected the food from mice, the weather, and who knows what else. Maybe the cave was one of the first structures families created and then lived in them until they could build a home? One of my first structures would have been an outhouse!

The state of Kansas was named after the Kanza Indians who came to the area now known as Kansas in the early 1800s from the Ohio River Valley. Kanza translates roughly as "The Wind People," or "People of the South Wind." The Kaw Nation—the official name of the Kanza Indians, purchased 170 acres four miles southeast of Council Grove in hopes of turning the land into a heritage park, and is trying to get their new land listed on the National Register of Historic Places. I remember my dad loved to fish and he would often take us to the "Kaw" river in the Kansas City area, which was actually the Missouri River. All the locals called it the "Kaw" river, and now I know why!

The city of Wichita was so named after a small tribe of Wichita Indians of only about 320 Indians that had first resided on a reservation in southern Oklahoma. With the white man moving in and the civil war breaking out the tribe migrated north to what is now known as Wichita, Kansas. The Wichita Indians called themselves Kitikitish, which literally means "raccoon eyelids," but better understood as "tattooed eyelids" because the men of that tribe had a custom of tattooing lines on their eyelids, and the women made tattoo lines on their chins or on their breasts.

The Wichita Indians have lived in the United States for more than three centuries. In my research I was captured by some Indian recipes for fried green tomatoes and another for wild onions and eggs. The Wild Onions and Eggs recipe required only three bunches of chopped up wild onions, a little bacon fat and two eggs. The Fried Green Tomato recipe requires two pounds of green tomatoes, four eggs, one and one fourth cups of corn meal, three quarters cup of water, one quarter cup minced chives, one tablespoon of salt, one quarter teaspoon of fresh ground pepper, and one quarter cup of butter.

The Santa Fe Trail ran through parts of Marion County, at least from the 1820s to the 1870s and was one of the most significant land routes. We know that Julius and his family lived not only in the Elk community but also in the Lost Springs area in Marion County, according to the 1915 census. Julius was listed as 69 years of age and his occupation was a blacksmith. Two of his sons, Henry age 37, and Emil age 30 were also listed as blacksmiths and living in the same household. Emil and Anna had three children at that time living there as well, Clyde age 5, Gilbert age 2, and Roy age six months. By the 1920 census widower Julius, age 74, was living in Cedar Point with his son Emil. Julius's second wife Ada had died in 1917. Emil and Anna now have their children Clyde, Gilbert, Roy and Bernal living there as well.

Lost Springs was one of the favorite camping spots on the Santa Fe Trail because it had such an ample supply of good water and was located about 15 miles west of Diamond Spring, which was about a day's travel for a wagon train. A few miles west of the town of Lost Springs is the site of the old Lost Spring on the Santa Fe Trail. You can actually see the ruts the great wagons made that are still there today. In 1887 the Chicago, Kansas and Nebraska Railway Company built a line right through Lost Springs but it was renamed the Union Pacific Railroad. The prairies are still home to pronghorn antelope, deer, foxes, coyotes, pheasants, prairie dogs, badgers, wild turkeys, rabbits, snakes, insects and rodents. You can see over 200 types of birds in the Flint Hills such as, meadowlarks, grasshopper sparrows, sandpipers and red-tailed hawks. The early settlers were able to use the honey-colored limestone for building foundations, homes, and even fence posts.

I was drawn to the area because I wanted to know of the struggles and hardships my family may have had to endure while living in such a desolate area of the state with very few trees, known as the Prairie Grove vicinity. The soil in the area was too thin to farm, and too rock-strewn to make good farmland. They had no electricity, no running water, no way of keeping their food cold during the hot summer months, and probably rode around in a covered wagon, or a horse drawn buggy. My grandma Piper once said that when she was young her family and the whole town would go down to the river in the winter time where the men would cut big blocks of ice out of the frozen parts of the river and creeks and would take those chunks home. They would store these chunks of ice in the floor of their barns and cover them with hay, and all the women would cook over bon fires on the river banks while the men cut out the ice chunks. She said the ice would sometimes be two or three feet thick, and it would take two or three days to get enough ice for everyone.

To preserve their vegetables the families would dig a hole and place their vegetables in it, placing a tarp over it, and then covering it with hay and dirt to keep them fresh most of the winter. When they wanted vegetables they would pick up one end of the tarp. My grandma Piper said that they had a big tub which they would partially fill with wax and build a fire under it, and when the wax melted, they would dip the vegetables in the wax. When the vegetables cooled down they stored them under that tarp, and the wax helped keep the vegetables fresher, longer. Some built caves

A man-made cave in Chase County that a family member built to live in and then store food in

made of natural stone from the area and covered the stone with dirt that would help preserve their vegetables and such. I visited one of those caves in Chase County and walked into it. The structure of it was so unique. Melvin Koegeboehn told us that his parents lived in that cave for two years, the very cave we had just discovered! Did my great-uncle Fred Conrad Piper also live in that same cave at some point, or was it another?

Most of my family in Chase County either attended or held family services at the old German Immanuel Evangelical Lutheran Church whose building sat near the Chase County line on highway K-150 west of Elmdale, and was a familiar landmark since 1886. Many people of German decent had settled in the community that was also known as the Prairie Grove and School District number 47, which was about one mile south of

German Immanuel Lutheran Church that was located in Chase County, KS

Elmdale and eight miles west on what is now highway K-150 and was one mile east of the Chase-Marion county line. The church building sat on the southeast corner of the southeast quarter section north of highway K-150 and west of the intersection of Wildcat Creek Road. In the early 1900's there were over 100 communicate members.

Up until 1943 the congregation shared its pastor with the Grace Lutheran Church in Strong City. The parsonage of this church was sold in 1943 and moved away after Our Savior Lutheran Church of Marion and the Immanuel Church became sister congregations and then the congregation at Immanuel disbanded due to the decline in the population and the church building was moved to Marion and added onto the Our Savior Lutheran Church. According to the Bureau of Statistics the church in Chase County had organized in 1886 and joined synod in 1921 and disbanded in 1959. It had survived about 73 years! I recently visited the church in the town of Marion and met some of their leadership and toured the grounds and buildings that once was the original church building in Chase County but was now all part of one beautiful church building in Marion, in Marion County, Kansas. What a joy I felt that I was walking through the same church building that my great-great ancestors worshipped in. Standing on the same platform that the preacher of their day stood on, and realizing that my ancestors saw the same view that I was seeing for the first time as I walked through that sanctuary. How can I possibly explain all the feelings that became apparent to me at that very moment in time?

SEVENTY FOUR

AUGUST AND MAMIE

My great grandpa, August Julius Piper

One of my great-great grandparent's sons was my great-grandfather, August Julius Piper. He was born in Gillman, Illinois on April 14, 1872 and his parents, Julius and Minna, came west in a covered wagon when he was about a year old. His family first stopped in Iowa because they had been robbed, and then they came on into Kansas where his parents could homestead land and he grew up near the community of Elk, Kansas. He married Mary (Mamie) Ada Giffler on September 4, 1895 in Florence, according to the Chase County Leader News dated September 12, 1895. Mary was born on April 29, 1878 in Albany, New York. 4012 August had built a neat cottage on his farm for himself and his new bride. He later served as the city Marshall in Florence, Kansas around but gave it up when his wife, Mary (Mamie) Ada (Giffler) Piper wanted him to stay home to help her with the children and take care

My great-grandparents, August and Mary Piper with five of their children, Fred, Charles, Will, Stella, and Laura

of their farm. Another reason he quit was because of the strong KKK influence and Masons in the area and he feared for his life because some of those members could have been neighbors of theirs. One of his sons, Charles, was a member of the Masons in Florence. August and his family were living on a ranch called the O. K. Ranch, northeast of Florence, in Morris County. Mary knew how to play the piano and organ and was very artistic. She was also a very good cook and taught her children the secrets of cooking. My cousin Betty remembers August as a very kind, gentle and soft spoken man.

A 1920 census showed August at age 47 and Mary age 41 living in Doyle Township in Marion County, Kansas. August was born in Illinois and his occupation was listed as a farmer. Living with them at that time was their son William Otto Julius age 23 and William's wife Goldie age 20 (my grandparents). August and Mary's other children living with them then were Charlie Emil Theodore age 21, Freddie Edward age 19, Laura Augusta age 17, Stella Mary age 14, Bertha Nellie Maggie age 10, Viola Minnie age 6, and Pauline Alberta age 4. By the 1925 census my grandparents William and Goldie had already moved out of William's parent's home. In fact, they had moved to Nebraska in 1923. All of August and Mary's children are listed except William and Goldie, and their daughter Geneva Marjory, age 2 was now listed, and they are now living in Fairplay Township, Marion County, Kansas. Fairplay was adjacent to Florence, Kansas on the west side.

My great aunt Laura, great uncle Charles, and great aunt Stella and great uncle Fred Piper

August died on January 4, 1942 in Dunlap, Kansas after suffering a heart attack while at the supper table, and his funeral service was held on

January 8th at the Christian Church in Florence. My dad and mom had just gotten married on January 3rd and mom told me that they attended August's funeral there in Florence. My mom told me that she hadn't met August but she did get to know his widow Mary. Mary (Mamie) died of congestive heart failure and diabetes at St. Mary's Hospital in Emporia, Kansas on August 1, 1950 at the age of 72.

When I visited the old homestead in Chase County recently and ducked under a fence with my cousin Milton, we found the remnants of an old stone foundation that had belonged to Herman in 1900 but had been occupied by Gustave and Bertha (Piper) Hahn, and William and Sara (Piper) Marquardt. Herman had moved in with his son William about 1910, and Herman died in 1912.

Remnants of my great-great uncle Herman's first stone foundation in Chase County, KS

One of my great-great grandparents' sons was Otto L. Piper, who was born in Streator, La Salle County, Illinois on February 8, 1874 and married Jenny (Jennie) Dornbush on March 13, 1895 in Florence, Kansas. Was Otto's middle name actually Lester since he named his youngest son John Lester? The clerk when filling out their marriage certificate had spelled Otto's last name as Pipper three times, and only on the seal was his name spelled Piper! This is a legal document for the probate court! Jennie's parents were Henry and Martha Ann (Paddock) Dornbush, and Martha's parents were William Paddock and Mary (Van Patten) (Paddock) Giffler. Her widowed mother Mary had become William Giffler's third wife when Martha's dad William Paddock died. Henry and Martha Dornbush lived in a home right next door to the Giffler's home in Swingtown, which was a small town created by the railroad employees just outside of Florence, Kansas. William Giffler and Jenny's father both worked for the railroad. William Giffler's daughter Sophia married a Cloverdyke and the Cloverdykes lived in Swingtown and were employees of the railroad as well.

According to the Chase County Leader News in May, 1902 Otto and Jenny Piper were living between Cottonwood Falls and Middle Creek townships when he brought in eight live wolves as large as young cats to the county clerk and demanded a dollar bounty for each of them. The clerk explained to Otto that he only wanted the skins and not the live wolf. Otto soon went off with eight dollars anyway! According to Otto's grandson John Bailor, Otto used to own a cattle ranch but lost it during the depression in the 1920s.

According to the Emporia Gazette Newspaper dated March 22, 1939 Otto Piper had bought his 26th set of license plates for a 1913 Model T Ford in Emporia. The car was still in good running condition and had a 1913 model chassis and was powered with a 1926 model motor. Otto told the employees at the county treasurer's office that he had been buying tags for his car for 28 years, a car that he had bought second-hand in 1913 from a man who admitted to him that the car was a 'wreck' and about to fall apart. The 1939 set of tags cost Otto only $4.00, with a $1.00 penalty fee added on for his buying the tags two months late!

The 1910 census for Chase County, Diamond Creek township showed Otto age 36, his wife Jennie age 30, and five children at that time were: Wilber age fourteen, Buddie age eight, Earl age six, Norma age five, and Allis was thirteen months old. Otto died at 9:10pm on Monday, February 16, 1948 at the Newman Memorial County Hospital in Emporia, Kansas. When he died he was survived by 10 children; Wilbur of Americus, Lyon County, Kansas who was born on May 16,

1896 in Marion, Kansas and died in April, 1949, Buddy F. of Espenola, New Mexico was born in 1902, Earl of Ramona, California was born in 1904, Mrs Norma Lee (Piper) Bailor of Allen who had married Logan L. Bailor, Lyon County, Kansas was born in 1905, Mrs. Allis (Piper) Bruner of Osage City, Kansas was born in March, 1910, Mrs. Ada (Piper) Williams of Allen, Lyon County, Kansas was born in 1913, James (John) of Allen, Kansas was born in 1914 and became a cowboy, Mrs. Grace (Piper) Aikman of Emporia was born in 1918, Mrs. Gladys (Piper) Staley of Admire, Lyon County, Kansas was born in 1921, and John Lester of Sydney, Australia. John Lester was born on March 11, 1923 in Dunlap, Kansas and married Veronica Dorothy Wade. Lester had become an alcoholic and eventually died on February 1, 1988 in La Palma, Orange County, California. According to John Bailor, his grandfather Otto's son James had become a cowboy. Texas cattlemen would drive their cows north, and pay James to help fatten their cows.

I was able to contact Norma (Piper) Bailor's son, who is my third cousin, John Bailor, age 82, who lives with his wife in Wichita. John told me that his dad, Logan L. Bailor's last name used to be spelled "Baylor," but because of a family squabble with cousins he changed the spelling of his last name to "Bailor." He told me also that many families changed the spelling of their name if they chose to back then because there were no laws specifying the legality of using one particular spelling of a name, or at least there were not the restrictions that we have today. I had mentioned that some Koegeboehn families had changed the spelling of their last name by taking out the "O's" and became Kegebehn!

Another son of my great-great grandparents was Henry Gustof Piper who was born on October 14, 1875 in Streator, Illinois and married Margaret (Maggie) Giffler and died on March 5, 1940. In the 1910 census for Elk County, Moline City, Kansas, it showed Henry Gusman

Piper age 33, and Maggie his wife as age 26. At that time they had William (Willie) Edward Piper age eight, who was born on November 24, 1901 in Florence and later married Lela Martin. One of William's sons was Milford Eugene Piper who was born on September 2, 1924 in Oil Hill, Kansas and married June Maxine Worthington on July 22, 1945. When June died on February 18, 1976 he married Mary Sawyer on September 3, 1977.

Milford had worked with Cities Service and Pester Refinery and retired in 1984. He had lived 10 years in Marion, Kansas before moving to Towanda. He was the former Mayor of Towanda, where he served on every seat in the city council. He was also the former police judge of Towanda and an explorer scout leader, and was the past president of the PTA in Towanda. Before he died he was an active member of the VFW in Marion. Milford served in the Air Force as a pilot of a B24 in WW II and was a member of the First Christian Church in El Dorado until he died at his home on January 4, 1989 at the age of 64. His funeral services were held at the Carlson Colonial Funeral Home in El Dorado and his burial was at the Towanda Cemetery. He left behind a daughter and son-in-law Carolyn and Jonnie Johnson of Leon, Kansas, step-sons Randy and Robert Sawyer of Marion, Kansas (sons of his second wife), and many grandchildren.

Henry and Maggie's son William (Willie) Edward Piper died in El Dorado, Kansas on July 29, 1929 and is buried there. Their son, Paul Henry Piper age six was born on December 21, 1903 in Florence. He married Pauline Vera Buick on August 11, 1931 and died on July 12, 1972 in Gravette, Arkansas and is buried in Tulsa, Oklahoma.

Twenty years later Henry and Maggie were living in El Dorado, Kansas, and in the 1930 census for El Dorado it showed their children as: Beulah Minnie (Piper) Davis age 19 and was born on May 31, 1910 near Howard, Kansas, and married Orla Benton Davis in Yates Center, Kansas, on August 11, 1931, a year after graduating from high school. She grew up in Oil Hill, Kansas and graduated with the class of 1930 at the El Dorado High School. She was a longtime, active member of the First United Methodist Church in El Dorado and enjoyed painting and the Home Arts Group and the Jolly Time Pinochle Club. Her husband Orla was born on July 9, 1908 in Milo, Grant County, Indiana and preceded her in death on February 8, 1981. She died on April 15, 2006 in El Dorado, Kansas and is buried at the Sunset Lawns Cemetery there.

Henry and Maggie's daughter Hazel (Tiny) Marie (Piper) Zang was age 16 in the 1930 census and she was born in 1914 in Chase County, and at the age of 18 married Bernard (Bernie) R. Zang on May 1, 1932. She and Bernard first met in the ninth grade. Hazel saw Bernard for the first time standing on the school stairs and thought he was extremely good looking but learned he was ornery. It was when Hazel and her friends were walking to a basketball game when she saw Bernard just

Hazel (Piper) Zang and her husband Bernie

ahead of them. He turned around and walked with Hazel and her friends to the game. Bernard must have been interested in Hazel because he started coming to her home, driving like a madman to see Hazel during his lunch hour at the A & P Grocers he worked at, and then hurrying back to deliver groceries. On dates he would take her to the movies, skating, and just hang out with Hazel and her friends. In high school Bernard and his friends would gather snakes or birds and place them into the water meter hole and place the lid back on before the meter reader came by. They hid around a corner to watch the meter reader jump and scream when he opened the cover and the birds would fly out, or a snake would be revealed when he lifted the cover.

I'm sending you a Valentine
As I did long ago
T'was all decked out
With silk and lace
and cupid, with his bow
The days have flown so quickly by
and in those days of yore
I told you that I loved you then
and now it's even more
Yes years have flown so quickly by
Since cupid with his dart
Once more I send a Valentine,
This time I send my heart

A poem written by Bernie to his wife Hazel

Soon Bernard asked Hazel to marry him and they drove to Newton, Kansas to get a marriage license. On the way their Essex automobile broke down and Bernard's brother Elton had to come and get them. Elton didn't know that his brother and Hazel were on their way to get a marriage license. Once they got their license they hid it under the rug at Bernard's mother's house for two weeks! After two weeks of Bernard constantly wanting to get married, Hazel gave in and they visited preacher Truesdell's house and he married them. Truesdell had to get his wife out of bed to be a witness and she came to the ceremony in bare feet! After they were married they both went back to their own separate homes and didn't tell anyone for a month. The truth came out when someone saw the listing of their marriage in the local newspaper! They were both 18 years old when they married.

Hazel and Bernard soon rented an apartment for $10.00 a week with all utilities included in the price. She quit school and started working at a local nickel and dime store for $12.00 a week. Bernard had been earning $15.00 a week at the A & P but was cut back to $2.00 a week. They could buy bread at .05 cents a loaf and they could get all their meat for about .07 cents a pound. They then rented a three room house that included a living room, kitchen, and bedroom. It was here that Bernard started working as a bookkeeper for the Gas Service Company. Early on he worked at a grocery store but throughout the rest of his life he worked for the Gas Service Company, owned a grocery store, and did a little auctioning on the side. He later worked at the Wesley Hospital in the shipping and receiving department. Every weekend Hazel and Bernard would go to Bernard's mother's to eat and the guys would play dominoes while the ladies cooked.

Hazel and Bernard's daughter Bernadine Carol (Zang) McColley was born on November 12, 1944 in El Dorado and married Jerry McColley. Bonnie Jean (Zang) Ballinger was born on May 31, 1934 in Oil Hill, Kansas and married Lawrence Ballinger. One of Bonnie and Lawrence's children was Robert Frank Ballinger who married Jan E. Willis. Robert and Jan's children were Melody Ann (Ballinger) McComas who was born on December 12, 1974 and married Scott McComas, and Sean Adam who was born on May 18, 1978 (never married) but had two children, Maddie and Sean Robert. Lawrence and Bonnie's other child was Laura Ellen (Ballinger) Barnes who married Ronald G. Barnes.

Robert Ballinger divorced Jan in 1979 and she died in 2005 of heart failure. Robert then married Joyce Darlene Stangle in 1980 and they had one child, Dezarae Renee (Ballinger) Smith who married Brian Smith and they had two boys, Trevor and Dylan. Robert and Joyce divorced in 1988 and he married widow Deborah Elaine Morgan in 2001 who had been married to Calvin Morgan that died of heart failure in 1999. Deborah and Calvin had had four children, Heather, Chantel, Michelle and Leon. Robert said he had been friends of both Deborah and Calvin back in 1980 and their kids grew up together, and when Calvin passed away, they became a blended family.

Robert Ballinger says he and Deborah have been together for almost 10 years. Some of their children live at their farm in Nevada, Missouri, some live in the Wichita, Kansas area, while some live in Newsport, Virginia. Robert and Deborah moved to Houston, Texas about six years ago because of work, and before that they lived in Tulsa, Wichita, Omaha, and Salina.

Hazel and Bernard's daughter Sherilyn Rae Zang was born on August 26, 1936 in Oil Hill, Kansas. I had no more information about Sherilyn.

Henry Gusman and Margaret (Maggie) (Giffler) Piper's other children were Andrew Frankie Piper age 13 in the 1930 census and was born in 1916 in Clements, Kansas, and married Ruby May Star, and Mamie Dorothy (Piper) Hirst was age 9 and was born in Oil Hill, Kansas in 1921 and married James (Tom) Thomas Hirst in San Francisco, San Mateo, California, and died on July 17, 1996 in Joplin, Missouri. Their son Kenneth Rodney Hirst was born on January 3, 1942 in San Francisco and married Meri Lou Kilbey. Their daughter Karren Lynn (Hirst) Varner was born on July 17, 1944 in Wichita, Kansas and married John Lester Varner. Mamie died and was buried on July 19th in Noel, McDonald County, Missouri. When the 1930 census was taken William (Willie) had already died on July 29, 1900 and was buried at the Sunset Lawns cemetery in El Dorado.

Henry and Maggie's son Andrew Frankie Piper who was born on August 2, 1916 in Clements, Chase County, Kansas, graduated from El Dorado High School and served in the U.S. Navy during World War II. He worked for Skelly, Getty, and Texaco Refinery where he worked on the blender unit. He married Ruby May Star on May 16, 1940 in Oil Hill, Kansas. Ruby was born on May 4, 1922. They lived in El Dorado for 57 years before moving to Wichita to be near their sons. He was a member of the First United Methodist Church in El Dorado, and a member of the Oil, Chemical and Atomic Workers Union. He was an outdoorsman who loved to fish and hunt. He lived at Fall River for a while so he could fish and hunt. He died on May, 21, 2007 at the age of 90.

According to the Wellington Daily News, Wellington, Kansas, dated March 6, 1940 announcing Henry Gustof's death, it stated that Henry had been a resident of Wellington, Kansas since last October and died unexpectedly from a heart attack shortly after dinner at his home located at 403 N. Park in Oil Hill, near El Dorado about 8:00 pm Tuesday evening. Funeral services were held at the El Dorado Lutheran Church with a quartet that sang "The Old Rugged Cross," "Beautiful Isle," and "In The Garden." Henry had been employed by the Cities Service Company as an oil field pumper and retired last October. The article stated that he was survived by two sons, Paul and Andrew, both from Wellington, and three daughters, Mrs. Orla Davis and Mrs. Bernard Zang, both from Oil Hill, and Mrs. James Marsh of Wellington. Also surviving Henry were his brothers Otto of Emporia, August of Bushing, and Fred Piper of Fort Riley. Henry and Maggie are buried at the Sunset Lawns Cemetery in El Dorado, Kansas along with their sons William and Andrew Piper. Their son William E. Piper was born on November 24, 1901 and died on July 14, 1929.

I was curious about the township of Oil Hill, which was part of the El Dorado history. In my research I found out that in 1916 El Dorado brought "Big Oil" to Kansas when it started producing about one percent of the nation's production, and by 1918 it was about 12.8 percent of national production. Cities Service organized the Empire Gas and Fuel to oversee and manage the El Dorado field. Company towns sprung up almost overnight such as Oil Hill, Midian, Keighley, Wilson, Smileyberg, and Oil Valley. Oil Hill was one of those towns complete with a swimming pool, golf course, school, gymnasium, stores, café, and a post office. It was the only town of its size in the U.S. without any form of municipal government. It was a town that oil built. All that remains today are the sidewalks peeking through the tall grass, abandoned flower beds, some old foundations and a company garage.

Apparently before my great-great grandpa Julius died, he had sold all his properties, including lots number eight, nine and ten, section three, in Cedar Point. We believe his family may have been very upset at him for what he did, and we believe that either Julius was buried without any stone marker with his name inscribed on it, or his tombstone had washed away during one of the many floods in the area. His family may have buried him in the same burial plot as his first wife Minna, and only her name appears on the tombstone. The Chase County Historical Society told me that he was probably buried on top of Minna's coffin, something that they practiced in those days, or maybe he is buried next to her, we don't know for sure. Maybe his family didn't have enough funds to purchase a tombstone after Julius died, we don't know for sure.

Emil William Piper was born in June of 1883 in Chase County, Kansas and married Anne (Anna) Butter, daughter of Carl and Ada Butter on February 10, 1909. Anne (Anna) was born in 1893. Ada, Anna's mother had married Emil's dad Julius, my great-great grandpa on June 10, 1909. Emil and Anna had six sons who were, in the order of their births: Clyde Edward was born on January 26, 1910 and married Mary A. Jones. Mary was born on June 23, 1911 and died October 2, 1996. Clyde died on February 4, 1991 and is buried at the Greenwood Cemetery in Clay Center, Kansas along with his wife Mary. Clyde and Mary's children were Lucy Ann Piper who died at birth on March 30, 1939, and Harley Gene, an adopted son who was born on February 27, 1943 and married Shirley Sypes.

Another son of Emil and Anna was Gilbert Lee Piper who was born on May 23, 1912 in Elk, Kansas and married Mabel Burkman on June 15, 1935 in Junction City, Kansas. One of their children was Robert (Bob) Lee Piper, Sr. who was born on July 26, 1936 and married Peggy Louise Hoeffner. Robert and Peggy's children were Robert Lee Piper, Jr. who married Dylynn Jorgenson, Rhonda Lynn (Piper) Cross married Kenny Cross, and Roxana L. (Piper) Greep married Kent Greep. Gilbert Lee had worked for the ADM Milling in Salina, Kansas and retired in 1973. He died on November 24, 1991 at the age of 79 at the Pinnacle Care Center in Salina, Kansas and was buried at the Roselawn Memorial Park.

Another son of Emil and Anna was Roy Lester Piper who was born on October 12, 1914 in Marion County and married Mildred Louise Turnbull on March 1, 1936 at the Zion Evangelical Church in Junction City, Kansas when Roy was 22 years of age. Roy used to work civil service as a chief Inspector of heavy equipment for 33 years. He retired in 1970. He then worked for the city of Junction City as a mechanic and retired from there in 1987. He was a lifetime member of the Eagles Auxiliary, he loved to travel, play bingo, and work on cars. Roy lived to be 96 years of age and died on February 2, 2011 in Salina, Kansas at his home, and his funeral services were held on February 10 at the Penwell-Gabel Johnson Chapel in Junction City. Roy was buried at the Highland Cemetery in Junction City. Roy's wife Mildred Louis (Turnbull) Piper was born on August 27, 1917 in Geary County on a farm on Clarks Creek. Mildred's parents were Peter and Ellen Turnbull. Mildred was a wonderful homemaker and loved to cook and was well known for her homemade pies and cinnamon rolls. She loved to travel and play bingo. She died on December 23, 2010 in Salina at their home at the age of 93 and is buried at the Highland Cemetery next to her husband in Junction City, Kansas.

Another son of Emil and Anna was Bernal (Bernie) Roy Piper who was born on November 13, 1917 and married Anna Mason. Bernal died on November 1, 1985. At one time he had owned a gas station in Paola, Kansas. I met Bernal when my parents had stopped by his gas station in Paola when I was just a teenager. Bernal served in the Army in WW II, according to his tombstone. Bernal is

Sons of Emil and Anna Piper as young men. Junior, Roy, and Homer.

buried at the Holy Cross Cemetery in Paola, Kansas. June (Junior) (Joe) or J.C.) C. Piper was born on June 12, 1922 in Elk, Kansas, and married Berniece Bishop. Junior and Berniece divorced and Junior married Dorothy Weaver on January 8, 1955. Junior and Dorothy had one son, Stephen Piper. Junior died on June 27, 1969 at Waynesville, Missouri at the age of 47 and is buried at the Waynesville Memorial Park. He served in WW II from August 29, 1940 to September 17, 1945.

Homer Glenn Piper was born on September 8, 1924 and married Bonnie Lee Wright on October 7, 1943. Bonnie was born on June 17, 1925 in Bald Knob, Arkansas. Her parents were Samuel David and Mildred Edith (Carlisle) Wright. Her family had moved to Detroit, Kansas where she attended grade school, and then her family moved to Longford, Kansas where she graduated from the Longford High School. Homer and Bonnie's only child was David Lee Piper who was born on November 13, 1945. I remember meeting David when I was in high school through my great-aunt Anna (Butter) Piper, who lived on Second Street in Junction City, Kansas. David lived with his parents until they died and now he lives at a senior center on 8th Street in Junction City,

Kansas. All I knew was that David had a learning disability. His mother Bonnie died on September 18, 2010 at the Geary Community Hospital in Junction City, Kansas. Bonnie is buried at the Highland Cemetery.

Emil died on December 21, 1949 and Anna died on October 23, 1980.

Emil Piper in his later years

SEVENTY FIVE

WILL AND GOLDIE

My great-grandparents August Julius and Mary (Mamie) Ada (Giffler) Piper were married in 1895 and had eleven children, one being my grandpa, William (Will) Otto Julius Piper. He was born on June 3, 1896 in Elmdale, Kansas. Elmdale has one building listed on the National Register of Historic places, the "Clover Cliff Ranch House," which is a bed and breakfast. William married my grandma, Goldie Ellen (Mallory) Piper. Goldie was born on November 7, 1899 in or near Culbertson, Nebraska, which is about 11 miles east of Trenton. She died from a car accident on October 19, 1966 after being taken to the hospital in Shawnee Mission, Johnson County, Kansas. When mom called me in New Jersey to tell me that my grandparents were involved in a car accident, I immediately called grandma at the hospital the day before she died. She told me she was bleeding on the inside and there was nothing they could do about it because of her heart. Grandpa William died on July 7, 1974 after having a stroke, and is buried next to my grandma Goldie at the old Monticello cemetery in Monticello, Kansas, not far from their home in Zarah, Kansas. Grandpa Will had to be placed in a nursing home in Desoto, Kansas before he died.

My grandpa Will remembered the Republican River in Nebraska when he and Goldie lived there, and how he got his first car by pulling it out of the river when the person who owned it left it there. Grandpa

Will had lived in Hitchcock County, Nebraska from at least 1923 through part of 1930. My dad told me he remembered living on a farm just east of Trenton. He lived there when he was age three to ten years of age and recalled the memories of living there. He said he remembered his sister Bernadine in the kitchen using the hand-pump to the well that came up through the kitchen floor. He took me to see that old stone foundation years later. I only wish I knew where that old stone foundation is located today.

August and Mary lived in several places during their marriage: the Patterson place, the O.K. Ranch, the Campbell place, and lastly they lived at the Carpenter's place.

My great-grandma Mary Ada (Giffler) Piper died on August 1, 1950 at St. Mary's Hospital at the age of 72 and is buried next to her husband August at the Florence Cemetery. She had spent her last days living in Dunlap with her daughter Geneva. Geneva then spent the rest of her life in Herington, Kansas and is buried there. According to the Emporia Gazette dated January 7, 1942 my great-grandpa August Julius Piper, age 70, died on Monday, January 4, 1942 at his farm near Dunlap after suffering a heart attack while at his supper table. The article stated that his funeral services were held on January 8, 1942 at the Christian Church in Florence at 2:30 pm and he was buried at the Florence cemetery. Before he died he had been working the previous four years on the Ben Bicker farm. My mother told me she and dad attended his funeral.

Another son of August and Mary (Ada) Piper was my great uncle Charles (Charlie) Emil Theodore Piper. He was born on July 20, 1898, and married Pauline Agnes Clark who was born on June 22, 1915. Pauline's parents were Clarence Austin and Mary Carolyn (Peterson) Clark. Charles and Pauline were living in Florence, Kansas when my great-uncle Charlie got a letter stating that he had been hired to work on the Beaver Lake Dam project in Arkansas, plus the fact that they were having legal problems with one of their sons, so they decided to move. They sold their home and bought the truck that their cousin Virgil had brought over for them. They left their younger children with their grandparents in Dunlap and were on their way to Arkansas when their truck struck a case of soda pop that had fallen out of a truck in front of them. The case of broken bottles blew several of their tires and they couldn't afford to replace them. Charlie was not able to get to the Beaver Lake Dam project in time to get the job. They stayed in Decatur and lived the rest of their lives there. He died on March 20, 1962 and is buried in Decatur, Arkansas.

My great uncle Charlie played acoustic guitar and harmonica. I met most of their children, my second cousins, when we would occasionally drive to Arkansas to spend time with them. Their children included Charles August Eugene Piper who was born on October 23, 1933 and married Wanda Thompson on August 14, 1956. Charles and Wanda's children were Charles, who was born on October 5, 1958 and died on October 6, 1958; Eva Marie (Piper) Barela was born on March 31, 1957 and married Samuel Barela on May 18, 1985; Paul Ray Piper was born on December 10, 1962 and married Alicia Barela on March 27, 1981 (Alicia is the sister of Samuel who married Eva); Norma Jean (Piper) Fossett was born on August 15, 1960 and married Daniel Fossett on July 14, 1984; Orville Wayne Piper was born on January 26, 1968 and married Georgina Bongmo on November 27, 1989; Rose Marie (Piper) (Reed) Williams was born on April 11, 1965 and was a twin to Rose Marlene Piper. Rose Marie's first husband was Jay Reed. Her second husband was William Williams whom she married on October 13, 1990. Rose Marlene (Piper) Winsea was born on April 11, 1965 and married Leland Winsea on September 11, 1993, and their brother

Marvin Anthony Piper Sr. was born on February 28, 1974. Their father Charles died on January 27, 1988.

Another child of great uncle great uncle Charles and Pauline Piper was Dorothy Denette (Piper) Lewellen who was born on May 31, 1944 and married Bobby Rae Lewellen on July 27, 1961. Dorothy and Bobby's children are Charlyn Raynette (Lewellen) Greathouse who was born on September 11, 1963 and married Darryl Greathouse, and Roberta Joy (Lewellen) Zapier who was born on November 10, 1964 and married Henry Zapier on April 15, 1989. Dorothy used to play organ in her church.

Great uncle Charles and Pauline also had a son Carl Dennis Piper who was born on September 19, 1939 and married Connie McChristian on July 2, 1960. Their children were Darrell Wayne Piper who was born on April 2, 1961, and Roger Dale Piper who was born on July 3, 1962 and married Karen Fortney on February 17, 1984. Carl Dennis Piper died on February 14, 1991.

Great uncle Charles and Pauline also had a daughter Euphama Verelene (Piper) Melton who was born on October 7, 1937 and married Hiriam Melton on February 4, 1956. Children of Euphama and Hiriam were Robert Eugene Melton who was born on March 10, 1957 and married Czella Diaprai; Rebecca Sue (Melton) (Quasa) Reed was born on January 30, 1959 and married Robert Quasa on December 15, 1974 and divorced. Rebecca then married John Reed on June 27, 1992. Euphama knew how to play the ukulele. Euphama died on February 22, 1981.

Great uncle Charles and Pauline's son Theron Dee Piper was born on October 9, 1941 and he married Linda Ruth Hickman on October 10,

1965. Their children were Joe Dee Piper who was born on November 22, 1966 and married Joleanne Marie Reagan on June 20, 1987, Terry Lee Piper was born on January 28, 1968 and married Paula Marie Vahlberg on February 14, 1987 and divorced, then married Jessica Dawn Crisman on November 30, 1996, and Troy Dean Piper who was born on November 19, 1969 and married Jeanette Kay Huston on November 11, 1995. Linda had been involved in a head-on collision and had to be taken care of in a nursing home. When Linda started getting better Theron was on his way to pick her up to bring her home when the nursing home called him and said that Linda had fallen and hit her head and died.

Less than two months later Theron married Beverly. They were married about five years when Tharens' health started failing. They were living in Idaho when Theron passed away.

Another son to great uncle Charles and great aunt Pauline Piper was Gailord (Skip) Leroy Piper who was born on October 15, 1947 and married Mia. Gailord and Mia's children were Sonya, who was born on June 11, 1970, and Sean who was born on June 10, 1975. They divorced and Gailard married Yong and they had a son Larry Piper. While Gailord was serving in Korea and was in a DMZ zone, which means a Demilitarized Military Zone, he was shot in the foot and was skipping down the road with bullets flying everywhere, and someone gave him the name "Skip." He wanted to be called Skip till the day he died. He once told me that he never liked his name Gailord because he said I am not 'gay' and I am not a 'lord.' Just call me Skip! Skip had a beautiful voice, once had a band and played the guitar. Skip loved the Lord and attended church on a regular basis.

Skip was an inventor and had created construction machinery. He once became a millionaire and lost it all when someone stole his blueprint plans and changed a few positions of where bolts were to be placed in the machinery he had created, and when he started telling people he was related to the inventors of the Piper Cub Airplane, he got sued. There was no proof of that. Those rumors have been handed down to us from one generation to another but the family members who started the rumors have all passed away. Gailord (Skip) passed away from complications of 'agent orange' from his service days, but I don't have a date.

Another daughter of great uncle Charles and great aunt Pauline was Mary Larue (Piper) Engleman who was born on September 16, 1935 and married Marvin Dean Engleman on March 17, 1954. Mary knew how to sing. Their children were Dorothy Larue (Engleman) Gore who was born on November 5, 1955 and married Robert Dale Gore on September 25, 1971; Sherry Ann (Engleman) Henkel who was born on August 10, 1956 and married Michael Henkel on August 26, 1972 and divorced in 1994; Debra Kay (Engleman) Worthy was born on June 17, 1958 and married Ernest Dale Worthy; Michael Dean Engleman was born on September 14, 1959 and married Carol Buchanan on July 29, 1995; and Ivan Eugene Engleman who was born on April 25, 1961 and died on May 12, 1961.

Great uncle Charles and Pauline's son Milton Emile Piper was born on April 2, 1956 and married Glenda Peters on March 7, 1981. Their children are Nathan Piper, who was born on September 9, 1981, and Preston Piper who was born on December 8, 1982. Milton and Glenda presently live in Independence, Missouri. Milton's brother Tharen and I palled around together for a while, attend Nebraska Christian College together, and drove to Las Vegas together. Their brother Gaylord, (Skip) as he wanted to be called, and his wife Yong, became close friends of both Phyllis and me. Both Tharon and Skip have since passed away. Now Milton and his wife Glenda have become close to us and have helped me in my family research. Milton has played drums and guitar, and once drew a picture of a one-room school that was located in Granite, Oregon.

My 2ⁿᵈ cousin Milton Piper's drawing of a one-room schoolhouse

My great uncle Charles Emil Theodore Piper died at the Gravette Medical Center in Gravette, Arkansas on March 20, 1963 after an extended illness. He had spent most of his early life in Florence, Kansas but in 1947 he moved his family to Decatur, Arkansas where he made his home with his wife and family until he died. His funeral service was held on March 23, 1963 at 3:30 pm at the First Baptist Church in Decatur with Reverend John Stell officiating. His burial was at the new addition of the Decatur Cemetery under the direction of the Wason Funeral Home of Siloam Springs, Arkansas. The pallbearers were: my dad, Bernard Piper, Edward Kister, Phillip Metcalfe, Cliff Mann, Bobby Norton and James Baker.

My great-uncle Fred Edward Piper, son of my great-grandparents August Julius and Mary Ada (Giffler) Piper was born on October 9, 1900 and married Shirley Rosetta Hinchman. Shirley was born on August 5, 1915. They were married on May 18, 1931 with Pete and Pauline Cornelius as witnesses (Pauline was Fred's sister). Shirley had fudged her age and had not even turned 16 years of age yet. Shirley was only 5'2" tall with very dark hair and light blue eyes. Fred and Shirley had 11 children with two sons dying at birth. Fred could play any stringed instrument, and played by ear. Fred also enjoyed dancing, and when he was younger, the girls would stand in line just to dance with him. Fred left home at the age of 16 to work on a ranch as a cowboy in McCook, Nebraska from 1916 to the 1920s. He also worked as an undercover revenuer in Kansas during the prohibition era. When he married Shirley they moved to Florence, Kansas and Fred started working at the Cloverleaf Dairy. He died at his home on October 4, 1972 at age 71 from a heart attack. His funeral service was held at the Rotz Chapel in Florence. Shirley died on December 26, 1995.

My 2nd cousin, Marion (Sarge) Piper from Florence, KS

One of Fred Edward and Shirley Piper's sons was Marion Lawrence Piper, who was known to his family as "Sarge". Marion Lawrence was born on May 29, 1932 in Florence, Marion County, Kansas. He died on April 18, 2007 in a fatal car accident when his car drove off a 180 foot embankment on highway 38, and landed upside down in the Umpqua River near Scottsburg, Oregon. He served in the Marine Corp. and became a Sergeant. He had received a Korean service medal, a United Nations service medal, two Purple Heart medals, a National Defense medal, a Distinguished Service Award, a Distinguished Citizenship Medal, and took training in CPR to become an instructor at the Bakersfield College. His many awards are just too numerous to mention here without my writing another book. For further information on Marion (Sarge) Lawrence Piper read my chapter titled "Buried Alive."

Another child of Fred and Shirley Piper was Betty Jane (Piper) (Mann) Criss who was born June 15, 1933 in Florence, Kansas. She married Clifford F. Mann on December 24, 1950 in Florence and lived on a farm just west of Florence. They divorced in 1972. On February 29, 1980 she married Ramon Daryl Criss in Las Vegas and joined with her husband in his business, Lewis & West, a ready-mix concrete and construction company located in El Dorado. They presently live in El Dorado, Kansas where Betty told me she worked 18 years in the oil industry prior to joining Ramon in his business. She served 9 years on the El Dorado Zoning and Planning Commission, 4 years as a City Commissioner, plus many other civic committees. She is presently completing 8 years on the Kansas Water Authority. Ramon and Betty used to be partners/owners of the El Dorado Country Club, which was sold to the city of El Dorado.

Another child of Fred and Shirley was Loretta Fern (Piper) (Cooksey) Klawitter who was born on September 12, 1934 and lived in Minneapolis, Minnesota with her husband Lawrence. Leland Lester Piper was born on November 19, 1935 and served in the Army in Korea and was killed as a result of an industrial accident in Wichita, Kansas on August 18, 1968 and is buried in Florence, Kansas. Earnest (Ernie) Wayne Piper was born on October 28, 1943 and presently lives in San Diego, California and has a doctorate of law. Ernie was in the Marines and served as Deputy Attorney General in California till his retirement. His daughter Heather (Piper) Strickland has gathered a lot of family history on the Giffler side of the family. Claude Dean Piper who was born on April 19, 1945, died at birth.

Fred and Shirley's other children were: Raymond Eugene Piper who was born on January 8, 1937 and died November 24, 2009 and his ashes are buried at the foot of Kenneth Leroy Piper. Kenneth was born on

December 31, 1940 and died on June 12, 2008. Kenneth had served in the Army. Irwin Eugene Piper was born on January 12, 1938 and died at birth. Rosetta Shirley (Piper) (Siebert) Humphrey was born on June 1, 1939 and died on December 29, 1993, Fred Junior Piper was born June 25, 1942 and date of death unknown.

My cousin Milton recently sent me a copy of an e-mail that he received from Ernest (Ernie) Piper who presently lives in San Diego, California where Ernie describes himself as being age five or six years of age when he traveled to the O.K. Ranch to visit his great-uncle Emil and aunt Anna with his own brother Fred and their parents Fred and Shirley. He recalled his dad driving on a country road northeast of Florence until they came to highway 150, which was a blacktop road back then, and his father turned east for some distance before turning north onto a long gravel driveway, which lead from the highway northward a distance to a small one-story wood frame home with a front porch and was situated on high ground. He states that he remembers that the house had no electricity, was somewhat of a mess, and smelled of coal and oil lamps. They had an outdoor toilet and a chicken coup just north of the house with chickens running around. He remembers being bored with nothing to do except go outside and play in the dirt.

My great-aunt Laura Augusta (Piper) Hinchman, was born on December 26, 1903 in Florence. She married Marion O. Hinchman. She died on December 31, 1988 and is buried in Dunlap next to her husband.

Another great-aunt was Stella Mary (Piper) (Kister) (Van Buren) Vaughn who was born on March 12, 1905 in Florence. She first ran away with Edward Kister to get married when she was quite young. They had been married only a few days when Stella's dad, August, came after them and had their marriage annulled, but in those few days of marriage Stella got pregnant with Eddie L. Kister, Jr. Eddie was born in 1924 and later joined the Marines. It was this son who accidentally shot himself to death in 1970 after playing with his gun, not realizing that his gun was cocked! Rumor has it that Eddie Kister, Jr. had a pet snake and Stella would not let him bring it into the house. They were living in Kansas City at the time.

Stella and her husband Robert Van Buren with their baby, Bonnie about 1938.

Stella's second husband was Robert (Bob) Harold Van Buren, who stood five foot four inches, was always chewing on a plug of tobacco, and was a hard worker. If he needed a plug of tobacco he would dress up in his white gloves and sporty hat and drive six miles into town in his buggy to purchase tobacco for about 10 cents a plug. Gas back then was only about 18 cents a gallon. Bob was born in 1906 and had been raised a Mennonite till he was about 10 years of age. He was an excellent student and never missed a day of school and received a plaque because of it. His son Harold told me that his dad never owned a car after he wrecked his first car shortly after his parents were married.

Bob was working at a farm house north of the town of Clements in Chase County, Kansas, in 1953 as a milker, which is a town just east of Cedar Point about five miles on highway 50 when tragedy struck. The town of Clements is well known for the old stone arch bridge that had been built in 1886 and was an architectural marvel for the Kansas plains.

To this day it still stands as a pedestrian bridge over the Cottonwood River.

Stella's husband Bob died when a fire broke out at the house where he and his son Lawrence were working near Clements in 1953. Bob was on the second floor and his son was on the roof. Bob told his son Lawrence to jump off the roof and go down and rescue two guys who were down below who he thought were still sleeping. What he didn't know was that they had become aware of the fire and had fled. Bob stepped out onto a stair landing and when he did, the landing gave way and Bob fell to his death in the flames below. Stella and two of her husbands, Robert Van Buren and Ralph Vaughn, plus her son Edward L. Kister, Jr. are all buried in Florence.

Stella and Bob's children were: Richard Van Buren who was born in 1931 and married Mary Stackley and lived in Clements, Kansas; Ronald Van Buren was born in 1933 and married Delores Yoakem and lived in El Dorado; Harold Van Buren was born on October 16, 1935 and married Peggy Hollingsworth and they live in Wichita; Bonnie (Van Buren) Romack was born in 1938 and married Claude Romack; Aldonna (Van Buren) (Bailey) Mickle was born in 1939 and first married James (Jimmie) Bailey. Her second husband was Jerry Mickle. Lawrence Van Buren was born in 1942 and married Virginia Klassen; Genevieve was a twin to Geneva and both were born in 1944 but Geneva died in 1978, Genevieve (Van Buren) Wacker married Marten Wacker; and Winifred (Van Buren) Boehrer was born in 1948 and married Alexander Boehrer.

Stella's third husband was Ralph Hayward Vaughn who was born in 1895 in Florence and became a railroad engineer in Newton. Rumor has it that Ralph and Stella could not stand each other, although Ralph kept telling Stella that if she married him and something happened to him, she would have his railroad pension. They married! Stella was very well known as being a good cook. Ralph died in 1973. Stella's son Ronnie lives in Texas but has a home in El Dorado as well. Stella's son Harald and his wife Peggy presently live in Wichita, Kansas. Stella herself died on August 23, 1984 at the age of 79 and is buried in Florence. Her funeral services were held at the Florence Christian Church, and the Draper-Cannon Funeral Home was in charge of the arrangements, (according to the El Dorado Times dated Saturday, August 25, 1984.)

Just recently my wife and I met my second cousin Harold Van Buren and his wife Peggy, my great aunt Stella's son, for the first time at their home in Wichita. One of the stories Harold told me was when he was just a baby and they lived in Florence, Kansas, his family would often provide food for the homeless and transients, and once in a while gypsies would stop by. One day a gypsy woman stopped by their home asking for food. Harold's mother left her newborn son in the living room while she went into the kitchen to gather up some food for the inquiring woman. However, when Stella came back with the food, the gypsy woman was gone, but so was her newborn son! Stella ran out the front door just in time to see the woman running down the street with her son in her arms. Stella yelled for help and her neighbors, hearing her frantic cry, came out just in time to catch the gypsy and return Stella's son to her.

Laura, Charlie, Stella, and Fred Piper–taken at the Carpenters farm just west of Florence, KS

My cousin Harold also told me of a family in Florence that had struck oil and became quite well-to-do but mismanaged their finances and ended up on a poor farm southeast of Hillsboro, Kansas. Back then there were no shelters, only county poor farms where many older people that had no social security or income would go where they would be provided with a bed and maybe a pot of beans to eat. There would be several beds in one room but these poor farms could house up to 30 to 40 people at one time.

Harold told us that he himself had been farmed out when he was quite young by his parents to work because his family just could not afford to feed and house all their own children. I can picture in my mind his widowed mother marrying again and now her children have a step-dad to deal with. The family that Stella's son Harold worked for treated him like a slave, working him several hours each morning before he tried to catch a school bus to school, which he often missed because of the hours, and frequently ended up walking to school no matter what the weather was like, and then upon returning to this family he would work all hours into the night. He never had any funds and hardly proper clothes to wear to school and never knew what a meat meal was until he was about 10 or 11 years of age! That family he worked for should have been horse-whipped, but that's my own opinion.

Great-uncle Stanley Piper was born on July 4, 1908 and died as an infant on August 20, 1908. Great-uncle Edward Piper was born in 1911 and died that same year. Great-aunt Bertha Margaret (Maggie) Nellie (Piper) Cole was born on June 17, 1913 in Florence. She married John Cole. They had lived in Topeka and then Dunlap. Bertha knew how to play the accordion. She died on March 4, 1998 at the age of 88 and is buried in Dunlap. Her services were held at the Dunlap Methodist Church. Great-aunt Viola Minnie (Piper) Metcalf was born on June 6, 1913 in Florence, and she married Virgil Metcalf and died on March 25, 1982 and is buried in Dunlap.

My dad's aunt Pauline (Piper) Cornelius, and her husband Pete

Great-aunt Pauline Alberta (Piper) Cornelius was born on November 25, 1915 in Florence, and she married Leslie (Pete) Allen Cornelius. When they married Pauline was only 16 and Pete was 14 years older. Pete was left-handed and had been afflicted with polio and always walked with a slight limp. Pete was born and raised in Dunlap, and his mother, Minnie Anna (Hoch) Cornelius whom they called grandma Waters, owned a local hotel which burned to the ground in 1950. Pete's dad's name was Joseph (Pete) Peter Cornelius. Pete knew how to play the piano, trumpet and cornet. Pete owned a repair shop where he could repair almost anything from appliances to automobiles, and even worked as a power lineman.

Pauline and Pete had five children: Ann Marie (Cornelius) Blythe was born on January 25, 1933 and married Andrew Kelly Blythe. Ann could play the accordion by ear. Leslie (Tyke) Lee Cornelius was born on April 6, 1934 and was divorced when he died on June 12, 1988, Frankie Ray Cornelius was born on June 30, 1938 and married Rosalie May Pitts, and their children are: Rex Randle Cornelius, born on October 8, 1957 and married Dina Downey but divorced, and then he married Bonnie Ann Nichols and they divorced. Robin Anita (Cornelius) Trent was born on March 7, 1960 and married Franklin Wayne Trent, Russell Wayne Cornelius was born on September 30, 1961 and married Jennie and they are divorced. Russell then married Cindy Lee (Bacon)

Rice. Frankie and Rosalie's son Radford Steven Cornelius was born on June 26, 1964 and married Shawn Lee (Mangold) Brown.

Another child of Pauline and Pete was Alice Kay (Cornelius) Blankley who was born on January 30, 1944 and married Kay Edward Blankley, and their children are Tammy Lynn (Blankley) Marlar who

Pauline and Pete with four of their five children

was born on November 4, 1963 and married Greg Marlar, and Troy Blankley who was born on October 29, 1965 and married Allison Young. Alice Kay could play the trombone.

Another child of Pauline and Pete was Susan (Sue) Elaine (Cornelius) Alexander and she was born on March 29, 1952 and married Jimmy Michael Alexander. Sue can play a trumpet. Their children are: Amber Dawn Alexander who was born on May 12, 1978 and teaches First grade, and Jackie LeAnn (Alexander) Carver who was born on July 20, 1985 and married Thomas Jonathan Carver. Jackie and Thomas have two sons,

My great-aunt Pauline Cornelius's home when it flooded in 1951. Dunlap, KS

Lance Cooper Carver who was born on June 6, 2008, and Stuart Wesson Carver who was born on July 4, 2010.

Dunlap flooded in 1951 and the Cornelius family moved everything up to their second story, including their refrigerator, so they wouldn't lose anything. Their daughter Susan (Sue) Elaine (Cornelius) Alexander told me that the flood was so high that the water came through the windows of their home.

Pauline and Pete also owned and operated two restaurants, one in Dunlap and one in Council Grove. Pauline played the piano, plus she told us that she could play any stringed instrument. She also knew how to do pin curling, barbering and permanents that she did for her family and her lady friends, charging only 25 cents a head.

My great aunt Pauline's daughter Susan (Sue) (Cornelius) Alexander told me that when she was quite young her nephew Bob came to live with them. Sue said that her mother was very much into storm watching, star gazing and whatever was in the old Farmer's Almanac. Sue remembers her mother would literally get up in the middle of the night and wake up Sue and Bob and have them go outside and lie on the hood of the car and gaze up into the night sky to watch the stars. It was during one of these nights when, wouldn't you have guessed, they witnessed a meteor shower. It looked like all the stars were falling from the sky! Sue said it was a wonderful sight.

In the spring time when stormy weather hit the area, Pauline was ready. As soon as the weather man reported a tornado, Pauline would load her kids into the car and go storm watching. She loved stormy weather! To this day Sue says her mother made a weather watcher out of her and she still enjoys storm watching. Sue's husband is a power lineman like Sue's dad was, and while he's out working on the lines, she's out watching the storm clouds.

Sue told me that all the children in their neighborhood loved her mom. Pauline made life fun, whether it was telling ghost stories or wild animal stories. She was always making homemade bread, hot donuts and cookies. There was always something cooking at the Cornelius house. Pauline loved to fish and hunt, and because of her love of the outdoors, she really hit it off with the boys in the neighborhood, and her grandson Bob who came to live with them.

At a Dunlap Fall Festival Pauline came dressed as Peter Pan, and Sue didn't even recognize her own mother! Pauline made quite a show! No one knew for sure what Pauline was going to do next. She had the spice of life right up until the day she died. She had to give up her driver's license in her old age when she got caught going 80 MPH in a 55 MPH zone. She told the patrolman that she was in a hurry. He didn't give her a ticket because she promised him she'd give up her license, which she did. Sue stated that she hopes to be half the mom her mother was, and the grandma that her mother had become. Pete died on June 30, 1977 and Pauline died on August 11, 2009 at the Morris County Hospital at age 93. Sue wrote a poem in memory of her mother titled "Give Me The Love."

"GIVE ME THE LOVE"

"Give me the love of a husband so gentle, sweet and true.
For all those years of love, I never could be blue.

Give me the love of children, let's make the number five.
For without all that love, I never could have survived.

Give me the love of my grands, that make my days so bright.
With all those hugs and kisses, and little sparkling eyes.

Give me the love of country life with meadows dark and green.

Where I shall plant my garden of tomatoes and green beans.

Give me the love of chickens and fishing on a river bank.
Give me the love of giving, with never a need for thanks.
Give me the love of memories, to plant deep inside.
In the heart of each of my loved ones, I never shall have died.

Give me the love of quilting, a gift from above.
To let you know each stitch I stitched was made with heart and love.
Give me the love of God who greets me with open arms.

To walk me through the gates of Heaven, where loved ones have all gone."

We were able to visit with my great aunt Pauline back in 2008 and she died the following year.

My great-aunt Geneva Marjory (Piper) Mustain, was born on October 4, 1922 in Florence. She married Jim Mustain and they lived in Herington when she died. She died on March 28, 1998 at the age of 75, and her funeral services were held at the Donahue Funeral Home. She is buried at the Greenwood Cemetery in Council Grove. My family went to visit my great aunt Geneva when I was quite young and all I can remember was that she had a hunch-back. They had a beautiful daughter by the name of Millie (Mustain) Stone, who we understand had later married Mr. Stone. Phyllis and I met Geneva at a Piper family reunion in 1990 in Cottonwood Falls, Kansas. We sat right next to her but she couldn't hear our conversation because she didn't have her hearing aids in. That was the last time we saw her, and she died in 1998.

My grandfather, William (Will) Otto Julius Piper, was born in Elmdale, Kansas on June 3, 1896. Elmdale is about 19 miles east of Florence, Kansas.

He enlisted in World War 1 in June of 1917 at the age of 21 and was in the 39th Infantry. During the war when Grandpa Will was in Europe, newspapers in the U.S. were asking people to write to the boys overseas, and my grandma, Goldie Ellen Mallory, from Trenton, Nebraska area picked the name of Piper and started writing to my grandpa Will. They wrote back and forth for over a year then they decided to get married when he got out of the service. Grandpa Will was discharged on April 14, 1919 and was paid a $60 travel bonus and went home to Florence, but shortly after he arrived home his parents moved to Doyle Township in Marion County, Kansas. Grandpa Will married my grandma, Goldie Ellen (Mallory) Piper on July 12, 1919 when he came to Nebraska. How he got to Nebraska we don't know, but it was either by covered wagon, horse, buggy, but who knows?

The story goes that when Will Piper showed up at the Mallory farm in Nebraska, Goldie's dad kept chasing Will off his property. Will and Goldie finally were married and it took about 14 days to get to the Doyle Township in Kansas where his parents had moved to. Will and Goldie first lived with his parents, in Doyle Township, Marion County, Kansas, according to the 1920 census, but by the 1925 census they were not living with grandpa's parents but in Nebraska. In fact, they had moved to Nebraska sometime in 1923 because that was where my aunt Marjie was born. The 1930 census showed they were living in Hitchcock County, Nebraska near Trenton on a farm, either living with the Mallory family or nearby. In that 1930 census my dad, Bernard, was only ten years of age, but he remembered when their large red barn caught fire. The fire and smoke could be seen for miles around. It was shortly afterwards that they moved back to Florence, Kansas, in the later part of 1930.

My grandparents had become members of the Florence Christian Church, but they moved to the Kansas City area and Grandpa Will worked at the Union Railroad Station in Kansas City, Missouri in his later years and was their mail handler. When a train pulled into the station his job was to take the large pouch of mail and distribute it to the right stations, and he ended up as their foreman. When Grandpa Will retired he would drive to the union station and stay almost all night hanging around the station visiting with his former employees. Grandpa must have loved his job but was forced into retirement? In his later years Grandpa Will had a stroke and had been moved to a nursing home in Desoto, Kansas. My second wife, Ina, and I had stopped in Desoto in 1972 to see my grandpa, and as soon as I walked in the door of his room he said "Hi Frankie!" With his stroke I was told he didn't recognize anyone, so I was thrilled he remembered me. When I left there I sat in our car and cried like a baby. I hadn't seen him in years, and now he was in this nursing home after his stroke and I knew I would probably never see him again. Grandpa Will died on July 7, 1974 at the Wadsworth Hospital in Leavenworth, Kansas. When he died Grandpa's oldest grandsons were pallbearers, including me.

Grandma Goldie died on June 19, 1966 a few days after she and grandpa were involved in a car accident, and her funeral services were held on June 23, 1966 at the Amos Family Chapel with Reverend Bill Keever from the Westside Christian Church in Kansas City, Missouri officiating. Songs played were "Goodnight, Goodmorning," and "Beyond The Sunset." Organist was Mrs. Richard Parks and the soloist was Mrs. Gilbert Haglin. Grandma Goldie Piper was buried next to grandpa at the old Monticello Cemetery in Johnson County, Kansas

When I was coming through Kansas City shortly after grandpa's death, my aunt Bernadine loaned us the keys to grandpa's old farm house in Zarah and told us we could take anything we wanted. We drove over to the farm and toured through the house and yard. Many childhood memories flooded my thoughts as we walked through the house. Still left in that house was a kitchen stove, a small kitchen table, their old dresser drawer in their bedroom with the large oval mirror on top, which I so wanted to take with us but had no tools to take it apart to transport back to Denver, and the old bed frame and box springs they had slept on for years. When we walked around the yard I saw the old lean-to's out back and found an old Minnesota Model A sewing machine that was over 100 years old and grabbed it. I found out later that that this sewing machine was given to Grandma Piper by the Mallory family as a gift. I tried crawling under their old home on the backside of the house where there was a crawl space, but it was so dark under there all I could see was an old wooden pickle barrel, which I took. Had I known that their old home was eventually going to be torn down I would have taken pictures of it and taken all that I could to remember them by.

What I was told was that my Grandpa Will had a trunk that contained the letters he had received from Goldie while he was in the service. His WW I uniform was in that trunk as well as service medals, plus pictures he had taken in Germany, including pictures of his grandparents' home there in Germany. He also had pictures drawn by his great-grandma Minna Ponto. Minna had been an artist. What happened to my Grandpa Will's trunk and the contents?

My cousin Gene told me about the times that our Grandpa Will used to stop by a local convenience store with a bar after work near their farm in Zarah, Kansas to have a beer or two. The owner was the same age as grandpa but was from France. One day they were talking about WWI and they found out that they both had been at one time in the same fox hole during the war! I was with my dad and my grandpa one time when they stopped by there for a drink. I wasn't very old, but can still remember the two of them drinking a beer together at the bar.

My grandparents had eight children. Their oldest son was my dad, Bernard (Bernie) Hobert Piper, born on March 19, 1920 in Florence, Kansas. According to my dad, he was named after a horse that came up to his parent's kitchen window. When I spoke to dad's only living sister, Joan (Piper) Patch, she said she only remembers their parents owning a mule. My dad married my mother, Pauline Evelyn (Day) Piper, in Burns, Kansas, on January 3, 1942. A week after they married, dad was drafted into the army, and had to report to Camp Barkley in Abilene, Texas. Because my dad was wounded while serving his country, he was presented with a purple heart for military merit, a medal for good conduct, along with many other medals, and for many years dad served in the Civil Air Patrol. I have no medals. Dad died in his sleep on November 19, 2002. He had become forgetful and our family decided to take him to a nursing home in Grand Junction, Colorado where my sister Debi was a nurse. He wasn't there but a few days when he was found dead. They said he had died sometime around 6:30AM because his body was still warm when he was found. When my sister came into work they told her. She could not go down into that section of the nursing home after that. We flew dad's body back to Denver for burial at the Ft. Logan Cemetery.

I, their oldest son, Bernard (Frank)(Frankie) Franklin Piper, was born in Kansas City, Kansas on November 7, 1942, and better known now as Frankie Valens. I have always loved music and drama and was quite a dancer growing up. My brother Douglas (Dougie) (Doug) Otto Piper, was born in Kansas City, Kansas on September 30, 1946. Dougie wasn't into music and wouldn't even wear shorts. Other than that I don't know what he liked. My sister Deborah (Debi) Paula Diane (Piper) Garner was born in Kansas City, Kansas on January 22, 1954.

My grandparents' other seven children were: Bernadine Hazel (Piper) Thomson, who was born at home in Florence, Kansas on December

8, 1921 and married George Thomson. They had two children, Kathy Louise (Thomson) Dunn, who married Dave Dunn, and Barbara Ellen (Thomson) Brice. Bernadine died at the age of 84 on April 5, 2006 from breast cancer and is buried next to her husband George at the old Monticello Cemetery in Shawnee, Johnson County, Kansas. George was born on January 22, 1918 and died on July 31, 2003. They leave behind three grandchildren, Stephanie (Dunn) Bruns, Stacey (Dunn) Noland, and Ryan Brice.

Grandpa Will and grandma Goldie's other children were, Louise Goldie (Piper) (Haney) (Fangrow) Barclift, who was born at home in Trenton, Nebraska on January 17, 1925 and married and divorced numerous husbands including William Haney, James Fangrow, and finally Rex Barclift. She had four sons, William (Gene) Eugene Haney, who lived most of his life with Will and Goldie our grandparents, and then David Fangrow, Johnny Fangrow and Roger Barclift. Marjie Maxine (Piper) Bowen was born at home in Palisades, Nebraska on June 2, 1923 and married Orlo Bowen, a full-blooded Indian. Marjie and Orlo's children were Pat (Bowen) McCarthy, Charlene, Leon, Marketa, Donna and Kathy. My aunt Marjie lived the rest of her life in Wichita, Kansas and is buried in Peabody, Kansas. We attended her funeral.

My dad's sister Marjie, and her husband Orlo

My uncle Bill (Billy) John Piper was born at home in Culberston, Nebraska on February 7, 1926 and married Phyllis Brice. Their children were Gary, Theresa (Terri) (Piper)

Carroll, Joe, and Pamela (Piper) Morse. Billy died on March, 10, 1978. He is buried at the old Monticello Cemetery in Shawnee, Johnson County, Kansas. Mary Jane Piper was born in Lindsey, Oklahoma and died three days later. What I've been told is that she was born after her brother Billy was born, and there are still conflicting stories as to where she died three days later. Some say Enid, and some say Lindsey, Oklahoma. My own dad tried to find Mary Jane's grave and couldn't find it.

Robert (Bobby) Doyle Piper was born at home on July 15, 1929 in Trenton, Nebraska. Bobby married Lois and they divorced. He never claimed his ex-wife's daughter, Nancy, as his own and he died of a massive heart attack on June 13, 1973 and is buried at the old Monticello Cemetery in Shawnee, Johnson County, Kansas. Joan (Annie) Ruth (Piper) Patch was born at home in Florence on December 16, 1931 and married Fred O. Patch. Their children are Mike and Patty. Donald (Donny) Eugene Piper was born at a hospital in Florence on April 20, 1933 and married an older woman, Nancy. Donny served in the U.S. Air Force in Korea. They had no children. Donny died on December 30, 1987 from complications of pneumonia and is buried at the Lewis Cemetery, Ramona, Marion County, Kansas. As of this writing the only living person of that whole generation of aunts and uncles of mine is my Aunt Joan (Annie) Ruth (Piper) Patch, my dad's sister, who presently lives in Kansas City.

I was the oldest of the three children of Bernard (Bernie) Hobert Piper and Pauline Evelyn (Day) Piper, and was born in Kansas City, Kansas on November 7, 1942. My favorite foods of all time are spaghetti, fried potatoes and home-made potato salad, beef tips and noodles, all types of fruit, most vegetables, crab legs dipped in hot butter, cherry pie or any pie with a graham cracker crust, and any meal served on a bed of rice. My favorite singers are Andy Williams, Celene Dion, Steve Perry from the group Journey, the Beatles as a group, and Paul McCartney as a solo singer. My favorite songs of all time are "My Heart Will Go On" from the movie Titanic, "Feed The Birds" from the movie The Sound Of Music, "Drive" sung by the group called The Cars, and "Unchained Melody" sung by the Righteous Brothers. My favorite gospel group is The Hoppers. My favorite books to read are "Heaven Is For Real" which was written about a 4 year old boy who spent time in Heaven and explains what he saw and who he met there, and the book "Within Heavens Gates" that was written by Rebecca Springer of the time she spent in Heaven in the late 1800s. Both books are such a blessing and will help bring hope to the lost.

I married Joyce Ann Biondo on July 1, 1963 in Hinton, Oklahoma. Our children are Jennifer Sue (Piper)(Cunningham) Biondo, born on July 1, 1964 in Las Vegas, Nevada, and Brian Franklin Piper, born on April 29, 1966 in Morristown, New Jersey. Brian married Christine Danielle Giordano and they have twin sons, James Marshall and Marshall James. Brian and Christine presently live in Flanders, New Jersey. Jennifer had been married to K.C. Cunningham and she had a miscarriage and they had their marriage annulled. She and Eric, her significant other, presently live in Parsippany, New Jersey. Joyce and I resided first in Henderson, Nevada, then in North Las Vegas before moving to New Jersey, and we divorced in 1971.

I met Ina Kay (Dawes) Donkersloot in 1971 in Whippany, New Jersey and we married in 1972 in Commerce City, Colorado. Ina Kay had been married to John (Jack) R. Donkersloot, Jr. Ina Kay had a son Jeffrey (Jeff) Allen Donkersloot whom I later adopted as my own son when he was about 5 years of age, and we changed his name legally to Jeffrey Bernard Piper. Ina's maiden name of Dawes stems back to the famous John Dawes who rode on another route as Paul Revere rode warning the people that the British were coming. Her grandfather was born and raised in England and came to the U.S. before WW1 but went to Canada to help fight because he was not a U.S. citizen at that time. My adopted son Jeffrey has a trunk that his great-grandfather used while in the war. Ina says she remembers as a child meeting Joshua O. Dawes from England who was one of the founders of soccer in the U.S.

Our first baby, as a newly married couple, was a miscarriage. We then had two more children, Mark Eric Piper, born on June 24, 1975 in Denver, Colorado, who married Ashleigh Wallace, and they had one son, Alec Craig (Piper) Wallace, and they are now divorced. Mark has a daughter, Zanna-Maryee Alexandra Cole, with Dawn Cole. Our second child was Heather Ann (Piper) (Sherman) Allen, born on January 27, 1977. Heather was first married to Matt Sherman, but they divorced. She is now married to Michael (Mikee) Patrick Allen. Mikee was born on October 28, 1977. Heather and Mikee have five children: Haley Ann Piper, born on June 13, 1993 in Denver; Heidi Ann Simpson, born on March 20, 1995 in Denver; Tyler Nichol Sherman, born on December 2, 2000 in Denver; Cody Ryan Sherman, born on January 13, 2005 in Denver; and Braedyn Patrick Allen, born on March 9, 2009 in Denver. Ina Kay and I resided in the Denver, Colorado area our whole married life, and we divorced in 1983.

I met Phyllis Jeanette (Cook) Warfel in Aurora, Colorado, and we married in 1985 in Denver, Colorado. Phyllis had been married to Sam Warfel and they divorced. Together they had two daughters, Deborah (Debbie) Renee (Warfel) Harmon, who was born on March 24, 1960 and married Meredith Harmon. They presently live in Lincoln, Nebraska. Their second daughter was Penny Lyn Warfel who was born on April 3, 1962 and presently lives in Lakewood, Colorado. Phyllis and I live in Clearwater, Kansas, which is southwest of Wichita.

My parent's second child was Douglas (Dougie) (Doug) Otto Piper, who was born on September 30, 1946 in Kansas City. He married Andrea (Linburg) Piper on July 19, 1987. Andrea had one daughter, Honey Lindberg, from a previous marriage, but Doug and Andrea had no children together, and they divorced in 1997. Doug presently lives in Wellston, Oklahoma with Carlotta Thompson, and our mother, Pauline Evelyn (Day) Piper.

My sister, Deborah (Debi) Paula Diane (Piper) Garner, was born on January, 22, 1954 in Kansas City, Kansas. Mom told me that she spent three days in labor with Debi. Debi married Rick Garner from Grand Junction, Colorado, and they had three children, Karlie, Aaron, and Brandon. Debi and Rick are now divorced, and Debi lives in the Denver, Colorado area. She is planning on a marriage to Peter Jovanovic from Chicago in June of 2011.

My dad, Bernard (Bernie) Hobert Piper, worked as a lumber yard foreman in his early years when I was a young boy. Later in life he became a preacher, with pastorates in Kansas, Oklahoma, Missouri, Louisiana, Colorado, and Texas until his retirement. The last church my dad preached at before he retired

My father preaching in Texarkana, TX in the 1980s

was the La Harpe Christian Church in La Harpe, Kansas. My mother, Pauline, has always been a housewife and a homemaker and never learned to drive a car.

616

Over the years I had always heard rumors that the Piper Cub airplane inventors were in our Piper family tree. Since there are so many branches of the Piper family originating from Germany and England, I have yet to find a direct link which would connect my family directly to the Piper Cub airplane. I'm not saying we are not related, I just haven't found the link. My cousin, Betty Criss, in El Dorado, Kansas had talked with one of the Piper families involved with the Piper Cub, and they told her that their ancestry originated in England. In my research I came across many Pipers that migrated to England from Germany in the late 1800s and early 1900s. Could there still be a connection? Maybe the William T. Piper on our 40-cent postage stamp is a shirt-tail relative? That William T. Piper, Sr. was born in Kingston, New York. His parents were from England. I have no one to ask in my family that knew the connections, because all of them have passed away.

William T. Piper, Sr. was a Spanish-American War veteran and a WW 1 captain in the Corps of Engineers, and in 1941 he proposed to the war department that light planes be used, and through his persistence the war department approved the trial use of light planes. At his own expense he supplied eight new J-3 Cub airplanes equipped with radios to the war department. He was convinced that small airplanes could aid the defense forces of his country, and went to considerable lengths to prove it. He died at age 89 and is buried in the Piper Family Mausoleum on top of a hill near Lock Haven University, overlooking the city of Lock Haven. His son, William T. Piper, Jr. then took over the family business. He did not live in the shadow of his more famous father, having made his own name in aviation and beyond. He died at age 96, but there is the Piper Aviation Museum in Lock Haven, Pennsylvania and the Piper family is very proud of the exhibits that record the Piper history that only a Piper would know. The museum's collection includes aircraft and equipment, an ever-expanding archives collection of the family records, flight journals, photographs, and memorabilia. The collection begins with the establishment of the Piper Aircraft back in 1937 and continues through history up until now at the Vero Beach plant in Florida. The town of Lock Haven, Pennsylvania is known as 'the home of the Piper Cub.' You can contact the museum by visiting their web site: "http://www.pipermuseum.com" www.pipermuseum.com.

The only other 'Piper' pilot I came across while searching the internet was an Allan Eugene Piper, Jr. who was born August 20, 1954 in Northampton, Massachusetts, the only son of Allan and Mary (Therrien) Piper. He graduated from Hopkins Academy in Hadley, Massachusetts in 1978. In 1979 he moved to Paradise, California where he started his training to become a pilot. He married Sheri Lea Queer and then opened the Piper School of Aviation in 1981. Allan was 54 when he died on December 27, 2008. His ashes were privately scattered on the Piper's 175 year old family farm in the North Hampton area. Is he another shirt-tail relative?

We may or may not be related to the Pipers in aviation but during my extensive research I also discovered through my Aunt Bernadine that there was heart disease and traveling arthritis in the Piper family, but I didn't take it seriously, until now! After so much research that I had to do into my family history I have now come to the conclusion that she was right. After I passed out recently and had to be rushed to the emergency room at a hospital in Wichita, I too realized that there was something seriously wrong. Tests showed that I had had a silent heart-attack earlier in my life and it had left permanent damage to my heart! I was placed on a strict diet and special medicines. This was a wake-up call for me.

I found out that my dad's brother Bobbie died of a massive heart-attack. His dad, my grandpa Will had a stroke and had to be placed in a nursing home until his death. My own sister Debi, had a stroke and has recovered. My cousin Gene Haney has had a stroke and recovered. My great-great grandma Minna died of a massive heart-attack. My cousin Milton said he has had heart attacks and has had heart surgery, and his brother Carl died of a sudden heart attack. Carl's son Darrel died of a sudden heart attack. Milton's brother Skip had three heart surgeries, and his brother Charles August Eugene had at least one heart surgery. My mother's sister Helen tried getting out of their car when they arrived home and she fell to the ground as soon as she got out. They said she was dead before she hit the ground! Fred Conrad Piper died of a massive heart-attack in Manhattan, Kansas after shoveling snow from his sidewalk.

Former home of Fred Conrad Piper in Manhattan, KS

I will continue to do extensive research into my family history and who knows what I might find yet. When my mother gave me a picture of her own mother as a three year old sitting on her mother's lap, and telling me she never remembered what her grandmother's name was, that ignited a flame within me to search all records until I could find the name of my mother's grandmother. My mother's grandmother died when her own mother was between the ages of three and four years of age, and then her grandpa remarried. Through my research I found the name of my mother's grandmother, including when she was born and when she died, and then I found who my great grandfather's second wife was. Read my chapter called "Hazel And The Butts Family."

SEVENTY SIX
GIFFLER'S THREE WIVES!

My dad's mother, grandma Goldie Ellen (Mallory) Piper's mother, my great-grandma Rosa Leuna (Fleming) Mallory was born on September 30, 1876 in Matoon, Illinois. She later married John Francis Mallory. Great-grandma Rosa was one of eight children born to my great-great-grandpa David Fleming and great-great grandma Rebecca Ellen (Davis) Fleming. Great-great grandpa David Fleming was born on November 8, 1851 in Shelby, Indiana. When he was a small boy, he and his parents moved to Jasper County, Illinois where they lived until 1883, when they came to Hitchcock County, Nebraska to live.

In the next few paragraphs I will lead you back to my great-grandma Rosa on her mother, Rebecca E. (Davis) Fleming's side of the family, which started with Christian Rhoads, who was born in Germany, and also died in Germany, and through his son Heinrich Rhoads' son, Henry Rhoads, Sr.! Heinrich himself died in Germany. Henry Rhoads, Sr. married Catherine Reinhardt, daughter of Ulrich and Catherine Reinhardt. Most of the family lines of Rhoads, Faust, Mathes and Reinhardt came from central Germany around Mannheim.

If someone were to check out the Rhoads family history online they will discover that Captain Henry Rhoads was a delegate from Pennsylvania in the First Continental Congress in Philadelphia in 1776.

He and his brothers were sent to Kentucky by Colonel Muhlenberg to survey and scope out the wilderness. They were instrumental in developing and setting McClain and Muhlenberg counties in Kentucky. Captain Henry Rhoads' original home that had been built in 1792 is still standing. In fact, his house in on the National Historical Register, and the family cemetery sits right across the street.

Captain Henry served in the Kentucky legislature for many years and was well-known as the 'Father of Muhlenberg.!' A beautiful historical marker was placed on the highway near his old historical house, and history books contain a lot of information about the Rhoads family. When the Rhoads family first migrated to America their last name was spelled either Rohdt, or Rodt. Those history files may go back as far as the early 1600's.

My cousin Barbara (Newman) Howard just recently purchased the book "The Rhoads Family In America" published by a descendent of Captain Henry Rhoads, and it mentions that Heinrich Rhoads, Sr. with his son, Heinrich Rhoads (Rode) Jr. and Daniel Rhoads, which was probably another son, was listed on October 31, 1737 on the passenger list of the ship William that was coming to America from Germany. Heinrich Rhoads was born in Manhiem, Germany in 1686 and married Catherine Cauble (Cabel) in 1707. Catherine was the daughter of Abraham Cauble and she was born in Manhiem, Germany in 1688. Heinrich Rhoads Sr. bought land in Frederick County, Maryland and died there in 1748. This Heinrich Rhoads is the son of Christian Rhoads (Rhodt) of Palatinate, Germany. Our direct line of Rhoads is through Daniel who was born on October 5, 1755 in Epharata, Pennsylvania and married Eva Elizabeth Faust, daughter of Nicholas Faust. Nicholas was born on February 10, 1777. Eva died in Nelson County, Kentucky in 1792 and Daniel later married Elizabeth Newman. Elizabeth was born on March 15, 1794. Daniel was raised in the Brothers Valley area of Pennsylvania and died in Edgar County, illinois on April 26, 1839 and is buried with many family members in the Ogden Cemetery south of Paris, Illinois.

Henry Rhoads, Sr. and Catherine's son Daniel married Eve Elizabeth Faust, daughter of Nicholas and Catherine (Mathes) Faust. Daniel and Eve (Faust) Rhoads' son, Jacob Rhoads, married Elizabeth Ripple. Elizabeth was the daughter of Micheal Ripple.

Jacob and Elizabeth (Ripple) Rhoads' daughter, Letita Rhoads, married Ballinger Maloney, son of John and Susan (Crawford) Maloney. Ballinger and Letita (Rhoads) Maloney's daughter Arminda, married George Wiley Davis. George Wiley Davis's parents were Presley and Wila Davis. George and Arminda (Rhoads) Davis's daughter Rebecca married David Fleming, and it was David and Rebecaa's daughter, Rosa Leuna Fleming who married John Mallory. Read on!

Great-great grandma Rebecca Ellen Davis was born on December 10, 1855 in Edgar County, Illinois. Rebecca Ellen (Davis) Fleming's parents were George Wiley Davis, who was born in Edgar County, Illinois on August 16, 1832 and died in St. Clair County, Missouri on January 15, 1911, and his wife Arminda (Maloney) Davis who was born in Edgar County, Illinois on December 21, 1832 and died in St. Clair County, Missouri on March 18, 1904 of Diphtheria. George Wiley Davis's parents were Presley and

George and Arminda (Maloney) Davis were the parents of my great-grandma Rosa Mallory

Wila (Kelly) Davis. Arminda (Maloney) Davis's parents were Ballinger and Letita (Rhoads) Maloney. Presley Davis's parents were George and Elizabeth (Abel) Davis, and Wila (Kelly) Davis's parents were William and Elsie (Eason) Kelly.

George and Arminda's children included: William A. Davis who was born on April 30, 1854 and died on July 4, 1878, Rebecca Ellen Davis (my ancestry line), was born on December 10, 1855 but we have no record of her death, Sylvester E. Davis was born on December 24, 1857 and died on March 7, 1889, Jacob M. Davis was born on December 23, 1859 and died in 1941, John H. Davis was born on March 29, 1862 and died on June 7, 1896, Jerry M. Davis was born on July 30, 1864 and died in 1876, Marian E. Davis was born on February 17, 1867 and died in 1924, Susan C. Davis was born on January 4, 1871 and died on August 25, 1892, Fred Riley Davis was born on July 7, 1874 and died in October, 1918, and Eddie S. Davis (Eddison) (Addison) was born on September 7, 1876 and died on October 17, 1876. A June 2, 1885 census that was taken for Blue Springs, Gage County, Nebraska showed they also had a daughter Elsie Davis who was born about 1884. She would have been born 8 years after her parent's last son Eddie was born in 1876!

David and Rebecca Flemings children were: Clement Samuel Fleming, born August 1, 1879 in Matoon, Illinois who later married Eliza Dewey. Clement had been in poor health for some time and his condition worsened. His wife Eliza died on January 16, 1926, and Clement died on October 14, 1959 in Hastings at the home of his daughter, Mrs. Gladys Thumser. It was reported that when Clement's wife died he made his daughters walk into town to sell eggs. He is survived by five daughters: Mrs. Neva (Fleming) Meyers and Mrs. Gladys (Fleming) Thumser of Culbertson, Mrs. Susan (Fleming) Eskew of Imperial, Mrs. Alice (Fleming) Brot and Mrs. Beulah (Fleming) Polackwich of California.

Census records show that the Davis family had come from Kentucky before migrating north to Edgar County, Illinois. Later, a branch of the Davis family migrated to California. One of my great-grandma Rosa's uncles had been a wagon master for the famous wagon train that was involved with the famed Donner Party. That branch of the family converted to the Mormon faith. The Donner Party, sometimes called the Donner-Reed Party, was a group of American pioneers who set out for California in wagon trains and was delayed with a series of mishaps and had to spend the winter of 1846-47 snowbound in the Sierra Nevada. You can find this information in the history books. Some of the family stopped in Sherman and Sheridan Counties in Kansas to settle down, although some became ill and died. It was then that some of the family wanted to return to Illinois, but when they were on their way they received a letter from their great-grandmother's brother in St. Clair County, Missouri and with that letter they decided to move there instead. A family member remembers that the family had traveled all winter long in a covered wagon pulled by oxen.

One daughter of my great-great grandparents David and Rebecca Fleming was Stella May (Fleming) Hinkle who was born on May 14, 1883 in Matoon, Illinois, and she later married William A. Hinkle. She died on April 29, 1969 in Benkelman, Nebraska and was buried at the Trenton Cemetery. Another daughter was Mary Arminda (Fleming) Silver, who was born on December 31, 1887 south of Trenton in Hitchcock County, Nebraska. She later married Clarence Artell Silver and had nine children: She died at the El Dorado Manor in Trenton on July 23, 1982. Another daughter was Della Florence (Fleming) Johnson who was born on February 25, 1891 in Hitchcock, Nebraska. She later married Frank Edward Johnson, and died on January 18, 1947 in Lincoln, Nebraska.

My great-great grandparent's son Frances (Doc) Fleming was born on July 11, 1894 in Hitchcock, Nebraska. He had a terrible accident, when he tripped trying to hop over a fence, and the gun he had in his hand discharged, causing a fatal wound. He was immediately taken to the home of the Johnson brothers, where three doctors were summoned to try to save his life. He only lived about twelve hours after being found. Another daughter was Dolly (Fleming) Beeney who was born on December 1, 1898 in Portis, Kansas. (Portis is a small town just south of Smith Center, Kansas.) She married Guy Sutton Beeney, and she died on February 7, 1972 in Lincoln, Nebraska.

Rosa Leuna (Fleming) Mallory, my great-grandmother, was born on September 30, 1876 in Matoon, Illinois. She married John Francis Mallory and she died on December 21, 1960 in Henderson, Nevada. My great grandma Rosa is buried at the Trenton cemetery, in Trenton, Nebraska.

My great-great grandpa David Fleming's parents were my great-great-great grandparents John and Elizabeth Fleming. We know they had at least four sons and one daughter: David Fleming, Samuel McConnell Fleming, James Albert Fleming, Isaac A. Fleming, and Martha (Fleming) Seaney.

My great-great uncle Samuel McConnell Fleming was born on July 2, 1849 in Scioto County, Ohio (near Portsmouth), and married my great-great aunt Mary Jane Hull on February 11, 1872. Mary Jane (Hull) Fleming was born near Belfast, Ireland on April 26, 1853 and died April 26, 1932. Mary Jane and Samuel were members of the Methodist Episcopal Church and a faithful follower of the Lord. Their children were: Nellie (Fleming) Thompson who was born on January 9, 1888. She married William R. Thompson, and she died on May 2, 1960. John

William Fleming was born on December 29, 1873 in Matoon, Illinois and married Jassamine Scott. He died on July 5, 1943. In 1883 he and his parents came to Nebraska in a covered wagon, but on the way one of his sisters and an infant brother died. The journey took the family till 1895 to arrive at the homestead in Hitchcock, Nebraska. John's occupation was farming and auctioneering. Everyone who knew him says he was fond of children and he had a sense of humor. Another son was Samuel O. Fleming who was born in October, 1896. A daughter Minnie Fleming Smith was born in 1878 and married O. C. Smith. She died on June 5, 1943 in Bremerton, Washington. A daughter, Lillie (Fleming) Taylor was born on December 4, 1894 and married Elmer Taylor. She died on June 5, 1943. Great-great Uncle Samuel died on March 29, 1935 in Trenton, Nebraska at the ripe old age of 85 years, eight months and 27 days.

My great-great uncle James Albert Fleming was born on January 13, 1833 in Scioto County, Ohio, and married Mary Susan Singer, who was born on May 18, 1844 in Tremble, Kentucky. Their children were: Willis Arthur Fleming, who was born in July, 1865. Frank Floyd Fleming was born in February 1867 and married Lizzie Brown. One of their sons, Ray Verner was born on July 31, 1892 and drowned on August 4, 1902 and is buried at the Fair Plains cemetery. Was Ray Verner his given name or was Mary Susan (Singer) Fleming married before? This cemetery is old and there are no roads leading to it. Great-great Uncle James Albert Fleming died on December 30, 1897 and great-great Aunt Mary Susan (Singer) Fleming died on December 7, 1912. Both are buried at the Fair Plains Cemetery near Hitchcock, Nebraska.

My great-great Uncle James and Mary Fleming's daughter Ida May (Fleming) Cox was born in September, 1874 and married Charles A. Cox. She died on December 26, 1902. Owen David Fleming was born in 1878 and married Josephine Clara Baker. Owen died on April 20,

1965. Owen and Josephine Clara (Baker) Fleming had one son, Joseph (Joe) Owen Fleming. Joseph was born on October 7, 1908 in the Stone Church Community on the Fleming homestead south of Culbertson, Nebraska. His mother Josephine Clara (Baker) Fleming died at their farm near Trenton, Nebraska.

I met Joe and Thelma (Phelps) Fleming when I was a young child still living at home. My parents took us to Trenton, Nebraska to a small farm house where I met Joe, my fifth cousin, and his wife Thelma. Joe had a train collection with circus animals and people that he had hand-carved. These trains were displayed high on their living-room walls. Joe had carved 704 baggage horses, 317 ring horses, 280 ponies and 92 elephants, many of which were hand-painted. Each horse is complete with rope or string tails painted to match. A few other beasts included in the menagerie were hyenas, a jaguar, apes, a wild hog, an ant eater and a giraffe. Joe's favorite train was a 20-car train with the mythical name of "Fleming Brothers."

Joe also branched out into constructing motorized circuses. He built two, each consisting of 12 truck and trailer rigs carrying the circus animals, tents and equipment. One of these he called "Jimmy Johnson," a name Joe's mother used to call him. Another circus-related hobby of Joe's was a hand-drawn parade he called "Flemings Parade." This hand-drawn parade fills 126 sheets of 4 ½ by 11 inch paper and it took him over a year to draw by coal-oil lamps in 1939. The sketching was first done with a lead pencil and the final outline and finishing touches were done with a fountain pen.

Joe used to tell the story about his family when they had moved to a farm in the valley southeast of Trenton, where he grew up and attended Trenton High School. Joe began farming the family farm, and on June

29, 1934 he married Thelma Phelps at Oberlin, Kansas. When Joe retired from farming because of his health, he and Thelma moved into Trenton.

Mr. Joe Fleming poses with the circus wagon he the years.
hand-made in 1937. This was the project that inspired   Fleming, a farmer by trade, used many evening and
the many circus trains, Fleming has constructed over   spare hours to build his collection.   (HCN Photo)

March 6, 1991
HCN

Circus dreams become reality

My fifth cousin, Joe Fleming

When Joe was younger he was an accomplished musician and played trumpet in the community band. His hobby and love was the circus and during his lifetime he hand-carved animals for several circus trains that he had carved and built. These trains are now in local museums. One 25 circus car train, known as the "Fleming and Orton" is displayed at the museum in Trenton. He had also given another train he carved to the High Plains Museum in McCook, and one to the Holdrege museum.

When Joe got older he started a new hobby of collecting baseball caps. The first cap that started the collection was given to him by a friend in California, Jack Kirby. In 1987 when Joe was interviewed by the NTV Network, he had 3,566 caps. His whole garage was nothing but shelves and shelves of caps all tucked away neatly in shoe boxes. Before Joe died there are over 13,000 caps in his collection. Phyllis and I visited Joe and Thelma while on tour several years ago and witnessed his cap collection first hand. Thelma kept an inventory sheet of each cap.

While visiting them, Joe had us drive out to their old farm where he and Thelma had lived and asked me to drive out into the open field towards a clump of trees off in the distance. When I had driven close to those trees, Joe had me stop. He pointed towards the trees in the gully and stated that his farm house used to sit down there amongst those trees. He and Thelma had planted those trees themselves, but when a flood came through, they had to have their home moved to higher ground. He showed us a couple of oil wells situated on his old property that still pump oil and told us that he and Thelma will always reap the benefits of those oil wells as long as they are alive, but after their death, the oil well profits will go to the new owners of their old farm.

It was during this visit that Joe rode with us in our van on an old gravel road and directed me to a corn field and pointed out a lone tree standing in the middle of the field. He told us that he had relatives buried near that tree. Since Joe was too old to trek across the field I decided to walk over and take a look for myself. As I was nearing the tree my heart began to beat a little faster with the excitement of maybe finding a tombstone or a marker. As soon as I walked up to that lone tree and looked under its branches, I saw natural stone markers standing upright right next to that tree that had the letter "P" on them. At first I thought the "P" meant that a Piper was buried there, but when I returned back to our van Joe told me that Frank Peyton was buried there. Frank was a cousin to Joe's father Owen David Fleming, and would have been Joe's second cousin. I don't remember if Joe told me that just Frank Peyton was buried there or Frank and his wife.

Joe died on Sunday, March 26, 1995 at the El Dorado Manor Home in Trenton, Nebraska at the age of 86. His services were held at the United Methodist Church in Trenton on March 30, 1995 with Pastor George Kilmer presiding. An organ selection was played of "Red Sails In The Sunset." Thelma Fleming, Joe's wife, was 93 years of age and was living in a nursing home in Trenton, Nebraska and had a tumor on her liver and had colon cancer. She died on January 3, 2011.

Another son of my great-great-great grandparents John and Elizabeth Fleming was my great-great uncle Isaac A. Fleming, who was born on February 24, 1831 in Scioto County, Ohio. He left home in October of 1850 and migrated west and ended up in Jasper County, Illinois where he met and married Rosa Walls. She was a devoted Christian all her life. On September 12, 1888 she died, and in 1890 he married Martha Bonder and he gave his heart to the Lord and joined the Christian Church and was a Christian the rest of his life. He died on December 15, 1916 at age 85 and is laid to rest at the Watson Cemetery, according to the Effingham Illinois Republican newspaper. This cemetery is a small, well-kept cemetery and is located south of Pittsfield, in Pike County, Illinois. No stone marker has been found to identify his grave.

I just found the records for my great-great-great grandparent's daughter, Martha (Fleming) Seaney. She was born in Scioto County, Ohio on July 29, 1844 and married William Riley Seaney and their children included: Ella Mae (Seaney) Crozier was born on October 23, 1871 in Crawford County, Illinois and married Ellis Benton Cozier. They had a least one son, Alva Ellis Crozier who was born on January 3, 1891 in Duncanville, Crawford County, Illinois and married Edna Aline (Lowrance) Crozier and Alva died on November 1, 1952 and is buried at the New Hebron Cemetery in Palestine, Crawford County, Illinois. Ella Mae died on June 15, 1944 and is buried at the New Hebron Cemetery in Palestine, Crawford County, Illinois.

The other children of Martha (Fleming) Seaney and William, was Annie Maude (Seaney) Neville, who was born on January 1, 1874 in Crawford County, Illinois and first married David Hamilton. Her second husband was Otis Neville. Annie died on September 29, 1958 and is buried at the Watson Cemetery, in Effingham County, Illinois. Clarence Albert Seaney was born on December 29, 1879 in Crawford County,

Illinois and married Alta Jane Funk. Clarence died on February 3, 1958 and is buried at the Seaney Cemetery in Flat Rock, Crawford County, Illinois. Martha's husband William was born in 1843 and died in 1910. Martha herself is buried at the Seaney Cemetery in Flat Rock, Crawford County, Illinois.

SEVENTY SEVEN
WHERE'S THE BUTTER?

Through my step great-great grandmother widow Ada Rocelia (Brundage) (Butter) Piper who was my great-great grandpa Julius's second wife, I wanted to share this story. My great-great step-grandmother Ada was married to Carl Hermann Butter who was born in 1856 and died in 1897 at the age of 41. One of Carl and Ada Butter's sons was Oscar Albert Butter and his wife Pearl Rose (Berry) Butter. Pearl Rose Berry's parents were Jacob (Jake) Henry Berry and his wife Minerva Alvira (Brundage) Berry. Jacob's sister Anna Eliza Berry married William Wiggins on November 27, 1870, and that's where this story begins. This story was written by a family member and I felt that the story of William Wiggins would help us to get a clearer picture of what life was like back in the late 1800s. (At the end of this chapter is a story about the Jacob Berry family, which leads back to Ada, my step great-great grandmother.)

William Wiggins was born in London, England on June 22, 1846. At the age of four years he came to America with his mother and six sisters in a large sail boat, taking three weeks for the trip. His father had come to America ahead of his family sending money back for them to take the trip. His family first lived in Illinois and then in Iowa. William was 24 when he and his sister Martha came to Kansas in 1870 with the Berry family caravan. The Berry family was comprised of a father and a mother, four sons and six daughters. After all, his 17 year old sweetheart was Anna Eliza Berry, who was the oldest. The caravan to Kansas was five covered wagons drawn by eight horses and one team of mules. They had six cows, one dog, 200 sheep and one Indian pony. Twenty miles was a full day's drive for this caravan and it took them four weeks to get from Iowa City to Morris County, Kansas. They would always stop every Saturday evening to rest for the week-end and bake bread for the coming week's journey. They had a four burner cook stove with an oven and a pipe to vent the smoke. They gathered wild fruits and nuts, since it was June and some of the fruit was in season.

Three of their girls, Anna, Mary and Martha took turns riding the pony and driving the sheep. When a sheep would die someone would skin it and tie the hide on the back of the side saddle. When Anna rode she would untie the hide and let it fall off because she didn't like the smell of it in the hot weather. Because the girls were hard workers their parents surprised them with about twelve yards of calico to make dresses and bonnets. The girls always had to ride side-saddle back then because it was not considered lady-like to ride astride.

They took a ferry at St. Joseph, Missouri downstream to Atchison. It was in Atchison that the family took a claim of 80 acres, and the railroad claimed every other section. William Wiggins built a 12x14 shanty on his claim and took his sweetheart Anna to be his wife on November 27, 1870. They had to go to Council Grove for their marriage license and asked Parson R. M. Wright on a Saturday to drive back home with them so they could get married outdoors on Sunday at the Berry homestead. They provided a big reception and invited all their neighbors and Parson Wright and his wife.

William and Anna's shanty had one window, one door, and a wooden floor, which was nice to have since most people only lived on dirt floors back then. They had one cow, five hens, one rooster, a team of mules, a

An old shanty

stove, a bed, a table that William made, and boxes to sit on. They began to plant grains, set hedge plants all around this 80 acres, planted apple trees, raspberry bushes and shade trees. They not only lived in the shanty but used the covered wagon as well.

William and Anna had four children that were born in this shanty, Mary Emily, Addie Jane, Wilmer Elmer, and Frankie. Baby Frankie died within 16 months with the summer complaints.

William learned to be a blacksmith by trade and learned to work on wheels even as a young boy back in Illinois. He ended up building his own shop and would barter to make ends meet. A fire broke out just after William had built his shop that burned down the shanty and burned sixteen miles wide taking everything in its path, also burning six people. Their son Fred was born in this shop because at that time, about 1878, William was building a four room stone house and had hired two stone masons, Charles Krouse and Mr. Young. They had to blast out rock to make the basement that would contain two rooms. The main floor would also contain two rooms. In 1940 that house was still standing. There are papers in the northeast corner of this house.

Their son Oscar was born in this new stone house. Then, about every two years or thereabouts, Clara, Anna, Willie, Elsie, Ollie, and Sarah were born with no doctor! Anna just seemed to be a nurse to everyone in the neighborhood.

William purchased 160 acres which joined the 80 acres on the north side that had belonged to Mr. Hansant. The 160 acres already had a shanty on it and a big yellow peach orchard. He then bought 60 acres from the railroad that also was adjacent to his 160 acres, but in order to get that land he had to mortgage his 80 acres.

At one time they had 15 milking cows and 400 chickens. Anna would make two buckets of butter every week, each holding three gallons of butter. She would take two crates of 15 dozen eggs each, and a bucket of butter, into town weekly where she was able to purchase sugar, coffee, corn meal and dry goods for her family. William would sell hogs and peaches, and would search for work to help pay the interest on his mortgage. Drought and grasshoppers plagued them many times.

Sometimes water was very hard to get in Morris County and he ended up going over to Franklin County looking for a new location to live. He found 360 acres on Appanoose Creek in Franklin County which provided lots of water. Sarah was eighteen weeks old when they moved from Morris County to Franklin County. William traded farms with a Mr. Jackson. William owned 320 acres but had mortgaged 60 acres from the railroad. William had to pay some cash difference, plus they bartered for a car and moved their household belongs and machinery while their sons Elmer and Fred drove the cattle over. They had lived in Morris County for 23 years!

This new farm was about eight miles north of Pomona and eighteen miles northwest of Ottawa. It was here that Edna and Alice were born, but this time with doctors. The one-story and a half house had been raised to be a two story and a half house, making it seven large rooms. A large kitchen was built on the north end of the house and it had a very large basement. William had brought peach seeds over from the farm in Morris County and planted them in the fall, but some had frozen that first winter and very few trees started that first year. The second year a large peach orchard was planted and in about three years those trees were loaded with luscious yellow peaches. The rabbits and mice did a lot of damage to the trees the following winter and many trees died. Some of the peaches were sold to people in Ottawa, some to neighbors and some were canned for home use. Walnut logs were cut from the timber and made lumber for the large barns.

There was a time when they had four or five teams of horses that were let out in the mornings to drink water and be harnessed for all kinds of farm work. The family planted wheat, corn, oats, barley, flax, cane, kaffir corn, and millet. When the work was done for the day, each horse had a place in the barn and the harness was taken off and hung behind each horse. The barn was always full of ears of corn for each horse plus a manger full of prairie hay or alfalfa. Each horse knew its name and teammate.

They had a large dinner bell that was rung every day at 11:30 am, and it was expected that every person stop whatever they were doing and get ready for the meal. William expected every person to all be seated about the same time and he would express thanks to the Lord before one bite was taken.

After William's big barn was built he held a big revival meeting in it. He himself was baptized in 1871, the second winter when the ice was cut from the pond, and Anna was baptized after Addie's birth. William then built a blacksmith shop with an implement shed and buggy shed combined. Attached to this shed was a corn crib and under the corn crib a place for the hogs. By this time they owned up to 350 hogs, which were always getting out and eating Anna's chickens and large grey geese. William made his own barb wire fencing to place around the hog pen. Maybe that's why the hogs kept getting out? They owned a spring buggy which hauled the produce to nearby towns. This buggy had two seats and a board in front of them that could hold a couple of their children.

Their children's whole world was about five miles square. The Dean School was about one and a half miles southwest, and when it got too cold to walk, the eight of them, Oscar, Ruben, Clara, Anna, Willie, Elsie, Ollie and Sarah would ride ole' Jennie the mule to school. Their school teacher was a prominent citizen and lawyer living in Ottawa, Ben Bowers. Ben had about 60 students at one time with some boys taller than himself.

Anna had a wonderful garden about as large as half a city block full of sweet corn. Their children enjoyed riding the horse on a one-horse plow and Anna hoed her garden a lot. She would store turnips, cabbage, and apples in pits, with many apples being stored in their basement. Their potatoes, pumpkins and squash were always planted near the creek.

They had large pine trees in their front yard and large maple trees all around their property. At one time they even had twenty four bee hives. William often worked with the bees with a mosquito net over his straw hat with his sleeves tied down, gloves on and his pant legs tied. He always used a smoker to run the bees off the hives so he could retrieve the honey.

On the east side of the barn was where they kept fifteen cows in special pens for milking. Four six gallon buckets of milk were brought in every evening and morning. Some was fed to the young calves while most was put in gallon crocks and stored in their big cool cellar.

Anna made lots of kraut in stone jars, and made lots of grape, apple and plum jelly. They used two apple peelers and cut and pared the apples in six pieces, enough to fill a clothes basket twice over. While this is being done, they butchered four hogs. They enjoyed the sausage, and many gallons of lard were produced. From the creek they enjoyed catching and eating catfish, suckers and perch.

At Christmas time not many presents were exchanged but they always had a large cedar tree in their home that reached all the way to the ceiling and was trimmed with strung popcorn balls made with molasses, and colored paper rings in a chain. Pears and apples were often wrapped special for their kids. One year they purchased an organ and Addie learned how to play it and ended up entertaining at the school and playing for their church. Their friend Jess Shoemaker was a beautiful tenor singer and belonged to the Dunkard Church. They are the ones that wore the net caps and plain black silk bonnets. Their dresses were hand-made and neat with a shawl effect with no lace or ruffles. William and Anna ended up buying family cemetery plots from the Dunkard Church and buried Elmer, Rubin and Alice there. William is now buried there as well.

After their son Rubin died at age 19, William lost interest in the farm and moved his family to Pomona in 1900. There he built a store adjacent to a bank, a dentist office and a doctor's office. William built three rooms onto a five room home in Pomona for his family. In 1917 they sold their home and quit the business in the store. They lived above the store for a while but loved spending their winters in Florida, then in 1922 they moved to Ottawa. William built a modern home on Mulberry Street.

His eyes were starting to fail him about 1928 and it was getting harder for him to drive their Ford. In Ottawa they still had their own vegetable and flower gardens. William passed away on November 27, 1936 on their 69th wedding anniversary at the age of 93. Before he died he pleaded to all of his children to "Seek ye first the Kingdom and all these things will be added to you." He gave his heart to the Lord back in Morris County and said that God had blessed him through Jesus Christ all the way.

The church in Ottawa was a great blessing and comfort to William and Anna. In 1940 she was still in good health and living with one of her children in Holton, Kansas and was 88 years of age. She was marveling at the modern day combine and how fast a car could go and how many miles one could travel in one day. Her favorite place was to be at home watching the wood burn in the fireplace." Anna Eliza (Berry) Wiggins, I pray that this chapter will be a tribute to you and to William for years to come.

Oscar and Pearl Butter

Where is the Butter? The story that made up this chapter began with my step great-great grandma Ada Rocelia (Brundage) (Butter) Piper's first husband Carl Hermann Butter. Their son Oscar Albert Butter had married Pearl Rose Berry. Pearl's father was Jacob (Jake) Henry Berry, and it was his sister Anna and her husband William Wiggins story.

SEVENTY EIGHT

JACOB BERRY'S LIFE

Jacob (Jake) Henry Berry was born on September 5, 1864 in Davenport, Boone County, Iowa to Peter Stephen and Tabitha (Waide) Berry. Jacob's family had moved to Wilsey, Kansas in June of 1870. The town of Wilsey is about 16 miles east of Herington, Kansas. Jacob Berry married Minerva Alvira Brundage and it was their daughter Pearl Rose who had married Oscar Albert Butter. Oscar's father was Carl Hermann Butter who married Ada Rocelia (Brundage) Butter, who became my great-great grandpa Julius Piper's second wife when Carl died. Minerva's grandparents had moved to Wilsey when Minerva was a very small child.

Jacob and Minerva were married by a probate judge in Council Grove on October 22, 1895. They started living on a farm that Jacob inherited from his mother, Tobitha (Waide) Berry, that was about two miles south and one mile east of Wilsey in the Walnut Grove district. They lived all their married life and raised eight children on this farm: Hazel Mary was born on September 23, 1896. Riley Buell was born on September 28, 1898. Pearl Rose was born on January 19, 1901. Agnes May was born on November 11, 1902. Iva Belle was born on December 20, 1904. Nellie Marie was born on April 1, 1907. It wasn't until January 4, 1910 that their son Harold Harmon was born, and then five years later Luella Tabitha was born on October 19, 1915.

Tragedy struck their home on August 4, 1908 when Minerva's Grandma Brundage died. She had come to live with them when her own husband had died. They are both buried at the cemetery two miles north of Wilsey along with two sons.

Their oldest daughter Hazel Mary (Berry) Lenners married Matthew James Lenners from Kelso, Kansas on August 7, 1918 in Council Grove. Pearl Rose (Berry) Butter married Oscar Albert Butter on February 23, 1919 at the home of Elzie Harrison. In 1920 Jacob Berry died and all of his children were able to be present for the funeral which was held at the Christian Church in Wilsey. His burial was at the Wilsey cemetery.

Jacob and Minerva's daughter Iva Bell (Berry) Parsons married Pearl Otis Parson of Parkerville, Kansas on November 26, 1924, and only six months later on May 30, 1925 Agnes May (Berry) Lawrence married George Lawrence of Elmdale, Kansas at the Christian Church parsonage in Wilsey.

On June 14, 1928 Nellie Marie (Berry) Parks married John Albert Parks in Marian, Kansas and started housekeeping at the Whiting Ranch just west of Wilsey.

Minerva Alvira (Brundage) Berry's parents were Hannah (Newton) Brundage who came from the state of Michigan and Hannah was born on November 18, 1835 and died on August 4, 1908 at the age of 73. Ed A. Brundage died on May 16, 1888 and both are buried at the cemetery north of Wilsey.

Hannah (Newton) Brundage's sister, Elizabeth (Newton) Brundage, married Ed A. Brundage's brother Steve Brundage. Steve and Elizabeth had three children, one being my step great-great grandmother Ada

Rocelia (Brundage) Butter, who first married Carl Hermann Butter and when he died she married my great-great grandfather Julius Piper. Before marrying my great-great grandpa Julius Ada and Carl had Flora, Emma, Anna and Oscar. Oscar married Pearl Rose Berry. Steve and Elizabeth's two other children were Sylvia (Brundage) Garretson and Ed Brundage.

And that's the Berrys!

SEVENTY NINE

CARL AND EMMA

This chapter in my book actually came from a story that my cousin Martha Velma (Mauderly) Brown had written about her parents Carl William and Emma Marie (Mau) Mauderly. Emma was one of Amelia (Piper) Mau's daughters and Amelia was my great-great grandpa Julius's sister and my great-great aunt. Here is what Martha Brown wrote some time ago. There is no date on her writing.

"Carl William Mauderly was born on July 14, 1895 in Antelope, Kansas. He came to Chase County at an early age with his parents, siblings, and his half-brothers. He spent his whole life in Chase County in the Middle Creek and Elmdale, Kansas areas, except for one year living in Delavan, Morris County, Kansas.

Carl married Emma Marie Mau, daughter of John and Amelia (Piper) Mau and they decided to live in the Middle Creek community. The Middle Creek community was a German settlement and German was often spoken in the homes, churches and schools. Dad and mother spoke German fluently in our home until WW II came along. It was then that they thought it best not to speak German. John and I never heard much of it spoken anymore.

Carl and Emma both attended school district 47 in Chase County, and also the Immanuel Lutheran parochial school. Carl served in WW I with the Private Co. F. development Battalion and received an honorable discharge at the end of the war.

Shortly after the war ended it was common for a young man to start out on his own and farming was what dad chose. It was then that he chose Emma to be his wife and they were married on March 13, 1921 at the Immanuel Lutheran Church in Chase County. Their wedding was one of the largest weddings held in that church.

The old German Immanuel Lutheran Church about 1905 in Chase County, KS

Carl and Emma started their married life together on the farm that they had rented. They had all kinds of hardships and had to borrow money or signed notes with someone on different occasions. They often had poor crops and poor prices that led to them having to have a sale to pay the notes off and move from their farm. This was hard on this pioneer family. They ended up having to move to another home in the same vicinity. Carl then became a common laborer and they moved several times, living in Delavan and Elmdale areas.

Dad always had a huge wood pile, all split for use in the cook stove and heating stove. Mother did domestic work both before and after marriage and continued until after John and I were grown.

My dad passed away at the age of 54 on October 12, 1949 at the Veterans Hospital in Wichita, Kansas. My mother passed away at the Chase County Nursing Home on May 6, 1977 at the age of 84. Both dad and mother were life members of the Lutheran Church and are both buried at the Elk Cemetery in Chase County.

Carl and Emma Mauderly

My parents, Carl and Emma, had three children, with their first daughter dying in infancy. I, Martha Velma (Mauderly) Brown was born in Elk in the Middle Creek vicinity on September 25, 1923. I attended school in Elmdale and graduated from high school in 1942, and on December 8, 1942 Dorman Doil Brown and I were married in Cottonwood Falls by Ed Forney, a Justice of the Peace. Dorman was born on February 11, 1907 in Mercer County, Missouri and died on June 19, 1985 in a hospital in Emporia, Kansas, and is buried at the Prairie Grove Cemetery. He had retired from the Chase County Highway Department.

I (Martha Brown) started at an early age working in domestic work, and for a time worked at the Chase County High School USD 284 as one of the custodians.

My brother, Ronald Glenn Mauderly was born on March 1, 1944 in Strong City, Kansas. He attended schools in Elmdale and graduated in 1962. He then attended Wichita Business College and later graduated from Vernons School of Cosmetology. As of this writing he works for the Marion County Highway Department in Newton. He is an avid marksman and belongs to the Newton Gun Club. He married Frances Anne Isenhardt on March 20, 1965 in Newton, Kansas and divorced. One of their daughters, Shannon Joey, was born on February 17, 1970.

My brother John Henry Mauderly was born on October 22, 1928 in the Middle Creek vicinity, not too far from where my mother was born and attended schools in Elmdale. He was a kind and caring son and helped our parents in many ways. John married Beulah Clara Hess of Burlington, Kansas at the First Christian Church in Emporia, Kansas on February 6, 1949. He saw numerous educational opportunities come his way, but he enjoyed being a carpet layer and seeing the fruits of his labor. His wife Beulah is a retired cosmetologist.

John, like his father, served his country in the United States Army in the Korean War at Fort Buckner in Okinawa. John received a Good Conduct Metal and a National Service Defense Metal. John passed away on August 3, 1995 and Beulah died on April 12, 2002."

Martha Velma (Mauderly) Brown is currently at the Salem Nursing Home in Hillsboro, Kansas.

EIGHTY

BURIED ALIVE!

My second cousin Marion (Sarge) Lawrence Piper was born in Florence, Kansas on May 29, 1932. His parents were my great uncle Fred Edward Piper and great aunt Shirley Rosetta (Hinchman) Piper. (Great uncle Fred was my grandpa Will's brother). Marion was an honor student at Florence High School which earned him a scholarship to attend Central College in McPherson, Kansas. His sister, Betty Criss, stays in touch with us and lives in El Dorado, Kansas. Marion not only had great academics but he was also a very good left-handed baseball pitcher at the college. He joined the Marines from 1951 to 1954 and served in Korea as a member of the third Battalion, fifth Marines, and the first Marine division where he received two Purple Hearts after being wounded twice, the Korean Service Medal, a United Nations Medal, and many others. After returning to the states in 1953 Sarge, as he was called, was stationed at the Marine base in San Diego, California when he got a week-end pass and decided to go visit his girlfriend in Bakersfield. Hitch-hiking he made it through Los Angeles and was on the north side of Las Angeles trying to thumb a ride when an old black 1937 Pontiac sedan stopped and the driver called, "Hop in." The driver was a 30 year old lean, red-haired craggy-faced man with a strange look around his eyes.

As much as Sarge tried to make conversation over the miles the driver only nodded and then told Sarge that he said he had to take a detour to visit his aunt. That's when the driver turned onto desolate highway 138, which snakes eastward over the mountains towards the Mojave Desert. After a few miles the driver turned onto what seemed like the world's most lonesome trail, the Old Ridge Road, and suddenly brought the car to a stop. That's when the driver muttered that he thought something was wrong with his headlights and got out to check.

Before long Sarge heard a loud explosion that seemed to be coming from the back seat. Something struck Sarge in the back so hard that it threw him forward against the windshield. At first he thought that someone had been hiding in the back seat and had shot him. The slug from a .22 caliber rifle that was lodged in the backseat hit a coil spring in the upholstery, which deflected it. But the hardened-steel spring was driven with bullet-like impact towards Sarge. When the driver saw that Sarge was still alive he went to get his hammer. Before Sarge could raise a hand to protect himself the driver came up with a hammer and swung it viciously, beating Sarge on the head again and again. Sarge collapsed in the front seat, unconscious.

The next thing he knew they were driving again. Sarge was dimly conscious with blood streaming down his face and into his eyes and was too groggy to move a muscle. He thought to himself, is this a robbery? He knew that he only had about six dollars in his wallet! Men in combat back then only earned $35.00 a month. They soon came to sudden stop. Sarge feigned unconsciousness and hoped that the hammer-swinging devil would leave him there. The driver started cutting Sarge's shoelaces with a knife and removed one of his shoes. Sarge tried to kick at him but missed. The driver cursed and said "Ain't you dead yet?"

The driver reached into the car and brought out a 12 gauge shotgun, aimed it and fired it at pointblank range, tearing a hole in Sarge's chest on the left side and he blacked out again. Sarge says that he was carrying a Gideon New Testament Bible in his left breast pocket and it gave his heart some protection from the shotgun blast. The next thing he remembers is being stripped of his clothing from the waist down and the driver was digging a hole with a shovel somewhere among the trees, but then Sarge blacked out again. It was during this time that the driver rolled Sarge onto his face and tried to commit sodomy. Soon the man totally stripped him and rolled him into a make-shift grave and started covering him up. The driver stripped Sarge of all his clothes, his wallet, dog tags, and wristwatch. By this time Sarge was semiconscious, and he knew that unless he played dead, there surely would be another shotgun blast again, so he made no effort to move.

Clods of dirt and sand hit Sarge in the face covering his face and body completely now. It wasn't the happiest choice he ever had to make but it was either his being shot dead or buried alive. Gasping for air he dimly heard the roar of an engine. Surely the man is gone now!

With great effort and a whole lot of pain, Sarge flexed his legs and arms, pushing the dirt from himself. As luck would have it, the grave was shallow and he was able to climb out of his own grave, stark naked, in the chill of the evening. He staggered to his feet and saw far ahead of him a light and he thought it might be a house where he could get help.

Ten months earlier while in Korea shrapnel had torn into his body and at that time he thought that was pretty bad! Now, naked and covered only with blood and dirt, gaping wounds in his chest, and bare feet torn by gravel, he staggered through the darkness to the light he saw. He walked when he could and then crawled the rest of the way on his hands and knees.

The house was the old Sandberg Lodge that had been converted to a home that was owned by Mr. and Mrs. Walter

The old Sanburg Lodge on Ridge Road in California where Sarge crawled to for help.

Stevens. Mrs. Stevens heard a noise and when she opened her front door she screamed because of a naked, bloody man at the door and her husband came running. They brought him in and placed him on a cot and covered him with warm blankets while Mr. Stevens called the Los Angeles County sheriff's station at Gorman.

Deputy Frank DeBernardi had taken the message and put out a quick call to the Newhall Hospital for an ambulance. When the first deputy arrived on the scene Sarge was still conscious and was able to gasp out the bare details of the story and give a description of the driver. That first deputy was James (Jim) Piper (not a relative that we know of), and he could hardly believe his ears about the assault and burial, and relayed the message to the sheriff's substation at Newhall where it was placed on the air. Another sergeant assigned to this case was Richard Dailey. Just before 10:00 pm two California highway patrolmen spotted a black 1937 Pontiac sedan traveling south towards Los Angeles about 30 miles from the scene on highway 99 near Castaic. When they pulled over the driver he was a red curly-haired guy wearing a wool plaid shirt that Sarge described.

The driver was Richard John Jensen, age 28, living in Tujunga, a Los Angeles suburb. In his car was a shotgun that had been recently fired. There was also a rifle with its stock sawed off, and a hammer. The rifle had been held securely in place in the back seat, ready to shoot the unsuspecting passenger through the upholstery. A cord rigged from the trigger, running under the front seat so that Jensen could pull it when so inclined to do so. When they fingerprinted Jensen and checked his records, what they found made their hair stand on end!

This Richard John Jensen was one of the most deformed personalities who ever walked this earth. He was already a criminal, a killer, a psychopath and had spent most of his life in and out of state institutions. As a boy he had committed a murder in his parent's basement, a murder that shocked the nation. Even though he had just assaulted a Marine and tried to bury him alive he was 'on leave' from confinement as a defective, and still had a murder indictment hanging over him.

Richard John Jensen was the son of a respected couple who lived in La Crescenta, a suburb of Los Angeles where his stepfather was the superintendent of a local dairy. In 1931 when he was only six, he began looting stores, always leaving a note behind reading "Thanks for the stuff.—The Hare." At age 11 he was sent to Pacific Lodge, a school for incorrigibles, but escaped a few months later. Soon he was caught in yet another burglary and was sent to a reform school in Whittier.

On August 22, 1939 Jensen had a 13 year old friend, Billy Williams, come over to play. Jensen's mother heard scuffling noises coming from their basement but thought that John was teasing their family dog. When she started to go downstairs Jensen came to meet her on the stairs. "Don't go down there Ma," he said. She asked him why not and his reply was

'Well, because I just killed Billy." He turned and raced to the garage where he grabbed his bicycle and rode off into the sunset.

When Jensen's mother went downstairs to investigate she was horrified to find Billy lying bleeding on the basement floor and beside him was a bloody hammer, a knife and a pair of pruning shears that were also bloody. Around Billy's neck was a thin copper wire that had been twisted several times. Young Billy was still alive but died on his way to the hospital. Jensen was found about 20 miles away riding his bike. Apparently Billy had called Jensen a convict and teased him about spending time at Whittier and that made Jensen mad. He said he hit him a couple of times with the hammer and then he didn't remember anything after that. He admitted to wanting to bury Billy in a hole in their back yard when it got dark out, but his mother walked in and spoiled it. His only reply was "I don't care what happens to me. I hate everybody. Let 'em hang me, let 'em bury me. I can take it. I'm not afraid to die." The coroner had found a dozen stab wounds in Billy's body. His skull had been crushed by nine visible hammer blows.

Four doctors who examined Jensen found him to be suffering from schizophrenia with pronounced homosexual tendencies. Richard John Jensen was committed to Camarillo State Hospital with a murder indictment pending again him. Rebelling against discipline he was soon transferred to another institution at Sonoma where he likewise defied the rules and tried to escape. He was finally sent to Mendocino State Hospital under maximum security for the criminally insane. He showed so much improvement that in 1941, at the age of 16, he was reported cured. He spent four years in Mendocino and on August 18, 1945, now age 20, he escaped. With him was an older inmate, the balding Harry Dunlap who had been confined after a career as a lovers' lane bandit. A series of holdups followed and he ended up in Columbus, Ohio stealing but was nabbed and had to return to California without Harry. Where was Harry? Did John murder him?

Through Jensen's parents' loyal efforts a hearing was held on August 18, 1950 trying to gain favor for their son to let him go free. The county jail physician was strongly opposed and was not convinced that his sexual abnormalities had been curbed sufficiently.

In the space of 15 years, Jensen had spent time in five different corrective institutions, and had appeared before numerous judges. He was still under indictment for Billy William's murder, and the court order demanding his detention on that charge still held. After the shooting of Marine Sergeant (Sarge) Piper authorities said angrily that they did not even know that Jensen was at liberty (free) or they would have pressed the murder charge.

Sarge became well-known as the man who climbed out of his own grave, was beaten savagely on the head with a hammer, and recipient of a shotgun blast to the chest, had no business being alive but was saved by a rugged constitution. One result of this attack was an order forbidding servicemen in uniform to hitchhike. He spent about 13 months in the hospital after the attack and was offered a medical discharge but he refused it to finish out his enlistment. It was during his stay at the hospital when someone asked Sarge how he survived and he said "You can't kill a Marine," which turned into a TV episode of Code 3, a TV sitcom. Following his discharge, he served another eight years in the Marine Corp Reserve.

When Jensen went to trial on March 1, 1954, the state tried him under California's "Little Lindbergh Law," which carries the death penalty for kidnaping, whether or not the victim survives. Sarge was able to appear in court to testify against Jensen and Jensen was found sane in a legal sense, but was convicted and sentenced to die. Jensen ended up confessing to the murdering of 16 year old Roger Raymond Lawson, a Malibu ranch hand, on September 13, 1953 near Moorpark!

A jury found Richard John Jensen guilty on each count of robbery, assault with intent to commit murder, and kidnaping for the purpose of robbery. What insidious crimes this man committed! The court ordered that the sentences for the first two offenses run concurrently, and for the last offence, the jury fixed the death penalty. Jensen was removed to death row at San Quentin Prison. On February 11, 1955 the guards escorted John Richard Jensen to the gas chamber to die, although by a newspaper article from the Oxnard Press Courier dated December 4, 1954 Jensen was supposed to get the gas chamber on Valentine's Day, February 14, 1955.

Sarge was discharged from the Marine Corp at the rank of sergeant in 1954.

After surviving all of this, Sarge met and married Ruth Tinkham and they decided to live in Frazier Park, California. There he worked for 33 years in the lightweight sand and gravel business and was sole owner of Hill Auto Parts. He also served 22 years as a sergeant of the Kern County Sheriff's Reserve in Kern County, California. Their children included Nora Louise (Piper) Orizaga of Bakersfield, California, who was born on January 25, 1959 and married Valentin Romero-Orizaga. Lorena (Rena) Susan (Piper) Linder was born on July 9, 1960 in Bakersfield, California and married Paul Edward Linder. Lorena and Paul's children are Susan Michele Linder, and Jennifer Rebecca Linder. Mathew Lawrence Piper was born on June 17, 1961 in Bakersfield, California and married Bonnie Lynn Johnston. Matthew and Bonnie's

children included Cheyenne Lynn Piper and Michael Lawrence Piper.
Sarge and Ruth adopted David August Piper as a son to complete their family. David was born on January 18, 1965 in Bakersfield, California and married Mona.

In 1971 Sarge and Ruth divorced. Sarge then married Patricia LaPine on November 25, 1971, in Las Vegas, Nevada and in 1995 moved to Brookings, Oregon. He helped train animals for the movies and even built tow bars for the B-36 bombers before he retired.

Marion (Sarge) Piper and his wife Ruth, with their children, Lorena, Nora, Matthew, and David

In his later years he served as a Chaplin for the Marine Corps League Detachment 578 for Oregon. He was twice awarded Marine of the Year and received a Legion of Honor Award from the Chapel of Four Chaplains. He served as Parish Assistant for Trinity Lutheran Church, Chaplain for the Curry County Chapter of the Gideon's International since 1956, Red Cross First Aid/CPR/AED instructor and Red Cross Blood Drive chairperson. He was active in the community, serving as a Meals On Wheels volunteer, and as a whale watch volunteer. He was a devout Christian and enjoyed teaching adult Bible studies.

He was ready to minister to any fellow Marines when asked. At one time, during a heavy storm, he was called by the Sutter Coast Hospital as a dying Marine had requested a fellow Marine to be at his bedside. It was late at night but Sarge drove to Crescent City and found the man in his hospital room twitching and nervous. With him were his family and a retired priest. Sarge read a few scriptures then suggested that everyone form a circle, holding hands to pray. It was during the prayer that the man's nervousness and twitching stopped. Sarge stayed at his bedside until his comrade in arms died quietly.

Marion (Sarge) Lawrence Piper died on April 18, 2007 in a fatal car accident when his car drove off a 180 foot embankment on highway 38, and landed upside down in the Umpqua River near Scottsburg, Oregon. His vehicle was reportedly discovered by a fisherman who notified the U.S. Coast Guard and called 911. After much investigation the officers told his wife, that they think that he either passed out or fell asleep at the wheel. A celebration of life service was held at 2:00 pm Saturday, April 28, 2007 at the Trinity Lutheran Church in Brookings, Oregon. Cremation was under the direction of the Redwood Memorial Chapel and Crematory.

A 'made for TV' movie was made about Sarge's attack called "You Can't Kill A Marine." This 30 minute Code 3 TV series in black and white aired on October 1, 1957 by director Paul Landres and starring Richard Travis as the assistant Sheriff, Dehl Berti as Erlinger, and Robert Rice as Dr. Crawdon. This episode of Code 3 was written by Jack Laird and filmed at the Hal Roach Studio in Culver City, California with the story line of Barnett trying to rescue a Marine who, while hitchhiking home, had been picked up by an angry, aggressive driver.

In 1971 Sarge's brother Ernie met with the Los Angeles County Sheriff Deputy Jim Piper asking him about the case. Jim Piper brought in an issue of True Detective Magazine that contained the story of Sarge in it. The story contained a picture of Sarge in his Marine uniform looking at the shotgun while on the witness stand during the Jensen trial. Ernie said he had asked his brother Sarge after the trial if he wanted a copy of the True Detective Magazine to keep, but he said Sarge declined. It was at Sarge's funeral that Ernie offered Sarge's son Matthew the copy of the magazine and Matt said he'd like to have it. Matt accepted and Jim mailed it to him.

I never had the chance to meet Sarge, and I have not met his brother Ernie, but I have met their sister Betty (Piper) Criss who presently lives in El Dorado, Kansas. From what I have read of Sarge and what I have received from his brother Ernie, I am proud to be a part of the Piper family. We have spent time with Betty at her home, sharing information about the family. The "Piper" family may not be a wealthy family, but we are a strong-willed and very determined family and we owe a lot to our ancestors who paved a way for us.

Many of our early family were God-fearing people that had come here from the old country, bringing with them their faith and determination to live and to prosper in a foreign land. They chose to live and raise their families in their 'promise land' of opportunities, learning a whole new language, homesteading land that was virtually untouched, building homes and foundations made from the natural stone found on the land, and creating a life for themselves and for their children which I am very much proud to be a part of. My thank you to my God-fearing great-great grandpa Julius, my great-grandpa August, my grandpa Will, and to my father, Bernie, for instilling in me a will and determination to know that I came from good stock and a will to pass what I have learned on down to my children and my children's children. I am no longer chasing an illusive dream for I have found my family roots and who I am in the Lord.

After writing my book I was so inspired to write a poem about the old stone foundations my cousin Milton and I discovered in Chase

County that had belonged to our ancestors. I titled the poem "Those Old Stone Ruins."

"Those Old Stone Ruins"

"What labor it took to stack these stones, to build a foundation so grand.
If only these stones could talk to me, and tell me who lived on this land.

These stones helped support a homestead of wood, that maybe my grandparents shared.
They raised a family on this very spot, in Chase County, Kansas with care.

I happened upon these ruins one day, when told where my ancestors built.
I walked around and cradled my heart, did I care enough, or—was it guilt?

Until I started to study my roots, did I come upon a wonderful past.
For they trotted upon unchartered land, and created a shared path at last.

Who placed each stone upon one another, did grandpa labor in vain?
No grandpa, I've visited those ruins, your legacy will live on in name!

What will happen to these old ruins, when weather and time take their toll?
The homestead ruins will decay away, and what will be left but a hole!"

I decided to use the following statement to sum up this book, which came from a dear pastor friend of ours in Iowa. "I work 60 hours a week and I know that you and Phyllis put in your time serving and traveling when most are already retired and playing golf. There was never a place too small or insignificant that you and Phyllis wouldn't perform at, and you never required the royal treatment. This always impressed me. When I say, "Jesus is coming soon," it has nothing to do with putting aside my labor for Christ. It has everything to do with living in a stinking world and the strength to hang on one more day because I tell myself I won't have to put up with the stupidity and suffering any longer—I can make it another day. Sometimes that's all I've got to hang onto. This world is so reprobate I don't claim it anymore. To live in this world as a Christian is to do battle and occupy. We take up arms every day. How pathetic things would be if we didn't. And, we see lots of so-called Christians that haven't a clue because they know nothing of the war that's being waged and they live defeated lives. I get up each day and labor. And, at the end of the day I say, "Even so, come Lord Jesus!" Be more concerned with your own character than your reputation. Your character is what you really are while your reputation is merely what others think you are! It's never too late to become what you might have been.

I have come to the conclusion that the 12 followers of our Lord, after facing violent opposition, never recanted their story of "He is risen, and He is Lord." It cost them their lives! In the face of persecution men will not die for a lie, but they will die for the Truth! The Gospel is truth, and I am committed to it and willing to die for it. Jesus died because he spoke the truth!

After Jesus died and rose again he appeared 40 days to hundreds of people. When He assembled with His Apostles, which by then numbered about 120, they asked Him, saying, "Lord, wilt thou at this time restore again the kingdom of Israel? And He said unto them, It is not for you to know the times, or the seasons, which the Father hath put in His own power. But ye shall receive power, after that the Holy Ghost is come upon you: and ye shall be witnesses unto me both in Jerusalem, and in all Judaea, and in Samaria, and unto the uttermost part of the earth. And when He had spoken these things, while they beheld, he was taken up; and a cloud received Him out of their sight." (Acts 1:6-9 KJV)

These followers witnessed Jesus's appearance after he had died! They also were there when Jesus rose up into the sky! Thomas doubted Jesus's appearance until he saw him face to face. "Jesus saith unto him, Thomas, because thou hast seen Me, thou hast believed: blessed are they that have not seen, and yet have believed." (John 20: 29

The man-pleasing church of today has a smorgasbord of worship styles and all claim to love and serve the Lord, but most churches today have been led away from her roots and bears no resemblance to the powerful first century New Testament Church. Most pastors are using whatever perversion of the bible that they feel will help their sermons, not realizing that they are getting further and further away from the truth. Why has the church embraced the new versions? Isaiah 30:10 says, "Prophesy not unto us right things, speak unto us smooth things, prophesy deceits." Mark 10:21 KJV says, "take up the cross, and follow me," but the new versions just say "come follow me." People just don't like to imagine 'taking up our cross daily." Some churches are getting away from even displaying a cross, and some are not even singing or mentioning anything to do with the 'blood' because it might offend someone.

When Phyllis and I re-read Rebecca Springer's book "Within Heaven's Gates" we were again blessed by her statements of what she saw and witnessed when she either had a vision or actually visited Heaven in the spirit. "But I saw no churches of any kind in Heaven. At first this somewhat confused me, until I remembered that there are no creeds or denominations in heaven. All worship together in harmony and love—the children of one and the same loving Father. Ah, I thought, what a pity that this fact, if no other in the great economy of heaven, could not be proclaimed to the inhabitants of earth! How it would do away with the petty contentions, jealousies, and rivalries of the church militant! No creeds in heaven! No charges of heresy brought by one professed Christian against another! No building up of one denomination upon the ruins or downfall of a different sect! But one great, universal brotherhood whose head is Christ and whose cornerstone is love."

You have read my life story and family history on the pages of this book. I have revealed myself and became vulnerable to the scrutiny of others by sharing my heart and my faith. I want to be remembered as that guy who had an awesome fear of the Lord and loved the Lord with all his heart.

Let me warn you . . .

There are many false apostles and prophets and deceitful workers in this world, transforming themselves into the apostles of Christ, but do not marvel, for Satan himself is transformed into an angel of light. Therefore it is no great thing if his ministers also be transformed or fashioned as the ministers of righteousness, whose end shall be according to their works. (taken from 2 Corinthians 11:13-15 KJV). Lies are being accepted into today's society as truth, but if you would only go to the truth source, God's word, it is a guide to live by. It is not ok to sleep with your own kind, as some movies depict. God made the differences for a reason! Knowing the truth will set you free.

I say, "what if we gave our illusive dreams the benefit of our attention and dusted them off, if just for a few fleeting moments, resuscitated them and really went for them? What if we acted as though they were achievable and not just elusive?"